Securities Industry Essentials

License Exam Manual

2nd Edition

At press time, this edition contains the most complete and accurate information currently available. Owing to the nature of license examinations, however, information may have been added recently to the actual test that does not appear in this edition. Please contact the publisher to verify that you have the most current edition.

This publication is designed to provide accurate and authoritative information in regard to the subject matter covered. It is sold with the understanding that the publisher is not engaged in rendering legal, accounting, or other professional services. If legal advice or other expert assistance is required, the services of a competent professional should be sought.

SECURITIES INDUSTRY ESSENTIALS LICENSE EXAM MANUAL, 2ND EDITION
©2020 Kaplan, Inc.

The text of this publication, or any part thereof, may not be reproduced in any manner whatsoever without written permission from the publisher.

If you find imperfections or incorrect information in this product, please visit www.kaplanfinancial .com and submit an errata report.

Published in February 2020 by Kaplan Financial Education.
Printed in the United States of America.

ISBN: 978-1-07-880324-3

CONTENTS

PART 3 **UNDERSTANDING TRADING, CUSTOMER ACCOUNTS, AND PROHIBITED ACTIVITIES**

INTRODUCTION

Thank you for choosing Kaplan for your educational needs, and welcome to the Securities Industry Essentials (SIE) License Exam Manual (LEM). This manual applies adult learning principles to give you the tools you'll need to pass your exam on the first attempt.

Why Do I Need to Pass the SIE?

All individuals interested in pursuing employment as representative-level registrants must take the SIE. Individuals do not have to be associated with a FINRA member firm to be eligible to take the SIE. However, passing the SIE alone will not qualify an individual for registration with FINRA. An individual who has passed the SIE will also need to pass the appropriate specialized knowledge examination associated with the registration category pertaining to the individual's job function to be eligible for registration with FINRA.

Specialized knowledge examinations are available for the following representative categories:

- Investment Company and Variable Contracts Products Representative (Series 6)
- General Securities Representative (Series 7)
- Direct Participation Programs Representative (Series 22)
- Equity Trader (Series 55)
- Investment Banking Representative (Series 79)
- Private Securities Offerings Representative (Series 82)
- Research Analyst (Series 86/87)
- Operations Professional (Series 99)

Are There Any Prerequisites?

There are no prerequisite exams to pass before sitting for the SIE.

What Is the SIE Exam Like?

The SIE exam is a 1 hour and 45 minute (105 minutes), 75-question exam. Each exam will contain 10 pretest questions, randomly distributed and unscored. Therefore, each exam contains 75 scored and 10 unscored questions. The SIE is administered by FINRA and offered as a computer-based exam at Prometric testing centers around the country.

What Score Must I Achieve to Pass?

All candidate test scores are placed on a common scale using a statistical adjustment process known as *equating*. Equating scores to a common scale accounts for the slight variations in difficulty that may exist among the different sets of exam items that candidates receive. This allows for a fair comparison of scores and ensures that every candidate is held to the same passing standard, regardless of which set of exam items they received. Currently, the score needed to pass is 70%.

What Topics Will I See on the Exam?

The questions you will see on the SIE exam do not appear in any particular order. The computer is programmed to select a new, random set of questions for each exam taker, selecting questions according to the preset topic weighting of the exam. Each SIE candidate will see the same number of questions on each topic, but a different mix of questions. The SIE exam is divided into four sections.

Test Topic	# of Questions	% of Exam
Knowledge of Capital Markets	12	16%
Understanding Products and Their Risks	33	44%
Understanding Trading, Customer Accounts, and Prohibited Activities	23	31%
Overview of the Regulatory Framework	7	9%

When you complete your exam, you will receive a printout that identifies your performance in each area.

PREPARING FOR THE EXAM

How Is the LEM Organized?

The LEM consists of units and unit tests. In addition to the regular text, each unit has some unique features designed to help with quick understanding of the material. When additional emphasis is valuable to your comprehension, the following distinctions are made.

TAKE NOTE

Each Take Note provides special information designed to amplify important points.

TEST TOPIC ALERT

Each Test Topic Alert reviews content that is especially likely to appear on the exam.

EXAMPLE

Each Example provides practical applications that convert theory into understanding.

KNOWLEDGE CHECK

Knowledge Checks are a quick interactive review of what you just read. These ensure you understand and retain the material.

Additional Study Resources

To accompany and supplement your LEM, your study package may contain additional study resources. Be sure to spend some time on your homepage, view the best practices video, and understand all that is available to help you study.

SecuritiesPro™ QBank—Coordinating with the LEM, the SecuritiesPro™ QBank includes a large number of questions that are similar in style and content to those you will encounter on the exam. You may use it to generate tests by a specific unit or combination of units. The

QBank also allows you to create Weighted Mock (Simulated) Exams that mimic your test. There is no limit on the number of QBank exams you can create.

Practice and Mastery Exams—Depending on the study package purchased, you may also have a fixed Practice Exam or a fixed Practice and Mastery Exam. These exams are designed to closely replicate the true exam experience, both in terms of the degree of difficulty and topical coverage. They provide scores and diagnostic feedback, but you will not be given access to (or be able to obtain from Kaplan) correct answers or question explanations. The Practice and Mastery Exams are sound indicators of potential actual exam scores—the better you do on these exams, the more likely you are to pass your actual exam. These may be taken just once each.

Video Library—You may also have access to various topics from our video library. These short, engaging videos cover key topics from your manual. If your package includes access to our video library, please review the topics as you complete your reading assignments in the study manual.

Online Updates

Exam Tips and Content Updates Link—Don't forget to monitor your Exam Tips and Content Updates. When rules and regulations change, or we want to share new information regarding your exam, it's posted there.

Corrections Link—Check the Corrections page regularly. If we find an error in our materials, that is where we will post a correction.

What Topics Are Covered in the Course?

The LEM consists of four parts, each devoted to the sections defined by FINRA that you will need to know to pass the SIE exam. Each part is divided into units devoted to more specific areas with which you need to become familiar.

Part	Topic
1	Understanding Products and Their Risks
2	Knowledge of Capital Markets
3	Understanding Trading, Customer Accounts, and Prohibited Activities
4	Overview of the Regulatory Framework

How Much Time Should I Spend Studying?

Plan to spend approximately seven to nine hours reading the material and carefully answering the questions in the LEM. Spread your study time over three to four weeks before the date on which you are scheduled to take the SIE exam. Your actual time may vary depending on your reading rate, comprehension, professional background, and study environment.

What Is the Best Way to Structure My Study Time?

The following schedule is suggested to help you obtain maximum retention from your study efforts. Remember, this is a guideline only, because each individual may require more or less time to complete the steps included.

Step 1: Read a part, unit by unit, and complete all exercises. Review rationales for all questions whether you got them right or wrong (time will vary based on the size of the unit).

Step 2: In the SecuritiesPro™ QBank, create exams of the designated length for each unit as you go. Carefully review all rationales. Use the LO number to locate additional or related information on the test topic in your LEM if needed (two to three hours per unit).

- Do not become too overwhelmed or bogged down in any one unit. You don't want to lose sight of the finish line because you're having trouble with one hurdle. Keep moving forward. It's a steady pace that wins the race.

- View rationales after each question initially and spend time studying each rationale to learn the concepts. Later, you will want to create exam scenarios in which scores and rationales are viewed at the end of each exam.

- Perfection is not the goal during the reading phase; scores in the mid-to-high 60s is good initially.

Step 3: When you have completed all the units in the LEM and their unit tests, using the SecuritiesPro™ QBank, concentrate on comprehensive exams covering all the material. With your comprehensive testing, it is best to view correct answers and rationales only after the test is completed. Plan to spend at least one week testing before a scheduled class (about two hours for every 100 questions).

- You should complete at least eight Weighted Mock Exams before class. Review your answers and rationales. Also, review your LEM and video library as needed.

- Your goal is to consistently score in the 80s.

Step 4: Complete the online practice and mastery exams. You should complete each exam while observing the time limits for the actual exam. Upon completing the exam, you will receive a diagnostic report that identifies topics for further review (about two hours per exam). We recommend taking the practice and mastery exams after a scheduled class.

Note: After completing the practice, mastery, and mock exams, be sure to review your Performance Tracker so you can identify areas of weakness. You can then create focused exams on topics as needed. Also, review your video library for additional help.

How Well Can I Expect to Do?

The exams administered by FINRA are not easy. You must display considerable understanding and knowledge of the topics presented in this course to pass the exam and qualify for registration.

If you study diligently, complete all sections of the course, and consistently score in the 80s on the tests, you should be well prepared to pass the exam. However, it is important for you to realize that merely knowing the materials will not enable you to pass unless you can apply your knowledge to the questions you are given and understand the essence of the information behind each question.

TEST-TAKING TIPS

Passing the exam depends not only on how well you learn the subject matter but also on how well you take exams. You can develop your test-taking skills—and improve your score—by learning a few techniques:

- Read the full question

- Avoid jumping to conclusions—watch for hedge clauses
- Interpret the unfamiliar question
- Look for key words and phrases
- Identify the intent of the question
- Memorize key points
- Use a calculator
- Beware of changing answers
- Pace yourself

Each of these pointers is explained next, including examples that show how to use them to improve your performance on the exam.

Read the Full Question

You cannot expect to answer a question correctly if you do not know what it is asking. If you see a question that seems familiar and easy, you might anticipate the answer, mark it, and move on before you finish reading it. This is a serious mistake. Be sure to read the full question before answering it. Mistakes are often made when assuming too much (or too little).

Avoid Jumping to Conclusions—Watch for Hedge Clauses

The questions on FINRA exams are embellished with distractors as choices. To avoid being misled by seemingly obvious answers, make it a practice to read each question and each answer twice before selecting your choice. Doing so will provide you with a much better chance of doing well on the exam.

Watch out for hedge clauses (e.g., *if*, *not*, *all*, *none*, and *except*) embedded in the question. In the case of *if* statements, the question can be answered correctly only by taking into account the qualifier. If you ignore the qualifier, you will not answer correctly.

Qualifiers are sometimes combined in a question. Some that you will frequently see together are *all* with *except* and *none* with *except*. In general, when a question starts with *all* or *none* and ends with *except*, you are looking for an answer that is opposite to what the question appears to be asking.

Interpret the Unfamiliar Question

Do not be surprised if some questions on the exam seem unfamiliar at first. If you have studied your material, you will have the information to answer all the questions correctly. The challenge may be a matter of understanding what the question is asking.

Very often, questions present information indirectly. You may have to interpret the meaning of certain elements before you can answer the question. Be aware that the exam will approach a concept from different angles.

Look for Key Words and Phrases

Look for words that are tip-offs to the situation presented. For example, if you see the word *prospectus* in the question, you know the question is about a new issue. Sometimes, a question will even supply you with the answer if you can recognize the key words it contains. Few questions provide blatant clues, but many offer key words that can guide you to selecting the correct answer if you pay attention. Be sure to read all instructional phrases carefully. Take time to identify the key words to answer this type of question correctly.

Identify the Intent of the Question

Many questions on FINRA exams supply so much information that you lose track of what is being asked. This is often the case in story problems. Learn to separate the story from the question.

Take the time to identify what the question is asking. Of course, your ability to do so assumes you have studied sufficiently. There is no method for correctly answering questions if you don't know the material.

Memorize Key Points

Reasoning and logic will help you answer many questions, but you will have to memorize a good deal of information. Some memorization will be automatic as you go over the material and answer questions; some you will simply have to do systematically.

Use a Calculator

Any math required to answer a question will be simple math: add, subtract, multiply, and divide. We recommend using a calculator for math. You may ask for a calculator or ask if you can use your own. If using your own, only simple math functions are allowed (add, subtract, multiply, and divide).

Beware of Changing Answers

If you are unsure of an answer, your first hunch is the one most likely to be correct. Do not change answers on the exam without good reason. In general, change an answer only if you:

- discover that you did not read the question correctly; or
- find new or additional helpful information in another question.

Pace Yourself

Some people will finish the exam early and some will not have time to finish all the questions. Watch the time carefully (your time remaining will be displayed on your computer screen) and pace yourself through the exam.

Do not waste time by dwelling on a question if you simply do not know the answer. Make the best guess you can, mark the question for *Record for Review*, and return to the question if time allows. Make sure that you have time to read all the questions so that you can record the answers you do know.

THE EXAM

How Do I Enroll in the Exam?

To take the exam, you should make an appointment with a Prometric Testing Center as far in advance as possible of the date on which you would like to take the exam.

You may schedule your appointment at Prometric 24 hours a day, 7 days a week on the Prometric secure website at www.prometric.com. You may also use the website to reschedule or cancel your exam, locate a test center, and get a printed confirmation of your appointment. To speak with a Prometric representative by phone, please contact the Prometric Contact Center at **1-800-578-6273**.

What Should I Take to the Exam?

Bring one form of personal identification with your signature and photograph as issued by a government agency. No personal items, food, or drink (including coffee and water) are permitted inside the testing room. Personal items include, but are not limited to, the following: pens, pagers, cellular phones, watches, hats, nonmedical electronic devices, outerwear, purses, and wallets. Personal items must be kept in your assigned locker or returned to your car before the start of your exam. As the testing vendor is not responsible for any personal items, they encourage you to bring only your identification into the center.

Erasable note boards and pens will be provided to you upon admittance to the testing room. If you need additional note boards or pens, please alert your proctor. The note boards and pens must be returned at the end of your exam or continuing education session.

If you need a calculator for your testing session, please see the test center administrator. You will be provided with a nonprogrammable, nonprinting calculator.

Additional Trial Questions

During your exam, you may see extra trial questions. These are potential exam-bank questions being tested during the course of the exam. These questions are not included in your final score.

Exam Results and Reports

At the end of the exam, you'll receive a printout of the results as you sign out with the test center administrator. FINRA will post your official results on Web CRD or report it to your regulator within three business days following your exam session. The exam printout will either show that you passed or your score, if it is below 70%.

PART 1

Understanding Products and Their Risks

Your exam will include 33 questions on the topics covered in Part 1.

There are six units in Part 1: Understanding Products and Their Risks

Unit 1: Individual Securities—Equities

Unit 2: Individual Securities—Debt

Unit 3: Derivatives

Unit 4: Packaged Investments

Unit 5: Other Investment Vehicles

Unit 6: Types of Risk

UNIT
1

Individual Securities—Equities

LEARNING OBJECTIVES

When you have completed this unit, you will be able to accomplish the following.

> LO 1.a   Define a security.
> LO 1.b   Name the two major types of securities.
> LO 1.c   Recall the characteristics of common stock.
> LO 1.d   Recall the cash dividend process.
> LO 1.e   Identify benefits and risks associated with common stock.
> LO 1.f   Differentiate rights and warrants.
> LO 1.g   Relate rules on control and restricted stock.
> LO 1.h   Recall the characteristics of American depositary receipts.
> LO 1.i   Recall characteristics of preferred stock.

INTRODUCTION

In Unit 1 you will be introduced to basic securities and will look deeper into equities: common and preferred stock. The common stock is the primary component of many investor's portfolios.

LESSON 1.1: THE BASIC SECURITIES

LO 1.a Define a security.

What is a security?

If you were to look up the definition of a security, you would find several different, but very similar, definitions. For this course, we are going to use this definition of a security:

Security: An intangible financial asset that may be bought, sold, or gifted between persons. It may be represented by a paper certificate or held in an electronic record.

TAKE NOTE   Commodities

There is often some confusion between commodities and securities. While a security is a financial asset, a commodity is generally a hard asset such as gold, beef, orange juice, or oil. There is an active market in a derivative investment in commodities called *futures*, but futures are based on commodities and so are not considered a security.

The legal definition of a security

In 1946, the U.S. Supreme Court ruled in favor of the government in *SEC v. W.J. Howey Co.* In the case, the SEC said that W.J. Howey had violated federal law by not registering its sale to the public of an interest in the profits of a section of the company's orange groves. Because Howey sold an interest in the profits of the grove, and not the grove or the produce directly, the court found that the interest that Howey sold was, in fact, a security.

The specifics of the case are not all that important for us, but what is important is that the *Howey* decision gave us a legal test for what is a security—the Howey Test.

The Howey Test is a four-part test, as described here.

A security is

1. an investment of money made into

2. a common enterprise

3. with the expectation of profit

4. through the efforts of a third party.

So, if people pool their money together with the expectation that a third party (usually a manager) will make a profit for them, a person's interest in that enterprise is a security.

Most of those things we normally think of as investments are some type of security. Here are a few examples of securities:

■ Stocks

■ Bonds, notes, and debentures (all types of debt)

■ Options

■ Mutual funds

■ Jumbo CDs

■ Depositary receipts

■ Units in an investment

■ Variable life and variable annuities

This list is far from complete, but it does cover most of the types of securities seen on the SIE Exam. We will take a closer look at all of these later.

It is helpful to remember some of the things that are not securities that do appear on the exam. Some examples are as follows:

■ Cash and currency

■ Fixed annuities

■ Life insurance (whole and term)

- A personal residence
- Commodities and futures contracts

TAKE NOTE   Cryptocurrencies

If you are wondering what bitcoin and the other cryptocurrencies are defined as, it is still an open question. It appears that cryptocurrency would likely meet our basic definition of a security, but you should note that there is no third-party management. Currently the Securities and Exchange Commission (SEC) treats cryptocurrency as a commodity. If you should see cryptocurrencies on the exam, remember that they are a commodity, *not* a security.

LO 1.b Name the two major types of securities.

Stocks and bonds: The building blocks of the securities industry

The two basic securities are called stocks (also called equities) and bonds (debt). Though there are several different types of debt, bonds are the most common.

KNOWLEDGE CHECK

1. All of the following are considered securities **except**
    A. U.S. minted gold coins.
    B. common stock of XYZ Corporation.
    C. 15 British pound put contracts.
    D. Treasury bonds.

2. Another term for stocks and bonds is
    A. equity and debt.
    B. shares and units.
    C. voting and nonvoting.
    D. taxable and tax free.

3. Which of the following is **not** a security that an investor would purchase?
    A. Common shares of ABC Petroleum, Inc.
    B. Debt issue by ABC Petroleum
    C. Bitcoins
    D. Windmill Growth Fund

Answers

1. **A**   Stocks, bonds, and options are all examples of securities. Gold and gold coins are a commodity, not a security. LO 1.a

2. **A**   Equity is a common term for securities that represent ownership interest, such as stocks. Bonds are the most common type of debt security. LO 1.b

3. **C**   Bitcoin is considered a commodity, not a security. LO 1.a

LESSON 1.2: COMMON STOCK

LO 1.c Recall the characteristics of common stock.

Individual investors, by purchasing shares of stock in a company, can participate in the company's success. They can benefit from an increase in the price of the shares (capital appreciation) and by sharing in earnings through a distribution of profits called dividends. They are called equities because they represent ownership in the company.

A company issues (sells) stock to raise capital (money). Investors who buy the stock buy a share of ownership in the company. These investors are called stockholders or shareholders; they are the company's owners.

Each share of stock entitles its owner to a portion of the company's earnings and a vote in major management decisions. In most corporations the stockholders regularly elect individuals to a board of directors (BOD) to oversee the company's business. By electing a BOD, stockholders have a say in the company's management but are not involved in the day-to-day details of its operations.

 EXAMPLE

If a corporation issues 100 shares of stock, each share represents an identical 1/100—or 1%—ownership position in the company. An investor who owns 10 shares of stock would own 10% of the company; an investor who owns 50 shares of stock would own 50% of the company.

Classes of common stock for a corporation

Common stock can be classified as

- authorized;
- issued;
- outstanding; and
- treasury.

Authorized stock

A corporation is a legal being. Corporations are formed through the preparation of a corporate charter. In many respects, corporations can do the same things as a natural person. What a corporation can do that individuals can't is raise money by issuing securities. The corporate charter specifies the number of shares the company is authorized to issue. It is a decision made by the founders of the business.

In most cases, a company does not issue all the authorized shares. It issues enough of them to raise sufficient capital for its expected needs. The company may sell the remaining authorized shares in the future or use them for other purposes. If the company wants to issue more shares than are authorized, the charter must be amended through a stockholder vote.

Issued stock

Issued stock is authorized stock that has been sold to investors. Those investors have bought the stock and the company has received the money. When a corporation issues, or sells, fewer shares than the total number authorized, it normally reserves the unissued shares for future needs, including

- raising new capital for expansion,
- paying stock dividends, or
- exchanging common stock for outstanding convertible bonds or preferred stock.

Authorized but unissued stock does not carry the rights and privileges of issued shares and is not considered in determining a company's total capitalization. Authorized but unissued stock is similar to the blank checks in your checkbook. They're ready to use when needed. Until then, they are just pieces of paper.

Outstanding stock

Outstanding stock includes any shares that a company has issued and are in the hands of investors. Isn't all issued stock outstanding? Sometimes it is, but other times it is not. As we will read next, sometimes a corporation buys back its outstanding stock. Sometimes, owners of the stock will donate it to the company. However the company gets it back, that stock is no longer outstanding.

Treasury stock

Treasury stock is stock a corporation has issued and subsequently reacquired. The corporation can hold this stock indefinitely or can reissue or retire it. Treasury stock does not carry the rights of outstanding common shares, such as voting rights and the right to receive dividends. For that reason, analysts are only concerned with outstanding shares.

Types of common stock

Common stocks are often classified by the size of the corporation. This measurement is called market capitalization, or just market cap. A corporation's market cap is determined by multiplying the number of outstanding shares by the current market value (CMV) of a share (outstanding × CMV).

Large-cap stocks

Large-cap stocks are the largest companies. These can be rapidly growing technology companies or big, long-established firms. These tend to be company names you have heard of. Large-cap companies that have a long history of steady dividend payments are often called **blue-chip stocks**.

Mid-cap stocks

Mid-cap stocks are still large by most standards, just not as huge as the large-cap stocks. A company that is too large to be a small cap, but not large enough to be large cap, are the mid caps. They tend to reflect characteristics of both small and large caps, as you might expect with a label like "mid cap."

Small-cap stocks

The smallest stocks that are still large enough to be listed on national exchanges are small caps. They tend to be oriented toward growth and produce very little dividends.

Penny stocks

A penny stock is an unlisted (not listed on a U.S. stock exchange) security trading at less than $5 per share. Equity securities defined as penny stocks are considered **highly speculative**. In this light, SEC rules require that customers, before their initial transaction in a penny stock, be given a copy of a risk disclosure document. The member must receive a signed and dated acknowledgment from the customer that the document has been received. Not surprisingly, the penny stock disclosure document fully describes the risks associated with penny stock investments.

Regardless of activity in the account, if the account holds penny stocks, broker-dealers (BDs) must provide a monthly account statement to the customer. This must indicate the market value and number of shares for each penny stock held in the account, as well as the issuer's name.

Penny stock cold-calling rules

SEC rules regarding cold-calling customers also state that when a BD's representative contacts a potential customer to purchase penny stocks (this is a solicitation to buy, such as those occurring during a cold call), the representative must first determine suitability on the basis of information about the buyer's financial situation and objectives. The customer must sign and date this suitability statement before any initial penny stock trades may be placed. In addition, the BD must disclose

- the name of the penny stock,
- the number of shares to be purchased,
- a current quotation, and
- the amount of commission that the firm and the representative received.

Established customers are exempt from the suitability statement requirement but not from the disclosure requirements. An established customer is someone who

- has held an account with the BD for at least one year (and has made a deposit of funds or securities) or
- has made at least three penny stock purchases of different issuers on different days.

TAKE NOTE

The provisions of the penny stock rules apply only to solicited transactions such as those that might occur during a cold call. Unsolicited transactions—those not recommended by the BD or the registered representative (RR)—are exempt from these rules on suitability and disclosure.

LO1.d Recall the cash dividend process.

Dividends from common stock

Dividends are distributions of a company's profits to its shareholders. Investors who buy stock or mutual funds, for example, are entitled to dividends if and when the BOD votes to make such distributions. Shareholders are automatically sent any dividends to which their shares entitle them. Dividends may be paid in any of three ways.

■ Cash dividends—Cash dividends are normally distributed by check if an investor holds the stock certificate, or they are automatically deposited to a brokerage account if the shares are held in street name (held in a brokerage account in the firm's name to facilitate payments and delivery). When declared, cash dividends are typically paid quarterly and are taxed in the year they are distributed.

■ Stock dividends—If a company wishes to reinvest its profits for business purposes rather than to pay cash dividends, its BOD may declare a stock dividend. This is typical of many growth companies that invest their cash resources in research and development. Under these circumstances, the company issues additional shares of its common stock as a dividend to its current stockholders instead of cash. The net result is that the shareholder now owns more shares after the distribution, but the cost per share is adjusted downward. The stock dividend itself is not taxable, but the adjusted cost per share (new cost basis) will impact the tax consequences when the shares are sold.

EXAMPLE

An investor buys 200 shares of XYZ at $60 per share for a total cost of $12,000. If XYZ were to declare and pay a 20% stock dividend, the investor would now have a total of 240 shares (200 shares × 20% = 40 additional shares). Dividing $12,000 by 240 shares results in a new cost basis of $50 per share. In this light, when the shares are later sold, the investor will list $50 per share as the cost. The difference between the cost and the sale price will be the investor's gain or loss per share.

■ Product dividends – Though rare, some companies will pay a dividend by sending a sample of the company's product to shareholders.

EXAMPLE

In years past, a large food manufacturer that specialized in baked goods would send a loaf of sliced bread to all its shareholders once per year. This product dividend was per shareholder (not per share) and was accompanied by a 1099 for the value of the bread. As the company grew, the practice became too cumbersome and the bakery stopped the product dividend.

Finally, cash dividends may be taxed as either nonqualified (taxed at the investor's ordinary income tax rate) or as qualified. The maximum tax rate on qualified dividends is specified by current IRS tax code and will depend on the investor's income tax bracket. The higher the investor's income tax bracket, the higher the tax on qualified dividends will be, up to the specified maximum. However, it will always be lower than the investor's ordinary income tax rate.

Dividend disbursement dates

There are four dates to remember that are associated with the dividend disbursing process: declaration, ex-dividend, record, and payable.

■ *Declaration date*—When a company's BOD approves a dividend payment, it is recognized as the date the dividend was declared. At this time, the BOD would also designate the payment date and the dividend record date, discussed as follows.

■ *Ex-dividend date (ex-date)*—On the basis of the dividend record date, Financial Industry Regulatory Authority (FINRA)—or the exchange if the stock is listed on an exchange—declares an ex-date. The ex-date is one business day before the record date. Because most trades settle the regular way—two business days after the trade date—a customer must purchase the stock two business days before the record date to qualify for the dividend. Or said another way, to receive the dividend, the stock must be purchased before the ex-dividend date.

Conversely, if the stock is purchased on or after the ex-date, the new owner has purchased the stock "ex" without the dividend and is therefore not entitled to receive it.

■ *Record date*—The stockholders of record (those who own the stock) on the record date receive the dividend distribution.

■ *Payable date*—On the payable date, the dividend disbursing agent sends dividend checks to all stockholders whose names appear on the books as owners as of the record date. Investors are taxed for the tax year the dividend is paid, based on the payable date.

TAKE NOTE

DERP will help you remember the order in which the dates involving dividend distributions occur. The order of dates is declaration, ex-dividend, record, and payable.

LO 1.e Identify benefits and risks associated with common stock.

Benefits of owning common stock

Common shareholders enjoy numerous benefits, including voting rights, the opportunity for capital appreciation, and current income, as well as limited liability. In the following paragraphs, we'll explore these benefits.

Rights of common stockholders—Common stockholders have the right to vote for corporate directors. Frequently, it is not possible for the stockholder to attend the stockholder's meetings to personally cast a vote. An absentee ballot, known as a proxy, is made available for those shareholders who want to vote but can't attend the shareholder meeting. Those voting by proxy can generally do so by mail or online. Common stock is **freely transferable** to anyone who wants to buy it or receive it as a gift. Shareholders have the right to sell or give away their shares without permission of the corporation. Without this feature, there would be no stock market.

Calculating the number of votes

A stockholder can cast one vote for each share of stock owned. Depending on the company's bylaws and applicable state laws, a stockholder may have either a statutory or a cumulative vote.

- **Statutory voting.** Statutory voting allows a stockholder to cast one vote per share owned for each item on a ballot, such as candidates for the BOD. A board candidate needs a simple majority to be elected.

- **Cumulative voting.** Cumulative voting allows stockholders to allocate their total votes in any manner they choose.

EXAMPLE   Statutory vs. Cumulative Voting

XYZ Corporation will be electing three directors at its annual meeting. Each XYZ shareholder has a number of votes equal to the number of shares owned times the number of directorships up for election. Assume that a shareholder owns 100 shares. Under statutory voting, the shareholder may use a maximum of 100 votes for any one seat on the board.

Under cumulative voting, the shareholder may allocate all 300 votes anyway they choose (i.e., to one director or split between two or more), giving the shareholder a greater impact.

EXAMPLE 1   Mr. X Owns 100 Shares

Statutory Voting	
Board of directors: seat 1	100
Board of directors: seat 2	100
Board of directors: seat 3	100

EXAMPLE 2   Mr. X Owns 100 Shares

Cumulative Voting			Cumulative Voting	
Board of directors: seat 1	175	**OR**	Board of directors: seat 1	300
Board of directors: seat 2	50		Board of directors: seat 2	0
Board of directors: seat 3	75		Board of directors: seat 3	0

TAKE NOTE

Cumulative voting benefits the smaller investor, whereas statutory voting benefits larger shareholders.

Common stockholders have a right to limited access to the corporation's books. For the most part, common stockholders have the right to examine the minutes of meetings of the BOD and the right to examine the list of stockholders. Usually, this right is not exercised unless the performance of the corporation's management declines seriously. Common stockholders also have the right to receive an audited set of financial statements of the company's performance each year (Form 10-K, normally made part of the annual report).

Finally, common stockholders usually have the preemptive right to maintain their proportionate share of ownership in the corporation. The word *preempt* means to put oneself in front of another. If a corporation wants to issue additional shares, existing shareholders have the right to purchase those shares in an amount that would keep their proportionate ownership in the corporation unchanged. More on preemptive rights will come later.

- *Growth (capital gains)*—An increase in the market price of securities is capital appreciation. Historically, owning common stock has provided investors with returns in well excess of the inflation rate. For this reason, most investors with a long-term investment horizon have included common stock in their portfolios as a hedge against inflation. Of course, it must be mentioned that stock prices can decline, particularly over the short run.

- *Income*—Many corporations pay regular quarterly cash dividends to stockholders. Dividends are declared by the BOD and may increase over time as profitability increases. Dividends, which can be a significant source of income for investors, are a major reason many people invest in stocks.

  Issuers may also pay stock dividends (additional shares in the issuing company) or property dividends (shares in a subsidiary company or a product sample).

- *Limited liability*—One of the most important features of equity ownership is limited liability. In the event of a corporation's bankruptcy, when corporate assets are not adequate to meet corporate obligations, a shareholder's personal assets are not at risk. One cannot be forced to sell any personal assets to help pay the debts of the business.

  If an individual invests $5,000 in the stock of a corporation that goes bankrupt, the investor may lose the entire $5,000 invested, but the investor will not be forced to pay out any more monies to take care of company debts. Shareholders are personally at risk only for the amount that they invested. By contrast, a partner or a sole proprietor risks not only the amount personally invested in the business but also personal assets should the business not be able to pay off its obligations.

In summation, why would you include common stock in a client's portfolio?

- Potential capital appreciation
- Income from dividends
- Hedge against inflation

Risks of owning common stock

Regardless of their expectations, investors have no assurances that they will receive the returns they expect from their investments. The risks of owning common stock are listed as follows.

- *Market risk*—The chance that a stock will decline in price is one risk of owning common stock. A stock's price fluctuates daily as perceptions of the company's business prospects change and influence the actions of buyers and sellers. Investors have no assurance whatsoever that they will be able to recoup the investment in a stock at any time. When investors wish to sell their shares, the price may be higher or lower than when the shares were initially purchased.

- *Decreased or no dividend income*—A risk of stock ownership is the possibility of dividend income decreasing or ceasing entirely if the company loses money. The common stockholders have the last claim on earnings, and there is no guarantee that dividends will be paid. The decision to pay a dividend rests with the BOD, and it is not guaranteed.

- *Low priority at dissolution*—If a company enters bankruptcy, the holders of its bonds and preferred stock have priority over common stockholders. A company's debt and preferred shares are considered senior securities. Common stockholders have residual rights to corporate assets upon dissolution. Once all debtholders and preferred shareholders are paid, residual funds would be paid out to the common stockholders. Common stockholders are the most junior class of investors in a company. Priority of payment in liquidation rules are covered later.

 KNOWLEDGE CHECK

1. Which of the following would **most** likely require shareholder approval?
    A. Declaring a dividend
    B. Firing the CEO
    C. Hiring a new CFO
    D. Changing the corporation's name

2. All Big Company, Inc., an NYSE-listed manufacturer of large objects, has declared a 50-cents-a-share dividend payable next month. All Big also has options available for trade. The actual ex-dividend date will be declared by
    A. the OTC.
    B. the NYSE.
    C. FINRA.
    D. the CBOE.

3. Which of the following securities would likely provide the greatest potential for capital appreciation?
    A. A preferred stock
    B. A U.S. Treasury STRIP
    C. A common stock
    D. A convertible bond

Answer

1. **D** Changing the corporation's name is a significant matter that will likely need shareholder approval. Declaring a dividend and the hiring and firing of senior executives is well within the board's power. LO 1.c

2. **B** Ex-dates are set by the market center where trades will likely take place. In the case of an NYSE-listed stock, the New York Stock Exchange will determine the ex-date. The fact that All Big has listed options is not relevant to the question. LO 1.d

3. **C** Common stocks would be the most suitable for investors seeking capital appreciation (growth). Bonds and preferred stocks are better suited for conservative investors because each is primarily an income investment and has limited growth prospects. LO 1.e

LESSON 1.3: RIGHTS, WARRANTS, AND RULE 144

LO 1.f Differentiate rights and warrants.

Stock rights (preemptive rights)

In the "Rights of common stockholders," we mentioned preemptive right. Stock rights, sometimes known as preemptive rights, or simply rights, entitle existing common stockholders to maintain their proportionate ownership shares in a company by buying newly issued shares before the company offers them to the general public.

A rights offering allows stockholders to purchase common stock below the current market price. The rights are valued separately from the stock and trade in the secondary market during the subscription period, which is typically 30–45 days.

Existing shareholders receive one right per share owned. The number of rights required to purchase one share of the new issue depends on the number of outstanding shares and the number of new shares offered.

A stockholder who receives rights may

- exercise the rights to buy stock by sending the rights certificates and a check for the required amount to the rights agent;

- sell the rights and profit from their market value (rights certificates are negotiable securities); or

- let the rights expire and lose their value (not a likely scenario).

EXAMPLE

Seabird Shipping, Inc., currently has 1,000,000 million common shares outstanding. The shares are trading at $50 a share. Seabird will raise money by selling an additional 100,000 shares via a rights offering. The right allows the shareholder to purchase shares of the new offering for 10 rights and $48 per share. If all the rights are exercised, Seabird will receive $4,800,000 ($48 × 100,000) and will have 1,100,000 shares outstanding.

Shane Seabird, Jr., owns 20% of Seabird Shipping's outstanding shares (200,000 shares). He will receive 200,000 rights (one per share he owns). In order to maintain his percentage of ownership, he will need to buy 20% of the new offering (20,000 shares) to bring his total up to 220,000 shares (20% of the 1,100,000 outstanding shares after the offer is complete). To do this, he will exercise all 200,000 rights and pay $960,000.

Warrants

A warrant is a certificate granting its owner the right to purchase securities from the issuer at a specified price, normally higher than the current market price at the time the warrants are issued, and at some time in the future. Unlike a right, a warrant is usually a long-term instrument that gives the investor the option of buying shares at a later date at the specified (exercise) price. Note that while the exercise price is higher than the current market value when the warrants are issued, it is hoped that the exercise price will be below current market value when the warrants are eventually exercised.

Warrants are usually offered to the public as sweeteners in connection with other securities, such as debt instruments (bonds) or preferred stock, to make those securities more attractive. Such offerings are often bundled as units. For example, an investor might buy a corporate bond and with it receive 10 warrants, allowing the investor to purchase 10 shares of common stock at a specified price on a later date.

EXAMPLE

Nokamura Industries is issuing a 20-year bond offering with warrants attached. Buyers of the bond will receive 10 warrants with the bond. Nokamura stock is trading at $50 a share. The warrants allow an investor to purchase shares of the company's common stock for $75 a share anytime before the warrant expires in 15 years.

TAKE NOTE

It pays to remember by comparison:

Rights—short term, given to existing shareholders, allows one to purchase shares below current market value

Warrants—long term, bundled with other securities, allows someone to purchase shares at a price that is above the current market value at the time the warrants were issued

---

LO 1.g Relate rules on control and restricted stock.

Rule 144: Restricted stock and control persons

Rule 144 applies to shares that are sold through a nonstandard offering and are subject to resale restrictions and to sales by persons who are classified as a control person (insider) of the issuer.

Restricted stock

Restricted securities are those acquired through some means other than a registered public offering. A security purchased in a private placement is a restricted security. Restricted securities may not be sold until they have been held fully paid for six months. According to Rule 144, after holding restricted stock fully paid for six months, an investor may begin selling shares. When issued, these shares will have a restrictive legend on the certificate warning about the holding period restriction. That is why these shares are sometimes referred to as legended, or legended certs.

Before these shares may be sold, the issuer must release (remove) the restriction, allowing the shares to trade freely. You may see the phrase "the sale effectively registers the stock" associated with this action. In other words, buyers of stock being sold that were subject to Rule 144 when issued are not subject to any restrictions if they choose to resell.

Control stock

Control stock are those owned by directors, officers, or persons who own or control 10% or more of the issuer's voting stock. Note that families will aggregate their positions to determine the percentage of ownership.

TAKE NOTE

If an unaffiliated individual owns 7% of the voting stock of XYZ, that person is not a control person. However, if that person's spouse owns 4% of the voting stock, then both would be considered control persons. In other words, if there is a 10% or more interest held by immediate family members, then all those family members owning voting stock are control persons.

When a control person (also called an affiliate) wants to sell shares, that person must complete a Form 144. The form is used to determine the number of shares the control person may sell over a 90-day period.

The volume limitations under Rule 144 are the *greater* of

■ 1% of the outstanding shares of the company or

■ the average weekly trading volume over the most recent four weeks.

PRACTICE QUESTION

Mrs. Davidson owns 8% of Copper Mountain Metals Corporation and her husband, Mr. Davidson, owns 4%. Mr. Davidson would like to sell some of his shares. When he files Form 144, he discovers that Copper Mountain has 2,400,000 outstanding shares. The recent trading volume of the company is as follows:

Week Ending	Volume
April 7	23,000
March 31	25,000
March 24	26,000
March 17	24,000
March 10	30,000

How many shares may Mr. Davidson sell in the next 90 days under Rule 144?

A. 24,000 shares

B. 24,500 shares

C. 32,000 shares

D. 26,250 shares

Answer: The answer is 24,500 shares and is found by first determining 1% of 2.4 million shares (2,400,000 × 0.01) 24,000 shares. The next step is to find the simple mean (average) of the *most recent* four weeks. In this question, you would not use the week of March 10 information. The average is 24,500 shares (23K + 25K + 26K + 24K = 98K; 98K / 4 = 24,500 shares). The volume limit is the higher of these two numbers, or 24,500 shares.

KNOWLEDGE CHECK

1. Under Rule 144, which of the following sales are subject to volume limitations on the number of shares sold?

    I. Control person selling registered stock held for 1 year

    II. Control person selling restricted stock held for 2 years

    III. Nonaffiliate selling registered stock held for 1 month

    IV. Nonaffiliate selling restricted stock held for more than 6 months

    A. III and IV

    B. I and II

    C. I and III

    D. I and IV

2. American Liquidators Corporation (Ticker LQDT) has 100 million outstanding common shares. The company would like to raise capital by selling 100 million new shares. In order to accomplish, this they would

    A. offer warrants to existing shareholders.

    B. suggest that existing shareholders go to the market and double their existing position.

    C. offer stock rights to existing shareholders.

    D. perform a stock split.

3. Squidco, Inc., is issuing 100 million dollars in 4 ½% bonds maturing in 20 years. When purchased at issue, the buyers will receive an additional security that allows them to purchase 20 shares of Squidco common stock at $50 per share anytime in the next 10 years. Squidco common is currently trading at $29.95 a share. This is an example of
   A.   a warrant.
   B.   a stock right.
   C.   a follow-on offering.
   D.   a call.

Answers

1. **B** Control persons (insiders) are always subject to volume limitations. Nonaffiliates have no volume (or any other restrictions) in the sale of registered stock. If the shares are restricted, the volume limits for nonaffiliates end after six months. Registered shares sold by nonaffiliates have no Form 144 filing requirement. LO 1.g

2. **C** LQDT would give the right to purchase a portion of the newly issued shares to existing shareholders sufficient to maintain their current percentage of ownership via a stock rights offering. Warrants are long term and normally attached to a fixed-income offer. Neither the stock split nor investors buying in the market generates capital for the company. LO 1.f

3. **A** A warrant is normally issued attached to a fixed-income security to attract more interest in the debt issue. Warrants are generally longer term (five or more years) and have an exercise price that is higher than the current stock price. LO 1.f

LESSON 1.4: AMERICAN DEPOSITARY RECEIPTS (ADRs) AND PREFERRED STOCK

LO 1.h Recall the characteristics of American depositary receipts.

American depositary receipts

Let's suppose an investor hears about an up-and-coming Chinese company that's going be the next Google. She's anxious to invest until she learns that the trade would need to be executed on the Chinese stock market and that she'll also need to convert her dollars into yuan (Chinese currency) before making the trade. At that point, the investor's enthusiasm wanes. There must be an easier way to invest in foreign companies.

The answer to this investor's dilemma is an American depositary receipt (ADR). ADRs are a type of equity security designed to simplify foreign investing for Americans. An ADR is created when common shares are purchased in the foreign company's home market. These shares are then deposited in a foreign branch of a U.S. bank, and a receipt (the ADR) is created. Each ADR may represent one or more shares of the foreign company's shares held on deposit. The ADR provides U.S. investors with a convenient way to diversify their holdings beyond domestic companies.

■   *Ease of use*—Typically, these ADRs will be listed on the NYSE or Nasdaq, but some may be traded over the counter (OTC). This U.S.-based trading means the investor gets to execute her trade in a familiar, well-regulated setting—and more importantly, the purchase is made in U.S. dollars. The ADRs trade and settle (T+2) in the same fashion as would a traditional U.S. common stock. This ease of use benefits the investor, but it also helps foreign companies attract a U.S. investor base. Many ADR issuers also file periodic reports with the SEC, which provides further comfort to the buyer.

■ *ADR taxation*—Dividends paid to a U.S. investor may be subject to a withholding tax by the home country of the underlying foreign stock issuer. In many cases, the amount of tax withheld by the foreign government is applied as a credit against the investor's U.S. tax liability. Any trading profits (capital gains) from the ADR would only be taxable in the United States.

■ *Currency and political risk*—ADRs are issued and pay dividends in U.S. dollars. That means these securities eliminate the complications of currency conversion. However, ADRs are still subject to currency risk. Why? The company pays dividends in its home currency and the issuing bank converts to and pays out those dividends in U.S. dollars. When the currency exchange rate changes, so will these dividends (in U.S. dollar terms). Also, the value of the ADR itself will rise and fall in conjunction with the value of the underlying foreign stock, which is also influenced by currency swings. Of course, if the ADR issuer is based in an unstable country, the investor is also exposed to political risk.

LO 1.i Recall characteristics of preferred stock.

Preferred Stock

Preferred stock is an equity security because it represents a class of ownership in the issuing corporation. Although it is an equity security, it shares some characteristics with a debt security. As with debt securities, the rate of return on a preferred stock is fixed rather than subject to variation, as with common stock. A preferred stock's annual dividend represents its fixed rate of return. This is a key attraction for income-oriented investors. Normally, a preferred stock is identified by its annual dividend payment stated as a percentage of its par value. Always assume preferred par value is $100 unless stated differently.

EXAMPLE

A preferred stock with a par value of $100 that pays $6 in annual dividends is known as a 6% preferred ($6 dividend / $100 par). The dividend of a preferred stock with no par value is stated as a $6 no-par preferred.

Two final characteristics of preferred stock are that, unlike common shareholders, preferred shareholders generally have no voting rights nor do they have preemptive rights. With few exceptions, the right to vote for board members or on other corporate issues is reserved for common shareholders.

TAKE NOTE

All corporations issue common stock, but not all corporations issue preferred stock.

Benefits of owning preferred stock

Although preferred stock does not typically have the same growth potential as common stock, preferred stockholders have some advantages over common stockholders.

■ *Dividend preference*—When the BOD declares dividends, owners of preferred shares must be paid before any payment to common shareholders.

Priority at dissolution over common stock—If a corporation goes bankrupt, preferred stockholders have a priority claim over common stockholders on the assets remaining after creditors have been paid.

Risks of owning preferred stock

Although they enjoy some preferences, owners of preferred stock face some risks.

■ *Purchasing power risk*—This is the potential that, because of inflation, the fixed income produced will not purchase as much in the future as it does today.

■ *Interest rate sensitivity*—Like a fixed-income security, when interest rates rise, the value of preferred shares declines. (This will be discussed in greater detail later in this unit.)

■ *Decreased or no dividend income*—As with common stock ownership, there is the possibility of dividend income decreasing or ceasing entirely if the company loses money. The decision to pay a dividend rests with the BOD, and while the dividend percentage is fixed, it is not guaranteed to be paid.

■ *Priority at dissolution*—While preferred shareholders are paid before common shareholders if a company enters bankruptcy, the preferred shares are paid behind all creditors.

In summation, why would you include preferred stock in a client's portfolio?

■ Fixed income from dividends

■ Prior claim ahead of common stock

■ Convertible preferred stock sacrifices income in exchange for potential appreciation (discussed shortly)

■ In doing so, the client would be incurring the following risks:

– Possible loss of purchasing power

– Interest rate (money rate) risk

– Business difficulties (leading to possible reduction or elimination of the dividend) and even bankruptcy (leading to loss of principal)

Types of preferred stock

Separate categories of preferred stock may differ in several ways, including dividend rate and profit participation privileges. However, all maintain preference over common stock.

■ *Straight (noncumulative)*—Straight preferred stock has no special features beyond the stated dividend payment. Missed dividends are not paid to the holder.

■ *Cumulative*—Cumulative preferred stock accrues payments due its shareholders in the event dividends are reduced or suspended.

Dividends due cumulative preferred stock accumulate on the company's books until the corporation's BOD decides to pay them. When the company resumes dividend payments, cumulative preferred stockholders receive current dividends plus the total accumulated dividends—dividends in arrears—before any dividends may be distributed to common stockholders.

EXAMPLE

In 2014, RST Corporation had both common stock and cumulative preferred stock outstanding. The common paid a dividend of $1, and the preferred paid a $2 dividend. Because of financial difficulties, the company stopped paying dividends during 2014. After resolving its problems in 2018, the company resumed dividend payments and paid the cumulative preferred shareholders an $8 dividend for dividends in arrears for years 2014, 2015, 2016, and 2017 plus the current year's (2018) $2 dividend ($10 total) before paying any dividends to the common stockholders.

■ *Callable preferred*—Corporations often issue callable (or redeemable) preferred stock, which a company can buy back from investors at a stated price after a specified date. The right to call the stock allows the company to replace a relatively high fixed-dividend obligation with a lower one when the cost of money has gone down. This is similar to refinancing a mortgage.

When a corporation calls a preferred stock, dividend payments cease on the call date. In return for the call privilege, the corporation may pay a premium exceeding the stock's par value at the call, such as $103 for a $100 par value stock.

■ *Convertible preferred*—A preferred stock is convertible if the owner can exchange the shares for a fixed number of shares of the issuing corporation's common stock.

Convertible preferred is generally issued with a lower stated dividend rate than nonconvertible preferred of the same quality because the investor may have the opportunity to convert to common shares and enjoy greater capital gain potential. The concept of a convertible security will be discussed in greater detail later in this unit when we cover convertible bonds.

TAKE NOTE

Because the value of a convertible preferred stock is linked to the value of a common stock, the convertible preferred share price tends to fluctuate in line with the common. For example, as a convertible preferred issue is convertible at $40, once the common stock crosses $40, the preferred will track the value of the common stock because investors assume that at some point, the preferred will be converted into the common.

■ *Adjustable-rate preferred*—Some preferred stocks are issued with adjustable (or variable) dividend rates. Such dividends are usually tied to the rates of other interest rate benchmarks, such as Treasury bills and money market rates, and can be adjusted as often as quarterly. Because the payment adjusts to current interest rates, the price of the stock remains relatively stable.

TEST TOPIC ALERT

For investors looking for income through preferred stocks, this would be their least appropriate choice.

■ *Participating preferred*—In addition to fixed dividends, participating preferred stock offers its owners a share of corporate profits that remain after all dividends and interest due other securities are paid. The percentage to which participating preferred stock participates is noted on the stock certificate.

EXAMPLE

If a preferred stock is described as XYZ 6% preferred participating to 9%, the company pays its holders up to 3% in additional dividends in profitable years if the BOD declares so.

KNOWLEDGE CHECK

1. Your client holds ADRs of Daikon Motors, Inc., an automobile manufacturer based in Asia. All of the following are true about the position **except**
   A. they will receive dividends in U.S. dollars.
   B. the security may be traded in U.S. markets.
   C. they have the same voting rights as an owner of the common stock.
   D. they have the right to request the underlying common shares be issued to them directly.

2. For this election cycle, Big Trucks, Inc., has three open board seats. Big Trucks operates under a cumulative voting system. Your customer owns 300 participating preferred shares of Big Trucks. He has
   A. 900 votes he can divide anyway he wants among the three seats.
   B. no voting rights.
   C. 300 votes each for the open seats.
   D. 300 votes total to spread among the three open seats.

3. In 2011, RST Corporation had both common stock and $100 par value 4% noncumulative preferred stock outstanding. The preferred, like the common stock, pay dividends on a quarterly basis. Because of financial difficulties, the company stopped paying dividends after 2011. After resolving its problems in 2015, the company resumed dividend payments in 2016. Before paying the first quarterly common stock dividend that year, the company would have to pay a quarterly dividend to the preferred stockholders of
   A. $1.00.
   B. $4.00.
   C. $17.00.
   D. $20.00.

Answers

1. **C**   It is important to remember that ADRs are issued by a depository bank and the bank is the registered owners of the shares. Depository banks are not required to pass voting proxies through to the ADR holders. LO 1.h

2. **B**   Your customer owns preferred stock. Preferred stock carries no voting rights. LO 1.i

3. **A**   In the case of a noncumulative preferred stock, skipped dividends are forever lost. So, when the company is able to pay a dividend, as is always the case, it must pay the current preferred dividend before paying to the common shares. The question states that dividends are paid quarterly. Therefore, the quarterly dividend on a stock paying $4.00 annually would be $1.00—an amount that must be paid before the quarterly common dividend can be paid. LO 1.i

UNIT 2

Individual Securities—Debt

LEARNING OBJECTIVES

When you have completed this unit, you will be able to accomplish the following.

- › LO 2.a   Recall the basic characteristics of bonds.
- › LO 2.b   Relate yields and interest rates.
- › LO 2.c   Define safety and volatility in bonds.
- › LO 2.d   Name the features of bonds.
- › LO 2.e   Define the features of a zero-coupon bond.
- › LO 2.f   Define the types of corporate debt and order of liquidation.
- › LO 2.g   Identify the benefits and risks associated with debt securities.
- › LO 2.h   Differentiate general obligation and revenue bonds.
- › LO 2.i   Calculate tax-equivalent yield.
- › LO 2.j   Recall the traits of T-bills, T-notes, and T-bonds.
- › LO 2.k   Recall the features of GNMA, FNMA, and FHLMC certificates.
- › LO 2.l   Recall how interest from different bonds are taxed.
- › LO 2.m   Define a money market security.
- › LO 2.n   Define mortgage and asset-backed securities.

INTRODUCTION

In Unit 2 we will focus on the other major asset class: debt. In addition to selling stock, corporations may issue debt in order to raise capital. Government entities also raise capital by issuing debt securities. Unlike stocks, debt securities come in a number of different forms: bonds, notes, bills, certificates, and various money market instruments, just to list a portion of these types of securities. The one characteristic that is true for all of these is that the issuer owes interest and principal to the owner of the debt.

LESSON 2.1: THE BASICS OF BONDS

LO 2.a Recall the basic characteristics of bonds.

Before we explore bonds from different issuers (corporate, federal government, and municipal governments), let's introduce some basic bond characteristics.

Par value

Most debt securities have a par value of $1,000. This is also called the principal or face value. The test will assume a par value of $1,000 for most debt. You should make this same assumption unless you are working with one of the specific exceptions discussed later on in this unit.

Maturities

Each bond has its own maturity date. This is the date the investor receives the loan principal back. While common maturities are in the range of 5–30 years, some can be much shorter (short-term debt securities), and others longer. Maturities come in different types: term, serial, and balloon.

- *Term bond*—A **term bond** is structured so that the principal of the whole issue matures at once. Because the entire principal is repaid at one time, issuers may establish a sinking fund account to accumulate money to retire the bonds at maturity.

- *Serial bond*—A **serial bond issue** schedules portions of the principal to mature at intervals over a period of years until the entire balance has been repaid.

- *Balloon bond*—An issuer sometimes schedules its bond's maturity using elements of both serial and term maturities. The issuer repays part of the bond's principal before the final maturity date, as with a serial maturity but pays off the major portion of the bond at maturity. This bond has a balloon, or serial and balloon, maturity.

 TAKE NOTE

The term *series* normally refers to types of savings bonds. Savings bonds are a type of debt issued by the federal government that may be purchased and redeemed at banks or from the Treasury Department. Savings bonds do not trade and are not considered a security. *Series* is not a type on maturity used with debt securities.

Coupons and accrued interest

The coupon represents the interest rate the issuer has agreed to pay the investor. At one time, bonds were issued with interest coupons attached to the certificate that the investor would detach and turn in to receive the interest payments. While bonds are no longer issued with physical coupons attached, the interest rate the bond pays is still called the coupon rate. It is also called the *stated yield* or *nominal yield*. It is calculated from the bond's par value, usually stated as a percentage of par. Par value, also known as *face value* for a bond, is normally $1,000 per bond, meaning that each bond will be redeemed for $1,000 when it matures. Therefore, a bond with a 6% coupon is paying $60 in interest per year (6% × $1,000 par value = $60).

Regarding **accrued interest**, what happens if the bond trades between coupon payments? The buyer (new owner) must pay the seller (old owner) the amount of interest earned to date at the time of settlement. This means the new owner gets paid the full coupon from the issuer in the next payment cycle. Corporate and municipal trades use a 30-day-month/360-day-year calculation for accrued interest. Treasury bonds and notes transactions employ the actual number of days elapsed when calculating the amount of accrued interest due. Please note that buyers of zero-coupon bonds do not pay accrued interest because these securities are not interest bearing.

TAKE NOTE

Interest is generally paid on a semiannual basis. Using the previous example, the 6% coupon bond would pay $30 in interest every six months—a total of $60 per year.

Pricing

Once a bond is trading in the secondary markets, it can trade at a price of par, a premium to par, or a discount to par. If par equals $1,000, an example of a premium bond might be one trading at $1,200, and an example of a discount bond might be one trading at $800. Bond pricing is measured in points, with each point equaling 1% of face value, or $10. For example, a bond trading at 90 is worth $900, while a bond trading at 103 is worth $1,030. Multiply the quoted price by 10 to get the dollar amount.

Market forces affecting bond prices

Bond prices can be impacted by the usual market forces that impact securities in general, such as supply and demand. However, because they are debt instruments, they have a particular sensitivity to changes in market interest rates. Remember that the interest rate the issuer pays is the cost of borrowing money. In that light, it makes sense that bond prices will rise and fall as interest rates fluctuate.

Generally, bond prices have an inverse relationship to interest rates. If interest rates go up, bond prices for those trading in the secondary markets will go down. Conversely, if interest rates are falling, bond prices for those trading in the secondary market will be going up. Think about it this way: If interest rates in the marketplace were at 6%, wouldn't a bond currently paying 8% trading in the secondary market look attractive? It would, and as investors were attracted to it, its price would push upward. On the other hand, if interest rates in the marketplace were at 6%, wouldn't a bond currently paying only 4% look less attractive? It would, and as investors moved to sell it, its price would move downward.

TAKE NOTE

Though the price of the bond will react to market forces (interest rate sensitivity and general supply and demand), the coupon is always the same. The coupon is a fixed percentage of par value; a 6% coupon pays $60 of annual interest, no matter what the current market value of the bond is.

LO 2.b Relate yields and interest rates.

Yields

A bond's yield expresses the cash interest payments in relation to the bond's value. Yield is determined by the issuer's credit quality, prevailing interest rates, time to maturity, and any features the bond may have, such as a call feature (which we'll discuss shortly). As noted earlier, a bond can be traded at prices other than par, so the price discount or premium from par is taken into consideration when calculating a bond's overall yield. You can look at a bond's yield in several ways.

■ *Nominal yield*—Coupon, nominal, or stated yield is set at the time of issue. Remember that the coupon is a fixed percentage of the bond's par value.

■ *Current yield (CY)*—CY measures a bond's annual coupon payment (interest) relative to its market price, as shown in the following equation:

annual coupon payment ÷ market price = current yield

■ *Yield to maturity (YTM)*—A bond's YTM reflects the annualized return of the bond if held to maturity. In calculating yield to maturity, the bondholder takes into account the difference between the price that was paid for a bond and par value received when the bond matures. If the bond is purchased at a discount, the investor makes money at maturity (i.e., the discount amount increases the return). If the bond is purchased at a premium, the investor loses money at maturity (i.e., the premium amount decreases the return).

TAKE NOTE

If you see a bond that is trading on a "basis of" and the question then provides you a yield, that yield is the yield to maturity (YTM).

Yields are measured in *basis points*. A basis point is a measurement of yield equal to 1/100 of 1%. A full percentage point is made up of 100 basis points (bps). Remember not to confuse basis points with points. As discussed previously, a point is a measurement of the change in a bond's price, which equals 1% of face value, or $10 per bond. YTM is sometimes called a bond's *basis*. For example, a bond trading at a 5.83 basis means the bond has a YTM of 5.83%.

EXAMPLE

If a bond is purchased for $900 (a discount) and is held to maturity, at maturity the investor will receive $1,000 (par). The amount of the discount ($100) increases the investor's total return. On the other hand, if a bond is purchased for $1,100 (a premium) and is held to maturity, at maturity the investor will receive $1,000 (par), and the amount of the premium paid ($100) reduces the investor's total return.

■ *Yield to call (YTC)*—Some bonds are issued with what is known as a call feature. A bond with a call feature may be redeemed before maturity at the issuer's option. Essentially, when a callable bond is called in by the issuer, the investor receives the principal back sooner than anticipated (before maturity). YTC calculations reflect the early redemption date and consequent acceleration of the discount gain if the bond was originally purchased at a discount, or the accelerated premium loss if the bond was originally purchased at a premium.

Recognizing the relationship these yields have to one another is important. Also, that relationship will depend on whether a bond is trading at par, a premium, or a discount. This is visualized in the following diagram, where you should note that while the coupon (nominal or stated) yield never changes regardless of price, the CY, YTM, and YTC do.

Figure 2.1: Inverse Relationship of Price and Yields

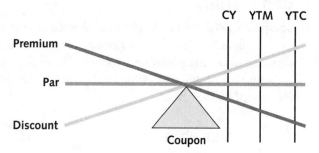

KNOWLEDGE CHECK

1. Your customer calls you with a question. The customer tells you that they received a phone call from the bond desk telling the customer that a trade to purchase 20 bonds at 100 has been executed for the customer's account. The customer would like to know how much they paid for the bonds before any commission or other charges. The answer to the customer's question is
   A. $2,000.
   B. $200,000.
   C. $1,000.
   D. $20,000.

2. A 6% corporate bond trading on a 7% basis is trading
   A. at a discount.
   B. at a premium.
   C. with a current yield above 7%.
   D. with a coupon rate below 6%.

3. A BB-rated 6% corporate callable bond that matures in 12 years that is trading at 100.25 is priced at
   A. a discount.
   B. a premium.
   C. with a current yield above 7%.
   D. with a coupon rate below 6%.

Answers

1. **D**   Paying "100" means they paid 100% of par ($1,000) per bond. They purchased 20 bonds, so a total of $20,000. Note that the question concerned "how much they paid for the bonds," not the price per bond. LO 2.a

2. **A**   The term "a 7% basis" means that the YTM is 7%. YTM is higher than the coupon rate (6%), so the bond trades at a discount. Current yield must be between the coupon rate and the YTM. LO 2.b

3. **B**   There are a lot of words, but the only thing you need to understand in order to answer this question is that the bond is trading at a price above par (100), so it's at a premium. LO 2.b

LESSON 2.2: BOND RATINGS AND FEATURES

LO 2.c Define safety and volatility in bonds.

Bond ratings

The purchase of a debt security is only as safe as the strength of the borrower. That strength can be enhanced if the loan has collateral. Because safety of the bond will frequently be a very important consideration for clients, most investors consult the rating services. There are a number of different rating organizations. The following Take Note describes the ones recognized by the SEC.

TAKE NOTE

There are three "major" credit rating agencies:

■ Fitch Ratings, Inc.

■ Moody's Investors Service, Inc.

■ Standard and Poor's Rating Service (S&P)

You may see a reference to A.M. Best Co., Inc., which is historically associated with rating insurance companies' ability to pay claims and their debt issues and, though a registered credit rating, is not one of the "majors."

The most important rating organizations for the exam are Standard & Poor's and Moody's. Both organizations have highly qualified personnel who analyze all the details of the debt issue and arrive at a letter rating indicating their opinion of the debt's quality (safety). You might see reference to the Fitch ratings and should note that they follow the same pattern as S&P.

The following chart (Figure 2.2) should give you all the information you need for the exam.

Figure 2.2: Bond Rating Chart

Standard & Poor's	Moody's	Interpretation
Bank-grade (investment-grade) bonds		
AAA	Aaa	Highest rating. Capacity to repay principal and interest judged high.
AA	Aa	Very strong. Only slightly less secure than the highest rating.
A	A	Judged to be slightly more susceptible to adverse economic conditions.
BBB	Baa	Adequate capacity to repay principal and interest. Slightly speculative.
Speculative (noninvestment-grade) bonds		
BB	Ba	Speculative. Significant chance that issuer could miss an interest payment.
B	B	Issuer has missed one or more interest or principal payments.
C	Caa	No interest is being paid on bond at this time.
D	D	Issuer is in default. Payment of interest or principal is in arrears.

PRACTICE QUESTION

According to Standard and Poor's rating system, the four highest grades of bonds (from best to lowest grade) are

A. Aaa; Aa; A; Baa.

B. A; Aa; Aaa; B.

C. B; A; AA; AAA.

D. AAA; AA; A; BBB.

Answer: D Choice A would be correct if the question referred to Moody's.

Investment-grade debt

In the industry, bonds rated in the top four categories (BBB or Baa and higher) are called investment grade. Investment-grade bonds are generally the only quality eligible for purchase by the institutions (e.g., banks or insurance companies) and by fiduciaries and, therefore, have greater liquidity than lower-grade instruments.

This is where the risk/reward concept comes into play. All other things being equal, the higher the rating, the lower the yield. Think of these ratings as your personal credit score. When your score is at 800, it is easy to borrow money. The rate you will be charged for the loan will be lower than for someone whose score is 600. The concept is that if the lender is going to have to take more risk that payments will not be made on time, there has to be a greater reward. That reward is in the form of a higher interest charge

High-yield bonds

Lower-grade bonds, known in the industry as junk bonds, are now more commonly called high-yield bonds. Because of their lower ratings (BB or Ba or lower) and additional risk of default, high-yield bonds may be subject to substantial price erosion during slow economic times or when a bond issuer's creditworthiness is questioned. Their volatility is usually substantially higher than investment-grade bonds, but they may be suitable for sophisticated investors seeking higher returns and possible capital appreciation from speculative fixed-income investments.

Once again, think risk/reward. The less creditworthy the borrower, the more risk to the lender. That requires a greater reward to the lender to compensate for that risk. That is why lower-rated bonds carry higher rates of return.

It is important to understand that when the raters evaluate a bond, they look at all the factors, including collateral. A mortgage bond is not necessarily safer than any debenture.

Nonrated

Finally, not all bonds are rated. Does that mean the risks are enormous? Not necessarily. The rating organizations rate those issues that either pay to be rated or have enough bonds outstanding to generate constant investor interest. The fact that a bond is not rated does not indicate its quality. Many issues are too small to justify the expense of a bond rating. In those cases, investors have to do their "homework."

Volatility

As discussed earlier, bond prices move in an inverse direction to interest rates. A bond's sensitivity to these movements is called "volatility." The more a bond moves in response to a change in interest rates, it is said to be more volatile; the less it moves, the less volatility it has.

As a rule, the more time left to maturity, the more volatile a bond's price will be given a change in interest rates. With little exception, a bond with 10 years to go until it matures will be more volatile than a bond with 5 years to maturity.

Secondarily, the lower a bond's coupon rate, the more volatile it is. A 3% bond with five years remaining will be more volatile than a 6% bond with the same five years left.

A way of measuring a bond's volatility that combines maturity and coupon rate is called "duration." A higher duration means a more volatile price; lower duration brings less price volatility. Duration may also be used to measure the overall volatility of a portfolio of bonds. You may need to recognize the concept of duration but will not need to calculate it.

LO 2.d Name the features of bonds.

Features

Bonds can be issued with different features attached. Among the most common are the following.

- *Call feature*—As noted previously, a call feature allows an issuer to call in a bond before maturity. Issuers will generally do this when interest rates are falling. From the issuer's perspective, why pay 6% interest to investors on an existing bond if current interest rates have fallen to 4%? It is better to call in the 6% bond and simply issue a new bond paying the lower current interest rate. This feature benefits the issuer. If called, the (former) bondholder now has the dilemma of finding a similar rate of return in a lower interest rate environment.

- *Put feature*—A put feature for a bond is the opposite of a call feature. Instead of the issuer calling in a bond before it matures, with a put feature, the investor can put the bond back to the issuer before it matures. Investors will generally do this when interest rates are rising. From the investor's perspective, why accept 6% interest on a bond one owns if current interest rates have risen to 8%? It is better to put the 6% bond back to the issuer, take the principal returned, and invest it in a new bond paying the current interest rate of 8%. This feature benefits the bondholder.

- *Convertible feature*—Much like our discussion of convertible preferred stock, convertible bonds are issued by corporate issuers, allowing the investor to convert the bond into shares of common stock. Giving the investor the opportunity to exchange a debt instrument for one that gives the investor ownership rights (shares of common stock) is generally considered a benefit for the investor.

If the related stock rises in value, convertible bonds may often track the value of the underlying shares that the bondholder would be entitled to upon conversion. Investors often engage in arbitrage transactions, which involves the simultaneous buying and selling of the bond and underlying stock in an attempt to capture price differentials between the related securities.

TAKE NOTE

When bonds are issued with features that benefit the issuer, such as a call feature, the issuer generally will need to pay a slightly higher coupon rate of interest to make the bond attractive to new investors. Conversely, when bonds are issued with features that benefit the bondholder, such as put or conversion features, the issuer will usually pay a slightly lower coupon rate of interest because the feature will compensate for the lower return.

KNOWLEDGE CHECK

1. Below which of the following S&P ratings would a bond be considered speculative?
    A. A
    B. B
    C. BB
    D. BBB

2. Which of the following bonds would have the **most** price volatility?
    A. 3% 10-year T-note
    B. 2% 5-year T-note
    C. 5% 20-year T-bond
    D. 5% 15-year corporate bond

3. If a bond has a feature that allows the issuer to pay off bondholders prior to maturity, the bond has
    A. a put feature.
    B. a call feature.
    C. a conversion feature.
    D. a presale feature.

Answers

1. **D** The investment-grade ratings, from highest to lowest, are AAA, AA, A, and BBB. All ratings below BBB are speculative bonds. LO 2.c

2. **C** The more time left to maturity, the more volatile the bond tends to be. Even though the 20-year T-bond is safer than the corporate, its price will be more volatile. LO 2.c

3. **B** A feature that allows an issuer to pay a bond off earlier than the maturity date is a call feature. A put feature allows the holder of the debt to force the issuer to pay off the bond. A conversion feature allows the owner to convert the bond to the issuer's common stock. A presale feature has nothing to do with bonds. LO 2.d

LESSON 2.3: ZEROS AND TYPES OF CORPORATE DEBT

LO 2.e Define the features of a zero-coupon bond.

Bonds are normally issued as interest-paying securities. **Zero-coupon bonds (zeroes)** are an issuer's debt obligations that do not make regular interest payments. Instead, zeroes are issued, or sold, at a deep discount to their face value and mature at par. The difference between the discounted purchase price and the full face value at maturity is the return, or accreted interest, the investor receives.

EXAMPLE

Lonsdale Corporation issue a zero-coupon bond at a price of 50 ($500 a bond) maturing in 20 years. The bond makes no interest payments. At maturity, it pays face value (par $1,000) to investors; $500 principal and $500 interest. This would calculate to an interest rate of 3.6%

The price of a zero-coupon bond reflects the general interest rate climate for similar maturities, going up and down in an inverse relationship with interest rates. As the coupon rate is zero, these bonds tend to be more volatile than other bonds with similar maturities.

Zero-coupon bonds are issued by corporations, municipalities, and the U.S. Treasury (Treasury-issued zeroes are called STRIPS) and may be created by broker-dealers from other types of securities. A more common form of broker-dealer-created zeroes is built from a basket of T-bonds. These zeroes, issued by a BD and not the Treasury, are called treasury receipts. Unlike a STRIP, a treasury receipt is not backed by the full faith and credit of the Treasury.

TAKE NOTE

Though the interest payment is paid at maturity, owners of zeroes will pay taxes on the interest annually. The total interest payment is divided by the years remaining to maturity and a 1099 Interest form will be sent to the owners. If the interest payment is $500 and 10 years remain to maturity, then the 1099 will reflect $50 every year. This is called "annual accretion of the discount" or "phantom income." You will not be required to do the calculation, but the concept of phantom income is a testable point.

LO 2.f Define the types of corporate debt and order of liquidation.

Corporate bonds

Corporate debt securities, like any other loan, may be either secured or unsecured. Secured debt securities are backed by various kinds of assets owned by the issuer, whereas unsecured debt securities are backed only by the reputation, credit record, and financial stability of the issuer. The latter is commonly referred to as being backed by the corporation's full faith and credit. These securities settle T+2 and pay accrued interest based on a 30-day month/360-day year.

Secured debt

Mortgage bonds

Just as the owner of a home pledges a real asset (the home and land) as collateral for a loan (the mortgage), a corporation will borrow money backed by real estate and physical assets of the corporation. Just as a home ordinarily would have a market value greater than the principal amount of its mortgage, the value of the real assets pledged by the corporation will be in excess of the amount borrowed under that bond issue. If the corporation develops financial problems and is unable to pay the interest on the bonds, those real assets pledged as collateral are generally sold to pay off the mortgage bondholders. Having the real assets as collateral for the loan puts the purchaser of a mortgage bond in a position of safety.

Equipment trust certificates

Corporations, particularly railroads and other transportation companies, finance the acquisition of capital equipment used in the course of their business. For example, railroads will issue equipment trust certificates to purchase their rolling stock and locomotives. Title to the newly acquired equipment is held in trust, usually by a bank acting as a trustee, until the certificates have been paid in full. When the railroad has finished paying off the loan, it receives clear title to its equipment from the trustee. If the railroad does not make the payments, the lender repossesses the collateral and sells it for his benefit. By lender we are referring to the trustee acting on behalf of the bondholders. Again, this is in an example of a secured loan; the obligation to pay the investor is secured by the equipment.

Collateral trust bonds

Sometimes, a corporation wants to borrow money and has neither real estate (to back a mortgage bond) nor equipment (to back an equipment trust) to use as collateral. Instead, it deposits securities it owns into a trust to serve as collateral for the lenders. The securities the corporation deposits as collateral for a trust bond can be securities issued by the corporation itself or by stocks and/or bonds of other issuers. Regardless of the issuer, all deposited collateral securities must be marketable (readily able to be liquidated). Collateral trust certificates are secured by the securities deposited—and obviously, the better the quality of the securities, the better the quality of the certificate.

Unsecured debt

Debentures

A debenture is a debt obligation of the corporation backed only by its word and general creditworthiness. Debentures are written promises of the corporation to pay the principal at its due date and interest on a regular basis. Although this promise is as binding as a promise for a secured bond such as a mortgage bond, debentures *are not* secured by any pledge of property. They are sold on the general good faith and credit of the company, unsecured.

TAKE NOTE

Although debentures are unsecured, there are issuers whose credit standing is so good that their debentures might be considered safer than secured bonds of less creditworthy companies.

Guaranteed bonds

Guaranteed bonds are backed by a company other than the issuing corporation, such as a parent company. The value of the guarantee is only as good as the strength of the company making that guarantee. The primary responsibility for the debt belongs to the issuer, but if the issuer defaults, the guaranty kicks in and the guarantying company must make the interest or principal payments. Because there is no asset held as security, these are unsecured debt.

TEST TOPIC ALERT

Never be fooled by the apparent strength of the word *guaranteed* as it relates to guaranteed bonds. These are unsecured debt securities.

Income bonds

Income bonds, also known as adjustment bonds, are used when a company is reorganizing and coming out of bankruptcy. Income bonds pay interest only if the corporation has enough income to meet interest on debt obligations and if the board of directors (BOD) declares that the interest payment be made. Obviously, income or adjustment bonds fall under the heading of unsecured debt securities.

TEST TOPIC ALERT

Income bonds are a true oxymoron. If an investor is seeking income, an income bond is not likely a suitable recommendation.

TAKE NOTE

All debentures (including income and guaranteed bonds) are senior to subordinated debt in order of priority.

Subordinated debt

Sometimes the term *subordinated* is used to describe a class of debt securities. This means "belonging to a lower or inferior class or rank; secondary." It is usually used in describing a type of debenture. A subordinated debenture has a claim that is behind (junior to) that of any other creditor. However, no matter how subordinated the debenture, it is still senior to any stockholder. Sometimes the term *senior debt* is used for debentures and *junior debt* for subordinated debentures.

Order of liquidation

Sometimes things just don't work out, and when things go seriously bad, a corporation may be unable to make payments to its creditors and vendors. When that happens, the only route out of the mess may be for the company to declare bankruptcy. The courts then step in and begin the process of liquidating the company (sometimes called liquidation). All assets are sold off, and those who are owed money line up to be paid. So who gets paid first? The law has a long-established order for creditors; it is called the order of liquidation.

- *Secured debt holders are first.* They are paid from the proceeds of the sale of the assets that secured the debt. If the assets are insufficient to pay what is owed, any additional amount is paid at the general creditor level.

- *Unsecured debt (debentures) and general creditors are second.* General creditors are those the company owes money to as part of its operations (typically vendors and other suppliers). Wages and taxes are often paid out at this level.

- *Subordinated debt (debentures) are third in line.* The increased risk for these investors is why these bonds will have a higher coupon rate.

- *Preferred stockholders come in next.* Preferred stock is an equity holding and will come after all creditors have been paid but will be before common shareholders.

- *Common stockholders are last.* The actual owners of the company are the last in line. This is the downside of being the investors that make the most when the company is successful. In a bankruptcy, it is extremely rare for the common stockholders to get anything at liquidation.

TAKE NOTE

The courts may shift some creditors up or down for different reasons. It is not uncommon for wages or taxes to be moved up in priority if it appears that there will be insufficient assets to pay them.

TAKE NOTE

You may see a question about administrative claim holders or administrative claimants. These parties (attorneys, the courts, property appraisers, auctioneers, and liquidators) are brought in to assist with the liquidation. They will demand assurance that they will be paid for their services. Their claim will be honored, and paid, before anyone else—even before secured creditors.

LO 2.g Identify the benefits and risks associated with debt securities.

Benefits of owning debt securities

Income

Bonds are considered the best way to produce current income for an investor. The nature of debt securities is that the issuer must make interest payments or go into default. These investments produce a steady and predictable income, unlike dividends from stocks, which are never guaranteed and are not an obligation of the issuer.

Safety

Bonds are higher in priority than equity securities. The bondholder's senior position combined with the obligation to make interest payments make these investments generally safer and with much less price volatility than stocks. More conservative investors often prefer the relative stability of bonds.

Risks of owning debt securities

Default

The primary risk when owning any debt security is that the issuer will fail to pay interest or principal when due. This is called default risk, financial risk, or credit risk. For most securities, we depend on credit rating agencies to rate the financial strength of an issuer. A default is the worst outcome of owning a bond.

TAKE NOTE

For test purposes, the default risk in debt backed by the U.S. Treasury is effectively zero. Treasury-backed securities are the safest investment for U.S. investors.

Interest rate risk

All debt securities will fluctuate in response to changes in prevailing interest rates.

Purchasing power risk (inflation)

Any security that produces a fixed payment is subject to purchasing power risk, or inflation risk. Inflation is a rise in the price of goods over time. As the fixed payment stays the same while prices are rising, the amount of goods the payment will buy decreases. Over a long period of time, this loss of purchasing power may become significant.

TAKE NOTE

Preferred stock, though not a debt, does produce a fixed payment and is subject to purchasing power risk.

EXAMPLE

Your customer owns one share of Lando Entertainment $8 preferred, which she purchased in 1985. In that year, the $8 annual dividend would pay for two tickets to a movie and two sodas, not a bad date. The average ticket to the movies today is around $10. So much for the date. By the way, which movie did your customer go to? *Back to the Future*, of course.

KNOWLEDGE CHECK

1. Interest from a zero-coupon bond
    A. pays monthly and is taxed annually.
    B. pays annually and is taxed at maturity.
    C. pays at maturity and is taxed annually.
    D. pays and is taxed at maturity.

2. Lando Entertainment, Inc., issues a bond collateralized by a trust holding the company's Las Vegas headquarters. This type of bond is called
    A. a collateral trust bond.
    B. a guaranteed bond.
    C. a headquarters debenture.
    D. a mortgage bond.

3. An investor who is seeking income might choose a corporate bond because
    A. a corporate bond pays a steady income and are generally reliable.
    B. bonds pay a higher dividend than stocks.
    C. bonds can grow faster than the rate of inflation.
    D. corporate bond interest is tax free.

Answers

1. **C** A zero is purchased at a deep discount and pays no interest until it matures; however, the interest is taxed on an annual basis, called "Phantom Income" LO 2.e

2. **D** A secured bond backed by real estate is called a mortgage bond. Collateral trust bonds hold other securities in trust as collateral. A guaranteed bond is an unsecured bond backed by a third party. A headquarters debenture is not a thing. LO 2.f

3. **A** Corporate bonds are, depending on rating, generally reliable producers of income through interest payments. Bonds do not pay dividends, nor do they grow in value with inflation. Corporate interest is fully taxable. LO 2.g

LESSON 2.4: MUNICIPAL BONDS

LO 2.h Differentiate general obligation and revenue bonds.

Municipal bonds

Municipal bonds are securities issued by state or local governments or by U.S. territories, authorities, and special districts. Investors who buy such bonds are lending money to the issuers for the purpose of public works and construction projects (e.g., roads, hospitals, civic centers, sewer systems, airports). Municipal securities are considered second in safety of principal only to U.S. government and U.S. government agency securities, but the safety of any particular issue is based on the issuing municipality's financial stability.

Interest on most municipal bonds is tax free on a federal level and tax free on a state level if the investor lives in the state of issuance. (Please note that capital gains or trading profits on these securities would still be taxable.) Municipal securities settle T+2 and pay accrued interest based on a 30-day month/360-day year.

Two categories of municipal securities exist: general obligation bonds and revenue bonds.

General obligation (GO) municipal bonds

General obligation (GO) bonds are municipal bonds issued for capital improvements that benefit the entire community. Typically, these projects do not produce revenues, so principal and interest must be paid by taxes collected by the municipal issuer. Because of this backing, GO bonds are known as full faith and credit issues and are backed by the municipality's taxing power. Bonds issued by states are backed by income taxes, license fees, and sales taxes. Bonds issued by towns, cities, and counties are backed by property (ad valorem or real estate) taxes, license fees, fines, and all other sources of direct income to the municipality. School, road, and park districts may also issue municipal bonds backed by property taxes.

Finally, the amount of debt that a municipal government may incur can be limited by state or local statutes to protect taxpayers from excessive taxes. Debt limits can also make a bond safer for investors. The lower the debt limit, the less risk of excessive borrowing and default by the municipality. If an issuer wishes to issue GO bonds that would put it above its statutory debt limit, a public referendum is required. In this light, GO bonds are often associated with requiring voter approval.

Revenue bonds

Revenue bonds can be used to finance any municipal facility that generates sufficient income. These municipal bonds are considered to be self-supporting debt because principal and interest payments are made exclusively from revenues generated by the project or facility for which the debt was issued, such as

- utilities (water, sewer, and electric);
- housing (public housing projects);
- transportation (airports, bridges, tunnels, and toll roads);
- education (college dorms and student loans);
- health (hospitals and retirement centers);

- industrial (industrial development and pollution control); and

- sports (stadium facilities).

Authorities—Revenue bonds are sometimes issued by authorities, which are quasi-governmental entities often tasked with building roads, tunnels, bridges, and other infrastructure. In many cases, a transit authority might own several bridges or tunnels. Bondholders must be aware that each bond may only be backed by a specific portion (not all) of the authority's overall revenues that is earmarked for that bond issue.

Keeping in mind that revenue bonds are not supported by the issuers' authority to tax, they are not subject to statutory debt limits and therefore do not require voter approval.

TAKE NOTE

The interest from bonds issued by or from a territory of the United States is tax free to U.S. taxpayers. Examples of territories are Guam, U.S. Virgin Islands, and Puerto Rico, among others.

Short-term municipal obligations (anticipation notes)

Municipal anticipation notes are short-term securities that generate funds for a municipality that expects other revenues soon. Usually, municipal notes have less than 12-month maturities, although maturities may range from 3 months to 3 years. They are repaid when the municipality receives the anticipated funds. Municipal notes fall into several categories.

- Municipalities issue tax anticipation notes (TANs) to finance current operations in anticipation of future tax receipts. This helps municipalities to even out cash flow between tax collection periods.

- Revenue anticipation notes (RANs) are offered periodically to finance current operations in anticipation of future revenues from revenue-producing projects or facilities.

- Tax and revenue anticipation notes (TRANs) are a combination of the characteristics of both TANs and RANs.

- Bond anticipation notes (BANs) are sold as interim financing that will eventually be converted to long-term funding through a sale of bonds.

- Tax-exempt commercial paper is often used in place of BANs and TANs for up to 270 days, though maturities are most often 30, 60, and 90 days.

- Construction loan notes (CLNs) are issued to provide interim financing for the construction of housing projects.

- Variable-rate demand notes have a fluctuating interest rate and are usually issued with a put option. This means that the investor could periodically (e.g., weekly, monthly) return the security to the issuer for its stated value.

- Grant anticipation notes (GANs) are issued with the expectation of receiving grant money from the federal government.

LO 2.i Calculate tax-equivalent yield.

An investor considering the purchase of a tax-exempt bond should compare its yield carefully with that of taxable securities. The tax savings of the tax-free bond may be more attractive than a taxable bond with a higher interest rate. This depends, in part, on the investor's tax bracket: the higher the tax bracket, the greater the tax exemption's value.

To determine a municipal bond investment's tax benefit, an investor must calculate the tax equivalent yield. To do so, divide the tax-free yield by 100% less the investor's tax rate.

When answering a tax-equivalent yield question, keep in mind that the municipal yield will always be less than the corporate yield.

EXAMPLE

An investor is in the 30% tax bracket. A municipal bond currently yields 7%. To offer an equivalent yield, what must a corporate bond yield?

Divide the municipal yield by 100% minus the investor's tax bracket.

This is known as the tax-equivalent yield formula.

$$7\% \div (100\% - 30\%) = 10\%$$

Assume that the same investor is in the 30% tax bracket. If a corporate bond currently yields 11%, what would be the equivalent municipal yield?

To find the answer, multiply the corporate yield by 100% minus the investor's tax bracket. This is known as the tax-free equivalent yield formula.

$$11\% \times (100\% - 30\%) = 7.7\%$$

KNOWLEDGE CHECK

1. Which of the following are considered sources of debt service for GO bonds?
    I.   Personal property taxes
    II. Real estate taxes
    III. Fees from delinquent property taxes
    IV. Liquor license fees
    A. I and IV
    B. II and III
    C. II, III, and IV
    D. I, II, III, and IV

2. The Alta Loma High School District is asking voters to approve a bond to fund the purchase of new computers and software. The bond will mature in 40 years, and the interest and principal payments will be funded from real estate taxes. This is an example of
    A. a GO bond.
    B. a revenue bond.
    C. a debenture.
    D. an equipment trust bond.

3. Your customer is in the 30% federal tax bracket. He is considering purchasing a 7% corporate bond. The after-tax yield would be
    A. 4.9%.
    B. 2.1%.
    C. 10%.
    D. 7%.

Answers

1. **D** All of these are taxes or fees that pay into the general fund of a municipality and may be used to service GO debt. LO 2.h

2. **A** If a municipal bond requires a vote, it is most likely a GO bond. Generally revenue bonds do not require a vote (note that there is no revenue-generating source

here). Debentures and equipment trust certificates are issued by corporations, not municipalities. LO 2.h

3. **A** The formula for the calculation is 7% (corporate rate) × (100% − 30% (tax bracket)). 7 × (1 − 0.3) = 7 × 0.7 = 4.9%. LO 2.i

LESSON 2.5: TREASURIES

LO 2.j Recall the traits of T-bills, T-notes, and T-bonds.

The U.S. Treasury Department determines the quantity and types of government securities it must issue to meet federal budget needs. The marketplace determines the interest rates those securities will pay.

The federal government is the nation's largest borrower, as well as its best credit risk. Securities issued by the U.S. government are backed by its full faith and credit, based on its power to tax. In this light, securities issued by the U.S. government are considered to be among the highest in quality regarding safety of principal. These securities are classified as bills, notes, and bonds, which distinguish each issue's term to maturity (short, intermediate, and long term).

Finally, government securities issued by the U.S. Treasury are all issued in book-entry form, meaning that no physical securities (paper certificates) exist and have a T+1 settlement cycle. Accrued interest on these securities is calculated based on actual calendar days elapsed.

Treasury bills (T-bills)

U.S. T-bills are direct short-term debt obligations of the U.S. government. They are issued weekly with maturities of 4 weeks, 13 weeks, 26 weeks, and at times, 52 weeks. Though the maximum maturity for T-bills is subject to change, they are always short-term instruments— that is, one year or less.

T-bills pay no interest in the way other bonds do; rather, they are issued at a discount from par value and redeemed at par. For example, an investor might purchase a $10,000, 26-week T-bill at a price of $9,800. She would receive no regular interest check, but at maturity, the Treasury would send her a check for $10,000. The difference between the $9,800 she paid and the $10,000 she received would be considered her interest income, though she never received a separate interest check.

TAKE NOTE

Key points to remember regarding T-bills include knowing that

- T-bills are the only Treasury security issued at a discount;

- T-bills are the only Treasury security issued without a stated interest rate;

- T-bills are highly liquid; and

- the 13-week (a.k.a. 90-day) T-bills are used in market analysis as the stereotypical risk-free investment.

Treasury notes (T-notes)

U.S. T-notes are direct debt obligations of the U.S. government. They pay semiannual interest as a percentage of the stated par value, and they mature at par value. T-notes have intermediate maturities (2–10 years).

Treasury bonds (T-bonds)

U.S. T-bonds are direct debt obligations of the U.S. government. They pay semiannual interest as a percentage of the stated par value and mature at par value. These government obligations have long-term maturities, greater than 10 years and up to 30 years.

Figure 2.3: Testable Features of T-Bills, T-Notes, and T-Bonds

Marketable Government Securities				
Type	Maturity	Pricing	Form	Accrued Interest
T-bills	Less than 1 year	Issued at a discount; priced on discount basis	Book entry	None
T-notes	2–10 years (intermediate term)	Priced at percentage of par	Book entry	Actual days elapsed
T-bonds	Greater than 10 years (long term)	Priced at percentage of par	Book entry	Actual days elapsed

Treasury receipts and Treasury STRIPS

- *Treasury receipts*—Brokerage firms can create a type of bond known as a treasury receipt from U.S. Treasury notes and bonds. BDs buy Treasury securities, place them in trust at a bank, and sell separate receipts against the principal and coupon payments. This separating of the coupon interest payments from the principal creates new securities and provides investors with several maturities to choose from. This stripping process also yields more profit for the BD versus selling the original Treasury securities outright.

  Although the Treasury securities held in trust collateralize the treasury receipts, the receipts (unlike Treasury securities) are not backed by the full faith and credit of the U.S. government.

- *Treasury STRIPS (Separate Trading of Registered Interest and Principal of Securities)*—The Treasury Department has its own version of receipts known as **Treasury STRIPS**. The Treasury Department designates certain issues as suitable for stripping into interest and principal components. Banks and BDs perform the actual separation of interest coupon and principal and trading of the STRIPS.

Both Treasury receipts and STRIPS are zero-coupon bonds.

Treasury Inflation Protected Securities (TIPS)

TIPS are a special type of treasury security. They are issued with maturities of 5, 10, or 20 years. They have a fixed coupon rate and pay interest every six months. What is different is that the principal value of the bond is adjusted every six months based on the inflation rate. The interest payments will increase with the principal during periods of inflation and decrease during periods of deflation. Also, the final principal payment at maturity will have been adjusted for inflation over the term of the bond. Note that the final principal payment will never be less than the original $1,000 par.

KNOWLEDGE CHECK

1. Treasury bills may be issued with all of the following maturities **except**
    A. 4 weeks.
    B. 13 weeks.
    C. 39 weeks.
    D. 52 weeks.

2. A newly issued treasury security that matures in five years is
    A. A T-bill.
    B. a T-note.
    C. a T-bond.
    D. a treasury receipt.

3. All of the following securities are issued the U.S. Treasury **except**
    A. treasury receipts.
    B. STRIPS.
    C. T-bills.
    D. TIPS.

Answers

1. **C** T-bills may be issued with 4-, 13-, 26-, and 52-week maturities. They are not issued with a 39-week maturity.

2. **B** T-notes are issued with maturities between 2 and 10 years. T-bills longest maturity is 1 year and T-bonds have maturities over 10 years. Treasury receipts are not issued by the Treasury.

3. **A** Treasury receipts are created and issued by broker-dealers acting as investment bankers. T-bills, STRIPS, and TIPS are issued by the U.S. Treasury.

LESSON 2.6: AGENCY ISSUES AND TAXATION

LO 2.k Recall the features of GNMA, FNMA, and FHLMC certificates.

In addition to the U.S.-Treasury-issued securities, T-bills, T-notes, and T-bonds, the U.S. Congress authorizes the following agencies of the federal government to issue debt securities:

- Farm Credit Administration

- Government National Mortgage Association (GNMA, or Ginnie Mae)

- Other agency-like organizations operated by private corporations, including the following:

  - Federal Home Loan Mortgage Corporation (FHLMC, or Freddie Mac)

  - Federal National Mortgage Association (FNMA, or Fannie Mae)

  - Student Loan Marketing Association (SLMA, or Sallie Mae)

The term *agency* is sometimes used to refer to entities that are not technically government agencies but that have ties to the government. For example, Fannie Mae is privately owned but government sponsored.

TAKE NOTE

The settlement of agency-issued securities occurs regular way—two business days (T+2). These securities are generally known as asset-backed securities or in the case of GNMA, FNMA, and FHLMC, mortgage-backed securities.

The agency securities most likely to appear on the exam are detailed in the following paragraphs.

Farm Credit System (FCS)

The Farm Credit System (FCS) is a national network of lending institutions that provides agricultural financing and credit. The system is a privately owned, government-sponsored enterprise that raises loanable funds through the sale of Farm Credit Debt Securities to investors. These funds are made available to farmers through a nationwide network of banks and Farm Credit lending institutions. The Farm Credit Administration (FCA), a government agency, oversees the system.

Government National Mortgage Association (GNMA, or Ginnie Mae)

The Government National Mortgage Association (GNMA) is a government-owned corporation that supports the Department of Housing and Urban Development. GNMAs are the only agency securities backed by the full faith and credit of the federal government. Although many of these securities have a stated 30-year life, GNMAs are typically sold based on an average life expectancy because the issues are backed by mortgages, which are often retired early. When a mortgage is paid off before its stated maturity, the GNMA investor will receive back all outstanding principal of that loan at par. This early payout is called prepayment risk.

Federal Home Loan Mortgage Corporation (FHLMC, or Freddie Mac)

The Federal Home Loan Mortgage Corporation (FHLMC) is a public corporation. It was created to promote the development of a nationwide secondary market in mortgages by buying residential mortgages from financial institutions and packaging them into mortgage-backed securities for sale to investors.

Federal National Mortgage Association (FNMA, or Fannie Mae)

The Federal National Mortgage Association (FNMA) is a publicly held corporation that provides mortgage capital. FNMA purchases conventional and insured mortgages from agencies such as the Federal Housing Administration (FHA) and the Veterans Administration (VA). The securities it creates are backed by FNMA's general credit.

TAKE NOTE

Fannie Mae and Freddie Mac are publically owned (held) corporations. They are sometimes called government-sponsored entities (GSEs).

LO 2.1 Recall how interest from different bonds is taxed.

Review of taxation on interest from bonds

Issuer	Federal	State & Local	Frequency
Treasury	Yes	No	At maturity or biannually
Municipality	No	Depends	Biannually
FNMA & FHLMC	Yes	Yes	Biannually
GNMA	Yes	Yes	Monthly
Territory bonds	No	No	Biannually

KNOWLEDGE CHECK

1. Which of the following securities is **not** backed by the full faith and credit of the U.S. Treasury?
    A. GNMA
    B. FNMA
    C. STRIPS
    D. Treasury bills

2. Your customer would like current monthly income from a very safe investment. Which of the following would you recommend?
    A. T-bonds
    B. FNMA
    C. GNMA
    D. T-notes

3. Your customer, Mr. Garcia, lives in Scottsdale, Arizona. He owns general obligation bonds issued by the city of San Juan, Puerto Rico. The interest from the bonds will be taxed at
    A. the federal, but not the state, level.
    B. the state, but not federal, level.
    C. neither the state nor the federal Level.
    D. both the state and federal levels.

Answers

1. **B** Federal National Mortgage Association is a government-sponsored entity. Its debt is not directly backed by the federal government. LO 2.k

2. **C** GNMA certificates pay monthly income and principal payments and are directly backed by the federal government. LO 2.k

3. **C** U.S. taxpayers pay no income tax on interest paid by U.S. territories and municipalities of those territories. LO 2.l

LESSON 2.7: MONEY MARKETS AND ASSET-BACKED SECURITIES

LO 2.m Define a money market security.

In the financial marketplace, a distinction is made between the capital market and the money market. The capital market serves as a source of intermediate-term to long-term financing, usually in the form of equity or debt securities with maturities of more than one year.

The money market, on the other hand, provides very short-term funds to corporations, banks, BDs, government municipalities, and the U.S. federal government.

Money market instruments are fixed-income (debt) securities with one year or less left to maturity. They are highly liquid and also provide a relatively high degree of safety. Consider that because they are short term, they have little time to default. In return for the safety, investors forgo a higher return for the lower returns generally associated with money market securities.

Finally, investors who purchase money market securities generally do not receive interest payments; instead, these securities are typically issued at a discount and mature at face value. The return is the difference between the discounted purchase price and the face value received at maturity. This is generally, but not universally, true.

In the following sections, we'll discuss the most widely used money market securities.

Certificate of deposit (CD)

Banks issue and guarantee certificates of deposit (CDs) with fixed interest rates and minimum face values of $100,000 (jumbo CDs), although face values of $1 million or more are common. Most mature in one year or less. Some that can be traded in the secondary market are known as negotiable CDs. Only these negotiable CDs are considered to be money market instruments. Another term for these is jumbo CDs.

A negotiable CD is a bank's version of an unsecured promissory note in the same way that commercial paper is for corporations. In other words, it is a bank's promise to pay principal and interest—secured by no physical asset and backed only by the bank's good faith and credit. They are sold at face value and pay interest at maturity.

TAKE NOTE

Do not confuse these with the typical CD that a customer would buy from a bank. Those CDs, called retail CDs, are difficult to transfer (not liquid), are often for specific amounts, and any minimum is set by the bank selling the CD.

Banker's acceptance (BA)

A banker's acceptance (BA) is a short-term time draft with a specified payment date drawn on a bank. Essentially, a BA is a postdated check or line of credit. The payment date of a BA is normally between 1 and 270 days (9 months). Corporations use BAs extensively to finance international trade; that is, a BA typically pays for goods and services in a foreign country.

Commercial paper (prime paper, promissory notes)

Corporations issue short-term, unsecured commercial paper, known as promissory notes, to raise cash to finance accounts receivable and seasonal inventory gluts. Commercial paper maturities range from 1 to 270 days, although most mature within 90 days. Typically, companies with excellent credit ratings issue commercial paper.

U.S. Treasury bills

U.S. Treasury bills are direct short-term debt obligations of the U.S. government. They are issued weekly with maturities of 4 weeks, 13 weeks, 26 weeks, and, at times, 52 weeks.

TAKE NOTE

Though T-notes and T-bonds are issued with longer maturities than T-bills, once the notes and bonds have only a year left to maturity, they are considered to be money market instruments.

Repurchase agreements (REPOs)

In a repurchase agreement (repo), a financial institution, such as a bank or a BD, raises cash by temporarily selling some of the assets it holds with an agreement to buy back the assets at a later date at a slightly higher price. Thus, a repo is an agreement between a buyer and a seller to conduct a transaction (sale) and then to reverse that transaction (repurchase) in the future. The contract would include the repurchase price and a maturity date. These agreements are often used by banks that need to raise capital, either with another bank or with the Federal Reserve Bank.

TAKE NOTE

There are also agreements known as reverse repurchase agreements, or reverse repos. In a **reverse repurchase agreement**, or **reverse repo**, a dealer agrees to buy securities from an investor and sell them back later at a higher price.

Federal funds loans

The Federal Reserve Board (FRB) mandates how much money its member banks must keep on reserve at the FRB. Any deposits in excess of the required amount are known as federal funds. These excess reserves or federal funds can be loaned from one member bank to another for the purpose of meeting the reserve requirement. These loans are very short term and, in most cases, can literally occur overnight.

TEST TOPIC ALERT

In summation, why would you place money market securities in a client's portfolio?

- Highly liquid

- Very safe

- A good place to invest money that will be needed soon (short term)

However, the rate of return is quite low, so these are not suitable for long-term investors.

Due to short-term maturities, principal is potentially being reinvested at a different rate each time the instrument matures (short intervals). In this light, the income not only is minimal but also will fluctuate with each new instrument purchased.

LO 2.n Define mortgage and asset-backed securities.

Collateralized mortgage obligations (CMO)

CMOs are a type of **asset-backed security**. Asset-backed securities are ones whose value and income payments are derived from or backed by a specific pool of underlying assets. These pools of assets can include expected payments from different types of loans, such as mortgages, as is the case with CMOs. Pooling the assets into financial instruments allows them to be sold to general investors more easily than selling them individually. This process is called securitization, and it allows the risk of investing in the underlying assets to be diversified because each security will now represent only a fraction of the total value of the diverse pool of underlying assets. CMOs pool a large number of mortgages, usually on single-family residences. A pool of mortgages is structured into maturity classes called **tranches**. CMOs are issued by private-sector financing corporations and are often backed by Ginnie Mae, Fannie Mae, and Freddie Mac pass-through securities. As a result, CMOs backed by government agency securities have historically been rated high.

A CMO pays principal and interest from the mortgage pool monthly; however, it repays principal to only one tranche at a time. In addition to interest payments, investors in a short-term tranche must receive all of their principal before the next tranche begins to receive principal repayments. Principal payments are made in $1,000 increments to randomly selected bonds within a tranche. Changes in interest rates affect the rate of mortgage prepayments and this, in turn, affects the flow of interest payment and principal repayment to the CMO investor.

Collateralized debt obligations (CDO)

CDOs are typically complex asset-backed securities. While CDOs do not specialize in any single type of debt, usually their portfolios consist of nonmortgage loans or bonds. The assets backing the CDOs can be a pool of bonds, auto loans, or other assets, such as leases, credit card debt, a company's receivables, or even derivative products of any of the assets listed.

While the individual assets may be small and not very liquid, pooling the assets facilitates them being sold to individual investors in the secondary markets. This pooling or repackaging of assets is sometimes called securitization. Securitization allows the risk of investing in the underlying assets to be diversified because each security will represent a fraction of the total value of the entire diverse pool of assets.

Similar in structure to collateralized mortgage obligations (CMOs), CDOs represent different types of debt and credit risk. Like CMOs, the different types of debt and risk categories are often called *tranches* or *slices*. Each tranche has a different maturity and risk associated with it. The higher the risk, the more the CDO pays. In practice, investors will choose a tranche with a risk and return combination that is suitable for them.

KNOWLEDGE CHECK

1. All of the following would most likely be found in a money market fund's portfolio **except**
   A. T-bills.
   B. T-bonds with less than one year to maturity.
   C. negotiable CDs.
   D. common stock.

2. Which of the following money market instruments are routinely used in import/export activities?
   A. GNMA
   B. BAs
   C. T-bills
   D. Repurchase agreements

3. CMOs are backed by
   A. mortgages.
   B. real estate.
   C. municipal taxes.
   D. the full faith and credit of the U.S. government.

Answers

1. **D**   Common stock does not meet the criteria for a money market. Though highly liquid, it has no maturity date nor is it relatively safe compared to debt instruments. LO 2.m

2. **B**   Banker's acceptances (BAs) are used for this purpose. LO 2.m

3. **A**   The "M" in CMO stands for *mortgage*. LO 2.n

UNIT 3

Derivatives

LEARNING OBJECTIVES

When you have completed this unit, you will be able to accomplish the following.

- › LO 3.a   Define a derivative.
- › LO 3.b   Identify the components of a call and a put option contract.
- › LO 3.c   Define premium.
- › LO 3.d   Calculate IV, TV, and premium.
- › LO 3.e   Differentiate equity, currency, and index options.
- › LO 3.f   Differentiate American and European exercise rules.
- › LO 3.g   Calculate break even, maximum gain, and maximum loss on an individual option contract.
- › LO 3.h   Determine how to best hedge risk with long options.
- › LO 3.i   Indicate how to generate premium income by selling.
- › LO 3.j   Determine the correct steps for adding options trading to a brokerage account.
- › LO 3.k   Recall the role of the Options Clearing Corporation.

INTRODUCTION

In this unit you will learn about derivative securities. Derivatives are a type of security whose value is based on its relationship to another asset or referenced value. They are used primarily for speculation or protection.

LESSON 3.1: BASIC OPTIONS

LO 3.a Define a derivative.

A derivative is a contract that derives its value from an underlying asset. There are two parties to the contract: a buyer and a seller. The buyer has the right to take an action (buy or sell) the underlying asset from the seller. In some derivative contracts (futures), the buyer will be obligated to buy the asset on a specific date. Derivatives are often used for commodities, such as oil, gasoline, or gold (these are called futures). Another asset class is currencies, often based on the value of a foreign currency versus the U.S. dollar. There are derivatives based on stocks and stock indices. Still others use interest rates, such as the yield on the 10-year Treasury note.

Options are derivative securities. This means that they derive their value from that of an underlying instrument, such as a stock, stock index, interest rate, or foreign currency. Option contracts offer investors a means to hedge, or protect, an investment's value or speculate on the price movement of individual securities, markets, foreign currencies, and other instruments.

TAKE NOTE

Futures are derivatives that have a commodity as the underlying asset. Futures are *not* classified as securities.

LO 3.b Identify the components of a call and a put option contract.

An option is a two-party contract, meaning that there are two parties involved in the contract—one party has the right to exercise the contract to buy or sell the underlying security, and the other is obligated to fulfill the terms of the contract. The amount paid for the contract when purchased, or received for the contract when it is sold, is called the contract premium.

The buyer (owner of the contract) who pays the premium for the contract is often called the owner, the holder, or the party who is long the contract. The buyer has the right to exercise the contract. Buyers risk losing the premium paid for the contract if the option expires as worthless.

Buyers begin the process with an opening purchase of the contract. If they decide to sell the contract later, the second transaction is called a closing sale. See Figure 3.1.

Opening purchase >>>> closing sale

The seller (writer of the contract) who receives the premium for the contract is called the writer or party who is short the contract. The seller will be obligated to perform if the buyer chooses to exercise the contract. Sellers can potentially profit by the amount of premium received for the contract if the option expires as worthless. See Figure 3.1.

Sellers begin the process with an opening sale of the contract. If they decide to buy back the contract later, the second transaction is called a closing purchase.

Opening sale >>>> closing purchase

Figure 3.1: Option Contracts Long vs. Short

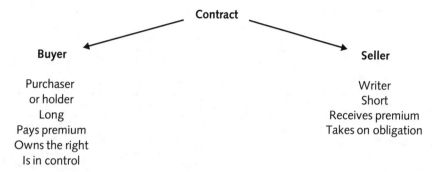

In theory, options can be created on any item with a fluctuating market value. The most familiar options are those issued on common stocks; they are called equity options. For the remainder of our discussion of options, we'll focus on equity options.

There are two types of option contracts: calls and puts. Because two types of options (calls and puts) and two types of transactions (purchases and sales) exist, four basic transactions are available to an option investor:

1. Buy calls

2. Sell calls

3. Buy puts

4. Sell puts

LO 3.c Define premium.

Basic calls and puts

As noted previously, investors can either buy or sell calls and puts. Buying and selling calls and puts are the basic option strategies. We'll look now at all four transactions.

Calls

An investor may buy calls (go long) or sell calls (go short). The features of each side of a call contract (long and short) are as follows.

■ *Long call (purchase)*—A call buyer owns the right to buy 100 shares of a specific stock at the strike price before the expiration if he chooses to exercise the contract. Therefore, a call buyer is a bullish investor (one who anticipates that the price of the underlying security will rise).

EXAMPLE

Long 1 XYZ Jan 60 Call at 3

Long	The investor has bought the call and has the right to exercise the contract.
XYZ	The single contract represents 100 shares of XYZ stock.
Jan	The contract expires on the third Friday of January at 11:59 pm ET.
60	The strike price of the contract is 60.
Call	The type of option is a call, and the investor has the right to buy the stock at 60 because he is long the call.
3	The premium of the contract is $3 per share. Contracts are issued with 100 shares, so the total premium is $300. The investor paid the premium to buy the call.

Buyers of calls want the market price of the underlying stock to rise. The investor who owns this call hopes that the market price will rise above 60. He then has the right to buy the stock at the strike price of 60, even if the market price is higher (e.g., 80).

■ *Short call (sale)*—A call writer (seller) has the obligation to sell 100 shares of a specific stock at the strike price if the buyer exercises the contract. Therefore, a call writer is a bearish investor (one who anticipates that the price of the underlying security will fall).

EXAMPLE

Short 1 XYZ Jan 60 Call at 3

Short	The investor has sold the call and has obligations to perform if the contract is exercised.
XYZ	The single contract represents 100 shares of XYZ stock.
Jan	The contract expires on the third Friday of January at 11:59 pm ET. If expiration occurs, the writer keeps the premium without any obligation.
60	The strike price of the contract is 60.
Call	The type of option is a call, and the investor is obligated to sell the stock at 60, if exercised, because he is short the call.
3	The premium of the contract is $3 per share. Options contracts are issued with 100 shares, so the total premium is $300.

Writers of calls want the market price of the underlying stock to fall or stay the same. The investor who owns this call (the buyer) hopes that the market price will rise or go above 60. Therefore, the writer hopes the market price will stay at or below 60 so that the contract would not be exercised. If the contract is unexercised by the time it expires, the writer keeps the premium of $300 with no further obligation.

Puts

An investor may buy puts (go long) or sell puts (go short). The features of each side of a put contract (long and short) are as follows.

■ *Long put (purchase)*—A put buyer owns the right to sell 100 shares of a specific stock at the strike price before the expiration if he chooses to exercise the contract. Therefore, a put buyer is a bearish investor because he wants the price of the underlying security to fall.

EXAMPLE

Long 1 XYZ Jan 60 Put at 3

Long	The investor has bought the put and has the right to exercise the contract.
XYZ	The single contract represents 100 shares of XYZ stock.
Jan	The contract expires on the third Friday of January at 11:59 pm ET.
60	The strike price of the contract is 60.
Put	The type of option is a put, and the investor has the right to sell the stock at 60 because he is long the put.
3	The premium of the contract is $3 per share. Contracts are issued with 100 shares, so the total premium is $300. The investor paid the premium to buy the put.

Buyers of puts want the market price of the underlying stock to fall. The investor who owns this put hopes that the market price will fall below 60. He then has the right to sell the stock at the strike price of 60, even if the market price is lower (e.g., 40).

- *Short put (sale)*—A put writer (seller) has the obligation to buy 100 shares of a specific stock at the strike price if the buyer exercises the contract. Therefore, a put writer is a bullish investor because he wants the price of the underlying security to rise or remain unchanged.

EXAMPLE

Short 1 XYZ Jan 60 Put at 3

Short	The investor has sold the put and has obligations to perform if the contract is exercised.
XYZ	The single contract represents 100 shares of XYZ stock.
Jan	The contract expires on the third Friday of January at 11:59 pm ET. If expiration occurs, the writer keeps the premium without any obligation.
60	The strike price of the contract is 60.
Put	The type of option is a put, and the investor is obligated to buy the stock at 60, if exercised, because he is short the put.
3	The premium of the contract is $3 per share. Options contracts are issued with 100 shares, so the total premium is $300.

Market attitude (bullish or bearish)

Depending on if investors are the buyers or the sellers of either a call or a put, they will have a particular market attitude about the underlying stock (bullish or bearish). See Figure 3.2. Though being bullish or bearish on the underlying security was noted earlier, let's revisit and sum up market attitude.

Calls:

A call buyer is a bullish investor because he wants the market to rise. The call is exercised only if the market price rises above the strike price.

A call writer is a bearish investor because he wants the market to fall (or remain unchanged). The contract is not exercised if the market price is below the strike price.

Puts:

A put buyer is a bearish investor because he wants the market to fall. The put is exercised only if the market price falls below the strike price.

A put writer is a bullish investor because he wants the market to rise or remain unchanged. The contract is not exercised if the market price is above the strike price.

Figure 3.2: Bullish and Bearish Options Positions

	Long	Short
Calls	Right to buy Bullish	Obligation to sell Bearish
Puts	Right to sell Bearish	Obligation to buy Bullish
	(Buyer, Holder, Owner)	(Seller, Writer, Grantor)

TAKE NOTE

Index options—Not all options are related to a single underlying stock. A stock index option tracks the performance of a particular group of stocks such as the S&P 500 Index or Dow Jones Industrial Average (DJIA). If an index option is exercised, no delivery of the underlying shares is made. Instead, the writer pays the options owner the differential in cash.

VIX options—The VIX Index is designed to measure expected volatility of the U.S. stock market and is based on pricing from the S&P 500 Index. Investors use these options to speculate on volatility of the equity markets. The VIX Index is often called the *fear index*, and tends to spike upward when the stock market experiences a severe downdraft. VIX options settle in cash with European exercise provisions.

KNOWLEDGE CHECK

1. A security that is a contractual obligation between two parties and whose value is based on the specifics of the contract in relation to a different security is
    A. a contractual plan.
    B. an investment company.
    C. a derivative.
    D. a hedge fund.

2. Which of the following statements regarding options are **true**?
    I.   Investors who are bullish on a stock should buy calls.
    II. Investors who are bullish on a stock should buy puts.
    III. Investors who are bearish on a stock should sell puts.
    IV. Investors who are bearish on a stock should buy puts.
    A. I and IV
    B. I and III
    C. II and III
    D. II and IV

3. Your customer, Mr. Newsome, recently purchased one put contract on Napa Valley Spirits, Inc., stock. The strike price is $50 and the premium was $4.50. He later executed the contract. How much did he pay for the contract?
    A. $5,000
    B. $500
    C. $4,550
    D. $450

Answers

1. **C** A contract that derives its value from its relationship to another security is a derivative. A contractual plan is a type of investment company that is no longer issued. LO 3.a

2. **A** Buying calls is bullish and buying puts is bearish. Buying puts is bearish and selling puts is bullish. LO 3.b

3. **D** The question asks what he paid for the contract, not what he received when he executed it or the breakeven price. One contract of 100 shares at $4.50 a shares is $450. LO 3.c

LESSON 3.2: INTRINSIC VALUE, TIME VALUE, AND THE OPTION PREMIUM

LO 3.d Calculate IV, TV, and premium.

In the money, at the money, out of the money, intrinsic value, and parity

Options contracts can be described using various terms unique to the options marketplace. One way to describe a contract is being in, at, or out of the money. Another would be to describe whether or not it has intrinsic value or is trading at parity. We'll look at all of these for both calls and puts.

Calls (in, at, or out of the money; intrinsic value; and parity)

- *In the money*—A call is in the money when the price of the stock exceeds the strike price of the call. A buyer will exercise calls that are in the money at expiration. Buyers want options to be *in the money*; sellers do not.

- *At the money*—A call is at the money when the price of the stock equals the strike price of the call. A buyer will not exercise contracts that are at the money at expiration. Sellers want at-the-money contracts at expiration; buyers do not. Sellers then keep the premium without obligations to perform.

- *Out of the money*—A call is out of the money when the price of the stock is lower than the strike price of the call. A buyer will not exercise calls that are out of the money at expiration. Sellers want contracts to be out of the money; buyers do not. Sellers then keep the premium without obligations to perform.

- *Intrinsic value*—The intrinsic value is the same as the amount a contract is in the money. A call has intrinsic value when the market price of the stock is above the strike price of the call. Options never have negative intrinsic value; intrinsic value is always a positive amount or zero. Options that are at the money or out of the money have an intrinsic value of zero. Buyers like calls to have intrinsic value; sellers (writers) do not. A call that has intrinsic value at expiration will be exercised by the buyer. A call that has no intrinsic value will simply be allowed to expire.

During the lifetime of an option contract, buyers want the contract to move in the money; sellers want the contract to move out of the money.

■ *Parity*—A call option is at parity when the premium equals intrinsic value.

EXAMPLE

ABC stock is at 62.

ABC June 60 call trading at 2

With ABC stock trading at 62, a 60 call has an intrinsic value of 2 (stock price 62 – strike price 60 = 2). Given this call contract is trading at a premium of 2, it is known to be trading at parity.

Puts (in, at, or out of the money; intrinsic value; and parity)

■ *In the money*—A put is in the money when the price of the stock is lower than the strike price of the put. A buyer will exercise puts that are in the money at expiration. Buyers want in-the-money contracts; sellers do not.

■ *At the money*—A put is at the money when the price of the stock equals the strike price of the put. A buyer will not exercise contracts that are at the money at expiration. Sellers want at-the-money contracts; buyers do not.

■ *Out of the money*—A put is out of the money when the price of the stock is higher than the strike price of the put. A buyer will not exercise puts that are out of the money at expiration. Sellers want out-of-the-money contracts; buyers do not.

■ *Intrinsic value*—Intrinsic value is the same as the amount a contract is in the money. A put has intrinsic value when the market price of the stock is below the strike price of the put. Remember that options never have negative intrinsic value; it is always a positive number or zero. Buyers like options to have intrinsic value; sellers do not. A put that has intrinsic value at expiration will be exercised. A put that has no intrinsic value at expiration will simply be allowed to expire.

■ *Parity*—A put option is at parity when the premium equals intrinsic value.

EXAMPLE

ABC stock is at 58.

ABC June 60 put trading at 2

With ABC stock trading at 58, a 60 put has an intrinsic value of 2 (strike price 60 – stock price 58 = 2). Given this put contract is trading at a premium of 2, it is known to be trading at parity.

Intrinsic value and the premium

The premium of an option consists of two parts, the intrinsic value and the time value. The basic formula for a premium is intrinsic value plus time value = premium (IV + TV = Pr).

You can see from the explanation of intrinsic value that IV is an objective number. If you know the details of the contract and the underlying asset's current value, you can calculate IV.

Time value is a subjective number that is determined by supply and demand. Because it is a subjective number, we can only find it by applying the formula. If we know intrinsic value and the premium, any difference must be time value.

There are two factors that affect time value: the amount of time to expiration and volatility. The more time until expiration, the more time value a given option will have. The more volatile the underlying asset's price, the more time value in the premium.

KNOWLEDGE CHECK

1.   An investor is long 1 XYZ May 40 call and XYZ stock has a current market value of 44. Which of the following is **true**?
    A.   The May 40 call is at the money.
    B.   The May 40 call is in the money.
    C.   The May 40 call is out of the money.
    D.   The May 40 call has no intrinsic value.

2.   An investor is long 1 August XYZ 30 put and XYZ is has a current market value of 25. Which of the following is **true**?
    A.   The August 30 put is in the money by 5 points.
    B.   The August 30 put is at the money.
    C.   The August 30 put is out of the money by 30 points.
    D.   The August 30 put has no intrinsic value.

3.   An investor writes (sells) a July 25 ABC call. Which of the following is **true**?
    A.   The investor has the right to purchase ABC stock at 25.
    B.   The investor has the right to sell ABC stock at 25.
    C.   The investor will be obligated to purchase ABC stock at 25 if the call is exercised by the owner (buyer).
    D.   The investor will be obligated to sell the ABC stock at 25 if the call is exercised by the owner (buyer).

4.   An investor writes a September 65 ABC put for $3 when the stock is trading at $63. Which of the following is **true**?
    A.   The Intrinsic value is $3.
    B.   The intrinsic value is $2 and the time value is $1.
    C.   The intrinsic value is $1 and the time value is $2.
    D.   The investor has the right to purchase ABC stock at 65.

Answers

1.   **B**   Options are in the money by the amount of their intrinsic value. This May 40 call has intrinsic value of 4 points and is therefore in the money by 4 points. Calls have intrinsic value when the current market value of the stock is above the strike price.

2.   **A**   Options are in the money by the amount of their intrinsic value. This August 30 put has intrinsic value of 5 points and is therefore in the money by 5 points. Puts have intrinsic value when the current market value of the stock is below the strike price.

3.   **B**   Writers of options incur an obligation if the option is exercised by the other party to the contract (owner or buyer). If the owner of a call exercises her right to purchase the stock, the writer will be obligated to sell the stock. Therefore, this investor will be obligated to sell the ABC stock at the strike price (25) if the call is exercised by the owner (buyer).

4. **B**   Puts are in the money when the price of the stock is lower than the strike price. In this example, the stock is at $63 and the strike price is $65; the put is $2 in the money (or has intrinsic value of $2). The premium is $3. Using the formula IV + TV = Pr, we know that the time value is $1: the difference between intrinsic value and premium. As the writer of a put, the investor has an obligation to buy the stock if the option is exercised.

LESSON 3.3: NONEQUITY OPTIONS

LO 3.e Differentiate equity, currency, and index options.

Nonequity (currency and index) options function nearly the same as equity options. However, because the underlying instruments are not shares of stock, nonequity options have different contract sizes and delivery and exercise standards.

Index options

Options on indexes allow investors to profit from the movements of markets or market segments and hedge against these market swings. They may be based on broad-based, narrow-based, or other indexes with a particular focus.

- **Broad-based indexes** reflect movement of the entire market and include the S&P 100 (OEX), S&P 500, and the Major Market Index (XMI).

- **Narrow-based indexes** track the movement of market segments in a specific industry, such as technology or pharmaceuticals.

Some indexes have a very particular focus, such as the VIX (Volatility Index). This index is a measure of the implied volatility of the S&P 500 Index options traded on the CBOE. VIX Index options, also traded on the CBOE, are designed to reflect investor expectations of market volatility over the next 30 days. It is often called the "fear" gauge or index. High readings are not bullish, nor are they bearish, but instead they are a measure of the expectation (fear) that the market will be volatile. The expectation of greater volatility generally translates into higher premiums for options contracts.

Index option features

Index options typically use a multiplier of $100. The premium amount is multiplied by $100 to calculate the option's cost, and the strike price is multiplied by $100 to determine the total dollar value of the index.

Purchases and sales of index options, like equity options, settle on the next business day. Index options stop trading at 4:15 pm ET if they are broad-based. Narrow-based index options stop trading at 4:00 pm ET.

The exercise of an index option settles in cash rather than in delivery of a security, and the cash must be delivered on the next business day. If the option is exercised, the writer of the option delivers cash equal to the intrinsic value of the option to the buyer.

When index options are exercised, their settlement price is based on the closing value of the index on the day of exercise, not the value at the time of exercise.

Index options expire on the third Friday of the expiration month, just as equity options do.

TAKE NOTE

With regard to settlement, there is one major difference between index options and equity options. The exercise of an index option settles next business day, whereas the exercise of an equity option settles regular way (two business days). With regard to trading (i.e., buying or selling), settlement is the next business day for both.

EXAMPLE

Following is an example to take you through the process from purchase through exercise, or through expiry, for an index option.

A customer buys 1 OEX Jan 460 call at 3.20 when the OEX index is trading at 461.

What is the premium?	$320 (3.20 × $100)
What is the breakeven point?	463.20 (strike price + premium)
What is the intrinsic value?	$100 (461 – 460)
What is the time value?	$220 ($320 – $100)

One month later, with the index at 472, the customer elects to exercise.

How much does the customer receive for the exercise? $1,200

Index 472 – strike price 460 = 12

12 × 100 = $1,200

Index options strategy

Index options may be used to speculate on movement of the market overall. If an investor believes the market will rise, he can purchase index calls or write index puts. If an investor believes the market will fall, he can purchase index puts or write index calls.

Hedging a portfolio is an important use of index options. If a portfolio manager holds a diverse portfolio of equity, he can buy a put on the index to offset loss if the market value of the stocks falls. This use of index puts is known as **portfolio insurance**. Index options protect against the risk of a decline in the overall market, which is **systematic** or **systemic risk**.

Interest rate options

Interest rate options are yield based (i.e., they have a direct relationship to movements in interest rates). These options are based on yields of T-bills, T-notes, and T-bonds. A yield-based option with a strike price of 35 reflects a yield of 3.5%. Assume an investor believes that rates on T-notes, currently at 3.5%, will rise in the near term. The investor could purchase a call option with a 35 strike price (at the money). If rates rise to 4.5%, the investor could exercise and receive cash equal to the intrinsic value of the option.

Rates have gone up by 10 points—35 to 45—so the investor would receive $1,000 because each point is worth $100. Profit would be the $1,000 received on exercise less the premium paid. On the other hand, the investor could have closed his position, profiting from the difference between the premium paid and the premium received on closing.

The strategy is straightforward. If a portfolio manager believes rates will fall, the manager will buy puts or write calls. If the manager believes rates will rise, buying calls and writing puts would be appropriate.

Unit 3

TAKE NOTE

All yield-based options are European-style exercise. That is, they may be exercised only on expiration day. European-style exercise options are discussed later.

Currency options

Currency options allow investors to speculate on the performance of currencies other than the U.S. dollar or to protect against fluctuating currency exchange rates against the U.S. dollar. Currency options are available for trading on U.S. listed exchanges on the Australian dollar, the British pound, the Canadian dollar, Swiss francs, Japanese yen, and the euro. Importers and exporters frequently use currency options to hedge currency risk. Currency options are often used by importers and exporters to hedge fluctuations in currency exchange rates.

- Currency options expire on the third Friday of the expiration month, just as equity options do.

- Currency options settle, like equity options, on the next business day. When a foreign currency option is exercised, settlement occurs on the next business day as well.

- Exchange-listed foreign currency options are European-style exercise only.

TAKE NOTE

If you are in the import/export business, which currency option should you use?

If you are an exporter, you are concerned with the value of the foreign currency dropping, so buy puts.

If you are an importer, you are concerned with the value of the foreign currency rising, so buy calls.

To keep it easy, remember that trade is EPIC!

Exporters buy Puts

Importers buy Calls

LO 3.f Differentiate American and European exercise rules.

American-style vs. European-style exercise rules

An **American-style** option allows the owner of a contract to exercise anytime before expiration. Nearly all equity and equity index options are American style.

European-style options can be exercised only on expiration day. Foreign currency and yield-based options are European style.

KNOWLEDGE CHECK

1. Your customer is a large exporter of electronic devices. They are delivering a large shipment to Japan and are concerned that the value of the Japanese yen may drop before they receive payment. In order to hedge this currency risk, your customer should
   A. buy yen calls.
   B. sell yen calls.
   C. buy yen puts.
   D. sell yen puts.

2. An investor might make money in a strong bull market by
   A. selling shares short.
   B. buying equity index puts.
   C. buying equity index calls.
   D. selling equity index calls.

3. If the owner of an option may only issue exercise instructions on the last day of trading, this is an example of
   A. a European-style option.
   B. an American-style option.
   C. an expiration-style option.
   D. a Eurasian-style option.

Answers

1. **C** U.S. exporters are concerned about the currency they will be paid dropping in value against the U.S. dollar. The best hedge against an asset dropping in price is to own puts. LO 3.e

2. **C** If the market is going up, you should own the bullish position, a long call. LO 3.e

3. **A** European-style option may only be exercised on the last trading day. An American-style option may be exercised at any time. We just made up the other two styles. LO 3.f

LESSON 3.4: OPTION CALCULATIONS

LO 3.g Calculate break even, maximum gain and maximum loss on an individual option contract.

Basic calculations (breakeven [BE], maximum gain [MG], and maximum loss [ML])

For each of the four basic options positions (long call, short call, long put, and short put), you will want to be comfortable with calculating the investor's breakeven (BE) point, maximum gain (MG), and maximum loss (ML). The BE point is the point at which the investor neither makes nor loses money. Realizing MG or ML has to do with the market attitude of the position (bullish or bearish), which direction the stock moves, and how far it goes in that direction. Remember that, in theory, a stock could go as high as infinity or as low as zero.

■ *Long call*—Remember that call buyers are bullish. By purchasing calls, an investor can profit from an increase in a stock's price.

■ *BE*—For calls, the BE is found by adding the strike price and the premium. For the call buyer, the contract is profitable above the BE.

■ *MG*—Theoretically, the potential gains available to call buyers are unlimited because there is no limit on how far a stock's price can rise. In theory, it can rise to infinity; thus, the potential gain is unlimited.

■ *ML*—The most the call buyer can lose is the premium paid. This will happen if the stock price is at or below the strike price of the option at expiration.

EXAMPLE

Long 1 July 40 call at 3

BE = strike price + premium (40 + 3) = 43

Above 43, the call buyer is profitable.

MG = unlimited, because the stock can rise to infinity

ML = premium paid (3 points) = $300

- *Short call*—Remember that call sellers (writers) are bearish. By writing calls, an investor can profit if the stock price falls.

- *BE*—Once again, for calls, the BE is found by adding the strike price to the premium, but for the call seller, the contract is profitable below the BE.

- *MG*—A call writer's MG is the premium received. The MG is earned when the stock price is at or below the exercise price at expiration.

- *ML*—A call writer's ML is unlimited because the writer could be forced to buy the stock at a potentially unlimited price, if the option is exercised by the buyer, for delivery at the strike price.

EXAMPLE

Short 1 July 40 call at 3

BE = strike price + premium (40 + 3) = 43

At or below 43, the call writer is profitable.

MG = premium received (3 points) = $300

ML = unlimited, because the writer can be forced to purchase the stock at an unlimited number; infinity

TAKE NOTE

Call Summary

BE is the same for both buyer and seller, while one investor's MG is the other's ML.

Call	Buyer	Seller
BE	Strike price + premium	Strike price + premium
MG	Unlimited	Premium
ML	Premium	Unlimited

Puts: BE, MG, and ML

- *Long put*—Remember that put buyers are bearish. By purchasing puts, an investor can profit from a decrease in a stock's price.

- *BE*—For puts, the BE is found by subtracting the premium from the strike price. For the put buyer, the contract is profitable below the BE at expiration.

- *MG*—The maximum potential gain available to put owners is the option's strike price less the amount of the premium paid (same as the BE). A stock's price can fall no lower than zero.

- *ML*—The most the put buyer can lose is the premium paid. This happens if the market price is at or above the strike price at the option's expiration.

EXAMPLE

Long 1 July 40 put at 3

BE = strike price – premium (40 – 3) = 37

Below 37, the put buyer is profitable.

MG = from the BE down to 0; the same as BE = 37 points ($3,700)

ML = premium paid (3 points) = $300

- *Short put*—Remember that put sellers (writers) are bullish. By writing puts, an investor can profit if the stock price rises.

- *BE*—Once again, for puts, the BE is found by subtracting the premium from the strike price. For the put seller, the contract is profitable at or above the BE at expiration.

- *MG*—A put writer's MG is the premium received. The MG is earned when the stock price is at or above the exercise price at expiration.

- *ML*—A put writer's ML is the put's strike price less the premium received (the same as the BE); it occurs when the stock price drops to zero. The investor is forced to buy the worthless stock at the option's strike price. The investor's loss is reduced by the premium received.

EXAMPLE

Short 1 July 40 put at 3

BE = strike price – premium (40 – 3) = 37

At or above 37, the put writer is profitable.

MG = premium received (3 points) = $300

ML = from the BE down to 0; the same as BE = 37 points ($3,700)

TAKE NOTE

Put Summary

BE is the same for both buyer and seller, while one investor's MG is the other's ML.

Put	Buyer	Seller
BE	Strike price – premium	Strike price – premium
MG	Strike price – premium	Premium
ML	Premium	Strike price – premium

TAKE NOTE

The breakeven calculations shown are for an option, and not for a combined position like a stock plus an option. If a question has a customer position that has both an option and a stock in it, the formulas above do not apply. The correct formula for those position will be covered later.

KNOWLEDGE CHECK

1. An investor is long 1 January 30 call at 2. Calculate the breakeven, maximum gain, and maximum loss.
   - A. BE 30, MG unlimited, ML 200
   - B. BE 32, MG 200, ML unlimited
   - C. BE 28, MG unlimited, ML 200
   - D. BE 2. MG 500, ML 32

2. An investor is long 1 January 15 put at 4. Calculate the breakeven, maximum gain, and maximum loss.
   - A. BE 11, MG 1100, ML 400
   - B. BE 19, MG unlimited, ML 400
   - C. BE 11 MG 400, ML unlimited
   - D. BE 19, MG 1100. ML 400

3. All of the following are true **except**
   - A. breakeven (BE) is always the same number for both buyer and seller of an option contract.
   - B. the maximum loss for options buyers is the premium paid.
   - C. the maximum gain for options buyers is always unlimited.
   - D. BE is calculated using the same formula for both buyer and seller.

Answers

1. **C** Breakeven = 32 (for a call, BE = strike price [30] + premium [2]); maximum gain = unlimited (market attitude for a long call is bullish; the stock could go to infinity); maximum loss = $200 (the most an investor can lose when purchasing options is the premium paid; 2 points = $200).

2. **A** Breakeven = 11 (for a put, BE = strike price [15] – premium [4]); maximum gain = $1,100 (market attitude for a long put is bearish; the stock can fall to zero leaving the investor with a gain from the BE point [11] down to 0); maximum loss = $400 (the most an investor can lose when purchasing options is the premium paid; 4 points = $400).

3. **C** BE is calculated using the same formula for both buyer and seller of an option contract. Therefore, BE is always the same number for both buyer and seller. The formula for calls is strike price plus premium, and the formula for puts is strike price minus premium. The most any options buyer can lose (maximum loss, or ML) for a call or a put is the premium paid. However, maximum gain (MG), while unlimited for a call buyer (bullish market attitude), is limited for a put buyer. Remember that the market attitude of a put buyer is bearish, and the farthest the stock could fall is to zero. Therefore, the put buyer's MG is limited to amount from BE point to zero.

LESSON 3.5: HEDGING RISK WITH OPTIONS

LO 3.h Determine how to best hedge risk with long options.

Sometimes, buyers of options are seeking to hedge (protect) a long or short stock position. These worried investors use options as an insurance policy in the event their core stock position moves it the wrong direction. The key thing to remember is that the insurance policy profits if the core stock moves in the wrong direction.

Protective puts

An investor who is long stock (bullish) could buy a put option as a hedge against the stock falling in value. The put would ensure that the client could sell the stock at no less than the option's strike price if the share price declines. Effectively, the put locks in a minimum sales price if the long position moves the wrong way. This position is sometimes called a "married put."

When calculating the breakeven of a protective put, you must remember that there are two parts to the position—a long stock and a long put.

In order for the customer to break even on the position, the value of the stock the customer owns must rise above what he paid for the stock by enough to cover the cost of the option position.

The formula: breakeven = stock price + premium

Protective calls

An investor who is short stock (bearish) could buy a call option as a hedge. The call would ensure that the client could buy the stock back at no more than the option's strike price if the shares rise in value. Effectively, the call locks in a maximum purchase price to cover the short if the short position moves the wrong way. A short stock position has unlimited risk. Using a call as a hedge controls the risk of selling a stock short.

When calculating the breakeven of a protective call, you must remember that there are two parts to the position—a short stock and a long call.

In order for the customer to break even on the position, the value of the stock the customer shorted must fall below what she paid for the stock by enough to cover the cost of the option position.

The formula: breakeven = stock price – premium

Summary

Core Position	Hedge
Long stock	Put option
Short stock	Call option

We are not expecting that you will need to calculate maximum gains or losses on hedge positions.

KNOWLEDGE CHECK

1. Which of the following positions/actions would cover a client who has 1,000 shares of the Seabird Coffee Company (Ticker BCC)?
   A. A long stock position
   B. Buying 10 BCC puts
   C. Buying 10 BCC calls
   D. A short stock position

2. Mr. Perez dislikes Seabird Airlines because of a bad experience on a flight to Portland. He thinks the company's stock is overvalued. He is currently short 1,000 shares of the company. He is concerned with the potentially unlimited risk he is exposed to and would like to use options to hedge that risk. His best option position would be
   A. buy 10 Seabird Airline calls.
   B. buy 10 OEX (S&P 100 index) calls.
   C. sell 10 Seabird Coffee calls.
   D. buy 10 Seabird Coffee puts.

3. Ms. Johansen purchased 100 shares of Natasha Publishing two years ago for $40 a share. The stock has risen to $62 a share. She is concerned that the recent death of the founder and CEO may negatively impact the stock. As a hedge she buys a 60 put on the stock for $2. Her breakeven price on this position is
   A. $64/share.
   B. $62/share.
   C. $58/share.
   D. $42/share.

Answers

1. **B** The best hedge for a long stock position is to own long puts. This gives a bottom price the customer can sell the stock for during the life of the put.

2. **A** Long Calls provide the best protection against a short stock position. The calls give the owner the right to exercise and buy the stock at the exercise price, thereby locking in the cost to replace the shares.

3. **D** The formula for breakeven on a long stock plus long call position is the cost of the stock plus the cost of the option on a per share basis. The original cost of the stock is $40, and the put cost $2, for a breakeven of $42/share.

LESSON 3.6: GENERATING PREMIUM INCOME

LO 3.i Indicate how to generate premium income by selling.

Selling options for premium income

As you read earlier, an investor can sell option (write) in order to generate income. However, writing an option obligates the investor to perform an action if the option is exercised. In the case of a call, the risk is theoretically unlimited. When writing a put, the risk is still significant, though not unlimited.

When we note a short option contract as being covered or uncovered, we are speaking to the writer's option position and whether or not the writer already owns the underlying security to be delivered (or have the cash available if the contract is cash settled) in the event that the owner exercises the contract.

Writing a call option

- *Covered*—If the contract is covered, the writer already owns the underlying security. This ensures the writer's ability to perform (deliver), should the owner exercise the contract.

- *Uncovered (naked)*—If the contract is uncovered (naked), the writer does not own the underlying security. If the contract is exercised by the owner, the writer will need to purchase the underlying security at the current market price to deliver it. As it is impossible to know what the price of the stock will be at that time, the risk is said to be unlimited.

TAKE NOTE

Uncovered (naked) contracts entail much more risk due to the uncertainty in price regarding purchase of the security in the current marketplace if the contract is exercised. Writers of naked calls are willing to accept that risk in return for taking in the premium when selling short (writing) the call.

EXAMPLE

Covered Positions

Covered call (client is already long the underlying shares)

Long 100 shares of XYZ at 40

Short 1 XYZ July 45 call @ 3

If the owner exercises the call, the writer will need to deliver the stock at the strike price (45). Already owning the stock at 40, this poses no risk because the client already owns the securities to be delivered. The breakeven on the position is $37 ($40 stock purchase price minus the $3 premium collected).

Uncovered Positions

Uncovered call (naked)

Short 1 XYZ July 45 call

If the owner exercises the call, the writer will need to deliver the stock at the strike price (45). Not owning the stock, the writer will need to purchase the stock in the open market to deliver it. The risk of this position is theoretically unlimited because there is no limit to how high the stock could rise in value.

TAKE NOTE

Of these positions, the covered call is the most common. It is a proven and relatively conservative way to generate income against a stock position.

Writing a put option

- *Covered*—If the contract is covered, the writer already has sufficient cash available to buy the stock. This ensures the writer's ability to perform (purchase), should the owner exercise the contract.

- *Uncovered (naked)*—If the contract is uncovered (naked), the writer does not have the cash on hand to purchase the stock at the strike price. If the contract is exercised by the owner, the writer will need to come up with the cash from somewhere.

- *Covered against a short stock*—You may see a reference to a covered put where the customer is short the stock and writes the put. If the option is exercised, the customer buys the stock from the option's owner and then delivers the stock to cover the short. This is still an unlimited risk position because the customer has no control over the option. If the stock goes up, the put will not be exercised and the customer is still short the stock. This is a theoretical hedge, and does not occur in the real world, but might on an exam.

EXAMPLE

Covered put (client has cash on hand)

$3,000 in the account

Short 1 XYZ July 30 put

If the owner (not our customer) exercises the put, the writer (our customer) will be required to buy the stock at the strike price (30) at a cost of $3,000. They are then the owners of 100 shares of XYZ stock.

Uncovered put (naked)

Short 1 XYZ July 30 put

If the owner exercises the call, the writer will be required to buy the stock at the strike price (30). If the stock falls in value to $0, the put writer would be forced to buy worthless securities for $3,000. The loss would be $3,000 (the cost of the worthless stock) minus the initial premium collected. This is substantial, but not unlimited because it would be in the naked call writer's case.

Covered put (client is already short the underlying shares)

Short 100 shares of XYZ at 40

Short 1 XYZ July 30 put

If the owner exercises the put, the writer will be required to buy the stock at the strike price (30). If the client has already shorted the stock at 40, this poses no risk because the client ends up with a net flat position after being forced to buy the stock back if the put is assigned. If the stock falls, the client profits on the short sale, which makes up for the loss on the mandatory stock purchase when the put is assigned.

KNOWLEDGE CHECK

1. Mr. Darcy owns 5,000 shares of English Manor Properties. It is his belief that the company is unlikely to grow much over the next year. He is curious how he might generate some additional income from the position because English Manor pays a paltry dividend and asks about covered calls. You tell him that
    A. writing calls against his stock position is a conservative strategy for generating income.
    B. writing calls against his stock position is a conservative strategy but is ineffective for generating income.
    C. selling covered calls is very aggressive but has a solid chance of generating substantial income.
    D. buy puts is the best hedge against this position.

2. If a customer had a large cash position and was interested in purchasing stock at prices below where they are today, and possibly generating some income in the process, an option strategy would be to
    A. write covered puts that are currently out of the money.
    B. write uncovered calls that are currently out of the money.
    C. buy out-of-the-money calls.
    D. place a buy stop order below the market.

3. Which of the following positions has unlimited risk?
    A. Short 5 BCC puts
    B. Long 500 BCC and short 5 BCC calls
    C. Short 500 BCC and short 5 BCC puts
    D. Short 500 BCC and long 5 BCC calls

Answers

1. **A** Only selling an option will generate income. Selling covered calls is an effective and very conservative way to do so.

2. **A** Writing the puts would generate premium income. If the stock declines in value and the option is exercised, he will by the stock at a price that's lower than where the market is at this moment. The short calls would force him to sell the shares if exercised. Buying out-of-the-money calls cost money, and the strike price would be higher than the market. The buy stop does not generate income.

3. **C** A put, whether long or short, does not generate unlimited risk. A long stock and a short call is a covered call and not unlimited risk. Short stock and a long call is a covered short and has limited risk. A short stock and a short put is exposed to unlimited risk because the put income provides very limited protection against a potentially unlimited loss.

LESSON 3.7: ADMINISTRATION AND COMPLIANCE

LO 3.j Determine the correct steps for adding options trading to a brokerage account.

The primary regulators for options are the Options Clearing Corporation (OCC) and for trading options, the Chicago Board of Options Exchange (CBOE).

The OCC provides an **options disclosure document** (ODD), which must be provided at or before the time of the account approval. This document explains options strategies, risks, and rewards and is designed to provide full and fair disclosure to customers before they begin options trading.

Before any trading can take place, an options account must be approved by a Registered Options Principal (ROP) of the firm.

Steps for setting up an account to trade options

A representative must believe that options are a suitable investment for a client based on the client's circumstances and objectives.

The representative provides the customer with a copy of the options disclosure document.

The account is approved for options trading by a Registered Options Principal.

Option trades may be entered.

Then, not later than 15 days after the account approval, the customer must return the signed options agreement.

The **options agreement** states that the customer has read the ODD, understands the risks of options trading, and will honor all rules regulations regarding options trading. By signing, the customer also agrees to advise the firm if any changes occur in his financial situation, investment objectives, and so forth that would impact whether or not the account should still be approved for options trading.

If the signed options agreement is not returned within 15 days of account approval, the investor cannot open new options positions. Only closing transactions are allowed if the options agreement is not returned as required.

TAKE NOTE

Note the chronological conundrum that exists. The options account must be approved before trading can occur. However, it is possible that the account has been approved, trades have occurred, and yet the customer, having 15 days after approval to do so, still has not returned the signed options account agreement.

EXAMPLE

Options Account Diagram

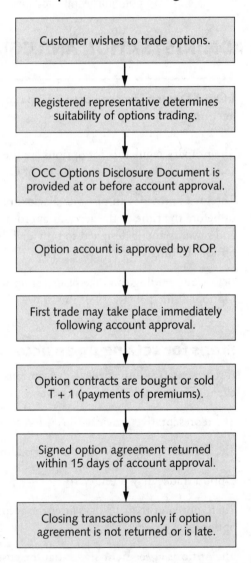

Customer wishes to trade options.

↓

Registered representative determines suitability of options trading.

↓

OCC Options Disclosure Document is provided at or before account approval.

↓

Option account is approved by ROP.

↓

First trade may take place immediately following account approval.

↓

Option contracts are bought or sold T + 1 (payments of premiums).

↓

Signed option agreement returned within 15 days of account approval.

↓

Closing transactions only if option agreement is not returned or is late.

LO 3.k Recall the role of the Options Clearing Corporation.

The OCC

The Options Clearing Corporation (OCC) is the clearing agent for listed options contracts—that is, those listed for trading on U.S. options exchanges. Its primary functions are to standardize, guarantee the performance of, and issue option contracts. The OCC determines when new option contracts should be offered to the market on an underlying security. It designates the contract specifications, such as strike prices and expiration months for new contracts, utilizing standards to maintain uniformity and liquidity. The following are some standards and characteristics of listed option contracts.

■ *Trading times*—Listed options trade from 9:30 am to 4:00 pm ET.

■ *Settlement*—Listed options settle on the next business day after trade date (T+1).

■ *Expiration*—Listed options expire on the third Friday of the expiration month at 11:59 pm.

■ *Exercise*—Listed options can be exercised by the owner from the time of purchase until they expire. The exercise process is guaranteed by the OCC. If a holder of an option wishes to exercise his contract, his BD notifies the OCC.

■ *Automatic exercise*—Any contract that is in the money by at least 0.01 will be exercised automatically at expiration for the holder unless the holder gives "do not exercise" instructions.

■ *Assignment*—When the OCC receives an exercise notice, it assigns the exercise notice to a short BD—that is, one who has a customer who is short the contract. The short BD assigns a short customer who is now obligated to perform (buy or sell the stock at the strike price).

The OCC assigns exercise notices to short BDs on a random basis. BDs may then assign exercise notices to their short customers on a random basis, on a first-in, first-out (FIFO) basis, or any other method that is fair and reasonable.

TAKE NOTE

Options contracts are traded without a certificate. An investor's proof of ownership is the trade confirmation.

Exercise and assignment

The owner of a call (party long the contract) has the right to buy the stock at the strike price. To do so, the owner must exercise the call. The writer of the call will then be assigned, meaning that the writer must now fulfill her obligation to sell the stock at the strike price.

The owner of a put (party long the contract) has the right to sell the stock at the strike price. To do so, the owner must exercise the put. The writer of the put will then be assigned, meaning that the writer must now fulfill her obligation to buy the stock at the strike price.

TAKE NOTE

Only owners of options contracts (those who are long the contracts) have the right to exercise them. Writers of contracts (those who are short the contracts) will be assigned to fulfill their obligation to perform; either sell, if short a call, or buy, if short a put.

KNOWLEDGE CHECK

1. A customer of a BD is opening a new options account. The customer must return the options agreement
   - A. signed before the account can be approved.
   - B. before the first transaction can occur.
   - C. signed and not later than 15 days after the account approval.
   - D. before he will be allowed to view the options disclosure document.

2. Regarding assignment of exercises notices, which of the following are true?
   - I. The Options Clearing Corporation (OCC) assigns short BDs randomly.
   - II. The OCC assigns short BDs using the first-in, first-out (FIFO) accounting method.
   - III. Short BDs can assign their short customers randomly only.
   - IV. Short BDs can assign their short customers randomly, using the FIFO accounting method or by any other fair method.
   - A. I and III
   - B. I and IV
   - C. II and III
   - D. II and IV

3. Listed options transactions settle regular way
   - A. on the third Friday of the expiration month.
   - B. on the next business day after trade date (T+1).
   - C. on the third business day after trade date (T+3).
   - D. when the option finally expires.

Answers

1. **C**   Once the account is approved by a principal of the BD, the customer has 15 days to return the signed options agreement. Remember that the customer must be given the OCC Options Disclosure Document before the account can be approved. Once approved, the customer may trade immediately but still has 15 days to get the signed options agreement back to the BD. LO 3.j

2. **B**   When an exercise notice is received, the OCC assigns short BDs on a random basis only. In turn, a short BD may exercise its short customers in 1 of 3 ways: randomly, using the FIFO accounting method, or by any other fair method. LO 3.k

3. **B**   Options transactions settle on the next business day after trade date (T+1). LO 3.k

UNIT 4

Packaged Investments

LEARNING OBJECTIVES

When you have completed this unit, you will be able to accomplish the following.

> LO 4.a   Classify the types of investment companies.
> LO 4.b   Differentiate open- and closed-end management companies.
> LO 4.c   Define variable annuity and variable life insurance contracts.
> LO 4.d   Differentiate A, B, C, and no-load share classes.
> LO 4.e   Recall the use of breakpoints, letters of intent, rights of accumulation, combination, and exchange privileges.
> LO 4.f   Define forward pricing.
> LO 4.g   Calculate NAV.
> LO 4.h   Define expense ratio.
> LO 4.i   Name the four types of mutual fund prospectus.
> LO 4.j   Define breakpoint sales.
> LO 4.k   Recall mutual fund taxation and the pipeline theory.

INTRODUCTION

In Unit 4 you will learn about different packaged investments. Packaged investments are portfolios that are made up of other investments, primarily stocks and bonds. Investors may buy interest in the portfolio (usually called shares or units). The most common of these are the investment companies, with mutual funds being the best-known example.

LESSON 4.1: INVESTMENT COMPANY ACT OF 1940

LO 4.a Classify the types of investment companies.

Investment companies

An investment company is a corporation or trust that pools investors' money and then invests that money in securities on their behalf. Investors are able to pool their money and have the investment company invest it based on a clearly defined objective, such as growth or income. By investing these pooled funds as a single large account, jointly owned by every investor in the company, the investment company is able to invest in many different securities and therefore reduce the overall risk associated with investing in only one or a few. These pooled investments can total hundreds of millions or even billions of dollars. They are very popular investment vehicles, because it is common for them to allow minimum investments of perhaps only $100 or even less. While investing $100 many times might not purchase a single share of stock or one bond, the ability to pool that $100 with thousands or millions of investors gives the individual investor a great advantage—purchasing power in the marketplace.

Like corporate issuers, investment companies raise capital by selling shares to the public. Investment companies must abide by the same registration and prospectus requirements imposed by the Securities Act of 1933 on other issuers. Investment companies are subject to regulations regarding how their shares are sold to the public, and they are regulated by the Investment Company Act of 1940.

Types of investment companies

The Investment Company Act of 1940 classifies investment companies into three broad types: face-amount certificate (FAC) companies, unit investment trusts (UITs), and management investment companies. See Figure 4.1.

Figure 4.1: Classification of Investment Companies

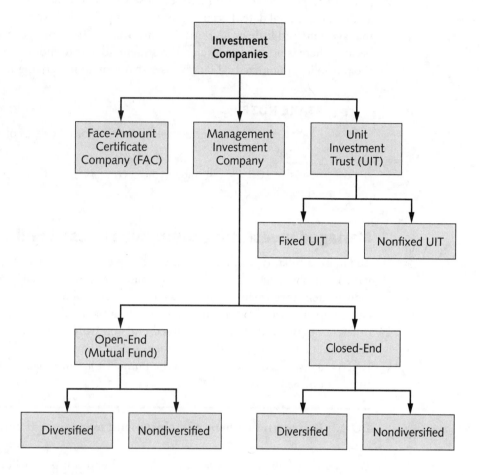

Classification of Investment Companies

 TAKE NOTE

Variable annuities have subaccounts that are defined as either UITs or open-end management investment companies.

Face-amount certificates (FACs)

A face-amount certificate (FAC) is a contract between an investor and an issuer in which the issuer guarantees payment of a stated (face amount) sum to the investor at some set date in the future. In return for this future payment, the investor agrees to pay the issuer a set amount of money, either as a lump sum or in periodic installments. If the investor pays for the certificate in a lump sum, the investment is known as a fully paid FAC.

Issuers of these investments are FAC companies. Very few FAC companies operate today.

Unit investment trusts (UITs)

A unit investment trust (UIT) is an investment company organized under a trust indenture. UITs do not have boards of directors (they have trustees).

UITs create a portfolio of debt or equity securities designed to meet the company's objectives. They then sell redeemable interests, also known as units or shares of beneficial interest, in their portfolio of securities. Each share is an undivided interest in the entire underlying portfolio.

A UIT may be fixed or nonfixed. A debt-fixed UIT typically purchases a portfolio of bonds and terminates when the bonds in the portfolio mature. An equity-fixed UIT purchases a portfolio of stocks and, because stocks don't have a maturity date, terminates at a predetermined date. Because a fixed UIT's portfolio is static, there is no need for active management and little or no portfolio turnover. UITs do not generally assess management fees because there is no need to hire an investment adviser to monitor and trade positions within the portfolio. A nonfixed UIT purchases shares of an underlying mutual fund.

TAKE NOTE

FACs and UITs are not managed; once the portfolios are composed, they do not change.

FACs and UITs do not trade in the secondary market; they are redeemable only through the issuer.

Managed investment companies (closed and open end)

The most familiar type of an investment company is the management investment company, which actively manages a securities portfolio to achieve a stated investment objective. A management investment company is either closed end or open end. Both closed- and open-end companies sell shares to the public in an initial public offering (IPO); the primary difference between them is that a closed-end company's initial offering of shares is limited (it closes after a specific authorized number of shares have been sold) and an open-end company is perpetually offering new shares to the public (it is continually open to new investors). In this section, we'll look at each.

LO 4.b Differentiate open- and closed-end management companies.

■ *Closed-end investment companies*—A closed-end company will raise capital for its portfolio by conducting a common stock offering, much like any other publicly traded company that raises capital to invest in its business. In the initial offering, the company registers a fixed number of shares with the SEC and offers them to the public with a prospectus for a limited time through underwriters. Once all the shares have been sold, the fund is closed to new investors. Many times, a fund elects to be a closed-end company because the sector in which it intends to invest has a limited amount of securities available. Closed-end investment companies may also issue bonds and preferred stock.

Closed-end investment companies are often called publicly traded funds. After the stock is sold in the initial offering, anyone can buy or sell shares in the secondary market (i.e., on an exchange or OTC) in transactions between private investors. Supply and demand determine the bid price (price at which an investor can sell) and the ask price (price at which an investor can buy). Closed-end fund shares may trade above (at a premium to) or below (at a discount to) the shares' NAV. Simply put, the fund's NAV is its assets minus its liabilities. The NAV per share is the fund's NAV divided by the number of outstanding shares.

TEST TOPIC ALERT

Closed-end investment companies are the only investment company security that trades in the secondary market.

Closed-end investment companies may issue common stock, preferred stock, and debt securities.

■ *Open-end investment companies (mutual funds)*—An open-end company only issues one class of security, which is common stock (no preferred shares or bonds). It does not specify the exact number of shares it intends to issue but registers an open offering with the SEC. In other words, mutual funds conduct a continuous primary offering of common stock. With this registration type, they can raise an unlimited amount of investment capital by continuously issuing new shares.

When investors want to sell their holdings in a mutual fund, the fund itself redeems those shares at the find's current NAV, discussed shortly. In this respect, mutual fund shares are like FACs and UITs in that they do not trade in the secondary market. When an investor sells shares back to the fund (the fund is redeeming the shares), the fund sends the investor money for the investor's proportionate share of the fund's net assets. Therefore, a mutual fund's capital shrinks when investors redeem shares but so does the number of outstanding shares; the value of each share does not fall as a result of the redemption. When a client acquires mutual fund shares, she pays the current public offering price (POP).

Mutual funds are priced at the end of each business day, with sellers receiving the next calculated NAV and buyers paying the next calculated POP. All transition requests must be entered by 4:00 pm. Any requests to buy or sell that are entered after 4:00 pm will receive the next business day's NAV or POP. For example, a seller who places an order after the close (4:00 pm ET on Friday) will receive Monday's NAV when liquidating her shares.

TAKE NOTE

You should understand that while mutual funds only issue common shares to their shareholders, the funds themselves can purchase common stock, preferred stock, and bonds for their investment portfolios. As noted, each fund has a stated investment objective, and which types of securities the fund portfolio purchases has largely to do with fulfilling that objective.

The table in Figure 4.2 summarizes the differences between open-end and closed-end fund companies.

Figure 4.2: Comparison of Open-End and Closed-End Investment Companies

	Open End	Closed End
Capitalization	Unlimited; continuous offering of shares	Fixed; single offering of shares
Issues	Common stock only; no debt securities; permitted to borrow	Common and preferred stock; debt securities
Shares	Full or fractional	Full only
Offerings and trading	Sold and redeemed by fund only; continuous primary offering; must redeem shares	Initial primary offering; secondary trading OTC or on an exchange; does not redeem shares
Pricing	NAV + sales charge; selling price determined by formula in the prospectus	CMV + commission; price determined by supply and demand
Shareholder rights	Dividends (when declared); voting	Dividends (when declared); voting; preemptive
Ex-date	Set by BOD	Set by the exchange or FINRA

Unit 4

KNOWLEDGE CHECK

1. Under the Investment Company act of 1940 all of the following are examples of management companies **except**
   A. S&P 500 Index Trust ETF.
   B. growth fund option for a VA.
   C. Windmill Income UIT.
   D. Windmill Income Fund, an exchange-listed closed-end fund.

2. One characteristic of an open-end investment company that distinguishes it from a closed-end one is that
   A. it may avoid taxation by distributing all of its net investment income to shareholders.
   B. it may be either diversified or nondiversified.
   C. there are a wide variety of objectives available for investors to select from.
   D. there is a continuous public offering.

3. An investor can take advantage of intraday price changes due to normal market forces when investing in
   I. closed-end funds.
   II. exchange-traded funds.
   III. hedge funds.
   IV. open-end funds.
   A. I and II
   B. I and IV
   C. II and III
   D. III and IV

Answers

1. **C** Unit investment trusts are investment companies, but not management companies, under the act. Closed-end funds, ETFs, and separate accounts are all types of management companies. LO 4.a

2. **D** The key difference between open-end investment companies and closed-ends is the fact that new shares are continuously being offered for open-end companies. In the case of the closed-end, once the IPO is over, the only way to acquire shares is in the secondary market. Both types of funds may operate as regulated investment companies and avoid taxation, both may choose to be diversified or not, and both offer a wide variety of investment objectives. LO 4.b

3. **A** Both closed-end funds and ETFs trade in the marketplace based on supply and demand. Open-end funds use forward pricing and generally price only once per day (usually at the end of the trading day). Most hedge funds are organized as private investment partnerships and are considered illiquid. Some have minimum holding requirements known as lockup provisions, and in that light, their interests do not reliably trade intraday. LO 4.b

LESSON 4.2: VARIABLE ANNUITIES AND LIFE INSURANCE

LO 4.c Define variable annuity and variable life insurance contracts.

Annuities

An annuity is an insurance contract designed to provide retirement income. The term *annuity* refers to a stream of payments guaranteed for some period of time. That might be for the life of the annuitant, until the annuitant reaches a certain age, or for a specific number of years. The actual amount to be paid out may or may not be guaranteed, but the stream of payments itself is. Because an annuity can provide an income for the rest of someone's life, the contract has a mortality guarantee. When you think about a retiree's greatest fear, it is typically outliving his income. This product can take away that fear.

Insurance companies introduced the variable annuity as an opportunity to keep pace with inflation. For this potential advantage, the investor assumes the investment risk rather than the insurance company. Because the investor takes on this risk, the product is considered a security. Individuals who are both insurance licensed and securities licensed are eligible to sell variable insurance products. These contracts also include the death benefit. Beneficiaries will receive the greater of the contribution amount or the current value if the owner dies during the accumulation period.

The premium payments for variable annuities are invested in what is called the separate account. The separate account comprises various subaccounts that behave like the diversified portfolios of mutual funds (we just can't call them mutual funds). These accounts will have various objectives to choose from, such as growth, income, and growth and income. The returns in the separate account are not guaranteed, and therefore, a loss of principal is possible.

If the investment manager of an insurance company is responsible for selecting the securities to be held in the separate account, the separate account is directly managed and must be registered under the Investment Company Act of 1940 as an open-end management investment company. However, if the investment manager of the insurance company passes the portfolio management responsibility to another party, the separate account is indirectly managed and must be registered as a UIT under the Investment Company Act of 1940. The performance of the separate account may be invested in one or more subaccounts that are managed separately. It is the performance of these subaccounts that determines the annuity's investment performance.

All fees directly related to the product must be disclosed to a variable annuity buyer. These product-specific charges include administrative fees, investment advisory fees, and custodial fees. Buyers must also be made aware of any surrender charges associated with the product.

There is no limit to the annual contribution amounts on commercial (nonqualified) contracts. Qualified variable contracts used in some employer-sponsored retirement plans are funded with pretax contributions, but these are limited to annual maximums similar to those found in 401(k) plans.

Annuitization

An investor who reaches retirement may choose to annuitize her contract. This is a one-time and irreversible election to give up ownership of the assets of the annuity in return for a lifetime guaranteed by the insurance company. The amount of the income is determined by the insurance company based on the annuitant's gender, age, account value, payout option, and an assumed interest rate (GAAPI). Though there are annuities that may adjust the rate for inflation, it is not a part of this initial calculation.

TAKE NOTE

A fixed annuity differs from a variable annuity. Though both are insurance company products and both guarantee a stream of income for life, a fixed annuity simply promises a stated rate of return. Therefore, it is the insurance company who is at risk to provide the rate of return it promised. The investor assumes no investment risk with a fixed annuity. With no investment risk for the investor to shoulder, the product is not considered a security.

KNOWLEDGE CHECK

1. When a customer chooses to annuitize a variable annuity, all of the following are factors the insurance company will use in calculating the initial payout amount **except**
   A. age of the annuitant.
   B. gender of the annuitant.
   C. balance of the separate account.
   D. historic inflation rate.

2. The investment return of a variable annuity comes from
   A. the performance of the selected subaccounts within the separate account.
   B. the assumed rate stated in the policy documents.
   C. computing the excess of the premiums received over the mortality experience.
   D. the insurance company's general account.

3. The decision to annuitize a variable or fixed annuity may be reversed within how many days of election?
   A. 30 days
   B. 7 days
   C. 0 days
   D. 90 days

Answers

1. **D** Insurance companies do not consider inflation when making this calculation. The components are GAAPI: gender, age, account balance, payout option, and interest rate (AIR).

2. **A** A key feature of the variable annuity is that most of the premium is invested in the insurance company's separate account rather than the general account. Within the separate account, there are a number of subaccounts that may be selected, depending on the investor's objectives. It is the performance of these subaccounts that provides the annuity's investment return.

3. **C** Annuitization is a one-time irrevocable action.

LESSON 4.3: SHARE CLASSES

LO 4.d Differentiate A, B, C, and no-load share classes.

Mutual funds

Here, we'll discuss the characteristics unique to mutual (open-end) funds. A mutual fund is a pool of investors' money invested in various securities as determined by the fund's stated investment objective. Mutual funds have several unique characteristics detailed in this section.

Unlike most other securities, mutual funds offer guaranteed marketability; if an investor wants to sell shares previously purchased in a mutual fund, it is the mutual fund that stands ready to buy them back. Mutual funds, therefore, are redeemable securities. You will recall that this means they do not trade in any secondary market.

Each investor in the mutual fund's portfolio owns an undivided interest in the portfolio. All investors in an open-end fund are mutual participants; no single investor has a preferred status over any other investor because mutual funds issue only one class of common stock. Each investor shares mutually with other investors in gains and distributions derived from the investment company portfolio.

Any distributions are typically done at net asset value (NAV) (the investor does not pay a sales charge) and provide a compounding effect to an investor's return. Mutual funds operate under the conduit theory of taxation, which means all taxable events flow down to the shareholders each year. Mutual funds permit shareholders to reinvest at NAV, but remember that all distributions (whether reinvested or taken) are taxable. Reinvestments will add to the investor's cost basis in the fund.

Each investor's participation in the fund's performance is based on the number of shares owned. Mutual fund shares may be purchased in either full or fractional shares—unlike corporate stock, which may only be purchased in full shares. Because mutual fund shares can be fractional, the investor can think in terms of dollars rather than number of shares owned.

EXAMPLE

Suppose a mutual fund's shares are priced at $12.34 per share and an investor wishes to invest $4,000. Given the share price and the amount the investor wants to invest, the purchase will be for 324.15 shares ($4,000 / $12.34 = 324.15). In other words, the investor doesn't need to specify purchasing any specific number of shares (e.g., 323, 324, or 325). Instead, the investor can simply decide on how much ($) she wants to invest, and however many shares that dollar amount will purchase will be the number of shares the investor will now own.

An investment company portfolio is elastic. Money is constantly being invested or paid out when shares are purchased or redeemed. The mutual fund portfolio's value and holdings fluctuate as money is invested or redeemed and as the value of the securities in the portfolio rises and falls. The investor's account value fluctuates proportionately with the mutual fund portfolio's value.

Here are several characteristics of mutual funds.

- A professional investment adviser manages the portfolio for investors.

- Mutual funds provide diversification by investing in different companies or securities.

- Most funds allow a minimum investment, often $500 or less to open an account, and they allow additional investment for as little as $25.

- An investment company may allow investments at reduced sales charges based on the amount of the investment.

- An investor retains voting rights similar to those extended to common stockholders, such as the right to vote for changes in the board of directors (BOD), approval of the investment adviser, changes in the fund's investment objective, changes in sales charges, and liquidation of the fund.

- Mutual funds must offer reinvestment of dividends and capital gains at NAV (without a sales charge), but these reinvestments are taxable.

- An investor may liquidate a portion of his holdings without disturbing the portfolio's balance or diversification.

- Tax liabilities for an investor are simplified because each year the fund distributes a Form 1099 explaining taxability of distributions.

- A fund may offer various withdrawal plans that allow different payment methods at redemption.

- Funds may offer reinstatement provisions that allow investors who withdraw funds to reinvest up to the amount withdrawn within 30 days with no new sales charge. This provision must be in the prospectus and is available one time only.

- Many mutual funds are part of a related (branded) family of funds or mutual fund complex. Switches between funds in the same family are taxable events.

Investors can purchase the same underlying mutual fund shares in several ways. Generally, investors can purchase Class A shares, Class B shares, and Class C shares. The differences among these shares are how much and in what way investors will pay sales charges (loads) and related expenses. In essence, these sales charges are the way the distribution services that a fund's underwriter provides are paid for. Some fund companies market their shares directly to the public without the assistance of underwriters. In these instances, the companies offer what are called no-load funds—a fund with no sales charges.

Class A (front-end load) shares

Class A shares have front-end sales charges (loads). With A shares, the sales charges are paid at the time an investor buys shares and the sales charge is taken from the total amount invested. Front-end loads are the most common way of paying for mutual fund shares.

EXAMPLE

Suppose a fund company offers a fund with a 5% sales charge and an investor wants to invest $10,000. Because 5% of the $10,000 investment must be allocated to the sales charge, only $9,500 is actually going to purchase fund shares ($10,000 × 0.05 = $500 sales charge; $10,000 invested – $500 sales charge = $9,500 available to purchase shares).

Class B (back-end load) shares

Class B shares have a back-end sales load, also called a contingent deferred sales charge (CDSC). A back-end sales charge is paid at the time an investor sells shares previously purchased (has them redeemed). The sales load, a declining percentage charge reduced annually (e.g., 8% the first year, 7% the second, 6% the third), is applied to the proceeds of any shares sold in that year. The back-end load is usually structured so that it drops to zero after an extended holding period—usually no longer than five years. At that time, the shares are converted to Class A shares, and no sales charge would be applied at the time of redemption.

TAKE NOTE

With Class B shares, the full investment amount is available to purchase shares because no sales charge is applied at the time of purchase, but it is instead deferred to the time of redemption. If an investor wants to invest $10,000, the entire amount is available to purchase shares.

While it might seem appealing to pay sales charges later—at the time of redemption instead of at the time of purchase as with A shares—it must be considered that if the shares grow in value as one hopes they will, the sales charges will be paid on amounts that are greater than the amount initially invested. This means that if the shares aren't held long enough to have the sales charge dissipate to zero, the sales charges can be costly as redemptions take place over time.

Class C (level-load) shares

Class C shares typically have a one-year, 1% CDSC, a 0.75% 12b-1 fee (fees used to promote the fund discussed later), and a 0.25% shareholder services fee. Because these fees never go away, C shares are commonly referred to as having a level load. Class C shares are appropriate for investors who have short time horizons because the annual charges make them expensive to own if investing for more than four to five years.

No-load shares

As noted earlier, some companies market their shares directly to the public, eliminating the need for underwriters and thus the sales charges used to compensate them. As the name no load implies, the fund does not charge any type of sales charge and the shares are purchased at NAV. However, not every type of fee passed on to shareholders is considered to be a sales charge. No-load funds are permitted to charge fees that are not considered sales charges, such as purchase fees, account fees, exchange fees, and redemption fees. Although a redemption fee is deducted from redemption proceeds just as in a deferred sales load, it is not considered a sales load because it is generally much smaller and often a fixed dollar amount instead of a percentage of the redemption.

TAKE NOTE

Among the load funds:

- A shares are best for investors with large investments (to get breakpoints) and longer time frames (spreading the one-time cost over several years).
- B Shares are best for investors with smaller investments and long time frames (to get past the contingent loads).
- C shares are best for investors with short time frames (but at least a year), not more than five years.

KNOWLEDGE CHECK

1. Which of the following is **not** true of no-load shares?
    A. They have fees associated with sales and redemptions.
    B. They are redeemed with no charges or fees of any kind.
    C. They are sold by the fund with no sales charges or fees of any kind.
    D. They offer more return per dollar invested versus load funds if investing results are the same.

2. Class B mutual fund shares are also called
    A. deferred-load shares.
    B. back-end load shares.
    C. CDSC shares.
    D. reverse load shares.

3. Class A shares are best for investors with
    A. larger investment amounts and short time frames.
    B. smaller investment amounts and long time frames.
    C. larger investment amounts and long time frames.
    D. smaller investment amounts and short time frames.

Answers

1. **A**   No-load shares have expenses that are not considered sales charges. Some broker-dealers may charge fees for transactions, but these fees are not from the fund.

2. **B**   Class B mutual fund shares are bought with no sales charge at the time of purchase. The sales charge is paid instead at the time of redemption, or at the "back end." Hence, they are known as back-end load shares. For this type of share, the sales charge percentage is reduced each year of ownership, typically becoming zero after five years. At this time, they convert to Class A shares.

3. **C**   The one-time cost and lower expense ratios make A shares better for investors with larger investments (to get breakpoints) and long time frames (to spread the impact of the front-end cost over many years).

LESSON 4.4: BREAKPOINTS

LO 4.e Recall the use of breakpoints, letters of intent, rights of accumulation, combination, and exchange privileges.

Breakpoints

Breakpoints are quantity discounts on open-end management company shares (mutual funds)—the greater the dollar amount of a purchase, the lower the sales charge. There is no industry standardized breakpoint schedule, so they can vary across mutual fund families.

EXAMPLE

Purchase	Sales Charge
$1–$9,999	8.5%
$10,000–$24,999	6.5%
$25,000–$49,999	4.0%
$50,000 +	2.0%

Using this sample breakpoint table, assume a customer had $23,000 to invest. At that level of investment, the sales charge would be 6.5%. Being close to the $25,000 breakpoint, an RR would be required to inform the customer that for $2,000 more, the investment amount would qualify for the next breakpoint, reducing the sales charge to 4%.

TAKE NOTE

Most mutual funds allow investors to combine orders among related accounts in order to achieve a better breakpoint. Individuals, spouses, and minor children may all combine an order to accomplish this. Corporations likewise may do this among the different divisions and subsidiary companies. One group, the investment clubs, may not get breakpoints.

Letters of intent

A person who plans to invest more money with the same mutual fund company may immediately decrease the overall sales charges by signing a **letter of intent (LOI)**. In the LOI, the investor informs the investment company of the intention to invest the additional funds necessary to reach the breakpoint within 13 months.

The LOI is a one-sided contract binding on the fund only. However, the customer must complete the investment to qualify for the reduced sales charge. The fund holds the extra shares purchased from the reduced sales charge in escrow. A customer who deposits the money to complete the LOI receives the escrowed shares. Appreciation and reinvested dividends do not count toward the LOI.

If a customer has not completed the investment within 13 months, he will be given the choice of sending a check for the difference in sales charges or cashing in escrowed shares to pay the difference.

EXAMPLE

Referring back to the sample breakpoint schedule, a customer investing $9,000 is just short of the $10,000 breakpoint. In this situation, the customer might sign an LOI promising an amount that will qualify for the breakpoint within 13 months from the date of the letter. An additional $1,000 within 13 months qualifies the customer for the reduced sales charge.

Unit 4

Rights of accumulation

Rights of accumulation, like breakpoints, allow an investor to qualify for reduced sales charges. The major differences are that rights of accumulation

- are available for subsequent investments and do not apply to initial transactions;
- allow the investor to use prior share appreciation to qualify for breakpoints; and
- do not impose time limits.

The customer may qualify for reduced charges when the total value of shares previously purchased and shares currently being purchased exceed a certain dollar amount. For the purpose of qualifying customers for rights of accumulation, the mutual fund bases the quantity of securities owned on the higher of current NAV or the total of purchases made to date.

Rights of accumulation allow an investor to combine previous investments in the fund with today's investment to determine today's sales charge. Referring back to the sample breakpoint schedule, once an investor accumulates $50,000 in the fund, each additional investment, no matter how small, qualifies for the lowest sales charge—in this case, 2%.

Combination privilege

A mutual fund sponsor frequently offers more than one fund and refers to these multiple offerings as its *family of funds*. An investor seeking a reduced sales charge may be allowed to combine separate investments in two or more funds within the same family to reach a breakpoint.

Exchange privilege

Many sponsors offer **exchange** or **conversion privileges** within their families of funds. Exchange privileges allow an investor to convert an investment in one fund for an equal investment in another fund in the same family, often without incurring an additional sales charge. This exchange is considered a taxable event, and there may be tax consequences.

LO 4.j Define breakpoint sales.

Breakpoint sales, on the other hand, is a term used in the securities industry that means sales just below the breakpoint. Allowing a sale to occur in an amount just below a breakpoint can be viewed as an effort by representatives to share in the higher sales charges.

This is inconsistent with just and equitable principles of trade. FINRA does not define near or just below a breakpoint or how close a purchase can be to a breakpoint triggering a violation. Therefore, members must make certain that customers are advised of a fund's breakpoint schedule. The rule is in place because members, and indirectly, RRs, could earn more concession dollars on a smaller customer investment (with a higher sales charge) than on a larger customer investment (with a smaller sales charge).

TAKE NOTE

It is not the order below the breakpoint that is a violation. It is the failure to *disclose* the breakpoint that triggers a breakpoint sale violation.

KNOWLEDGE CHECK

1. Which of the following statements regarding a letter of intent and breakpoints are **true**?
    I.   The letter of intent can be backdated a maximum of 30 days.
    II.   The letter of intent is valid for 13 months.
    III. The investor is legally bound to meet the terms of the agreement.
    IV.   The fund holds the additional shares in escrow.
    A. I and II
    B. II and III
    C. II and IV
    D. III and IV

2. All of the following investors can take advantage of breakpoints **except**
    A. an individual.
    B. an investment club.
    C. a trust.
    D. a corporation.

3. An investor is purchasing $48,000 of the Windmill Alternative Energy Fund. The fund has a breakpoint at $50,000. The least appropriate action would be to
    A. place the order.
    B. explain breakpoints.
    C. explain letters of intent.
    D. discuss combination privilege.

Answers

1. **C** The letter of intent may be backdated 90 days. The investor is not required by law to satisfy the letter of intent, although in the case of default, he will pay a higher sales charge.

2. **B** Breakpoint advantages are available only to individuals. An investment club is not considered an individual, but trusts and corporations are.

3. **A** All the other options introduce breakpoint to the customer. Not disclosing the breakpoint would make this a breakpoint sale.

LESSON 4.5: PRICING

LO 4.f Define forward pricing.

The NAV of a fund share is the amount the investor receives upon redemption. It must be calculated at least once per business day. A typical fund calculates its NAV at the end of each business day. The price the customer receives is the next NAV calculated after receipt of his redemption request. This practice is known as forward pricing; we always have to wait until the next available calculation to determine the value of shares redeemed or, for that matter, the number of shares purchased.

The purchase price of a fund share is called the public offering price (POP). For the class of fund shares known as front-end loaded shares, it is simply the NAV plus the sales charge: NAV + SC = POP.

As noted earlier, the sales charge is paid as compensation to the underwriters for marketing or bringing the shares to the public. And as a reminder, sales charges can be levied at the time of purchase (front-end load), at the time of redemption (back-end load), or over the course of ownership (level load); or there can simply be no sales charge (no load), meaning that shares are both purchased and redeemed at NAV.

The NAV changes daily because of changes in the market value of the securities in a fund's portfolio. This table illustrates which events increase, decrease, or do not affect the fund's NAV.

LO 4.g Calculate NAV.

Because mutual funds don't trade in the secondary market, the value of shares is not determined by supply and demand, but rather by formula. Everything begins with net asset value (NAV) per share.

To calculate the NAV of a fund share, the fund starts with its total assets and subtracts out its total liabilities: total assets – total liabilities = total NAV of the fund.

The fund then divides the total net assets by the number of shares outstanding. This gives the NAV per share: NAV of the fund / shares outstanding = NAV per share.

EXAMPLE

The ABC fund has total assets of $100 million and $5 million in liabilities. If it has 10 million shares outstanding, what is its NAV per share?

Net assets: $100 million (total assets) – $5 million (total liabilities) = $95 million total NAV. NAV per share: $95 million ÷ 10 million shares outstanding = $9.50 per share.

LO 4.h Define expense ratio.

A fund's **expense ratio** compares the management fees and operating expenses, including any 12b-1 fees, with the fund's net assets. All mutual funds, both load and no load, have expense ratios. The expense ratio is calculated by dividing a fund's expenses by its average net assets.

Stock funds generally have expense ratios between 1% and 1.5% of a fund's average net assets. Typically, more aggressive funds have higher expense ratios. For bond funds, the ratio is typically between 0.5% and 1%.

A fund's expense ratio includes the following:

- Manager's fee
- Administrative fees (trading, transfer agents, accountants, attorneys, etc.)
- Board of directors' costs
- 12b-1 fees

This list is not exhaustive. The fund's expenses are a direct charge against the assets of the fund and are a drag on the fund's returns. Everything else being equal, a fund with higher expenses will provide lower returns.

TAKE NOTE

The expense ratio does not include sales charges or loads.

EXAMPLE

A fund with an expense ratio of 1.25% deducts $1.25 for every $100 of the fund's assets annually.

KNOWLEDGE CHECK

1. A mutual fund's public offering price is $10.50. An investor who wishes to invest $1,000 in the fund will purchase how many shares?
    A. 95 shares with $2.50 left
    B. 96 and owe $8.00
    C. Partial shares not allowed
    D. 95.238

2. Which of the following would cause a change in the net asset value of a mutual fund share?
    A. The market value of the portfolio declines.
    B. Many shares are redeemed.
    C. Securities in the portfolio are sold for a capital gain.
    D. The fund takes a new position.

3. Which of the following would **not** be included in a mutual fund's list of expenses?
    I.   Shareholder records and service
    II.   Investment adviser's fee
    III. Broker-dealer sales charges
    IV.   Underwriter's sales loads
    A. I and II
    B. III and IV
    C. I and III
    D. II and IV

Answers

1. **D** Mutual funds may be purchased in even dollar amounts, and partial shares may be issued. LO 4.f

2. **A** A decline in the market value of the portfolio would reduce the assets of the fund without changing the number of outstanding shares. Sales and redemptions of shares change the net assets but also change the number of shares outstanding to the same degree, leaving the NAV per share unchanged. Buying or selling securities for a capital gain simply replaces securities in the portfolio with an equivalent amount of cash, leaving the NAV unchanged. LO 4.g

3. **B** Costs to maintain shareholder records, costs to provide services to shareholders, and the investment adviser's fees are all expenses to the fund. The costs paid in the form of sales charges (loads) to an underwriter or broker-dealers selling mutual funds to the public may never be treated as an expense to the fund. They are expenses to the investor. LO 4.h

LESSON 4.6: DISCLOSURE AND TAXATION

LO 4.i Name the four types of mutual fund prospectus.

There are four disclosure documents (prospectus) associated with a mutual fund. See Figure 4.3.

Full or statutory prospectus

This is the full and fair disclosure document that provides a prospective investor with the material information needed to make a fully informed investment decision. If using a prospectus to solicit a sale, it must be distributed to an investor before or during the solicitation. The front of a mutual fund prospectus must contain key information to appear in plain English in a standardized order. Information in this clear and concise format includes the fund's objective, investment policies, sales charges, management expenses, and services offered. It also discloses 1-, 5-, and 10-year performance histories, or performance over the life of the fund, whichever is shorter.

EXAMPLE

If a fund has been in existence for eight years, it will show performance for one, five, and eight years; if it has been in existence for only four years, it will show one and four years.

The delivery of any type of sales literature is considered a solicitation of sale and therefore must be accompanied or preceded by the delivery of a prospectus.

Summary prospectus

A mutual fund can provide a summary prospectus to investors who may include an application that investors can use to buy the fund's shares.

The summary prospectus is a standardized summary of key information in the fund's full or final prospectus. Investors who receive the summary have the option of either purchasing fund shares using the application found therein or requesting a full (statutory) prospectus. An investor who purchases fund shares on the basis of the summary prospectus must be able to access a full prospectus no later than the confirmation of the sale. Delivery may be made online.

There are some very specific requirements for a summary prospectus. The following must be included on the cover page of the summary prospectus or at the beginning of the summary prospectus:

- The fund's name and the class or classes of shares

- The exchange ticker symbol for the fund's shares; and if the fund is an exchange-traded fund (ETF), identification of the principal U.S. market or markets on which the fund shares are traded

- A legend, which must appear on the cover page, that refers to the summary nature of the prospectus and the availability of the fund's full (statutory) prospectus; the legend must provide a toll-free number to request paper delivery of prospectus or a website where one may be downloaded

Additionally, the summary must provide specific information in a particular sequence, such as investments, risks, and performance; fee tables; investment objectives, investment strategies, and any related risks; the portfolio holdings and details regarding management; shareholder information; and any financial highlights.

Statement of additional information (SAI)

Mutual funds (open end) as well as closed-end funds are required to have an SAI available for delivery within three business days of an investor's request without charge. Investors can obtain a copy of the SAI by calling or writing to the investment company or by contacting a BD that sells the investment company shares, or by contacting the Securities and Exchange Commission (SEC).

While a prospectus is always sufficient for the purpose of selling shares, some investors may seek additional information not found in the prospectus. This additional information is not considered mandatory to make an informed investment decision, but it may be useful to the investor.

The SAI affords the fund an opportunity to have expanded discussions on matters such as the fund's history and policies. It will also typically contain the fund's consolidated financial statements, including

- the balance sheet;

- statement of operations;

- an income statement; and

- a portfolio list at the time the SAI was compiled.

TEST TOPIC ALERT

A prospectus may not ever be altered in any way. This means that no highlighting, writing in, or taking any measure to bring attention to any specific passage or section is permitted.

Omitting prospectus (Rule 482)

Omitting prospectus is another term for a fund advertisement. An advertisement does not contain enough information to qualify as "full and fair disclosure." Delivery of an omitting prospectus is not sufficient to solicit a trade. You can't just hand them an ad and say, "give me a check."

Figure 4.3: Prospectus Types

Document	Purpose	Contains	Presented
Summary prospectus	Rule 498: short form that may be used to make the sale	Summary of key information in the prospectus	Before or with the solicitation
Prospectus (statutory)	Sale document	Full and fair disclosure of all material facts for investment decision	Before or with solicitation or if a summary prospectus is used, no later than confirmation of the sale
Statement of additional information (SAI)	SAI: more data for the investor	Additional details about the fund not necessary for the prospectus	Within three business days of customer request
Omitting prospectus	Raise awareness	Not much	Published advertisement

LO 4.k Recall mutual fund taxation and the pipeline theory.

Because an investment company is organized as a corporation or a trust, one might assume that its earnings are subject to tax. Consider, however, how an additional level of taxation shrinks a dividend distribution's value.

Triple taxation of investment income may be avoided if the mutual fund qualifies under Subchapter M of the Internal Revenue Code (IRC). If a mutual fund acts as a conduit, or pipeline, for the distribution of net investment income (NII), the fund may qualify as a regulated investment company, subject to tax only on the amount of investment income the fund retains. The investment income distributed to shareholders escapes taxation at the mutual fund level.

Subchapter M requires a fund to distribute at least 90% of its net investment income to shareholders. The fund then pays taxes only on the undistributed 10%. If the fund distributes 89%, it pays taxes on 100% of net investment income.

EXAMPLE

The Windmill Balanced Fund holds a mix of stocks and bonds. In the current year, it received $500,000 in dividends from stocks and $600,000 in interest from bonds. Over the year, it has had $100,000 in expenses.

Dividends	$ 500,000
Interest	$ 600,000
Total Income	$1,100,000
Expenses	$ 100.000
Net Investment Income	$1,000,000

The fund must distribute $900,000 (90% of NII) to avoid taxes on the amount it distributes to shareholders. It will still pay taxes on the NII it retains. If the fund distributes less than $900,000, the tax bill is based on the entire NII ($1,000,000). The fund's shareholders pay tax on the amount they receive.

KNOWLEDGE CHECK

1. In order to qualify as a conduit a mutual fund must pay out a minimum of
    A. 90% of gross investment income.
    B. 90% of net expenses.
    C. 90% of net investment income.
    D. 95% of net investment income.

2. Before an order to purchase a mutual fund can be taken, an investor must be provided with
    I. a full prospectus.
    II. a statement of additional information.
    III. a Rule 482 prospectus.
    IV. a summary prospectus.
    A. I and IV
    B. II or III
    C. I or IV
    D. III and IV

3. In order to clear up confusing language and highlight a fund's features, a registered representative may
    A. highlight the financial results in the statutory prospectus.
    B. highlight the breakpoint chart in the summary prospectus.
    C. not change a prospectus in any way.
    D. provide a magazine article that explains the fund prior to taking an order to purchase.

Answers

1. **C**   An investment company must distribute a minimum of 90% of net investment income in order to qualify for the tax break given to conduits. LO 4.k

2. **D**   Either a full or a summary prospectus is required to solicit and accept a mutual fund order. You may deliver both, but that is not the requirement. LO 4.i

3. **C**   No fooling with the prospectus, no fooling! LO 4.i

UNIT
5

Other Investment Vehicles

LEARNING OBJECTIVES

When you have completed this unit, you will be able to accomplish the following.

> LO 5.a   Differentiate 529 college savings and prepaid tuition plans.
> LO 5.b   Recall the use of local government investment plans.
> LO 5.c   Identify the qualification for an ABLE account.
> LO 5.d   Recall the structure of a general partnership.
> LO 5.e   Recall the structure of a limited partnership.
> LO 5.f   Recognize the tax treatment of DPPs.
> LO 5.g   Identify risks associated with limited partnerships.
> LO 5.h   Differentiate the three types of REITS.
> LO 5.i   Differentiate public and private REITS.
> LO 5.j   Identify the suitability and risk issues of investing in a hedge fund.
> LO 5.k   Define ETFs and ETNs.
> LO 5.l   Recall the advantages and disadvantages of ETFs.
> LO 5.m   Identify the risks of ETNs.

INTRODUCTION

Unit 5 will cover a collection of different investment vehicles and specialized account types. Many of these are collectivized baskets of different securities.

LESSON 5.1: 529 PLANS

LO 5.a Differentiate 529 college savings and prepaid tuition plans.

A Section 529 plan is a specific type of education savings account available to investors. The plans allow money saved to be used for qualified expenses for K-12 and post-secondary education. Qualified expenses include tuition at an elementary or secondary public, private, or religious school for up to $10,000 per year. Because they are state sponsored, they are defined as a municipal fund security. As such, the sale of these plans must be accompanied or preceded by an official statement or offering circular (similar to a prospectus) in the same way other municipal securities sales would be.

TAKE NOTE

The $10,000 spending limit does not apply to post-secondary (after high school) education. A $10,000-a-year limit on college costs would not be enough to cover costs at most colleges, but is sufficient for most precollege (K-12) education.

There are two basic types of 529 plans: prepaid tuition plans for state residents and savings plans for residents and nonresidents. See Figure 5.1. Prepaid plans allow resident donors to lock in current tuition rates by paying now for future education costs. The more popular option is the savings plan, which allows donors to save money to be used later for education expenses.

Any adult can open a 529 plan for a future college student. The donor does not have to be related to the student. (An adult student may also contribute to her own 529 plan.) With a 529 plan, the donor can invest a lump sum or make periodic payments. When the student is ready for college, the donor withdraws the amount needed to pay for qualified education expenses (e.g., tuition, room and board, and books). Withdrawals for nonqualified expenses will be subject to taxes on any gains and a 10% penalty on the gains.

Contributions, which are considered gifts under federal tax law, are made with after-tax dollars, and earnings accumulate on a tax-deferred basis. Withdrawals are tax free at the federal level if they are used for qualified education expenses. Most states permit tax-free withdrawals as long as the donor has opened an in-state plan. In addition, some states allow contributions to in-state plans to be tax deductible. Therefore, if one of your customers wishes to open an out-of-state plan, you must advise the customer that certain tax advantages, such as the one just noted, may not be available to out-of-state donors.

If a beneficiary does not need the funds for school, there are no tax consequences if the donor changes the designated beneficiary to a family member of the original beneficiary. For example, if the original beneficiary chooses to not attend college, the donor can transfer the funds from that child's 529 plan into a sibling's plan without penalty. Also, if the current beneficiary receives a scholarship, the donor may withdraw the equivalent value from the plan without penalty. Income taxes on the gains would still apply.

Other relevant points regarding Section 529 plans are as follows.

- Overall contribution levels can vary from state to state.
- Assets in the account remain under the donor's control, even after the student becomes of legal age.
- There are no income limitations on making contributions to a 529 plan.
- Plans allow for monthly payments if desired by the account owner.
- Account balances left unused may be transferred to a related beneficiary.
- Rollovers are permitted from one state's plan to another state's plan, but no more than once every 12 months.

Figure 5.1: Summary of the Savings and Prepaid Tuition Plan Differences

	Savings Plan	Prepaid Tuition Plan
Inflation hedge	Maybe, depends on performance	Yes
Outpace inflation	Maybe, depends on performance	No
School/system	Any	Specific

KNOWLEDGE CHECK

1. Mr. Hermosillo would like to save money for his 10-year-old daughter's college tuition costs. She has her heart set on a small liberal arts school with a growing reputation in the arts. His biggest concern is the potential increase in cost over the next several years. The program best suited to hedge against the increasing cost of college tuition at the school is
   A. a 529 prepaid tuition program.
   B. a 529 college savings program.
   C. a Coverdell ESA account.
   D. a custodial account in the child's name.

2. Your customer, Mr. Hortzman, has been saving money in 529 college savings plans for his three nephews. The oldest nephew is awarded an athletic scholarship valued at $15,000 at a major university. Mr. Hernandez may do any of the following **except**
   A. withdraw the value of the scholarship tax free.
   B. transfer the account to one of the brothers.
   C. withdraw the value of the scholarship penalty free.
   D. leave the money in the account for that nephew's future use.

3. Which of the following does **not** have regulatory jurisdiction over the structure or sale of 529 plans?
   A. SEC
   B. IRA
   C. MSRB
   D. Department of Education

Answers

1. **A**   The 529 prepaid tuition plan is designed to pay tuition costs at today's rate to be used later. It is the best suited to cover tuition inflation. Both the college savings and the ESA account allow for investing that has good growth potential, but not specifically locking down costs in today's dollars. A custodial account has similar issues, plus the account is in the child's name, potentially harming scholarship and grant eligibility.

2. **A**   If the money is withdrawn for a nonqualified use, it is still subject to taxes on the growth, but the penalty is waived for the amount of the scholarship. The customer may also move the funds to a 529 plan for a family member of the original beneficiary, or just leave the funds in the account.

3. **B**   The Department of Education does define what is or is not a school, but that is it as far as a 529 plan goes. The 529 plan is a type of securities account (SEC) that is sponsored by the individual states (MSRB), and provides certain tax incentives (IRS).

LESSON 5.2: LGIPs AND ABLEs

LO 5.b Recall the use of local government investment plans.

Local government investment pools

States establish local government investment pools (LGIPs) to provide other government entities, such as cities, counties, school districts, or other state agencies, with a short-term investment vehicle to invest funds. The LGIPs are generally formed as a trust in which municipalities can purchase shares or units in the LGIP's investment portfolio.

While not a money market fund, most LGIPs operate similar to one. For instance, an LGIP may be permitted to maintain a fixed $1 net asset value (NAV). Maintaining a stable NAV, similar to a money market mutual fund, facilitates liquidity and minimum price volatility.

LGIPs are not required to register with the SEC and are not subject to the SEC's regulatory requirements, given that LGIPs fall within the governmental exemption, just as municipal securities do. Therefore, investment guidelines and oversight for LGIPs can vary from state to state.

With no SEC registration required, there is no prospectus. However, LGIP programs do have disclosure documents, which generally include information statements, investment policy, and operating procedures. The information statement typically details the management fees associated with participation in the LGIP.

LO 5.c Identify the qualification for an ABLE account.

Achieving a Better Life Experience (ABLE) accounts

Achieving a Better Life Experience (ABLE) accounts are tax-advantaged savings accounts for individuals with disabilities and their families. They were created as a result of the passage of the ABLE Act of 2014. The beneficiary of the account is the account owner, and income earned by the accounts is not taxed.

The ABLE Act limits eligibility to individuals with significant disabilities where the age of onset of the disability occurred before turning age 26. In this light, remember that one need not be under the age of 26 to be eligible to establish an ABLE account. One could be over the age of 26, but as long as the onset of the disability occurred before age 26, one is eligible to establish an ABLE account.

If an individual meets the age/onset criteria and is also receiving benefits either through Social Security insurance (SSI) and/or Social Security disability insurance (SSDI), he is automatically eligible to establish an ABLE account. Only one ABLE account per person is allowed.

Contributions to these accounts, which can be made by any person, including the account beneficiary, as well as family and friends, must be made using after-tax dollars and is not tax deductible for purposes of federal income taxes. Some states, however, do allow income tax deductions for contributions made to an ABLE account. Contributions by all participating individuals are limited to a specified dollar amount per year, which may be adjusted periodically to account for inflation.

KNOWLEDGE CHECK

1. An investment established by states to provide other government entities such as cities or counties a place to invest funds short term is
   A. an FDIC.
   B. an ABLE.
   C. an LGIP.
   D. a REPO.

2. All of the following are true for an Achieving a Better Life Experience account **except**
   A. the account must be opened before the beneficiary turns 26.
   B. the account owner and the beneficiary must be disabled.
   C. the income is tax free.
   D. the onset of the disability must have occurred before the owner turned 26.

Answers

1. **C** Local government investment pools (LGIPs) are established by states to provide other government entities such as cities, counties, school districts, or other state agencies with a short-term investment vehicle to invest funds. LO 5.b

2. **A** The account does not need to be opened before the owner turns 26, but the qualifying disability does need to have begun before that age. Income from an ABLE account is received tax free. LO 5.c

LESSON 5.3: DIRECT PARTICIPATION PROGRAMS

LO 5.d Recall the structure of a general partnership.

Partnerships

A partnership is an unincorporated association of two or more individuals. Partnerships frequently open accounts necessary for business purposes.

The partnership must complete a partnership agreement stating which of the partners can make transactions for the account. If the partnership opens a margin account, the partnership must disclose any investment limitations.

An amended partnership agreement (similar to a corporate resolution) must be obtained each year if any changes have been made.

Partnerships are classified into two broad categories: general partnerships and limited partnerships.

In a general partnership, all partners in the business have responsibility to manage the business. Ownership of a general partnership may be unequal, and specific responsibilities may be assigned to specific partners. The partnership agreement would detail the specifics of the partnership.

All owners may be held liable for actions of the partnership; there is no liability protection. The business results of the partnership flow through to the partners for tax purposes proportional to their ownership interest. The partnership is a tax-reporting entity (they report their business results) but not a tax-paying entity (the owners would pay any taxes).

LO 5.e Recall the structure of a limited partnership.

Direct participation programs

Direct participation programs (DPPs) are unique forms of business that raise money to invest in real estate, oil and gas, equipment leasing, and other similar business ventures. DPPs are not taxed directly as a corporation would be; instead, the income or losses are passed directly through to the owners of the partnership—the investors. The investors are then individually responsible for satisfying any tax consequences.

There is virtually no secondary market for an investor to divest interest in a DPP, and in this regard, DPPs are considered highly illiquid. Therefore, on the point of liquidity alone, they are not suitable for many investors.

Limited partnerships

The most common type of DPP in the securities industry is a limited partnership (LP). LPs are investment opportunities that permit the economic consequences of a business to flow or pass through to investors. The businesses themselves are not tax-paying entities. These programs pass through to investors a share in the income, gains, losses, deductions, and tax credits of the business entity. The investors (partners) would then have the responsibility to report individually to the IRS.

The greatest disadvantage to limited partners is the lack of liquidity in the partnership interest. The secondary market for LP interests is extremely limited; investors who wish to sell their interests frequently cannot locate buyers (i.e., interest in the business is not freely transferable).

An LP involves two types of partners: the general partner and the limited partner. An LP must have at least one of each. Property in these partnerships is usually held in the form of a tenants in common (TIC), which provides limited liability and no management responsibilities to the limited partners.

General partners (GPs)

General partners (GPs) have unlimited liability, meaning that they can be held personally liable for business losses and debts. Their role is to manage all aspects of the partnership and have a fiduciary responsibility to use the invested capital in the best interest of the investors. In managing the partnership, they make decisions that legally bind the partnership, and they buy and sell property for the partnership; they are compensated for fulfilling these duties. They may not compete personally with the business, borrow money from the partnership, or commingle the partnership funds with their personal assets.

Limited partners

As their title implies, limited partners have limited liability, meaning that they can't lose more than they invested. They have no business management responsibilities, and in fact, should they participate in any day-to-day management of the business, they can lose their limited liability status and be considered a GP. Limited partners have the right to vote on overall business objectives and the right to receive cash distributions, capital gains, and tax deductions generated by the business. They have the right to inspect all books and records, and if the GP does not act in the best interest of the business, limited partners have the right to sue the GP.

Limited partners enjoy several advantages:

■ An investment managed by others (the GP)

■ Limited liability (can only lose the amount invested)

■ Flow-through of income and certain expenses

Partnership sales and dissolutions

LPs may be sold through private placements or public offerings. If sold privately, investors receive a private placement memorandum for disclosure. Generally, such private placements involve a small group of limited partners, each contributing a large sum of money. These investors must be accredited investors (meeting income and net worth criteria) and must have substantial investment experience. The general public generally does not meet this description.

In a public offering, LPs are sold by prospectus for disclosure. In a public offering distribution, a larger number of limited partners each making a relatively small capital contribution ($1,000–$5,000) is more likely because they do not need to be accredited investors.

Generally, LPs are liquidated on a predetermined date specified in the partnership agreement. Early shutdown may occur if the partnership sells or disposes of its assets or if a decision is made to dissolve the partnership by the limited partners holding a majority interest. When dissolution occurs, the GP must settle accounts in the following order:

1. Secured lenders

2. Other creditors

3. Limited partners—first, for their claims to shares of profits and then for their claims to a return of contributed capital

4. GPs

Types of limited partnerships

Real estate programs

Real estate programs can invest in raw land, new construction, or existing properties. Depending on the properties held by the program, they can provide investors with the following benefit opportunities:

■ Capital growth potential—achieved through appreciation of property

■ Cash flow (income)—collected from rents

■ Tax deductions—from mortgage interest expense and depreciation allowances for "wearing out the building" and capital improvements

■ Tax credits—for government-assisted housing and historic rehabilitation (tax credits are very strong incentives because they reduce tax liability dollar for dollar)

Which real estate program would be best for a client? That depends on the client's objective. For example, a raw land program would offer a chance for capital appreciation but would not provide current income. Conversely, an existing property would be better suited for an investor who desires current cash flow, but it likely offers less capital appreciation potential.

Oil and gas programs

Oil and gas programs include speculative or exploratory (wildcatting) programs to locate new oil deposits (generally considered the riskiest developmental programs that drill near existing producing wells in hopes of locating new deposits) and income programs that invest in producing wells (generally considered the least risky). Unique tax advantages associated with these programs include the following.

- Intangible drilling costs (IDCs)—These are costs associated with drilling, such as wages, supplies, fuel, and insurance that have no salvage value when the program ends. These IDCs can be written off (deducted) in full in the first year of operation. In contrast, tangible drilling costs are associated with items that have some salvage value at the end of the program, such as drilling equipment. These types of tangible costs, instead of being immediately deductible, are deductible over several years. The deduction is taken as depreciation. In other words, each year, the asset is worth a little less, and that depreciated amount can now be deducted.

- Depletion allowances—These are tax deductions that compensate the program for the decreasing supply of oil or gas (or any other resource or mineral) after it is taken out of the ground and sold.

Which oil and gas program would be best for a given client? Again, it depends on his objective. A drilling program offers the greatest chance for capital appreciation but would not provide current income. Conversely, an income program would be better suited for an investor who desires current cash flow, but it likely offers less capital appreciation potential.

Leasing programs

Equipment leasing programs are created when DPPs purchase equipment leased to other businesses. This type of equipment can be as far ranging as jetliners or railcars leased to airlines and railroads, trucks leased to shipping companies, or computers leased to any business in need of them. Investors receive income from lease payments, as well as a proportional share of write-offs from operating expenses, interest expense, and depreciation of the actual equipment owned by the program. The primary investment objective of these programs is tax-sheltered income (the income being sheltered by the write-offs).

 KNOWLEDGE CHECK

1. The **most** common type of direct participation program (DPP) in the securities industry is
   A. a limited partnership (LP).
   B. a real estate investment trust (REIT).
   C. a collateralized mortgage obligation (CMO).
   D. an investment company.

2. All of the following are benefits for the limited partners in a direct participation program (DPP) **except**
   A. passive losses.
   B. flow-through of income.
   C. unlimited liability.
   D. an investment managed by the general partner (GP).

3. Which of the following statements regarding a general partnership is **correct**?
   A. Partners participate in the gains and losses of the business and are fully liable for the businesses actions.
   B. Partners participate in the gains and losses of the business and are partially shielded from the businesses liabilities.
   C. Partners participate in the gains and losses of the business and are fully shielded from the businesses liabilities.
   D. Partners participate in the gains but not the losses of the business and are fully shielded from the businesses liabilities.

Answers

1. **A** The most common type of DPP in the securities industry is an LP. LO 5.e

2. **C** As the name implies, a limited partner has limited liability. In other words, a limited partner can't lose more than what was initially invested. The same cannot be said, however, of the GP. LO 5.e

3. **A** In a general partnership, the results of the business flow through to the partners and there is no liability protection in this type of organization. LO 5.d

LESSON 5.4: DPP SUITABILITY AND TAXATION

LO 5.f Recognize the tax treatment of DPPs.

Historically, some limited partnerships were called tax shelters. The structure of the limited partnership allows for the investor to receive income that is sheltered from taxes. Through the use of depreciation and depletion (depletion in natural resource program such as oil and gas) create a deduction for tax purposes that is not an actual cost of the partnership.

EXAMPLE

Revenue and costs for taxes

Revenue	$300,000
Costs:	
Maintenance	$ 50,000
Loan Interest	$ 70,000
Operations	$160,000
Depreciation	$ 50,000
Profit/Loss	$–30,000

Note that depreciation is not an actual cost. To find the cash flow, add the depreciation back into the business results.

Profit/loss	$–30,000
Depreciation	$ 50,000
Cash Flow	$ 20,000

TAKE NOTE

Income from an LP is called passive income and is added to ordinary income for tax purposes. Losses from an LP are called passive losses. Passive losses offset passive income only. However, if an LP generates tax credits, those may be used to offset income taxes directly; tax credits are not a type of income.

LO 5.g Identify risks associated with limited partnerships.

There are specific risks to limited partners.

Liquidity

There is effectively no secondary market for limited partnership interests. Any transfer of interest in an LP requires permission of the general partner. An investor in a limited partnership should assume she will own the program until it ends.

Audit/recapture of tax benefit

If the IRS disallows a prior tax benefit, the consequences flow through to the limited partners. If in the example above, if an audit resulted in the depreciation deduction being disallowed, the limited partners would find themselves having an extra $30,000 of income for that tax year. The IRS will likely impose taxes and penalties for the underreporting of income plus interest on the unpaid taxes. The limited partners would have to pay for the problem. Remember, the LP is a tax-reporting, but not a tax-paying, entity.

KNOWLEDGE CHECK

1. All of the following would be considered tax advantages relating to a DPP investment **except**
    A. depreciation recapture.
    B. depletion.
    C. intangible drilling costs.
    D. accelerated depreciation.

2. Each limited partner's share of partnership losses
    A. may be used to reduce ordinary income.
    B. may be used to offset passive income.
    C. is deductible up to $3,000 per year.
    D. cause a dollar-for-dollar decrease in the market value of the limited partnership units.

Answers

1. **A**   Depreciation recapture can occur when an investor sells his interest in a real estate program. If, at the time of the sale, the amount of accelerated deprecation taken exceeds the straight-line depreciation amount, the difference (called recapture) must be reported by the investor as ordinary income. LO 5.g

2. **B**   It is important to remember that passive losses can be used to offset only passive income. An investor with $500,000 worth of passive income could write off up to $500,000 of passive loss (if he had that much loss). Do not confuse this with the $3,000 maximum deduction against income for capital losses. There is no maximum passive loss that can be written off against passive income. LO 5.f

LESSON 5.5: REITs

LO 5.h Differentiate the three types of REITS.

A real estate investment trust (REIT) is a company that manages a portfolio of real estate, mortgages, or both to earn profits for shareholders. REITs pool capital in a manner similar to that of an investment company but are not investment companies, neither open nor closed end. Shareholders receive dividends from investment income or capital gains distributions. REITs normally

- own commercial property (equity REITs),
- own mortgages on commercial property (mortgage REITs), or
- do both (hybrid REITs).

REITs are organized as trusts in which investors buy shares or certificates of beneficial interest, either on stock exchanges or in the OTC market.

Under the guidelines of Subchapter M of the IRC, a REIT can avoid being taxed as a corporation by receiving 75% or more of its income from real estate and distributing 90% or more of its net investment income to its shareholders.

LO 5.i Differentiate public and private REITS.

Many REITs are registered with the SEC and, therefore, are subject to all disclosure requirements. These are known as public REITs. However, there are REITs that are not registered with the SEC, known as private REITs. Nonregistered REITs are not subject to the same disclosure requirements as public REITs and, therefore, are subject to greater risk.

Many REITs are traded on a stock exchange. These are known as exchange-traded or **listed** REITs. For those that are not listed on an exchange and trade instead of in the OTC market, unique risks exist. Many nonlisted REITs are difficult to price and have far less liquidity versus a listed product.

TEST TOPIC ALERT

The following are five important points to remember about REITs.

1. An owner of REITs holds an undivided interest in a pool of real estate investments.
2. REITs may or may not be registered (public or private) with the SEC.
3. REITs may or may not be listed (trade) on exchanges.
4. REITs are not investment companies (open end or closed end).
5. REITs offer dividends and gains to investors but do not pass through losses like LPs and, therefore, are not considered DPPs.

KNOWLEDGE CHECK

1. All of the following are types of real estate investment trusts **except**
   A. mortgage.
   B. oil and gas.
   C. equity.
   D. hybrid.

2. A REITs is taxed as
   A. a corporation.
   B. a partnership.
   C. a municipal bond.
   D. as a conduit.

3. Your client is considering the Newport Land and Farming REIT and notes in the description that it is listed. What does "listed" mean in this context?
   A. The REIT is registered and likely trades OTC.
   B. The REIT is unregistered and trades only in the primary market.
   C. The REIT is registered and likely trades on an exchange.
   D. The REIT is unregistered and is likely trading OTC bulletin board.

Answers

1. **B** Oil and gas limited partnerships are common. The others are all types of REITs. LO 5.h

2. **D** REITs fall under the conduit (or pipeline) tax theory. LO 5.h

3. **C** A listed security is one that has been accepted for trading on an exchange. Only registered securities are listed. LO 5.i

LESSON 5.6: HEDGE FUNDS

LO 5.j Identify the suitability and risk issues of investing in a hedge fund.

Many companies rely on one of the exceptions from the definition of being an investment company under the Investment Company Act of 1940. They are not classified as FAC companies, UITs, or management companies (open end or closed end). These companies are commonly known as private investment companies. Some private investment companies can be what are known as hedge funds.

Hedge funds are often organized as limited partnerships and are sold as private placements.

Hedge funds are similar to mutual funds in that investments are pooled and professionally managed, but they differ in that the hedge fund has more flexibility in the investment strategies employed. While hedging is the practice of attempting to limit risk, most hedge funds specify generating high returns as their primary investment objective. In attempting to achieve these returns, they tend to shoulder a substantial amount of risk. Hedge funds are typically aggressively managed and often construct portfolios of high-risk investments. Hedge funds use advanced and sometimes complicated investment strategies.

Some of the more common strategies employed by hedge funds are

- highly leveraged portfolios (borrowing to purchase securities);
- the use of short positions (selling securities the portfolio does not own);
- the utilization of derivative products such as options and futures;
- currency speculation;
- commodity speculation; and
- the investment in politically unstable international markets.

Most hedge funds are organized as private investment partnerships, allowing them to limit the number of investors or require large initial or minimum investments if they so desire. Some also require that investors maintain the investment for a minimum length of time (e.g., one year) and to that extent they can be considered illiquid. These minimum holding requirements are known as lockup provisions.

KNOWLEDGE CHECK

1. A private, unregulated investment company organized in such a way so as to invest and achieve high returns utilizing debt leverage and derivative products such as options and margin is best described as
    A. a mutual fund.
    B. a direct participation program (DPP).
    C. a real estate investment trust (REIT).
    D. a hedge fund.

Answer

1. **D** Hedge funds are unregulated investments with a goal of achieving high returns. They do this by primarily utilizing strategies associated with risk, such as trading in commodities, currencies, and derivatives, and utilizing debt leverage and margin.

LESSON 5.7: EXCHANGE-TRADED FUNDS AND EXCHANGE-TRADED NOTES

LO 5.k Define ETFs and ETNs.

Exchange-traded funds (ETFs)

An exchange-traded fund (ETF), considered an equity security, invests in a specific group of stocks and generally does so to mimic a particular index, such as the S&P 500. In this way, an ETF is similar to a mutual fund that tracks an index. The difference is that the ETF trades like a stock on the floor of an exchange and, in regard to how it trades, is similar to a closed-end investment company rather than an open-end mutual fund. They are registered, however, as either an open-end fund or as a UIT, but they are obviously different in many ways.

Because of the way they trade, an investor can take advantage of intraday price changes due to normal market forces, rather than just the underlying value of the stocks in the portfolio. And, unlike mutual funds, ETFs can be purchased on margin and sold short.

Expenses tend to be lower than those of mutual funds, and the management fee is also low. Consider that the portfolio is designed to track an index, and just as the securities contained in the index are unlikely to change, so are the securities in the fund portfolio. In other words, there is little trading activity required to keep the fund securities aligned with those in the index it is intended to track. This generally results in greater tax efficiency for the investor.

On the other hand, every time a person purchases or sells shares, there is a commission, and those charges can add up over time.

Understanding that ETF shares are not mutual fund shares but are registered as open-end funds, it should be expected and is common that they are often compared to mutual fund shares. In that light, ETFs have some advantages and disadvantages to be considered when compared with open-end mutual funds.

Exchange-traded notes

Exchange-traded notes (ETNs) are senior, unsecured debt securities issued by a bank or financial institution. Therefore, they are backed only by the good faith and credit of the issuer.

The notes track the performance of a particular market index, but do not represent ownership in a pool of securities the way share ownership of a fund does.

ETNs are bond-like instruments with a stated maturity date, but they do not pay interest and offer no principal protection. Instead, ETN investors receive a cash payment linked to the performance of the underlying index minus management fees when the note matures. Because the returns of ETNs are linked to the performance of a market index or a basket of securities, investors are also exposed to market risk.

LO 5.1 Recall the advantages and disadvantages of ETFs.

The following are some advantages of ETFs when compared with open-end mutual funds.

- *Pricing and ease of trading*—Because individual ETF shares are traded on exchanges, they can be bought or sold anytime during the trading day at the price they are currently trading at as opposed to mutual funds, which use forward pricing and are generally priced once at the end of the trading day.

- *Margin*—ETFs can be bought and sold short on margin like other ETPs. Mutual funds cannot be bought on margin, nor can they be sold short.

- *Operating costs*—ETFs traditionally have operating costs and expenses that are lower than most mutual funds.

- *Tax efficiency*—ETFs can and sometimes do distribute capital gains to shareholders like mutual funds do, but this is rare. Understanding that these capital gains distributions are not likely, there are no further tax consequences with ETF shares until investors sell their shares. This may be the single greatest advantage associated with ETFs.

The following are some disadvantages of ETFs when compared to open-end mutual funds.

- *Commissions*—The purchase or sale of ETF shares is a commissionable transaction. The commissions paid can erode the low-expense advantage of ETFs. This would have the greatest impact when trading in and out of ETF shares frequently or when investing smaller sums of money.

- *Overtrading*—Given the ability to trade in and out of ETFs easily, the temptation to do so is possible. Excessive trading can eliminate the advantages associated with investing in a diversified portfolio and add to overall commissions being paid by the investor, further eroding any of the other expense and operating-cost advantages associated with ETFs.

- *Market influences on price*—Because ETFs trade on exchanges, share prices can be influenced by market forces such as supply and demand, like any other ETP. In this light, investors need to recognize that just as they might receive less than book value per share when selling corporate shares of stock, they might also receive less than NAV per share when selling ETF shares.

LO 5.m Identify the risks of ETNs.

Exchange-traded notes (ETNs) are senior, unsecured debt securities issued by a bank or financial institution. Therefore, they are backed only by the good faith and credit of the issuer.

The notes track the performance of a particular market index, but do not represent ownership in a pool of securities the way share ownership of a fund does.

ETNs are bond-like instruments with a stated maturity date, but they do not pay interest and offer no principal protection. Instead, ETN investors receive a cash payment linked to the performance of the underlying index minus management fees when the note matures. Because the returns of ETNs are linked to the performance of a market index or basket of securities, investors are also exposed to market risk.

While the market price of an ETN, in theory, depends on the performance of the underlying index or benchmark, the ETN has an additional risk compared with an ETF; if the credit of the underwriting bank should falter, the note might lose value in the same way any other senior debt of the issuer would. Additionally, there are limits to the size of ETN issues. This means, with limited availability, there are times when an ETN might trade at a premium to its inherent valuation. Investors purchasing at a premium could be subject to losses later depending on the value of the note at maturity.

TAKE NOTE

The primary risk associated is default risk. Liquidity risk is also a common concern. Even though they are called "exchange traded," very few of them have ever actually been listed on an exchange.

KNOWLEDGE CHECK

1. All of the following are true for exchange-traded funds (ETFs) **except**
    A. ETFs can be bought or sold throughout the trading day.
    B. ETFs are not marginable securities.
    C. ETF share prices are subject to market forces like supply and demand.
    D. ETF transactions are commissionable trades.

2. An investor has placed money in a debt-like instrument issued by a financial institution and linked to the performance of the S&P 500 Index. From the investment, which has a stated maturity date but makes no interest payments, the investor anticipates receiving a cash payment minus any applicable management fees when the instrument matures. This describes which of the following investments?
    A. Municipal bond
    B. Direct participation program (DPP)
    C. Exchange-traded note (ETN)
    D. Variable annuity

Answers

1. **B** ETFs trade as all other exchange-traded products (ETPs) do. Commissionable transactions can occur throughout the trading day where prices are subject to all normal market forces. They can be purchased on margin. LO 5.m

2. **C** ETNs are debt-like instruments issued by banks and other financial institutions that trade on exchanges. Their performance is generally linked to a specific market index. At maturity of the note, investors receive a cash payment minus any management fees. LO 5.n

UNIT
6

Types of Risk

LEARNING OBJECTIVES

When you have completed this unit, you will be able to accomplish the following.

> LO 6.a   Define systematic risk.
> LO 6.b   Recognize systematic risks.
> LO 6.c   Define nonsystematic risk.
> LO 6.d   Recognize nonsystematic risks.
> LO 6. e   Identify ways to mitigate systematic and nonsystematic risk.

INTRODUCTION

In general terms, the greater the risk that investors are willing to assume with an investment, the greater the potential reward should be. For example, safe investments tend to offer lower yields, but investments where considerable risk is attached should offer much higher potential yields.

Additionally, different types of risk can be associated with different investments and securities. In all cases, investors should be aware of the risks they shoulder with any investment, be able to afford the risk, and be comfortable with doing so.

For our part as securities industry professionals, understanding the many types of risk and ensuring that our customers understand these risks lends itself to the topic of determining suitability. Just as every investment is different, so is every investor. Several types of risk must be considered in determining whether or not any investment is suitable for any investor.

Risk can generally be broken into two categories: systematic risk and nonsystematic risk.

LESSON 6.1: SYSTEMATIC RISK

LO 6.a Define systematic risk.

Systematic risk is the risk that changes in the overall economy will have an adverse effect on individual securities, regardless of the company's circumstances. It is generally caused by factors that affect all businesses, such as war, global security threats, or inflation.

TEST TOPIC ALERT

No matter how diversified a portfolio of investments is, it will still be subject to systematic risk. Said another way, one cannot diversify away systematic risk.

LO 6.b Recognize systematic risks.

Market risk

Market risk is the risk that when the overall market declines, so too will any portfolio made of securities the market comprises.

EXAMPLE

If the Dow Jones Industrial Average (DJIA), or any other market index, were to plummet substantially, so too would a portfolio of common stock. Regardless of the number of stocks and the diversity of their makeup, they could not escape a large fall in the market without being affected.

Interest rate risk

Interest rate risk is defined as a potential change in bond prices caused by a change in market interest rates after an issuer offers its bonds. If interest rates rise post-issuance, existing bonds (with a lower coupon) will be viewed as less attractive and will be priced in the market at a discount. Conversely, if rates fall, the existing bonds (with their higher coupons) will be viewed as desirable and will trade in the market at a premium. As you can see, there is an inverse relationship between the direction of rates and bond price moves.

Regarding duration, if rates move up or down, the prices of bonds with longer maturities will fluctuate more than bonds with shorter maturities, because this interest rate differential is potentially longer lived. *Duration* is a word often used to express a bond's price sensitivity to interest rate swings.

If market conditions or the Federal Reserve push interest rates higher, the market price of all bonds will be affected. When interest rates rise, the market price of bonds falls, and that is why this is a systematic risk for fixed-income securities. This risk is sometimes called the market risk for bonds.

Reinvestment risk

This is a variation of interest rate risk. When interest rates decline, it is difficult to reinvest proceeds from redemptions, securities that have been called (call risk), or investment distributions and maintain the same level of income without increasing credit or market risks.

Inflation risk (purchasing power risk)

Sometimes called purchasing power risk, inflation risk is the effect of continually rising prices on investment returns. If an investment's yield is lower than the inflation rate, the purchasing power of the client's money diminishes over time. Conversely, deflation is a prolonged period of falling prices. Falling prices would make fixed-income payments more valuable because bond investors could buy more goods and services with their coupon payments.

EXAMPLE

An investor has purchased a 30-year bond yielding 5%. Inflation rates push upward over time to levels above 5%. The interest payments are no longer sufficient to purchase the goods and services that they had been initially. This diminished buying power would also be true for the principal amount returned in 30 years.

KNOWLEDGE CHECK

1. When the interest rate paid on a debt security is less than the current inflation rate, the investor suffers from which of the following risks?
    A. Liquidity risk
    B. Call risk
    C. Purchasing power risk
    D. Currency risk

2. Your customer has carefully researched the purchase of stock in Green Shoe Company. After the purchase, the equity markets dropped 20%, and Green Shoe stocked dropped along with it. Green Shoe gave up 15% during the drop. This is an example of
    A. business risk.
    B. interest rate risk.
    C. market risk.
    D. nonsystematic risk.

Answers

1. **C**   Purchasing power risk is a systematic risk that impacts fixed-income investments. It is the risk that a fixed payment from an investment will lose purchasing power due to inflation.

2. **C**   All stocks in the market are effected when the market moves. The sensitivity of a given security to its market is measured by beta.

LESSON 6.2: NONSYSTEMATIC RISK

LO 6.c Define nonsystematic risk.

Unlike systematic risk, which is nondiversifiable, these risks can be reduced through diversification. They are risks that are unique to a specific industry, business enterprise, or investment type.

Beta measures the volatility of an asset. The market (using the S&P 500 Index as proxy) has a beta of 1.00. If a security has a beta that is greater than 1.00, it is more volatile than the market. If an asset has a beta of less than 1.00, it is more stable than the market as a whole. The bottom line is that a high beta security is considered riskier. The following are some of the most common nonsystematic risks.

LO 6.d Recognize nonsystematic risks.

Default risk (financial risk)

Default risk is the potential for an investor to lose some or all of their money—their invested capital—under circumstances related to an issuer's financial strength. Default risk includes the risk that a debt security fails to make interest payments.

TAKE NOTE

Capital risk is simply the risk that an investor will be unable to get all the investment back. It varies depending on the type of security and the specific issuer. Capital risk is minimal to none when investing in securities backed by the federal government, such as T-bills, but could be far greater when investing in derivative products such as options or businesses such as DPPs.

Business risk

This is an operating risk, generally caused by poor management decisions. At best, earnings are lowered; at worst, the company goes out of business and common stockholders could lose their entire investment.

EXAMPLE

Introducing a new product that turns out to have a very narrow market or underestimating a competitor's new product and failing to compete are both examples of poor business decisions that impact the price of a company's stock.

Financial risk

Often confused with business risk (it is similar), financial risk relates primarily to those companies that use debt financing (leverage). An inability to meet the interest and principal payments on those debt obligations could lead to bankruptcy and, once again, total loss for the stockholders. For that reason, this is sometimes called credit risk or default risk.

Call risk

Call risk is the risk that a bond might be called before maturity and an investor will be unable to reinvest the principal at a comparable rate of return. In this light, the occurrence of call risk can lead to reinvestment risk, as discussed earlier. When interest rates are falling, bonds with higher coupon rates are most likely to be called. Investors concerned about call risk should look for call protection—a period during which a bond cannot be called. Most corporate and municipal issuers generally provide some years of call protection.

EXAMPLE

An investor holds a callable bond yielding 5%. Because interest rates have fallen to 3%, the issuer of the bond calls it in and the investor receives his principal. The investor is now left to reinvest the proceeds of the called bond, on which he had been earning 5%, at the now lower current interest rate of 3%.

Prepayment risk

Prepayment risk is the risk that a borrower will repay the principal on a loan or debt instrument (bond) before its maturity and thus deprive the lender of future interest payments. This risk is often associated with call risk, as discussed earlier. Securities such as GNMAs are subject to prepayment risk because the underlying mortgages may be refinanced when interest rates fall. The refinancing will result in a partial paydown of principal to the GNMA holder, who now needs to find a suitable reinvestment in a lower interest rate environment.

Currency risk

Currency risk is the possibility that an investment denominated in one currency could decline if the value of that currency declines in its exchange rate with the U.S. dollar. Fluctuating currency exchange rates become an important consideration whenever investing in a foreign security or any security denominated in a foreign currency. Currency is quoted at the spot rate, meaning a given currency's current market value. Currency is always quoted in relative terms between two currencies. For example, the euro could be getting stronger or weaker versus the U.S. dollar.

Liquidity risk

The risk that an investor might not be able to sell an investment quickly at a fair market price is known as liquidity risk or marketability risk. The marketability of the securities a registered representative (RR) recommends must be consistent with the client's liquidity needs.

EXAMPLE

Most stocks and money markets are liquid. This means that the asset can be easily bought or sold without dramatically affecting its price. Other fixed assets such as real estate, fine art, or collectibles are not generally liquid. These assets may be difficult to quickly buy or sell, and transaction costs might be significantly higher.

Regulatory risk

A sudden change in the regulatory climate can have a dramatic effect on the performance of a business and entire business sectors. Changes in the rules that a business must comply with can devastate individual companies and industries almost overnight.

Common examples of this risk are rulings made by the Environmental Protection Agency (EPA) or the Food and Drug Administration (FDA). Rule changes for affected businesses to follow can sometimes upset their business models and their ability to be profitable.

EXAMPLE

An investor owns shares of XYZ stock in a pharmaceutical company. The U.S. Food and Drug Administration (FDA) orders an immediate halt to all sales of the company's best-selling drug. Shares of XYZ stock begin to fall as a result of the news, and the investor is left with a decision to either sell at the now-depressed price or hold the shares in hopes of a price correction sometime in the future.

Legislative risk

It is common to lump together regulatory and legislative risk, but there is a difference. Whereas regulatory risk comes from a change to regulations, legislative risk results from a change in the law. A government agency, state or federal, may pass certain regulations, but only a legislature can pass a law. Changes to the tax code are the most obvious legislative risks.

EXAMPLE

The implementation of a luxury tax on higher-priced items such as automobiles and boats severely impacts those industries.

Political risk

While political risk can be interrelated with legislative risk, most attribute this risk specifically to the potential instability in the political underpinnings of the country. While this is particularly true in emerging economies, it can occur even in highly developed societies.

Sovereign risk

Sovereign risk ratings capture the risk of a country defaulting on its commercial debt obligations. When a country is at risk of defaulting on its debt, the impact is felt on financial markets worldwide.

LESSON 6.3: RISK MITIGATION

LO 6.e Identify ways to mitigate systematic and nonsystematic risk.

Mitigating systematic risk

Systematic risk is risk that is built into the system. The only way to mitigate or hedge systematic risk is to find an asset that will move in the opposite direction of the markets as a whole. Portfolio managers will use derivative securities to hedge the portfolio risk.

EXAMPLE

In order to offset the market risk in a portfolio of large-cap stocks an investment adviser buys into the portfolio puts on the S&P 500 index.

Mitigating nonsystematic risk

The most common way to hedge risks that a specific security may carry is to build a portfolio that consists of securities of several different issuers. The term for this is *diversification.*

KNOWLEDGE CHECK

1. One of the advantages of a security being traded on a listed stock exchange is the ready availability of buyers and sellers. This has the tendency to reduce or even eliminate
    A. inflation risk.
    B. liquidity risk.
    C. market risk.
    D. price risk.

2. Before making an investment, it is wise to evaluate the potential risk involved. It is safe to assume that
    I.   the greater the risk, the greater the potential reward.
    II. the greater the risk, the lower the potential reward.
    III. the lower the risk, the greater the potential loss.
    IV. the lower the risk, the lower the potential reward.
    A. I and III
    B. I and IV
    C. II and III
    D. II and IV

Answers

1. **B** Liquidity risk is the uncertainty that an investor will be able to find a buyer for a security when the need to sell arises. Listed securities virtually always have ready marketability.

2. **B** One of the primary axioms of investing is the relationship between risk and reward. Basically, when an investor takes more risk, it is in the expectation of a greater reward. Reducing the risk should result in a lower reward.

PART 2

Knowledge of Capital Markets

Your exam will include 12 questions on the topics covered in Part 2.

There are nine units in Part 2: Knowledge of Capital Markets.

UNIT 7

The Securities Act of 1933 and the Primary Markets

LEARNING OBJECTIVES

When you have completed this unit, you will be able to accomplish the following.

- ❯ LO 7.a Recall the purpose of the primary markets.
- ❯ LO 7.b Recall the types of primary market offerings.
- ❯ LO 7.c Name the participants in the primary market.
- ❯ LO 7.d Order the process for offering a nonexempt issue.
- ❯ LO 7.e Recall the types of exempt issues and issuers.
- ❯ LO 7.f Name the types of disclosure documents.
- ❯ LO 7.g Determine the prospectus delivery requirements after issuance.
- ❯ LO 7.h Define shelf offerings and the green shoe option.

INTRODUCTION

In this unit, you will learn how securities are sold and why those who issue securities choose to do so. The primary markets are a vitally important part of the economy, allowing issuers to raise capital and investors to participate in their success.

LESSON 7.1: THE PRIMARY MARKETS

LO 7.a Recall the purpose of the primary markets.

The primary market is where securities are sold to the investing public in what are known as issuer transactions. In other words, the issuer of the securities receives the proceeds generated by the sale of the securities. By contrast, the secondary markets are where securities trade between investors. Another term for these two markets is the *capital markets.*

When you see the term *primary offer* or *primary market,* you know that we are talking about an issuer (corporation or a government) that is selling a security to raise capital. The sale of securities to the public allows for corporations to raise capital relatively quickly to take advantage of changes in the economy. This activity is a key piece of a modern economy, allowing corporations to raise the money needed to build factories, buy equipment, and expand the demand for labor, creating jobs. At the same time, it allows investors, from the wealthiest billionaire to the regular person saving in a 401(k), to grow their assets alongside the economy as a whole. The person who owns a mutual fund share that holds a partial share of a corporation earns the same return, on a per share basis, as the largest stockholder of that company.

Governments also use the capital markets to raise money for infrastructure projects (such as bridges, roads, dam, ports, etc.) as well as funding other programs for the public good. Take a look at a bridge over a river that ties two cities together and benefits both. Who built that bridge? Well, construction workers built it, engineers designed it, and it was paid for by investors who believed the project was worth supporting.

As a representative in the securities industry, you take on an important role in providing the capital needed to grow the economy, create jobs, and fund the projects that improve everyone's lives.

LO 7.b Recall the types of primary market offerings.

A primary offering is one in which the proceeds raised go to the issuing corporation. Primary offerings are done in the primary (new issues) market. The corporation increases its capitalization by selling stock (either a new issue or previously authorized but unissued stock). It may do this at any time and in any amount, provided the total stock outstanding never exceeds the amount authorized in the corporation's bylaws.

Public offerings of securities are regulated under the Securities Act of 1933. In a public offering, securities are offered and sold to the investing public. To facilitate this, companies will use the services of investment bankers and BDs, known as underwriters of the securities. The offerings can be advertised to the public, raise relatively large amounts of capital via the sale of stocks or bonds, and may attract investors with smaller budgets and less investment sophistication. Typically, they are more tightly regulated under the Securities Act of 1933 and are subject to the more stringent federal registration and prospectus requirements than private securities offerings. Registration of securities to be offered to the public will be discussed later in this unit.

TAKE NOTE

The primary purpose of the Securities Act of 1933 is to require full and fair disclosure in connection with the sale of securities to the public. The act requires that a new issue, unless specifically exempted from the act, be registered with the SEC before public sale. All investors must receive a detailed disclosure document known as a *prospectus before purchase.*

Initial public offering (IPO)

The first time an issuer distributes securities to the public, it is called an initial public offering (IPO). Any subsequent money raises are known as *follow-on offerings*. These follow-on offerings are sometimes called additional public offerings (APOs). Follow-on offerings are popular methods for companies to raise additional equity capital in the capital markets through a stock issue.

EXAMPLE

The first time that ABC Shoe Co. issued shares to the public, it engaged in an IPO. Let's assume ABC Shoe received the entire proceeds from that initial offering. Four years later, ABC Shoe raised additional capital through a follow-on offering in which it also received the entire deal proceeds. Both offerings are primary because only the issuer is receiving proceeds, and both the IPO and the follow-on shares must go through a registration process with the SEC.

IPO rules and regulations

Designed to protect the integrity of the public offering process and public investors, the rules ensure that

- members make a bona fide public offering of securities at the public offering price (POP);

- members do not withhold securities in a public offering for their own benefit or use such securities to reward persons who are in a position to direct future business to the member; and

- industry insiders, such as members and their associated persons, do not take advantage of their insider status to gain access to new issues for their own benefit at the expense of public customers.

Essentially, the rules apply to IPOs of common stock. The rules prohibit member firms from selling a new issue to any account where restricted persons are beneficial owners. Before selling an IPO to any account, representatives are required to obtain a written representation from the account owner(s) that the account is eligible to purchase a new common stock issue at the POP. Restricted persons, those not allowed to purchase shares at the POP, are defined as follows:

1. Member firms

2. Employees of member firms

3. Finders and fiduciaries acting on behalf of the managing underwriter, including attorneys, accountants, financial consultants, and so on

4. Portfolio managers, including any person who has the authority to buy or sell securities for a bank, savings and loan association, insurance company, or investment company

5. Any person owning 10% or more of a member firm

Further, any immediate family member of any person in items 2–5, as listed here, is also restricted. Immediate family includes parents, in-laws, spouses, siblings, children, or any other individual to whom the person provides material support.

TAKE NOTE

Aunts and uncles, as well as grandparents, are not considered immediate family. If, however, one of these individuals lives in the same household as a restricted person, that individual would be a restricted person.

Finally, there is a de minimis exemption. If the beneficial interests of restricted persons do not exceed 10% of an account, the account may purchase a new equity issue. In other words, restricted persons will be able to have an interest in an account that purchases new equity issues as long as no more than 10% of the account's beneficial owners are restricted persons.

EXAMPLE

Daryl Smith is a restricted person. He is a member of an investment club and has a 5% interest in the investment club account. Because his interest in the club account does not exceed 10%, the investment club account is not considered a restricted account.

If Larry Smith (Daryl's brother) bought an interest in the account that brought his ownership to 6%, then the Smith brothers would own 11%. Because more than 10% of the account is owned by restricted persons, this account may no longer purchase stocks at the IPO. Finally, there is a de minimis exemption. If the beneficial interests of restricted persons do not exceed 10% of an account, the account may purchase a new equity issue. In other words, restricted persons will be able to have an interest in an account that purchases new equity issues as long as no more than 10% of the account's beneficial owners are restricted persons.

Additional public offers (APOs, follow-on offers)

As mentioned above, a corporation may offer additional shares of stock to the public as a primary market transaction. These follow-on offerings go by several names: APO, subsequent public offering, or follow-on offerings. There may be multiple APOs over time. The two defining characteristics are that these are *primary offerings* (the proceeds go to the issuer) and they come *after* the IPO (this class of shares are already available to the public). The "P" may also be "primary," as in "initial primary" or "additional primary" or "subsequent primary" offering.

KNOWLEDGE CHECK

1. How many primary offerings can a corporation issue?
    - A. 1 primary offering
    - B. 2 primary offerings
    - C. 3 primary offerings
    - D. Unlimited

2. What federal law regulates the initial sale of securities to the public?
    - A. The Securities Act of 1933
    - B. The Securities Exchange Act of 1934
    - C. The Investment Company Act of 1940
    - D. The Truth in Investing Act

3. Which of the following may purchase an IPO at the POP?
    - A. Jim, a registered representative for Seacoast Securities
    - B. Jim's brother Robert, a contractor
    - C. Jim's niece Amber, a chef
    - D. Jim's father Roy, a retired engineer.

Answers

1. **D**   A corporation can sell as many shares, and have as many offerings, as it can get people to buy the stock. LO 7.b

2. **A**   The rules for registering a new issue come primarily from the Securities Act of 1933. LO 7.a

3. **C**   Jim, an employee of a broker-dealer, is a prohibited person, as are his spouse, parents, siblings, children, and various "in-laws." Aunts and uncles are not on the prohibited list, nor are nieces and nephews. LO 7.b

LESSON 7.2: PARTICIPANTS IN THE PRIMARY MARKET

LO 7.c Name the participants in the primary market.

In this section, we will discuss the participants in the primary market and their respective roles.

TAKE NOTE

In securities, the term *person* refers to a natural person (human being) *or* a legal entity (such as a corporation or a government). Any entity that can legally enter into a contract is a *person*.

Issuers

Corporations

An issuer is a corporation, government, or other entity that is selling a security to raise capital for itself. They are *issuing* the security. Corporations may issue both equities and debt issues (stocks and bonds). A government entity may issue debt.

Larger corporations' stock (after issued) that trade on a national exchange (listed) or the Nasdaq system are called National Market System securities. Those whose stock will not be listed are non-NMS securities. More detail on these parts of the secondary market are covered later in this unit; it is just important to introduce the terms.

Municipalities

Municipal governments issue municipal bonds and other types of debt. As a reminder, municipalities are governments at the state or lower level, such as counties and cities. This debt is sometimes called *munis.*

The Federal government and agencies

The largest issuer of debt in the United States is the Treasury Department. We have already discussed different types of Treasury debt. Debt issued by the government is sometimes called *govies.*

Underwriters (broker-dealers, investment bankers)

Underwriters are groups of BDs or investment bankers that work with an issuer to bring its securities to the market and sell them to the investing public. Investment bankers help the issuer to structure capital raises and, at times, form syndicates with other underwriters to facilitate this money-raising process.

Underwriting commitments

Different types of underwriting agreements require different levels of commitment from the underwriters. This results in different levels of risk for the underwriters and the issuer.

Best efforts underwriting (investment banker acting as agent)

A **best efforts underwriting** calls for the underwriters (syndicate) to buy securities from the issuer acting simply as an agent, not as the principal. This means that the underwriters are not committed to purchase the shares themselves and are therefore not at risk. Best efforts deals are closed by collecting client funds into an escrow account, so no underwriter capital is at risk in these types of offerings. The underwriter is acting as an agent contingent on the underwriter's ability to sell shares in either a public offering or a private placement. The underwriter is not at risk for the shares, but the issuer is. If all of the shares cannot be sold, the issuer will not raise the needed capital.

The following are two types of best efforts underwritings to be familiar with.

- All-or-none (AON)—In an AON underwriting, the issuing corporation has determined that it wants an agreement outlining that the underwriter must either sell all the shares or cancel the underwriting. Because of the uncertainty over the outcome of an AON offering, any funds collected from investors during the offering period must be held in escrow pending final disposition of the underwriting.

- Mini-max—A mini-max underwriting sets a floor or minimum (the least amount the issuer needs to raise to move forward with the underwriting), as well as a ceiling or maximum on the dollar amount of securities the issuer is willing to sell. The underwriter must locate enough interested buyers to support the minimum (floor) issuance requirement. Once the minimum is met, the underwriter can expand the offering up to the maximum (ceiling) amount of shares the issuer specified.

Firm commitment underwriting (investment banker acting as principal)

Firm commitment underwriting is a widely used type of underwriting contract. Under its terms, the underwriters contract with the issuer to buy the securities. The underwriter buys shares from the issuer and resells the securities to the public at a higher price—the POP—and earns this price differential (spread) for its efforts. Here, the underwriters are acting as principals rather than agents. They are committing to purchasing any unsold shares for the syndicate account. In this type of underwriting, it is the underwriters who are at risk for any shares they cannot sell to the public, not the issuer. If the shares cannot be sold, the underwriter must place the securities into his inventory and runs the risk of losing money, should the position fall in value. The issuer knows that ultimately all the securities will be sold and all the capital needed will be raised. Please note that a firm may never guarantee to a customer that it will agree to repurchase the shares at the POP if the deal subsequently trades lower.

Syndicates

In large firm commitment underwritings, it is common for a group of BDs to form a syndicate. A syndicate is a type of joint venture where the BDs form up to share both the risk and the profits from the offering. One of the members of the syndicate will take on a lead role and provide significant resources to the venture. This role is called the *managing underwriter*.

Often syndicates will bring in other BDs to assist the syndicate in the sale of the securities. This is the selling group. The members of the selling group do not commit capital, nor do they hold the securities in inventory the way a syndicate member does. Selling group members take on no liability for unsold shares.

Investors

Investors in the primary markets are those who are purchasing the new issue with the intent to hold the security for a period of time. They may be divided into three groups: institutional, retail, and accredited.

Institutional investors

An **institutional investor** is an entity that pools money to purchase securities and other investment assets. Institutional investors can include banks, insurance companies, pensions, hedge funds, investment advisers, and mutual funds.

Some institutional investors are called **qualified institutional buyers** (QIBs). This generally means that the QIB owns and invests a minimum of $100 million in securities on a discretionary basis.

Retail investors

Your typical retail investor is investing his own assets. Any investor that does not qualify as an institution should be treated as a retail investor. Though these investors may be quite large, most are smaller investors. As they tend to be less knowledgeable than institutional investors, sales to retail investors have higher communication and disclosure expectations.

Accredited investors

Accredited investors are a subset of investors made up of all institutional investors and certain retail investors.

Retail investors who are accredited investors are

- insiders of the security's issuer (officers, board members, major stockholders) or
- meet certain financial criteria:
  - An income of at least $200,000 or more the past two years and expected to meet that criteria in the current year (if the purchase is in a joint name, this number is increased to $300,000)
  - Or have a net worth of $1,000,000 or more (not including equity in the primary residence)

Note that the investor must meet at least one of the above criteria but does not need to meet both.

The assumption is that the accredited investor will have a higher sophistication level than the average retail investor and does not need the same level of protection.

TAKE NOTE

Retail and Institutional investors are active participants in the secondary markets (Unit 8), but the designation of accredited investor is used exclusively in primary market transactions.

Municipal advisors

Municipal advisors are a type of investment banker that advises municipalities on the issuing of municipal debt and other types of municipal securities. Municipal advisors work under a contract with the municipality to provide advice on issues such as debt structure, bond features, and other issues involved with raising capital.

Municipal advisors may assist in some of the underwriting functions, such as preparing the official notice, but they may not be compensated as part of the underwriting (sale) of any issue they provide advice on. (In other words, they may not switch roles from advisor to underwriter.)

KNOWLEDGE CHECK

1. An investment banking firm that enters into a contract with a municipality to provide advice and direction on raising capital for the municipality is
   A. a syndicate member.
   B. a muni dealer.
   C. a municipal advisor.
   D. a bond dealer.

2. A corporation that seeks to sell its own stock to raise money for building a new factory is an example of
   A. a selling group member.
   B. an underwriter.
   C. a market maker.
   D. an issuer.

3. An underwriter that assists a corporation on the sale of a new issue without taking the security into inventory is underwriting on what type of underwriting?
   A. Best efforts
   B. Firm commitment
   C. Partial commitment
   D. Full or none

Answers

1. **C** This relationship between a municipality and an adviser is the role of a municipal advisor. The other terms are for investment bankers involved in the actual sale of the issue or in the secondary markets.

2. **D** The company selling its own securities to raise capital is the issuer.

3. **A** The underwriter who does not commit capital and take the issue into its inventory is acting on a best efforts basis.

LESSON 7.3: NONEXEMPT REGISTRATION

LO 7.d Order the process for offering a nonexempt issue.

Issuing a new security and the Securities Act of 1933

The main purpose of the Securities Act of 1933 (also called the **Paper Act)** is to ensure that the investing public is fully informed about a security and its issuing company when the security is first sold in the primary market. The Securities Act of 1933 protects investors who buy new issues by

■ requiring registration of new issues (unless exempt under the act);

■ requiring an issuer to provide full and fair disclosure about itself and the offering;

■ requiring an issuer to make available all material information necessary for an investor to judge the issue's merit;

■ regulating the underwriting and distribution of primary issues; and

■ providing criminal penalties for fraud in the issuance of new securities.

TAKE NOTE

The Securities and Exchange Commission is the primary federal regulator in the securities industry. The SEC will be covered in more detail in a later unit.

The registration statement

When an issuer desires to sell a security that does not meet one of the exemptions to registration under the 1933 Act (detailed later in this unit) the issue must first be registered with the Securities and Exchange Commission (SEC). The first step in this process is for the issuer to file a **registration statement** (called an S-1) with the SEC.

The **statement** discloses material information about the issue. Part of the registration statement is a disclosure document called a **prospectus**, which must be provided to all purchasers of the new issue.

The registration statement must contain

■ a description of the issuer's business;

■ the names and addresses of company officers and directors, their salaries, and a five-year business history of each;

■ the amount of corporate securities company officers and directors own and identification of investors who own 10% or more of the company;

■ the company's capitalization, including its equity and debt;

■ a description of how the proceeds will be used; and

■ whether the company is involved in any legal proceedings.

Underwriters (BDs and investment bankers) may assist the issuer in preparing and filing the registration statement and prospectus. However, the accuracy and adequacy of these documents is the responsibility of the issuer.

The cooling-off period

After filing the registration statement, the cooling-off period begins. The cooling-off period lasts for a minimum of 20 calendar days, though the period is often longer. If the SEC finds that the registration statement needs revision or expansion, the SEC may suspend the review and issue a deficiency letter to the issuer of the securities. The 20-day cooling-off period would resume when the issuer submits a corrected registration statement. Note that it resumes where it had left off and does not begin anew.

During the cooling-off period, no one can solicit sales of the securities. However, there are several activities that are allowed during the cooling-off period.

During the cooling-off period, the following are allowed.

The issuer may place a tombstone advertisement

Certain types of advertisements relating to a new issue are allowed to be run before the effective date. These are known as tombstone ads because of the bare-bones/minimum information provided. Tombstone ads are an announcement and description of the securities to be offered.

Tombstone ads are the only form of advertising that is permitted during the cooling-off period. Remember that the cooling-off period is the time between the registration filing with the SEC and the effective date (when the SEC allows the security to be sold). While tombstone ads may run to announce a new issue during the cooling-off period, they are not required, and the ad does not need to be filed with the SEC.

Tombstone ads may be placed by the issuer directly or with the assistance of the underwriters. They are limited to the following information:

- Name of the issuer
- Type of security being offered
- Number of shares to be sold
- Public offering price (POP), or a range if the POP is not yet set
- Names of the underwriting members (when placed by the underwriters instead of the issuer)

All tombstone ads must contain the following advisory: "This announcement is neither an offer to sell nor a solicitation of an offer for any of these securities. This offer is made only by prospectus."

A preliminary prospectus may be delivered (also called a red herring)

The **preliminary prospectus**, or **red herring**, can be used as a prospecting tool, allowing issuers and underwriters to gauge investor interest and gather indications of interest. There is no final price included in the preliminary prospectus, though a range is often included. The preliminary prospectus must be made available to any customer who expresses interest in the securities during the cooling-off period.

Indications of interest may be gathered

An indication of interest is an investor's declaration of potential interest in purchasing some of the issue from the underwriter after the security comes out of registration. An investor's indication of interest is not a commitment to buy because sales are prohibited until after the registration becomes effective (the **effective date**). An indication of interest from an investor is neither a commitment to buy from the investor nor a promise to sell by the underwriter; it is nonbinding to either party. Also, no money changes hands. It is, in essence, an investor saying, "I might be interested."

Due diligence takes place

Underwriters and selling group members examine the issue to determine which customers the issue is suitable for. Often, the managing underwriter and the issuer will have *due diligence meetings* to make a formal presentation to those representatives that may offer the security to their customers.

State registration requirements (blue sky filings)

In addition to federal law the individual states have securities laws. The process of coordinating the federal and the state registrations is called "blue sky". When the proper forms have been filed the security is registered in the states at the same time it is released for sale by the SEC.

Release (or effective) date

Sometime on or after (usually after) 20 days, the SEC will allow the security to be offered to investors. It is important to note that the SEC does not "approve" the issue. The SEC avoids language that sounds like an endorsement, preferring to say it "allows" the issue to be "released." Starting on the release date, investors may purchase the issue. Generally it will begin the secondary markets shortly after the IPO.

Final prospectus

The final prospectus is also available at release. The final prospectus will be delivered to all who purchase the new security at the IPO. It will contain the same information as the preliminary prospectus plus two additional items: the release date and the POP.

A copy of the final prospectus must precede or accompany all sales confirmations. The prospectus must include the

- description of the offering;
- offering price;
- selling discounts;
- offering date;
- the use of the proceeds;
- description of the underwriting, but not the actual contract;
- statement of the possibility that the issue's price may be stabilized;
- history of the business;
- risks to the purchasers;
- description of management;
- material financial information;

- legal opinion concerning the formation of the corporation; and
- SEC disclaimer.

TAKE NOTE

The SEC does not approve or endorse any offering for sale; the SEC simply clears, or releases the offering for sale. The standard **SEC disclaimer** reads as follows: "These securities have not been approved or disapproved by the SEC nor have any representations been made about the accuracy or the adequacy of the information."

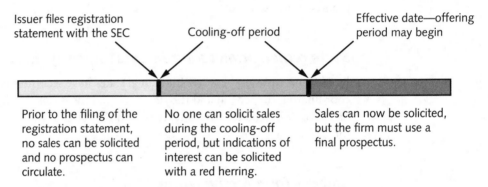

Issuer files registration statement with the SEC

Cooling-off period

Effective date—offering period may begin

Prior to the filing of the registration statement, no sales can be solicited and no prospectus can circulate.

No one can solicit sales during the cooling-off period, but indications of interest can be solicited with a red herring.

Sales can now be solicited, but the firm must use a final prospectus.

You will note that on the effective date, it says "offering period may begin." We tend to think of IPOs in terms of the "hot offering," where all the securities are sold almost instantly. This is not true for most offers. It may take days, or even weeks, to sell the entire offer. Note that anyone who buys from the offering pays the POP and receives the final prospectus.

Additional primary offering (subsequent primary offering, follow-on offering)

When a corporation issues stock to sell to the public for the first time, this is called an IPO. If after (usually years after) the IPO, the corporation chooses to sell more shares of the company, this is called an additional primary offering (or one of the terms in the title line, above). Though the process differs somewhat from the IPO, an APO still requires a filing with the SEC and a prospectus. This may be accomplished as a rights offering as covered in Part 1.

TEST TOPIC ALERT

If the issuer of the security is receiving the funds from an offering, this is a primary market transaction. Whether an IPO, APO, or something else, if the issuer is getting the money, it is a primary offering.

TAKE NOTE

You may see the term *hybrid* or *combination offering*. When a corporation sells shares through a primary offering, it may allow some of the existing shareholders to sell their shares along with the new issued shares. Usually these are early investors, founders, or key managers. This is a hybrid offer, with most of the money going to the corporation for the new shares, and some to individuals for their shares. It is actually fairly common in large IPOs for hot companies, but the hybrid part is largely ignored by the press.

LO 7.h Define shelf offerings and green shoe offerings.

There are two special types of offerings that may appear on the test: the shelf offering and the greenshoe offering.

The shelf offering

Through a shelf offering registration, an issuer who is already a publicly traded company can register new securities without selling any of the shares until later or some of the shares initially, and waiting to sell the remaining portion of the shares. Once filed, the registration is good for two years and allows the issuer to sell portions of a registered shelf offering over a two-year period without having to reregister the security. This provision under the Securities Act of 1933 allows issuers to quickly raise capital when needed or when market conditions are favorable.

An issuer that meets the criteria of a well-known seasoned issuer (called a WKSI) may extend the shelf offering to three years. Though the WKSI criteria are not tested, be aware that any security listed on a major exchange will meet the WKSI criteria.

TAKE NOTE

For securities offered via a shelf registration, a supplemental prospectus must be filed with the SEC before each sale.

Green shoe option

The prospectus for a stock offering will list the number of shares to be sold. The greenshoe option (formally known as an over-allotment option) allows the underwriters to increase the number of shares offered up to an additional 15% if there is sufficient demand. This is a fairly common option for offerings where heavy demand is expected.

EXAMPLE

This option was first used by the Green Shoe Manufacturing Company in 1960. The initial offering was for 2,000,000 common shares, but high interest during the cooling-off period allowed for the underwriters to expand the offering to 2,200,000 shares.

The Green Shoe Manufacturing Company changed its name in 1966 to Stride Rite Corporation. This point is not testable, but it is interesting.

KNOWLEDGE CHECK

1. Seabird Airlines is selling shares to the public for the first time. The company intends to use the proceeds from the sale of its stock to purchase several new passenger aircraft. This offering is an example of
   A. a secondary offering.
   B. a rights offering.
   C. an initial public offering.
   D. a subsequent primary offering.

2. The Hew Lumber Company's common stock is currently trading at $32 in the market. Hew is preparing to sell additional shares to raise money for a new mill. This is an example of
   A. a secondary offering.
   B. a hybrid offering.
   C. an initial public offering.
   D. a subsequent primary offering.

3. During the cooling-off period, an underwriter may do all of the following **except**
   A. gather binding indications of interest.
   B. distribute red herrings to interested parties.
   C. perform due diligence.
   D. file required forms for state registration.

Answers

1. **C** This is the first time this company has made its stock available to the public, so this is an *initial public offering*. This transaction is in the primary market (the issuer is receiving the proceeds). LO 7.d

2. **D** The company is already trading in the market, so its IPO is sometime in the past. This sale of shares by the company is an APO (or subsequent primary offering). LO 7.d

3. **A** There are no *binding* indications of interest. Indications of interest are *nonbinding*. All the other functions mentioned are allowed during the cooling-off period, as are nonbinding indications of interest. LO 7.d

LESSON 7.4: EXEMPTIONS TO REGISTRATION

LO 7.e Recall the types of exempt issues and issuers.

When securities are required to be registered in order to be sold to the public, they are known as **nonexempt** securities (not exempt from registration and must be registered). However, there are exemptions from the registration requirements, which we will discuss now.

Exempt issuers

Certain securities are exempt from the registration and prospectus requirements of the Securities Act of 1933 because the issuer is the federal government, an agency of the federal government, a municipal government, or because another government regulatory agency has jurisdiction over the issuer.

These exempt securities include

- U.S. government securities;
- municipal securities;
- commercial paper, banker's acceptances, and other securities that have maturities of 270 days or less;
- fixed life insurance policies (such as term or whole life) and fixed annuity contracts (but not variable annuities or variable life policies);
- national and state bank (not bank holding company) securities;

- building and loan and savings and loan (S&L) securities;
- charitable, religious, educational, and nonprofit association securities;
- interests in common carriers (example: railroad equipment certificates); and
- banks.

Certain securities are exempt from the registration statement and prospectus requirements of the Securities Act of 1933, either because of the issuer's level of creditworthiness or because another government regulatory agency has jurisdiction over the issuer.

These exempt securities include

- U.S. government securities;
- municipal bonds;
- commercial paper and banker's acceptances that have maturities of 270 days or less;
- insurance policies and fixed annuity contracts (but not variable annuities);
- national and state bank (not bank holding company) securities;
- building and loan (S&L) securities;
- charitable, religious, educational, and nonprofit association issues;
- interests in railroad equipment certificates; and
- banks.

TAKE NOTE

The bank exemption applies only to the securities of banks, not to the securities of bank holding companies. Securities issued by the First National Bank of Bigtown (example: CDs) are exempt. The bank is owned by the Bigtown Bank Holding Company, Inc. The holding company's securities are not exempt.

Insurance policies are not included in the definition of security; however, variable annuities, variable life insurance, and variable universal life insurance are funded by separate accounts investing in securities. Therefore, these products must be registered as securities with the SEC. For the exam, if you see the word "variable" or the phrase "separate account product," the product must be registered.

Exempt Transactions

Some securities are exempt from registration requirements due to the nature of the transaction. Often these are smaller offerings or have restrictions on who may invest.

Regulation A+: small- and medium-sized offerings

With the passage of the JOBs Act, a rule was put into place that would ease the requirements for small- and medium-sized companies to raise capital. Previously known as Regulation A, the new rule is Regulation A+.

Regulation A+ provides two offering tiers for small- and medium-sized companies that will allow the companies to raise capital in amounts substantially more than the $5 million previously allowed under Regulation A.

Tier 1: Securities offerings up to $20 million in a 12-month period will be allowed. Of the $20 million, no more than $6 million can be sold on behalf of existing selling shareholders. The offering would be subject to a coordinated review by individual states and the SEC.

Tier 2: Securities offerings up to $50 million in a 12-month period will be allowed. Of the $50 million, no more than $15 million can be sold on behalf of existing selling shareholders. These offerings are subject to SEC review only and none at the state level. Tier 2 offerings are still subject to rigorous disclosure requirements to the SEC, including audited financial statements, annual, semiannual and current reports.

Offerings under both tiers are open to the public, and general solicitation (advertising) is permitted for both tiers. However, Tier 2 investors must be "qualified" investors, and there are two ways to qualify:

- Be an accredited investor as defined in Rule 501 of Regulation D (found in LO 7.c Name the participants in the primary market)

- Limit the investment to a maximum of the greater of 10% of the investor's net worth or 10% of the investor's net income per offering. Note that self-certification for Tier 2 as to net worth and income is all that is required with no burdensome filings.

Tier 1 has no investment limits.

Finally, remembering that the new Regulation A+ is intended for small- and medium-sized companies, the regulation specifically excludes investment companies (i.e., private equity funds, venture capital funds, and hedge funds).

In a Regulation A+ offering, the issuer files an abbreviated **notice of sale**, or **offering circular**, with the regional SEC office. Investors are provided with this offering circular rather than a full prospectus.

Rule 147: The Intrastate Offering Rule

Under **Rule 147**, offerings that take place entirely in one state are exempt from registration when the issuer has its principal office (headquarters) in the state and all purchasers are residents of the state.

In addition, the company must meet one of the following criteria:

- It receives at least 80% of its income in the state.

- At least 80% of the issuer's assets are located within the state.

- At least 80% of the offering proceeds are used within the state.

- The majority of the company's employees must work in the state.

Also, if there is a broker-dealer acting as underwriter, the BD must be based in the state.

Securities sold under Rule 147 may not be resold to nonresidents of the state for six months after the initial purchase.

Regulation D: Exempt Transactions (private placements)

The SEC does not require registration of an offering under Regulation D so long as there are no more than 35 nonaccredited investors. There is no limit to the number of accredited investors that may invest in the private placement. The definition of an accredited investor is found under LO 7.c Name the participants in the primary market.

Purchasers must have access to the same type of information they would receive if the securities were being sold under prospectus in a registered offering. The amount of capital that can be raised is unlimited.

A private placement investor must sign a letter stating that he intends to hold the stock for investment purposes only. Private placement stock is called **lettered stock** due to this investment letter. The certificate may bear a legend indicating that it cannot be transferred without registration or exemption; therefore, private placement stock is also called **legend stock**.

The SEC requires that all companies raising capital in a nonpublic offering that qualify under the Regulation D exemption file the information on Form D electronically via the internet. The SEC also specifies the instances when an amended Form D be filed, such as to correct a mistake of fact or error or to reflect a change in information.

General solicitations and advertising private placements

In order to solicit or advertise private securities offerings (private placements), a business will need to meet certain requirements regarding the intended investors. First, meeting the requirements assumes that the securities are in fact being offered under the Regulation D registration exemption. Beyond that assumption, the requirements are as follows:

- All purchasers of the advertised securities must be accredited investors, or the business must reasonably believe that the investors are accredited investors at the time of the sale. In other words, while businesses may sell to up to 35 nonaccredited investors, in order to solicit or advertise, all purchasers must be accredited.

- The business must take reasonable steps to verify that all purchasers are accredited, considering background, relevant facts (such as reported income), and particular circumstances of each purchaser.

TEST TOPIC ALERT

Sometimes it is difficult to identify private placement stock in a question because of the many terms that can be used to describe it. Recognize all of the following terms as synonymous with private placement stock:

- Restricted (because it must be held for a six-month period)

- Unregistered (no registration statement on file with the SEC)

- Letter stock (investor agreed to terms by signing an investment letter)

- Legend stock (a special inscription on the stock certificate indicates restricted transfer)

KNOWLEDGE CHECK

1. A Regulation A+ exemption covers
    A.   an offering of $50 million or less in 12 months.
    B.   an offering of letter stock.
    C.   a private offering.
    D.   an offering of $50 million or more in 12 months.

2. Which of the following are considered to be nonexempt offerings according to the Securities Act of 1933?
   I.   Government securities
   II. Private placements
   III. Public offering of $60 million by a brokerage firm
   IV. Sales of corporate bonds of $52 million
   A. I and II
   B. I and III
   C. II and IV
   D. III and IV

3. Under the intrastate offering rule (Rule 147), when may a resident purchaser of securities resell them to a nonresident?
   A. Three months after the first sale made in that state
   B. Six months after the last sale made in that state
   C. At least six months after the date of purchase
   D. None of these

Answers

1. **A** Regulation A+ filing under the Securities Act of 1933 exempts the security from registration and limits offerings to $50 million or less within a 12-month period.

2. **D** The Securities Act of 1933 exempts U.S. government bonds and private placements from registration. Public offerings of less than $50 million, and in some cases $20 million, are also exempt (under Regulation A+), so an offering of $60 million and sales of corporate bonds are not exempt; they must be registered with the SEC.

3. **C** In an intrastate offering, a purchaser of the issue may not sell the securities to a resident of another state for at least six months from the date of purchase.

LESSON 7.5: DISCLOSURE DOCUMENTS

LO 7.f Name the types of disclosure documents.

Disclosure documents for corporate issues

Some of this material was covered earlier in this unit.

Preliminary prospectus

The preliminary prospectus is covered in lesson 7.2 under the actions that can take place during the cooling-off period.

Final prospectus

When the registration statement becomes effective, the issuer amends the preliminary prospectus and adds information, including the final offering price for the **final prospectus**. Registered representatives may then take orders from those customers who indicated interest in buying during the cooling-off period.

A copy of the final prospectus must precede or accompany all sales confirmations. The prospectus must include the

- description of the offering;
- offering price;
- selling discounts;
- offering date;
- use of the proceeds;
- description of the underwriting, but not the actual contract;
- statement of the possibility that the issue's price may be stabilized;
- history of the business;
- risks to the purchasers;
- description of management;
- material financial information;
- legal opinion concerning the formation of the corporation; and
- SEC disclaimer.

TEST TOPIC ALERT

The SEC does not *approve* or *endorse* any offering for sale; they simply clear, or release, the offering for sale. The standard **SEC disclaimer** reads as follows: "These securities have not been approved or disapproved by the SEC nor have any representations been made about the accuracy or the adequacy of the information."

For those who have noticed we already covered this point, yes, we know. It's important.

Disclosure documents for mutual funds

Some of this material was covered in Part 1, Unit 4: Packaged Investments.

Full (statutory) prospectus

This is the full and fair disclosure document that provides a prospective investor with the material information needed to make a fully informed investment decision. If a prospectus is being used to solicit a sale, it must be distributed to an investor before or during the solicitation. The front of a mutual fund prospectus must contain key information that appears in plain English in a standardized order. Information in this clear and concise format includes the fund's objective, investment policies, sales charges, management expenses, and services offered. It also discloses 1-, 5-, and 10-year performance histories, or performance over the life of the fund, whichever is shorter.

EXAMPLE

If a fund has been in existence for eight years, it will show performance for one, five, and eight years; if it has been in existence for only four years, it will show one and four years.

The delivery of any type of sales literature is considered a solicitation of sale and, therefore, must be accompanied or preceded by the delivery of a prospectus.

A mutual fund is said to have an ongoing prospectus. Recall from Unit 1 that mutual funds are open-end managed investment companies. Because all purchases in a mutual fund are primary market sales of new shares, there must always be a prospectus available.

TAKE NOTE

A mutual fund prospectus is updated annually. It may be used for sales solicitations for a period of 16 months from the date of publication. The 16 months allows for a 4-month overlap to throw out the old prospectus and stock the new ones. This rule is a throwback to the day that all of these documents were in paper form.

TEST TOPIC ALERT

A prospectus may not ever be altered in any way. This means that no highlighting, writing in, or taking any measure to bring attention to any specific passage or section is permitted.

Summary prospectus

A mutual fund can provide a summary prospectus to investors who may include an application that investors can use to buy the fund's shares.

The summary prospectus is a standardized summary of key information in the fund's full prospectus, *Investors* who receive the summary have the option of either purchasing fund shares using the application found therein or requesting a full (statutory) prospectus. An investor who purchases fund shares on the basis of the summary prospectus must be able to access a full prospectus no later than the confirmation of the sale. Delivery may be made online.

There are some very specific requirements for a summary prospectus. The following must be included on the cover page of the summary prospectus or at the beginning of the summary prospectus:

- The fund's name and the class or classes of shares.
- The exchange ticker symbol for the fund's shares.
- A legend, which must appear on the cover page, that refers to the summary nature of the prospectus and the availability of the fund's full (statutory) prospectus; the legend must provide a toll-free number to request paper delivery of prospectus or a website where one may be downloaded.
- Additionally, the summary must provide specific information in a particular sequence, such as investments, risks, and performance; fee tables; investment objectives, investment strategies, and any related risks; the portfolio holdings and details regarding management; shareholder information; and any financial highlights.

Statement of additional information (SAI)

Mutual funds and closed-end funds are required to have an SAI available for delivery, without charge, within three business days of an investor's request. Investors can obtain a copy of the SAI by calling or writing to the investment company or by contacting a BD that sells the investment company shares, or by contacting the Securities and Exchange Commission (SEC).

While a prospectus is always sufficient for the purpose of selling shares, some investors may seek additional information not found in the prospectus. This additional information is not considered mandatory to make an informed investment decision, but it may be useful to the investor.

The SAI affords the fund an opportunity to have expanded discussions on matters such as the fund's history and policies. It will also typically contain the fund's consolidated financial statements, including

- the balance sheet;
- statement of operations;
- an income statement; and
- a portfolio list at the time the SAI was compiled.

 TAKE NOTE

An investment company must send a copy of its balance sheet to any shareholder who requests one in writing between semiannual reports.

Omitting prospectus (Rule 482 prospectus)

The omitting prospectus is the official name for an advertisement for a mutual fund. These will often take the form of a tombstone advertisement for a new fund. The key to remember is that an omitting prospectus omits most of the information an investor would need to make an investing decision. Omitting prospectuses are *not* sufficient for soliciting a sale.

Other disclosure documents

Municipal securities

The primary disclosure document for a municipal security is the *official statement*. It contains much of the same sort of information you would find in a prospectus.

Private placements, Regulation A+, and other exempt securities

The common term for the disclosure document for other types of exempt securities is the *offering circular*, sometimes the term *notice of sale* is used. This document is very similar to a prospectus but is often not as detailed in its disclosures.

LO 7.g Determine the prospectus delivery requirements after issuance.

These rules are specific to a *prospectus* for a corporate offering. As discussed, any offering of a corporate security in a primary market transaction requires the delivery of a prospectus to the investors that purchase the security. In addition to those investors that buy shares at the IPO (or APO), investors that purchase these shares in the secondary market are also entitled to the final prospectus if the purchase is made within a certain number of days of the release date.

As noted in Part 1, stocks that are listed on an exchange or the Nasdaq are National Market System (NMS) securities. Those that are not so listed are non-NMS.

An investor that buys a new security in the *secondary* market will be entitled to the final prospectus if the purchase occurs within the following timelines:

- For IPOs of NMS securities—25 days
- For APOs of NMS securities—zero days (no requirement)
- For IPOs of non-NMS securities – 90 days
- For APOs of non-NMS securities—40 days

KNOWLEDGE CHECK

1. In order to solicit the purchase of a mutual fund, a registered representative must provide the investor with
    I. the summary prospectus.
    II. the Rule 482 prospectus.
    III. the statutory prospectus.
    IV. the statement of additional information.
    A. I and II
    B. I or III
    C. II or III
    D. II and IV

2. An investor that purchases Big City 3½% general obligation bonds of 2040 in the primary market should receive
    A. an official statement.
    B. a preliminary prospectus.
    C. a final prospectus.
    D. a statutory circular.

3. Your customer has purchased shares of the Littleton Lumber Company (a nonlisted stock) in the secondary market. Littleton Lumbar recently completed an APO. Your customer will receive a prospectus for the APO if the purchase is within how many days of the APO date?
    A. 5 days
    B. 25 days
    C. 40 days
    D. 90 days

Answers

1. **B** A representative may deliver either a summary or a full prospectus to meet the disclosure requirement. LO 7.f

2. **A** The most common term for the disclosure document for a municipal security is the *official statement*. LO 7.f

3. **C** Littleton Lumber is a non-NMS security. The question specifies that the company recently completed an APO (follow-on offering). The delivery requirement is 40 days. LO 7.g

UNIT
8

The Securities Exchange Act of 1934 and the Secondary Markets

LEARNING OBJECTIVES

When you have completed this unit, you will be able to accomplish the following.

- › LO 8.a   Recognize the purpose of the secondary markets.
- › LO 8.b   Define the major market centers.
- › LO 8.c   Recall the participants in the secondary markets.
- › LO 8.d   Differentiate exchanges and the OTC market.

INTRODUCTION

This unit will examine trading activities both on the exchanges and OTC. It presents many terms and rules that are used by the industry and are critical for exam success.

The trading of securities in the secondary market is regulated by the Securities Exchange Act of 1934. The Act of 1934 created the Securities and Exchange Commission and gave it the authority to regulate securities exchanges and the OTC market.

Exchanges, such as the NYSE, operate as auction markets where stocks listed on the exchange are traded. The OTC market is an interdealer computer and telephone network where market makers in stocks show the bid and ask price for stocks in which they make a market.

LESSON 8.1: THE SECONDARY MARKETS

LO 8.a Recognize the purpose of the secondary markets.

The short answer to "Why are there secondary markets?" is that they provide a place for the buyers and the sellers of securities to connect and transact business. There is a longer answer: the secondary markets support the primary markets. Imagine an economy without stock exchanges or securities dealers. Very few people would be likely to own stocks. Most investors that buy stocks do so with the intent of holding them for a time and, hopefully, sell them for a nice gain. They then use that money for more useful things such as food, shelter, clothing, education, or a host of other things. They aren't even limited to useful things; you could blow it on a boat if you wanted.

If there was no place to easily sell stocks for a fair price, very few people would buy them in the first place. If very few people would buy, then it would be much more difficult for corporations to raise capital this way. Even with bonds, the ability to sell them is a significant advantage. If there were no secondary markets, there would be very little, or no, primary market. If there were no primary market, it would be much more difficult to grow a business and enjoy the economic expansion and job growth that goes with a growing economy.

You, as a representative of a broker-dealer, are a vital part of this system—helping your customers achieve their financial goals while supporting the economy as a whole.

TAKE NOTE

The ability to buy or sell a security easily is called liquidity. The secondary markets provide liquidity to investors. A security that is easily sold (liquidated) is said to be very liquid, or have little liquidity risk. Treasury bills and stocks listed on exchanges are examples of securities that are very liquid. Limited partnership units are extremely difficult to liquidate and are called illiquid.

TEST TOPIC ALERT

In the primary markets, the seller is always the issuer; in the secondary markets, the seller is never the issuer. An investor sells securities in the secondary markets and keeps the money for its own use.

LO 8.b Define the major market centers.

The Market Centers

The locations, both physical and electronic, where buyers and sellers may gather and place trades are called *market centers*. The secondary markets in the United States have four types of market centers.

Exchanges

The **exchange market** is composed of the New York Stock Exchange (NYSE) and other exchanges on which listed securities are traded. This market is also known as an **auction market**. The term **listed security** refers to any security listed for trading on an exchange. The NYSE is the largest of the exchanges and is the model used for the exam.

Each stock exchange requires companies to meet certain criteria before it will allow their stock to be listed for trading on the exchange.

- *Physical location.* Listed markets, such as the NYSE and other exchanges, have central marketplaces and trading floor facilities.

- *Pricing system.* Listed markets operate as **double-auction** markets. Floor participants compete among themselves to execute trades at prices most favorable to the public.

The over-the-counter market (OTC)

OTC markets also have criteria that a company must meet to be traded on a particular OTC venue, just as exchanges do. While historically these criteria were not as stringent as those imposed by the exchanges, over time the quality of issues-traded OTC closed the gap and today equal exchange-traded issues.

- *Location.* No central marketplace facilitates OTC trading. Trading takes place over the phone, over computer networks, and in trading rooms across the country.

- *Pricing system.* The OTC market works through an **interdealer network**. Registered market makers compete among themselves to post the best bid and ask prices. The OTC market is a negotiated market.

The third market (Nasdaq Intermarket)

The **third market**, or **Nasdaq Intermarket,** is a trading market in which exchange-listed securities are traded in the OTC market. Broker-dealers registered as OTC **market makers** in listed securities can do transactions in the third market. All securities listed on the NYSE and most securities listed on the regional exchanges are eligible for OTC trading as long as the trades are reported to the **Consolidated Tape** within 10 seconds of execution.

The fourth market (the ECNs)

The **fourth market** is a market for institutional investors in which large blocks of stock, both listed and unlisted, trade in transactions unassisted by broker-dealers. These transactions take place through **electronic communications networks (ECNs)**. ECNs are open 24 hours a day and act solely as agents.

TAKE NOTE   The Dark Pools

Dark pools, sometimes called dark pools of liquidity or simply dark liquidity, is trading volume that occurs or liquidity that is not openly available to the public. The bulk of this volume represents trades engaged in by institutional traders and trading desks away from the exchange markets. Generally, these are large-volume transactions.

Institutional trading desks that choose to use dark pools are able to execute large block orders without impacting public quotes or price, or revealing their investment strategy regarding any of their holding accumulations or divestitures. Additionally, orders can be placed anonymously so that the identity of the entity placing the order is unknown to the general investing public, along with the volume and price for the transaction. The concern with dark pools is that some market participants are left disadvantaged because they cannot see the trades, volume, or prices agreed upon within the pools, and thus market transparency is darkened.

TAKE NOTE   Trading Hours

The NYSE trades between 9:30 am and 4:00 pm ET each business day. Normal hours for retail OTC trading are the same as those of the NYSE, although many market makers remain open until 6:30 pm in extended hours trading. The after-hours market is much less liquid because order flow is limited. As a result, the spreads between bid and ask prices are wider and there is greater price volatility.

KNOWLEDGE CHECK

1. Which of the following statements regarding the third market is **true**?
    A. It is composed of listed securities traded OTC.
    B. It is composed only of unlisted securities.
    C. The services of a brokerage firm are not used.
    D. It refers to the block trading of unlisted securities.

2. A large-volume transaction for an institutional investor has occurred on an alternative trading system or network. Entered anonymously, the general public will see no information regarding the volume, price, or who the institutional investor was. This transaction scenario is generally referred to as having occurred
    A. on a U.S. exchange.
    B. in a dark pool.
    C. in the over-the-counter (OTC) market.
    D. in the third market.

3. The SEC regulates the trading of all of the following **except**
    A. the New York Stock Exchange.
    B. the Chicago Board of Options Exchange.
    C. the London Stock Exchange.
    D. the U.S. over-the-counter market.

Answers

1. **A** The third market is composed of OTC market makers (dealers) that deal in and provide liquidity for exchange-listed stocks. Though most of the trading of listed stocks takes place on the exchanges it is listed on, there is no rule that prevents OTC market makers from providing liquidity for these stocks as well. LO 8.b

2. **B** Dark pools are designed to help institutional traders operate in a less transparent setting than the exchanges (lit markets). This allows the institutions to trade with less disruption of the secondary markets. It also helps these institutional money managers make it more difficult to determine the strategies they are using. LO 8.b

3. **C** The SEC is a U.S. government regulator of securities. The London Stock Exchange is located in London, England, the United Kingdom. It is not in the United States nor under U.S. authority. LO 8.a

LESSON 8.2: EXCHANGES AND THE OTC

LO 8.c Recall the participants in the secondary markets.

Those who engage in the secondary markets fall into two broad categories: investors and facilitators.

Investors

Investors are the persons who are buying and selling securities in the secondary markets. They are trading in order to accomplish their objectives, whatever they may be. In the secondary markets, the seller of a security is not the issuer.

TAKE NOTE

In most secondary market transactions, the issuer of the security is not involved. However, in the case of a buyback, the issuer of a security may buy the security from investors through the secondary markets. This is an exception to the concept of "no issuers in the secondary market."

Retail investors

Retail investors are the normal people who are investing their own money to accomplish their own objectives. They may be people of modest means, or very wealthy, but they are the investors that are generally not professional investors. Most of the rules on disclosure, communications, and recommendations are designed to help the retail investor.

Day trader

The day trader is generally a type of retail investor that trades rapidly in and out of positions. Most day traders will have all positions closed and will close the day "flat" (no open positions).

Accredited investors

These investors are were covered in Unit 7. The classification of accredited is used in primary market transactions, particularly for Regulation A+ and Regulation D private placements. The term has no specific use in secondary markets, but it is sometimes used to identify a wealthier or more sophisticated retail investor.

Institutional investors

An institutional investor is a large investor such as a mutual fund, a pension fund, a bank, an insurance company, or some other financial service organization. The investment decisions for these institutions is often made by a professional, such as an investment adviser, who is paid by the institution to manage the institution's portfolio.

Fiduciaries: custodians and trustees

Certain types of accounts are managed by a custodian or a trustee. Don't try to find a specific difference between these two; the terms are used within the securities industry in different ways. However, both of these roles are fiduciaries.

TEST TOPIC ALERT

A fiduciary is a person that manages assets (usually financial) for another person, a beneficiary. A fiduciary has a legal and moral obligation to perform her duties in the best interest of the beneficiary, placing the beneficiary's interest before her own.

■ *Custodian.* On the exam, custodian refers to a custodian on a minor's account under the Uniform Transfer to Minors Act (UTMA) or the Uniform Gift to Minors Act (UGMA). *Custodian* may also refer to a firm that holds assets in a qualified retirement account such as an IRA.

■   *Trustee.* A trustee is a fiduciary that oversees a trust. This might be a living trust, a pension trust, or any other sort of trust. If there is a trust, there will be a trustee. A trustee is a trustee of a trust.

■   *Guardians and executors.* These persons are normally court-appointed custodians over a minor, an incapacitated adult, or an estate (executor in that case). These roles might appear on the exam but are less common.

TAKE NOTE

A fiduciary may or may not be a professional, depending on the role and the type of account he oversees. Note that an investment adviser is always a fiduciary.

Investment advisers

Anyone who

■   gives investment advice

■   as a regular part of their business,

■   for compensation,

must register as an investment adviser (IA) under the Investment Advisers Act of 1940.

BDs who provide advice for a fee are subject to registration under this act. Agents of investment advisers must register and pass the Series 65 exam or Series 66 exam (for representatives with a Series 7). When acting in the capacity of an IA, the adviser is acting as a fiduciary for a customer.

EXAMPLE

An RR who is registered under the Securities Exchange Act of 1934 and has been charging commissions for transactions now wants to charge separately for investment advice, regardless of whether a transaction takes place. To do so, though already registered under the Securities Exchange Act of 1934, the RR would need to register under the Investment Advisers Act of 1940 by passing the appropriate exam (Series 65 or 66).

TAKE NOTE

When acting as an IA, the IA represents the customer; if the same firm is also a BD, it can also place the trade but is acting in its BD capacity when executing a trade. It might be said that this adviser has "switched hats" from IA to BD. The representative who does this will be "dual-registered" (IA representative and a RR) and will be working for a "dually registered" firm (IA and BD).

Facilitators

Facilitators help customers in performing transactions in the secondary markets. There are a number of different types of companies involved in the process of buying and selling securities.

Broker-dealers

Broker-dealers (FINRA member firms) perform securities transactions for their own accounts or for their customers. Their primary source of revenue is from transaction fees like commissions and loads.

Each member firm BD operates under an individualized membership agreement with FINRA and possibly other self-regulatory organizations (SROs). The membership agreement explains what lines of business the BD undertakes. Once becoming a member, firms (and their associated persons) may never state that they are endorsed, approved, or recommended by a regulator. This prohibition extends to both verbal and written communications.

Some BDs offer all types of investment products, such as stocks, bonds, mutual funds, options, and many others, while some limit the products they offer to only a few. BDs can also incorporate proprietary trading—that is, to trade the firm's own capital. These firms stand ready to buy and sell specific securities hoping to profit from price swings. Other firms will publish quotes to buy and sell securities and are known as *market makers*. Most firms service retail customers, but some specialize in dealing solely with institutional investors.

There are three types of broker-dealer firms on the exam.

Carrying firms (clearing firms)

A **carrying firm** carries customer accounts and accepts funds and securities from customers. Carrying firms and clearing firms typically rank among the larger BDs. They have the capability to do trade executions, clear and settle transactions, take custody of customer funds and securities, and handle all back-office tasks, such as sending trade confirmations and statements.

A firm carrying customer funds and securities clearly has a line of business that is inherently risky, and it is required to maintain levels of net capital higher than that of firms that do not accept custody of funds or securities.

 TAKE NOTE

Carrying firms must segregate (hold separately) customer funds and securities held in their custody from the firm's capital and securities. They may not comingle the firm's assets with client assets.

Fully disclosed (introducing) firms

A **fully disclosed firm**, or **introducing BD**, is one that introduces its customers to a clearing firm. The clearing firm holds funds and securities of the introducing firm's customers and performs related functions, such as sending confirmations and statements for its correspondent firms. Essentially, the clearing firm acts as the introducing firm's back office. Because the risk associated with holding customer funds and securities is not present, net capital requirements are lower for introducing BDs than they are for self-clearing or carrying BDs.

TAKE NOTE

Introducing firms may take orders from customers and pass those orders to a fully disclosed firm for execution. However, an introducing firm does have the ability to execute trades for its customers (and often do), but the settlement (clearing) of the trade falls to the carrying firm.

EXAMPLE

Firms sometimes called full-service firms are carrying firms or clearing firms that clear their own transactions. Smaller, regional BDs are typically introducing firms or fully disclosed firms that introduce their transactions to larger carrying firms to clear their transactions. In other words, firms such as Merrill Lynch, in addition to clearing their own transactions, may accept transactions from other smaller, fully disclosed firms—and in so doing so, act as the smaller firms' clearing firm.

Prime brokers

To understand a prime broker's role, you must first understand what a prime account is. This type of account allows a customer—generally, an institution—to select one member firm (the prime broker) to provide custody and other services, while other firms—called executing brokers—handle all trades placed by the customer.

To open a prime brokerage account for a customer, a member (the prime broker) must sign an agreement with the customer, spelling out the terms of the agreement, as well as names of all executing brokers the customer has contracted with. The prime broker will then enter into written agreements with each executing broker named by the customer. The customer receives trade confirmations and account statements from the prime broker, who facilitates the clearance and settlement of the securities transactions. Responsibility for compliance of certain trading rules rests with the executing brokers.

The key advantage of a prime brokerage account is that it usually provides a client with the ability to trade with multiple brokerage houses while maintaining a centralized master account with all of the client's cash and securities. A prime brokerage account often includes a list of specialized services, such as securities lending, margin financing, trade processing, cash management, and operational support. Prime brokerage accounts are likely to be offered to a BD's more active trading clients, such as hedge funds, who may require a number of executing broker outlets to conduct their transactions and who can benefit by having margin requirements that are netted across all of the prime broker's positions.

TEST TOPIC ALERT

Broker-dealers make money from processing transactions. A BD may act as a broker or as a dealer on a transaction, but may never be both on the same transaction.

Broker (Agent/Agency)	Dealer (Principal/market maker)
Trade on behalf of customers	Trade with customers from own inventory
Charge commission	Maintain inventory
	Profit on spread (markup and markdown)

Remember: A BD is both a broker and a dealer, but may not act in both capacities on the same transactions.

Transfer agents

The transfer and registration of stock certificates are two distinct functions that, by law, cannot be performed by a single person or department operating within the same institution. Issuers typically use commercial banks and trust companies to handle these functions.

The transfer agent for a corporation is responsible for

- ensuring that its securities are issued in the correct owner's name;
- canceling old and issuing new certificates;
- maintaining records of ownership; and
- handling problems relating to lost, stolen, or destroyed certificates.

Registrars

The registrar is always a separate firm than the issuer or a transfer agent. Registrars are licensed by the states and provide audit and oversight services for the transfer agents. The transfer agent maintains a count of the total number of shares of a company that are authorized and outstanding.

Depositories and clearing corporations

A clearing agency is an intermediary between the buy and the sell sides of a transaction. The clearing agency receives and delivers payments and securities on behalf of both parties. Any organization that fulfills this function, including a securities depository, is considered a clearing agency. Conceptually, this is similar to the way a bank clears checks between two parties.

In addition to BDs, commercial banks can act as clearing agencies and depositories, as well as corporations that are set up for the purpose of clearing securities transactions and taking custody of funds and securities. The Depository Trust & Clearing Corporation (DTCC) is the world's largest securities depository. It provides custody services for virtually all securities *except* those subject to transfer or ownership restrictions (restricted securities).

TAKE NOTE

The DTCC is a member of the Federal Reserve System and is not in the retail banking business (one can't open a savings or checking account there). The DTCC provides automated clearing and settlement services in book-entry format to banks and BDs for stock and bond trades and employs a continuous net settlement (CNS) system. The DTCC and its subsidiaries also function as a central securities depository by providing custody and safekeeping services in more than 60 countries worldwide.

Another is the Options Clearing Corporation (OCC). The OCC is the clearing agent for listed options contracts—that is, those listed for trading on U.S. options exchanges. Its primary functions are to standardize, guarantee the performance of, and issue option contracts. The OCC determines when new option contracts should be offered to the market on an underlying security. The OCC also designates the contract specifications, such as strike prices and expiration months. These standardized features for options help to maintain uniformity and liquidity in the marketplace.

LO 8.d Differentiate exchanges and the OTC market.

Trading in the secondary markets takes place on either an exchange (listed) or in the OTC market (nonlisted). The Nasdaq system tracks and provides trading for the largest OTC-traded companies. It is important to note that securities that trade on Nasdaq are considered listed.

Exchanges

One of the defining characteristics of exchanges is that they have a physical location, often called a floor. This is not as universally true as it was in the past, but it is still a point of difference from the OTC market. Members (not employees) of the exchanges transact business (trades) on the floor of the exchange.

The exchanges are sometimes called **double-auction markets** because both buyers and sellers call out their best bids and offers in an attempt to transact business at the best possible price.

The members of the exchange are as follows.

Designated market maker

The DMM (sometimes called a specialist) is the member that acts as the dealer on the floor for a specific security. The DMM maintains an inventory of the security and guarantees liquidity. The DMM is responsible for maintaining a "fair and orderly" market in the assigned security.

Floor broker

Floor brokers represent their firms and their firm's clients on the floor. If your customer places a trade that will execute on an exchange, a floor broker will handle it.

Two-dollar broker

If the floor brokers become overwhelmed by trades, they enlist the services of the $2 brokers. These members place trades for the floor brokers and receive a fee for performing the service.

Floor traders

The floor traders (also registered floor traders, FTs, or RFTs) are members that buy and sell on the floor for their firm's accounts (not outside customers). They help maintain liquidity on the exchange.

TEST TOPIC ALERT

Trading on an exchange happens between the members, not employees. Employees on an exchange support the exchange and its members, but are not involved in trading.

To establish the best bid, a buying broker-dealer must initiate a bid at least $0.01 higher than the current best bid. The best offer by a selling broker-dealer must be at least $0.01 lower than the current best offer.

EXAMPLE

A quote might look like this:

Last	Bid	Ask	Size
$46.71	$46.66	$46.74	30 × 14

Quotes are a bid and an ask (sometimes called an offer). The *bid* is the price that a *seller* would receive for his security. The *ask* is the price a *buyer* would have to pay to buy that security. The bid is always lower than the ask. The *last* is the last price a trade took place. The size (in 100s) represents the number of shares available on a given side of the market.

In the example, the last trade was at $46.71. Currently, there is demand for up to 3,000 shares at a price of $46.66. There are people willing to sell up to 1,400 shares at $46.74.

TAKE NOTE

There are over a dozen registered exchanges in the United States. Though the rules vary, they perform trades in much the same fashion. The test uses the New York Stock Exchange (NYSE) as the model for exchanges.

The over-the-counter market (OTC)

The over-the-counter market trades unlisted stocks, as well as most bonds, including municipals and treasury debt that trades in the secondary markets.

TAKE NOTE

Most corporate debt issues trade OTC. There is a small number of corporate debt issues that trade on an exchange, but that has not been a test topic.

OTC trading occurs between market makers in a decentralized electronic market. There is no "floor" in the OTC market. A market maker is a broker-dealer that maintains an inventory in a given security and buys and sells the security throughout the day. The OTC market maker's function is very similar to the DMM on the exchanges. However, in the OTC market, there are multiple market makers dealing in the same security and competing to attract orders from BDs.

When a customer places an order with a broker to purchase an OTC security, the broker chooses a market maker (called a dealer, if it is a debt security) to complete the trade. The broker, who represents the client, chooses a market maker to get the customer a fair price.

When a customer *sells* a security in the OTC market, the customer is selling to a dealer (with the assistance of the broker) at the *bid* price. So, that means that the dealer is purchasing at the *bid* from the customer.

A customer that *buys* a security in the OTC market is buying from a dealer (with the assistance of the broker) at the *ask* price. So, that means that the dealer is selling at the *ask* to the customer.

The difference between the *bid* and the *ask* is the *spread*, and it represents the market maker's income.

Quotes in the OTC market represent the highest *bid* and lowest *ask* posted in the system.

KNOWLEDGE CHECK

1. When a broker-dealer maintains an inventory in a particular stock and trades that stock in the OTC market, it is acting as
   A. an agent.
   B. a market maker.
   C. a broker.
   D. an underwriter.

2. To fill a customer buy order OTC, your broker requests a quote from a market maker. That dealer responds, "15 bid, ask 15¼". If the trade order is entered, the market maker must
   A. sell the shares for $15.
   B. buy the shares for $15.
   C. sell the shares for $15.25.
   D. buy the shares for $15.25.

3. All of the following are true for a designated market maker **except**
   A. is a member of an exchange.
   B. is charged with maintaining a fair and orderly market.
   C. maintains an inventory of the assigned stock.
   D. guarantees the customer will get a profitable trade.

Answers

1. **B** A market maker is a dealer in the OTC market that maintains an inventory in a stock and provides liquidity for customers seeking to buy and sell the security. LO 8.c

2. **C** This is an order to *buy*, so the market maker is selling. The customer sells at the *bid* price. With this quote, the market maker is committing to selling at the bid price of $15.25. LO 8.d

3. **D** Nobody can guarantee a profit in securities trading. A DMM is an exchange member that maintains an inventory in a stock, provides liquidity, and is responsible for maintaining a fair and orderly market in its assigned securities. LO 8.d

UNIT
9

The Government Regulators

LEARNING OBJECTIVES

When you have completed this unit, you will be able to accomplish the following.

› LO 9.a   Define the role and authority of the Securities Exchange Commission.
› LO 9.b   Name the branches of the Treasury that have regulatory authority over the securities industry.
› LO 9.c   Recall the role of the Federal Reserve Bank.
› LO 9.d   Recall the purpose of the Securities Investor Protection Corporation.
› LO 9.e   Determine the protection provided by the FDIC.
› LO 9.f   Define the state administrators and NASAA.

INTRODUCTION

The securities industry is heavily regulated. Following the First World War, the United States began to knit together, becoming less a simple union of separate states and more a single nation. It became clear in the years after the war that the nation needed federal rules on how capital markets functioned. The stock market crash of 1929 caused significant government response to the functioning of the securities business. The government took an active interest in implementing legislation to protect the public and correct abusive practices by industry practitioners.

This unit presents an overview of the major pieces of federal legislation, the federal regulators, and state securities law. It is important to know the general boundaries of these rules and regulations for success on the exam.

LESSON 9.1: THE SEC AND THE TREASURY

LO 9.a Define the role and authority of the Securities Exchange Commission.

The Securities and Exchange Commission (SEC)

Created under the Securities Exchange Act of 1934, the **Securities and Exchange Commission** (SEC) is the securities industry's primary regulatory body. BDs that transact securities business with customers or with other BDs must apply and receive registration from the SEC. Additionally, the SEC regulates all exchanges and trading markets. The SEC also has regulatory authority over licensing of securities representatives, a role it has delegated to FINRA. Securities information providers (SIPs) also fall under the SEC's regulatory authority.

BDs must comply with SEC rules and regulations when conducting business. A BD that does not comply is subject to

■ censure;

■ limits on activities, functions, or operations;

■ suspension of its registration (or one of its associated person's license to do business);

■ revocation of registration; and/or

■ a fine.

Other issues covered by the Securities Exchange Act of 1934

The act is concerned with the secondary markets. It is designed to provide a fair market place for all investors. It was written in conjunction with the Securities Act of 1933.

Some additional areas that fall under the 1934 act are

■ regulation of insider transactions, short sales, and proxies;

■ regulation of client accounts;

■ a customer protection rule;

■ a net capital rule and financial responsibility for broker-dealers; and

■ reporting requirements for issuers (e.g., annual reports).

TAKE NOTE

Although a BD must register with the SEC, the BD may not claim that this registration in anyway implies that the SEC has passed upon or approved the BD's financial standing, business, or conduct. Any such claim or statement is misrepresentation.

LO 9.b Name the branches of the Treasury that have regulatory authority over the securities industry.

Besides the SEC, several other branches of the U.S. Treasury have some regulatory authority over the securities industry.

Financial Crimes Enforcement Network (FinCEN)

The mission of the Financial Crimes Enforcement Network is to safeguard the financial system from illicit use, to combat money laundering, and to promote national security through the collection, analysis, and dissemination of financial intelligence. Most financial services companies are required to report suspicious or unusual activity to FinCEN.

Internal Revenue Service (IRS)

The IRS is the primary tax enforcement agency of the federal government. In that role, they have significant power to investigate potential tax evasion. As part of licensing, most financial services companies (including BDs) are required to provide the IRS with customer and firm information on demand. The IRS does not make tax law, but its enforcement of the law is seen as a vital national interest.

Office of the Comptroller of the Currency

The Comptroller supervises nearly 1,400 national banks, federal savings associations, and federal branches and agencies of foreign banks operating in the United States. The mission of the Comptroller is to ensure that national banks and federal savings associations operate in a safe and sound manner, provide fair access to financial services, treat customers fairly, and comply with applicable laws and regulations.

The comptroller also serves as a director of the Federal Deposit Insurance Corporation and member of the Financial Stability Oversight Council and the Federal Financial Institutions Examination Council.

TEST TOPIC ALERT

On the exam, the Office of the Comptroller of the Currency will either use the full name, or possibly Comptroller of the Currency. If you see the abbreviation OCC, that is the Options Clearing Corporation, a self-regulator discussed in a later unit. Don't get them mixed up.

Unit 9

TAKE NOTE

Here is a list of the major federal legislative acts governing the securities industry.

Year	Which Act?	What's the Act's Purpose?
1933	Securities Act of 1933	■ Governs the new issuance (primary) market, which involves the money-raising activities of issuers ■ Requires issuers to register their securities when selling to the public
1934	Securities Exchange Act of 1934	■ Governs trading markets for existing securities and registration requirements of BDs, BD employees, and exchanges
1940	Investment Company Act of 1940	■ Governs the regulation of packaged products such as mutual funds, closed-end funds, and unit investment trusts
1940	Investment Advisers Act of 1940	■ Governs the regulation of firms that earn fees for providing investment advice
1970	Securities Investor Protection Act of 1970 (SIPA)	■ Covers the protection thresholds for customers in the event of a BD's bankruptcy
1988	Insider Trading and Securities Fraud Enforcement Act of 1988	■ Defines penalties for the misuse of material, nonpublic information by both firms and individuals
2001	The USA PATRIOT Act (Partially based on the Bank Secrecy Act of 1970)	■ Covers anti-money laundering (AML) policies and procedures that must be followed by financial firms

KNOWLEDGE CHECK

1. The SEC has the power to do all of the following **except**
   A. revoke a registration.
   B. arrest those in violation of the regulations.
   C. impose fines.
   D. limit a firm's activity.

2. The SEC is the primary federal securities industry regulator in the United States. It was created by
   A. the Securities Act of 1933.
   B. the Securities Exchange Act of 1934.
   C. the Investment Advisers Act of 1940.
   D. the Uniform Securities Act.

3. Financial activities and large cash transactions are reported to which of the following federal agencies?
   A. SEC
   B. OCC
   C. Federal Reserve
   D. FinCEN

Answers

1. **B** The SEC may investigate suspected violations, impose fines, limit a firm's activities, and revoke or suspend registrations. It does not have the authority to arrest those suspected of criminal activity. If the SEC uncovers illegal activity, it refers the case to the Justice Department for that level of law enforcement activity. LO 9.a

2. **B** The SEC was created by the Securities Exchange Act of 1934. The 1933 act does give oversight of the primary markets to the SEC, but the commission itself was not formed until the 1934 act passed. The Investment Advisers Act governs IAs. The USA is a template for state securities laws. LO 9.a

3. **D** FinCEN is the intelligence agency within the federal government that tracks suspicious financial activities. It both collects from and provides information to the other federal agencies, such as the Federal Reserve Board (FRB) and the SEC. The OCC is the Options Clearing Corporation. LO 9.b

LESSON 9.2: THE FEDERAL RESERVE BOARD

LO 9.c Recall the role of the Federal Reserve Bank.

The Federal Reserve Board (FRB)

The Federal Reserve Act of 1913 established the Federal Reserve System as the central bank of the United States to provide the nation with a safer, more flexible, and more stable monetary and financial system. The law sets out the purposes, structure, and functions of the system, as well as outlines aspects of its operations and accountability.

The **Federal Reserve Board** (FRB) consists of 12 regional Federal Reserve Banks and hundreds of national and state banks that belong to the system. The FRB determines monetary policy and takes actions to implement its policies. Because the FRB (through its actions) determines how much money is available for businesses and consumers to spend, its decisions are a critical aspect of the U.S. economy. We will cover the FRB in more detail in a later unit.

LESSON 9.3: SIPC, FDIC, AND NASAA

LO 9.d Recall the purpose of the Securities Investor Protection Corporation.

The Securities Investors Protection Corporation (SIPC)

The **Securities Investor Protection Corporation** (SIPC) was created under the **Securities Investor Protection Act of 1970**. The corporation is a nonprofit membership organization. SIPC members pay assessments into a general insurance fund that is used to meet customer claims in the event of a BD bankruptcy.

TAKE NOTE

All BDs registered with the SEC must be SIPC members except

- banks that deal exclusively in municipal securities;

- firms that deal exclusively in U.S. government securities; and

- firms that deal exclusively in redeemable investment company securities.

If the SEC or any SRO finds indications that a BD is in financial difficulty, SIPC will be notified immediately. If SIPC determines that the member has failed or is in imminent danger of failing, it may petition a federal court to take action by appointing a trustee to liquidate the firm and protect its customers. A customer can be broadly defined as anyone who has cash or securities in the possession of a BD.

The court, upon receipt of SIPC's petition, will issue a protective decree if the BD is, in fact, insolvent and will then promptly appoint a trustee for the liquidation of the BD's business.

Once a trustee has been appointed, the member firm is prohibited from engaging in business as a BD. It also is prohibited from attempting to conceal assets, file false statements, or alter securities records to defraud the trustee or SIPC.

SIPC coverage and disclosures

The basic coverage under SIPC is no more than $500,000 per separate customer, not per separate account. Of that $500,000 total, SIPC covers no more than $250,000 in cash. How an account is titled will determine if it represents a separate customer. See Figure 9.1.

Figure 9.1: Sample SIPC Customer Coverage Limits

Examples of Customer Coverage Limits	
John Doe—cash account John Doe—margin account	1 customer = $500,000 coverage
John and Mary Doe—joint account	1 customer = $500,000 coverage
John Doe as custodian for Jane Doe	1 customer = $500,000 coverage

 TAKE NOTE

Cash and margin accounts for the same customer are combined for the purposes of determining SIPC coverage. However, only the equity in a margin account is covered, not the full market value.

If a BD fails, any customer with claims in excess of SIPC coverage limits becomes a general creditor of the BD for the uncovered amount. It should also be noted here that commodities and commodities futures contracts are not covered by SIPC, nor are futures contracts or losses related to currencies, because they are not considered securities.

Regarding disclosures, BDs must include their SIPC membership on all advertising but may not imply that SIPC coverage is more than it actually is or that its benefits are unique to only that BD. The term *SIPC* may not appear larger than the firm's own name. Also, all member firms must post a sign on their premises that indicates SIPC membership.

In addition, SIPC members must provide written disclosure to customers that they may obtain information about SIPC, including the SIPC brochure, by contacting SIPC. This disclosure must be made to new customers at the time an account is opened and to all customers at least once each year thereafter.

LO 9.e Determine the protection provided by the FDIC.

The Federal Deposit Insurance Corporation (FDIC)

Created during the Great Depression of the 1930s in response to widespread bank failures and massive losses to bank customers, the **Federal Deposit Insurance Corporation** (FDIC) is an independent agency of the U.S. federal government that preserves public confidence in the banking system by insuring deposits. The funds for the agency are provided in the same way as the funds for a private insurance company; premiums are paid by all participating institutions.

In the event of the failure of a member financial institution, the FDIC may do any of several things. Usually, customer deposits and loans of the failed institution are sold to another institution, and in this way, the depositors become customers of the new institution.

The FDIC provides deposit insurance guaranteeing the safety of a depositor's accounts in member banks up to $250,000 for each deposit ownership category in each insured bank.

EXAMPLE

Gabriel Jones has $200,000 deposited with an FDIC member bank. Gabriel and Lisa Jones have $450,000 deposited in a joint account at the same bank. Titled differently, each of these accounts is recognized as a separate account and each is entitled to FDIC insurance. If the bank were to fail, Gabriel's individual account would be covered in full, and the Jones's joint account would be covered up to $450,000 ($225,000 for Gabe and $225,000 for Lisa).

The FDIC covers the traditional types of bank deposit accounts, including checking and savings accounts, money market deposit accounts and certificates of deposit (CDs), and self-directed IRA accounts. Investment products that are not deposits, such as mutual funds, annuities, life insurance policies, and stocks and bonds, are not covered by FDIC deposit insurance.

TEST TOPIC ALERT

You may have noticed how the FDIC and the SIPC account coverage is different. The FDIC ownership categories are per owner per account (a joint account with two owners would be covered up to $250,000 per owner). The SIPC covers per separate account. Each account, no matter how many people are on the account, is covered up to the $500,000. However, accounts with differing registrations, say an individual account, a joint account, and an IRA, would each be covered up to $500,000, even though the same person owns all three accounts.

LO 9.f Define the state administrators and NASAA.

The state administrators

The Uniform Securities Act (1956) is a template for state securities laws. The federal government requests that the states adopt the template in order to create uniform securities laws at the state level. All the states have adopted the USA, a few with some minor variations.

One of the provisions of the USA is that each state have a state securities administrator (the administrator). The method of selection, whether by appointment or election, is left to the states. The official title of the administrator varies from state to state, but they are known as the administrators. Administrators have significant authority within their states regarding the registration of securities, broker-dealers, investment advisers, and representatives.

North American Securities Administrators Association

The North American Securities Administrators Association (NASAA) represents state and provincial securities regulators in the United States, Canada, and Mexico. NASAA has no specific regulatory authority, but it is still a major force in state securities regulations. The association often produces guidelines that the state administrators use in the enforcement of state regulations. Note that NASAA also has members that are the equivalent to state administrators from Canada and Mexico.

KNOWLEDGE CHECK

These questions apply to material covered in Lesson 9.2 and Lesson 9.3.

1. The Federal Reserve Board was established by
   A. the Securities Act of 1933.
   B. the Uniform Securities Act.
   C. the Federal Reserve Act of 1913.
   D. the Trust Indenture Act.

2. The FDIC insures customer assets held at
   A. banks.
   B. broker-dealers.
   C. depositary trusts,
   D. investment advisers,

3. In order to register a broker-dealer firm to do business in a state, you would register with
   A. the SEC.
   B. the administrator.
   C. NASAA.
   D. FINRA.

Answers

1. **C** The Federal Reserve Board was established by the Federal Reserve Act in 1913. LO 9.c

2. **A** The Federal Deposit Insurance Corporation (FDIC) insures bank deposits. Assets held at broker-dealers are covered by the Securities Investor Protection Corporation (SIPC). Investment advisers do not typically hold deposits. How the depository trusts insure assets is beyond the scope of this exam. LO 9.e

3. **B** Registration of broker-dealers at the state level is under the authority of each state's administrators. Broker-dealers do register at the federal level with the Securities and Exchange Commission (SEC) and join Financial Industry Regulatory Authority (FINRA), but the question specifies state registration. The North American Securities Administrators Association (NASAA) is not a regulator. LO 9.f

UNIT
10

The Self-Regulatory Organizations

LEARNING OBJECTIVES

When you have completed this unit, you will be able to accomplish the following.

› LO 10.a Recall the scope of authority of the Financial Industry Regulatory Authority.
› LO 10.b Recall the Municipal Securities Rulemaking Board's scope of authority and enforcement powers.
› LO 10.c Recognize the Exchange's regulatory authority.

INTRODUCTION

The securities industry is also regulated by a number of self-regulatory organizations, the foremost of which is the Financial Industry Regulatory Authority (FINRA). The purpose of the self-regulators is just that, for the industry to take a hand at policing itself. The idea behind these organizations is that the industry is in the best position to understand what rules are needed to protect the public while still allowing for robust and effective capital markets.

LESSON 10.1: FINANCIAL INDUSTRY REGULATORY AUTHORITY

LO 10.a Recall the scope of authority of the Financial Industry Regulatory Authority.

The Financial Industry Regulatory Authority (FINRA)

The **Financial Industry Regulatory Authority** (FINRA) regulates all matters related to investment banking (securities underwriting), trading in the over-the-counter (OTC) market, trading in exchange-listed securities, and the conduct of FINRA member firms and associated persons.

FINRA's purpose and objectives are to

- promote the investment banking and securities business, standardize principles and practices, promote high standards of commercial honor, and encourage the observance of federal and state securities laws;

- provide a medium for communication among its members and between its members, the government, and other agencies;

- adopt, administer, and enforce rules designed to prevent fraudulent and manipulative practices, as well as to promote just and equitable principles of trade; and

- promote self-discipline among members and investigate and resolve grievances between the public and members and between members.

FINRA has numerous rules designed to protect the integrity of securities markets. These can be broken down into four sections.

- **Conduct Rules** establish the relationship between firms and their customers. These rules cover areas such as fair dealing with customers, compensation-related issues, standards for communications, and various sales practice violations. Violations of the Conduct Rules are serious violations.

- The **Code of Procedure** (COP) covers the enforcement of FINRA rules and details the punishment of members who violate the Conduct Rules. FINRA's Department of Enforcement (DOE) investigates suspected violations. Such investigations normally arise out of a FINRA audit or, more frequently, a customer complaint. The DOE will hold a hearing to determine the outcome of any violation. FINRA may do any of the following to a member firm or an associated person upon a finding of a violation:

  - Suspend, expel, or bar from membership

  - Impose fines

  - Censure

  - Any other action deemed appropriate

  Note that FINRA does not have arrest powers, but it is certainly able to refer issues to law enforcement. COP decisions may be appealable to the National Adjudicatory Council (a FINRA division), then to the SEC, and from there to the appellate courts.

- **Uniform Practice Code** (UPC) rules cover technical aspects of trading and payment for securities transactions. Examples of UPC issues include good delivery of securities, the payment procedures for dividends on common stocks, and interest on bonds. Each of these topics will be discussed later in the manual.

- The **Code of Arbitration** (COA) is a FINRA-run dispute resolution process to settle monetary disputes. The goal of the COA is to provide a faster and cheaper resolution versus going through the traditional court system. COA decisions are final and binding.

TAKE NOTE

If a customer is involved in a monetary dispute with a BD, the customer must agree to arbitration, though such an agreement may have been made prospectively (before the incident). Most new account forms include a predispute arbitration agreement.

Broker-dealer firms apply for membership to FINRA, and, if granted, they agree to abide by FINRA's rules and regulations. These are often called member firms. Those who work for FINRA firms also agree to FINRA rules; these people are called associates. A FINRA member firm may only do business with another FINRA member firm unless it meets one of the exceptions. Here are a couple of the more common exceptions:

- A bank in the underwriting of a municipal issue
- A foreign firm that is a member of its nation's FINRA equivalent

FINRA has been delegated authority by the SEC to administer qualification tests for associates of member firms and investment advisers.

LESSON 10.2: OTHER SROs

LO 10.b Recall the Municipal Securities Rulemaking Boards scope of authority and enforcement powers.

The Municipal Securities Rulemaking Board (MSRB)

The **Municipal Securities Rulemaking Board** (MSRB) is the primary industry (SRO) regulator for underwriting and trading of state and municipal securities. The MSRB writes the rules but does not have enforcement powers—it depends on other regulators for the enforcement of its rules. In this light, it should be noted that it has no regulatory power over the municipalities that issue municipal securities.

MSRB rules are enforced on the banking industry primarily through the comptroller of the currency, The Federal Reserve, and the FDIC.

MSRB rules on securities firms are enforced primarily by the SEC and FINRA.

TAKE NOTE

MSRB creates the rules for municipal securities, not just municipal debt. 529 plans and ABLE accounts are examples of non-debt municipal securities covered by the MSRB.

EXAMPLE

The City of New Orleans is issuing municipal bonds. To do so, it is using the services of several BDs acting as underwriters (syndicate members) to sell the new bonds. It's important to recognize that the MSRB has no enforcement power regarding its municipal securities rules. Those rules will be enforced by FINRA. FINRA will ensure that the BDs underwriting these new bonds abide by all securities rules and regulations (including those of the MSRB) regarding the sale of new securities to the public.

LO 10.c Recognize the Exchange's regulatory authority.

The exchanges are also regulators, in addition to their role as a market center. The exchanges regulate trading activity that occurs on the exchange and have some authority over the securities that are listed on the exchange, as well as the issuers of those securities.

The exchanges have the power to remove a listed security (delisting), as well as suspending trading on a listed security. The NYSE is the model used for this exam.

KNOWLEDGE CHECK

These questions apply to material covered in Lesson 10.1 and Lesson 10.2.

1. The city of Los Angeles is issuing 20-year GO bonds at 8%. MSRB rules regarding this underwriting may be enforced by all of the following regulators **except**
    A. FINRA.
    B. SEC.
    C. MSRB.
    D. the comptroller of the currency.

2. Registered representative Thomas Jones has been found by a DOE hearing to have violated the Code of Procedure. He believes that the hearing panel did not have all the facts and wants to appeal the ruling. His appeal goes to
    A. the SEC.
    B. the DOE.
    C. the NAC.
    D. the arbitration panel.

3. An arbitration panel has found that Seacoast Securities owes $7,500 to its customer Mr. Garcia. Seacoast does not believe that the panel ruled correctly and desires to appeal the ruling. Such an appeal
    A. is not possible; there is no appeal to an arbitration award.
    B. is filed with the NAC.
    C. is filed with the SEC.
    D. is filed with the courts.

Answers

1. **C**   MSRB has no enforcement division. MSRB rules are enforced by other regulators like the SEC, FINRA, and the Comptroller. LO 10.b

2. **C**   DOE rulings may be appealed: First to the National Adjudicatory Council (NAC), then to the SEC, then to the courts.

3. **A**   There is no appeal to an arbitration finding. Arbitration is final and binding.

UNIT 11

LEARNING OBJECTIVES

When you have completed this unit, you will be able to accomplish the following.

> LO 11.a Define GDP, CPI, and GNP.
> LO 11.b Classify other indicators as leading, coincident, or lagging indicators.
> LO 11.c Define price movement indicators (e.g., inflation, deflation, stagnation, and hyperinflation).

INTRODUCTION

Economics is the study of supply and demand. When people want to buy an item that is in short supply, the item's price rises. When people do not want to buy an item that is in plentiful supply, the price declines. This simple notion, the foundation of all economic study, is true for bread, shoes, cars, clothes, stocks, bonds, and money. Several economic indicators are used to get the "pulse" of the economy. In this unit, we discuss the most widely used of the economic indicators.

LESSON 11.1: ECONOMIC INDICATORS

LO 11.a Define GDP, CPI, and GNP

Gross domestic product (GDP)

A nation's annual economic output—all the goods and services produced within the nation— is known as its **gross domestic product (GDP)**. The United States' GDP includes personal consumption, government spending, gross private investment, foreign investment, and net exports. GDP counts all activity that occurs within the confines of the nation's boundaries, even if the activity is generated by a foreign entity.

In the United States, GDP figures are released quarterly by the Commerce Department. A positive figure indicates that the economy is growing. A negative figure indicates that the economy is contracting.

Consumer Price Index (CPI)

The most prominent measure of general price changes is the **Consumer Price Index (CPI)**. The CPI measures the rate of increase or decrease in a broad range of consumer prices, such as food, housing, transportation, medical care, clothing, electricity, entertainment, and services. The CPI is computed each month.

When comparing the economic output (GDP) of one period with that of another, analysts use the CPI to account for changes in the costs of goods to adjust for inflation (or deflation). This way the GDP figures reflect actual growth. This is called real GDP, and it is a *constant dollar* (inflation adjusted) measurement. The term *constant dollar measurement* is sometime used for CPI.

Gross national product (GNP)

GNP is very similar to GDP but is based not on the activity that occurs within the country but on the activity of the citizens and entities of the nation, wherever it may occur. This figure is also published by the Commerce Department on a quarterly basis. GNP sees significantly less use (outside of economists) than GDP.

EXAMPLE

Foreign Motor Corporation, based in Japan, builds a new auto assembly line in Texas. This economic activity would add to GDP (it was built in the United States), but it would not add to GNP because the company is not a U.S. entity.

If the Dearborn Motor Corporation, based in Michigan, builds a new auto plant in Germany, that would add to GNP (the company is a U.S. company) but would not add to GDP (the activity happened outside the United States).

LO 11.b Classify other indicators as leading, coincident, or lagging indicators.

There are several other economic indicators. These are broadly classed by when they change direction in relationship to the overall economy: leading, coincident, or lagging indicators.

Leading economic indicators

Leading indicators are those indicators that tend to change direction ahead of the overall economy. The change of direction may lead the economy by a very long time frame (months) to very short (weeks), but they have proven to be reliable. Here is a list of the leading indicators that may appear on the exam:

- Money supply (M2)
- Building permits (housing starts)
- Average weekly initial claims for state unemployment compensation
- Average work week in manufacturing
- New orders for consumer goods

- Machine tool orders
- Changes in inventories of durable goods
- Changes in sensitive materials prices
- Stock prices
- Changes in business and consumer borrowing

Coincident economic indicators

Coincident indicators change direction along with the economy as a whole. Because these indicators are often published after the time period has passed, they are good confirmation tools of the leading indicators. Here is a list of coincident indicators that may appear on the exam:

- Number of hours worked (as a proxy for personal income)
- Employment levels
- Nonagricultural employment
- Personal income
- Industrial production
- Manufacturing and trade sales
- GDP

Lagging economic indicators

Lagging indicators are those indicators that change after the economy has begun a new trend but serve as confirmation of the new trend. Lagging indicators help analysts differentiate long-term trends from short-term reversals that occur in any trend. Lagging indicators that may appear on the exam include the following:

- Corporate profits
- Average duration of unemployment
- Labor cost per unit of output (manufacturing)
- Ratio of inventories to sales
- Commercial and industrial loans outstanding
- Ratio of consumer installment credit to personal income

LO 11.c Define price movement indicators (e.g., inflation, deflation, stagnation, and hyperinflation).

The indicator used to measure price movements is CPI. There are different definitions of what a particular set of movements are called. Below are the most common definitions.

Inflation

Inflation is a general increase in prices. Mild inflation can encourage economic growth because gradually increasing prices tend to stimulate business investments. High inflation reduces a dollar's buying power, which hurts the economy.

Deflation

Deflation is a general decline in prices. Deflation usually occurs during severe recessions when unemployment is on the rise.

Stagnation

Economic stagnation refers to prolonged periods of slow or little economic growth, accompanied by high unemployment.

Hyperinflation

In hyperinflation, the pace of inflation is extremely high and accelerating. This severely erodes the purchasing power of a currency. In hyperinflation, investors often move cash away from the nation and the currency experiencing it, worsening the devaluation of the currency. Hyperinflation is a very rare occurrence.

Stagflation

Stagflation is the term used to describe the unusual combination of inflation (a rise in prices) and high unemployment. This generally occurs when the economy isn't growing and there is a lack of consumer demand and business activity, but prices for goods are still rising. Note that inflation does not need to be high, just present, along with high unemployment.

 KNOWLEDGE CHECK

1. An economic environment with little or no economic growth, but where inflation is present, is best described as
    A. deflation.
    B. depression.
    C. Stagflation.
    D. Stagnation.

2. Which of the following would be a leading economic indicator?
    A. S&P 500 Index
    B. Industrial production
    C. Duration of unemployment
    D. Gross domestic product (GDP)

3. A measure of the change in economic activity that occurs over a given time frame within the boundaries of a nation is that nation's
    A. gross domestic product.
    B. gross national product.
    C. Consumer Price Index.
    D. industrial production.

Answers

1. **C**   The presence of inflation in an environment of high unemployment is stagflation. It is unusual and difficult to resolve. Deflation occurs when prices are dropping, and most likely occurs in a recession or a depression, along with high unemployment. Stagnation indicates a slow economy, often increasing unemployment, but with very little price movement. LO 11.c

2. **A**   The stock market, as measured by the S&P 500, is a leading indicator, usually in the three-to-six-month time frame. Industrial production and GDP are coincident indicators. Duration of unemployment is a lagging indicator. LO 11.b

3. **A**   The measure of activity within the boundaries of a nation is GDP. GNP is a measure of this activity by the citizens and entities of a nation. CPI measures inflation. Industrial production is a more limited measure of activity LO 11.a

UNIT 12

The Business Cycle

LEARNING OBJECTIVES

When you have completed this unit, you will be able to accomplish the following.

> LO 12. a Put the five phases of the business cycle in proper order.
> LO 12.b Define the five phases of the business cycle.
> LO 12.c Define recession and depression.
> LO 12.d Associate inflation with expansion.

INTRODUCTION

The economy fluctuates between growth and contraction in a regular cycle—the business cycle. Understanding the business cycle, and where we are in it, is part of providing good advice and recommendations to customers.

LESSON 12.1: THE BUSINESS CYCLE

LO 12.a Put the five phases of the business cycle in proper order.

TAKE NOTE

Some economists break the expansion phase into two separate phases, recovery and expansion. This creates a five-phase cycle. If you see recovery and expansion on the exam remember this:

■ Recovery is the period of growth from the trough to the prior peak.

■ Expansion is when the economy reaches the prior peak and continues to grow.

Business cycles go through four stages, or phases:

■ Expansion

■ Peak

■ Contraction

■ Trough

Figure 12.1: Four Stages, or Phases, of a Business Cycle

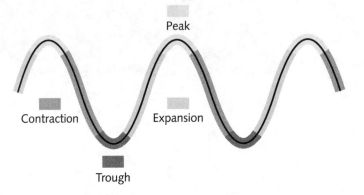

LO 12.b Define the four phases of the business cycle.

Expansion

Expansion in the business cycle tends to be characterized by

■ increased consumer demand for goods and services,

■ increases in industrial production,

■ rising stock prices,

■ rising property values, and

■ increasing GDP.

Peak or prosperity

A peak is characterized by

■ very low unemployment,

■ a slowdown in inflation,

■ a slowing of GDP, and

■ steady consumer demand.

Contraction

Downturns (contractions) in the business cycle tend to be characterized by

■ rising numbers of bankruptcies and bond defaults,

■ higher consumer debt,

■ falling stock prices,

- ▓ rising inventories (a sign of slackening consumer demand in hard times), and

- ▓ decreasing GDP.

Trough

A trough is characterized by

- ▓ high unemployment;

- ▓ flat GDP;

- ▓ low inflation; and

- ▓ low, but not decreasing, consumer demand.

LO 12.c Define recession and depression

Recession

When the economy enters an extended period of contraction that continues for six months or longer, it is called a recession. Recession may be mild (as occurred in the early 1990s) or severe (as in the Great Recession of 2008).

Depression

If a contraction continues for 18 months, it is now called a depression. This sort of a severe downturn is thankfully rare.

TAKE NOTE

These definitions of *recession* and *depression* are very simplistic. Economists today have significantly more accurate (and complex) methods of determining when we are in one of these economic downturns. However, the exam sticks to the simpler definitions. FINRA wants you to have a grasp of economics, not to be economists.

EXAMPLE

The recession of the early 1990s began in July of 1990 and lasted about eight months. GDP for the first three quarters of 1991 were –0.95%, –0.54%, and –0.10, respectively. This was seen as a mild recession.

The recession of 2009 began in the fourth quarter of 2008 with a GDP reading of –2.75%. The first three quarters of 2009, GDP readings were –3.29%, –3.92%, and –3.05%. This was called the Great Recession, and for good reason. It ended within two months of meeting our definition of a depression.

What about the depression? From 1930 through 1933, the economy contracted about 35% and unemployment peaked at 25%. Even the Great Recession was mild by comparison.

LO 12.d Associate inflation with expansion.

In normal economic cycles, we tend to see inflation be very low, or even deflation, when the economy is contracting. As the economy recovers, inflation increases but generally stays mild. A more serious inflation period is more common during the expansion phase of the economy. During an expansion, most of the existing productive capacity is already in use (all the workers are working and all the factories are producing). As demand increases, the production side has trouble increasing to meet the demand, and prices tend to rise.

KNOWLEDGE CHECK

1. Which state of the business cycle is characterized by rising consumer demand and higher wages?
    A. Contraction
    B. Expansion
    C. Recession
    D. Trough

2. Economic data shows that the gross domestic product (GDP) has been declining steadily over the past two quarters. This would suggest
    A. expansion.
    B. inflation.
    C. a depression.
    D. a recession.

3. Inflation is **most** commonly found during which phase of the business cycle?
    A. Expansion
    B. Peak
    C. Contraction
    D. Trough

Answers

1. **B** When both wages and consumer demand are increasing, you are in an expansion LO 12.b

2. **D** When the economy contracts for a period of 6 months (two quarters), it is likely sliding into a recession. If the recession goes on for 18 months, it becomes a depression. LO 12.c

3. **A** Inflation is most likely to occur when demand for goods is growing faster than supply of goods. Increasing demand is typical of an expansion. LO 12.d

UNIT
13

The Federal Reserve

LEARNING OBJECTIVES

When you have completed this unit, you will be able to accomplish the following.

> LO 13.a Define the purpose of the Federal Reserve.
> LO 13.b Define the measures of money supply and their use.
> LO 13.c Recall the active measures used by the Federal Reserve.
> LO 13.d Define the four prominent interest rates.

INTRODUCTION

Though we touched briefly on the role of the Federal Reserve Board earlier, in this unit, we review the purpose and tools of the Federal Reserve in more detail.

LESSON 13.1: THE FEDERAL RESERVE

LO 13.a Define the purpose of the Federal Reserve.

The Federal Reserve System is the central bank of the United States. It is sometimes called the Federal Reserve Bank, or simply the Fed. The system is directed by the Federal Reserve Board. The most common acronym on the exam is FRB. Though the FRB has several functions, the FRB's most important duty is twofold:

■ Conduct the nation's monetary policy to promote maximum employment.

■ Promote a stable price environment, keeping inflation under control.

Though the FRB's other duties are very important, they are all part of and support the two primary duties listed. They perform these functions by managing the money supply: the amount of cash available within the U.S. economy. This is called monetary policy.

TEST TOPIC ALERT

Milton Friedman, Ph.D. is considered the founder of monetarism (or monetarist) theory. Much of work of the Federal Reserve is based on his theories.

Increasing the money supply expands the economy and creates jobs, but if the economy expands too quickly (overheats), it may trigger high levels of inflation. High inflation is hard on the consumer, hurting the same people that a healthy economy helps.

In order to perform these duties the FRB has a number of tools at its disposal. Some of these tools are diagnostic tools (those that "read" the economy) and active (those that directly impact the economy). Another way to think of this is that diagnostic tools are like a ruler or a level, used to measure the economy. The active tools are a wrench, used to loosen or tighten the money supply.

LO 13.b Define the measures of money supply and their use.

One of the most important diagnostic tools of the FRB is the measures of money supply: M1, M2, and M3.

- M1 is the measure of the most readily available money to spend: cash (actual cash and coinage) and money in demand deposit accounts (DDAs), such as checking accounts. This is the money that is closest to being spent and turned into economic activity.

- M2 consists of M1 plus "consumer savings deposits"—those assets that are easily move to a DDA and spent. Among the "consumer savings deposits" are savings accounts, retail (non-negotiable) CDs, money market funds, and overnight repurchase agreements. Remember, M1 is also part of M2.

- M3 consists of M2 plus "large time deposits"—those assets that are a bit harder to move into a DDA and be spent. Examples include negotiable (jumbo) CDs and multiday repurchase agreements. Again, don't forget that M2 is part of M3, so by extension is M1 because it is part of M2.

Figure 13.1: Federal Reserve Board's Diagnostic Tools

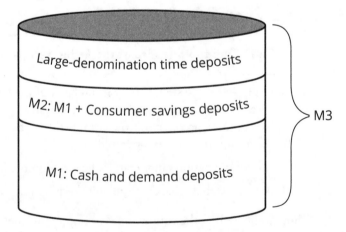

EXAMPLE

Seabird Airlines has money in a long-term CD that it is saving to purchase a new airliner. When the CD matures, Seabird will deposit the money into a checking account in preparation for purchasing the new plane. What effect will this have on the money supply? The funds are moved from M3 to M1, so M1 increases, but M3 does not change because the funds never left M3.

LO 13.c Recall the active measures used by the Federal Reserve.

In addition to its diagnostic tools, the FRB has several ways of influencing the money supply through active tools.

Federal open-market operations

The FRB, acting as an agent for the U.S. Treasury Department, influences the money supply by buying and selling U.S. government securities (Treasury bills, notes, and bonds) in the open market. These actions will expand or contract the money supply, depending on which they are doing (buying or selling). The **Federal Open Market Committee** (FOMC) meets regularly to direct the government's open-market operations.

When the Fed wants to expand (loosen) the money supply, it buys securities from banks. The securities come out of the economy, and money goes into the economy through the bank. The increase of reserves (cash) allows banks to make more loans and effectively lowers interest rates. By buying securities, the Fed pumps money into the banking system, expanding the money supply and reducing rates.

When the Fed wants to contract (tighten) the money supply, it sells securities to banks. Now, cash comes out of the respective banks (to pay for the securities) and the securities go in as each sale is charged against a bank's reserve (cash) balance. This reduces the bank's ability to lend money, which tightens credit and effectively raises interest rates. By selling securities, the Fed pulls money out of the system, contracting the money supply and increasing rates.

TEST TOPIC ALERT

The following list outlines the FRB's buying or selling of securities in the open market and its impact on the economy.

- *Buying*—Securities come out of the economy, and money goes in. The money supply goes up, interest rates go down, borrowing and spending for consumers is easier, and the economy expands.

- *Selling*—Securities go into the economy, and money comes out. The money supply goes down, interest rates go up, borrowing and spending for consumers becomes more difficult, and the economy contracts.

Regulation T

As part of the FRB's regulatory authority, the Fed set the minimum amount an investor must deposit when using credit to buy a security. Under Regulation T, the current initial deposit is 50% of the purchase price. If the FRB lowered the initial deposit requirement and allowed more borrowing, the extra cash available would likely raise stock prices. This would result in more merger activity, as well as investors using the additional wealth to make purchases, expanding the economy. Increasing the amount required at purchase (thus limiting credit) would have the opposite effect, slowing the economy. In practice. the Fed leaves Regulation T requirements as they are. The current 50% has been in place since 1974.

The discount rate

Banks that need additional capital to meet their reserve requirement may borrow money from the Federal Reserve System. This is often done through a repurchase agreement. In a repurchase agreement, the Fed holds some of the bank's assets (usually loans the bank holds) as collateral for a short-term loan, usually overnight, though some times longer. This increases the bank's cash reserves. The interest rate the Fed charges the bank is the discount rate. When you hear news stories about the Federal Reserve raising or lowering interest rates, it is the discount rate they are referring too. The discount rate is seen as the base rate for the nation. Raising the discount rate tends to lift interest rates throughout the economy; lowering the discount rate tends to cause rates to drop.

The reserve requirement

The reserve requirement is the amount a bank must maintain on deposit with the Federal Reserve. Reserves dropping below this number indicate that the bank may have insufficient cash to meet depositors' demands. Lowering this number frees up cash at the banks to fund loan activity, expanding the economy. Raising this number decreases the amount available for loans. Because changes in the reserve requirement have a dramatic impact throughout the banking system, hitting all the banks at once, the Fed rarely changes the reserve requirement.

LO 13.d Define the four prominent interest rates.

The cost of doing business is closely linked to the cost of money. The cost of money is called **interest**. In large measure, the supply and demand of money determines the rate of interest that must be paid to borrow it. When the money available for loans exceeds demand, interest rates fall; when the demand for money exceeds the supply, interest rates rise. The level of a specific interest rate can be tied to one or more benchmark rates, such as the federal funds rate, the discount rate, the prime rate, and the broker call loan rate. Let's look at each of these now.

Federal funds rate

The **federal funds rate** is the rate that the commercial money center banks charge each other for overnight loans of $1 million or more. It is considered a barometer of the direction of short-term interest rates, which fluctuate constantly and can be considered the most volatile rate in the economy.

Prime rate

The **prime rate** is the interest rate that large U.S. money center commercial banks charge their most creditworthy corporate borrowers for unsecured loans. Each bank sets its own prime rate, with larger banks generally setting a rate that other banks use or follow. Banks lower their prime rates when the FRB (or Fed) eases the money supply, and they raise rates when the Fed contracts the money supply.

Broker call loan rate

The **broker loan rate** is the interest rate that banks charge BDs on money they borrow to lend to margin account customers. Margin accounts allow customers to purchase securities without paying in full. The amount not paid is essentially loaned to the customer by banks and BDs. The broker loan rate is also known as the **call loan rate** or **call money rate**. The broker loan rate usually is a percentage point or so above other short-term rates. Broker call loans are callable on a 24-hour notice.

The discount rate

The **discount rate** (covered earlier in this unit) is the rate the Federal Reserve charges for short-term loans to member banks. The discount rate also indicates the direction of FRB monetary policy—a decreasing rate indicates an easing of FRB policy, and an increasing rate indicates a tightening of FRB policy.

TAKE NOTE

The **discount rate** is the only rate of these four set by a unit of the federal government. The other three are set by the bank that is making the loan.

EXAMPLE

If the FRB wants to ease its monetary policy to allow consumers to borrow more easily, it can lower the discount rate. This allows member banks to borrow from the FRB at a lower rate, which in turn allows consumers to borrow money at a lower rate from the member banks. Consumers' ability to borrow at lower interest rates helps to fuel or push the economy forward because they are now in a position to purchase more goods and services.

In Summary

Federal Reserve Policy Tactics	
Easy Money Policy	**Tight Money Policy**
To expand credit during a recession to stimulate a slow economy:	To tighten credit to slow economic expansion and prevent inflation:
■ Buy U.S. government securities in the open market	■ Sell U.S. government securities in the open market
■ Lower the discount rate	■ Raise the discount rate
■ Lower reserve requirements	■ Raise reserve requirements

KNOWLEDGE CHECK

1. Which of the following is added to M2 to arrive at M3?
    A. Large time deposits
    B. Currency in circulation
    C. Checking accounts
    D. Gold and silver bars in bank storage vaults

2. Which of the following actions of the Federal Reserve Board (FRB) would likely have the effect of causing interest rates to increase?
    I. The Federal Open Market Committee (FOMC) buying securities
    II. Raising the reserve requirements
    III. Raising the discount rate
    IV. Raising the prime rate
    A. I and II
    B. II and III
    C. II and IV
    D. III and IV

3. Which of the following rates is set by the Federal Reserve?
    A. Fed funds rate
    B. Discount rate
    C. Broker call rate
    D. Prime rate

Answers

1. **A**   One of the key additions to M2 in order to reach M3 is the negotiable time deposits of $100,000 or more, generally known as jumbo CDs.

2. **B**   When the FRB raises the reserve requirements, it reduces the available funds for banks to lend. Having fewer dollars to lend will lead to higher interest rates. When the discount rate is increased, it costs more for banks to borrow, and that increase is passed along to consumers. The FRB does not set the prime rate, and it is only when the Federal Open Market Committee (FOMC) sells securities that the money supply shrinks.

3. **C**   The discount rate is set by the Fed. All the other rates shown here are set by the financial institution making the loan.

UNIT
14

Fiscal Policy and Trade

LEARNING OBJECTIVES

When you have completed this unit, you will be able to accomplish the following.

> LO 14.a Define the purpose of fiscal policy.
> LO 14.b Differentiate demand- and supply-side theories.
> LO 14.c Recall the impact of exchange rates on trade and prices.
> LO 14.d Define the balance of trade.

INTRODUCTION

Two distinctive types of policies impact our economy: monetary and fiscal. Monetary policy is what the FRB engages in when it attempts to influence the money supply. Fiscal policy refers to the government's budget decisions and tax policy as enacted by our president and Congress. Fiscal policy is based on the assumption that the government can control such economic forces as unemployment levels and inflation by adjusting overall demand for goods and services.

Because the political process determines fiscal policy, it takes time for conditions and solutions to be identified and implemented. Due to the length of time it may take to enact fiscal policy decisions, fiscal policy is not considered the most efficient means to solve short-term economic problems.

Trade is an important part of a healthy economy. Trading with other nations allows our economy to take advantage of differing strengths of our trading partners. The relative value of a notions currency directly affects international trade.

TAKE NOTE

Monetary policies are those enacted by the FRB to influence the money supply. Fiscal policies are those enacted by our president and Congress, such as tax laws and federal spending appropriations.

LESSON 14.1: FISCAL POLICY

LO 14.a Define the purpose of fiscal policy.

Fiscal policy attempts to do much of the same work as monetary policy. However, its tools for managing the cash supply are quite different. Fiscal policy depends on the use of taxation and federal spending to increase or decrease the money supply through encouraging or discouraging consumer and business spending.

There are numerous different economic theories regarding how the economy should be viewed and how it should be impacted by government. We have already explored monetary theory in the work of the Federal Reserve. In the following paragraphs, we'll explore two of the prominent fiscal theories: Keynesian (pronounced *Kanes-ian*) and supply-side.

LO 14.b Differentiate demand- and supply-side theories

Keynesian (demand-side) theory

The economist John Maynard Keynes (later 1st Baron Keynes; he was British) held that active government involvement in the economy was vital to the health and stability of a nation's economy. Keynesians believe that demand for goods ultimately controls employment and prices. Insufficient demand for goods causes unemployment; too much demand causes inflation. Keynes believed it was the government's right and responsibility to manipulate overall demand (and therefore artificially manipulate the economy) by changing its own levels of spending and taxation.

According to Keynes, a government's fiscal policies determine the country's economic health. Fiscal policy involves adjusting the level of taxation and government spending. The government is expected to intervene in the economy as a major force in creating prosperity by engaging in activities that affect aggregate demand.

Government affects individual levels of spending and saving by adjusting taxes. Increasing taxes removes money from the private sector, which reduces private-sector demand and spending. Government spending puts money back into the economy. To increase private-sector demand for goods, the government reduces taxes, which increases people's disposable income.

Keynesian theory is also called demand-side theory. Demand-side focuses on directly increasing the supply of money to the consumer. Increasing money in the consumer's pocket encourages spending (increasing the demand for goods and services), decreasing the money supply of the consumer discourages spending (so deceases demand for goods and services).

Supply-side theory

Supply-side economics holds that government should allow market forces to determine prices of all goods. Supply-siders believe the federal government should reduce government spending, as well as taxes. In this way, sellers of goods will price them at a rate that allows them to meet market demand and still sell them profitably.

Supply-side focuses more on creating a healthy environment for business by decreasing the tax and regulatory burden on business. The theory suggests that healthy businesses will grow, expanding their workforce efficiently and creating a strong and steady demand for labor. Further, employed people will have the capital to spend and will grow the economy, thereby creating more demand. Through this approach, supply-siders believe that more sustainable expansions are achieved.

In Summary

Both theories believe that decreasing taxes encourages economic activity and increasing discourages economic activity.

Demand-side sees government spending as encouraging economic activity. Supply-side sees government spending as an inefficient and temporary approach, and that holding down government debt is better overall.

Demand-side focuses stimulus on the consumer. Supply-side believes that encouraging businesses to be successful and expand is a more sustainable long-term approach.

LESSON 14.2: CURRENCY RATES AND THE BALANCE OF TRADE

LO 14.c Recall the impact of exchange rates on trade and prices.

The value of one currency against another is known as the exchange rate. The value of the U.S. dollar against foreign currencies affects the balance of trade.

TEST TOPIC ALERT

This is a U.S.-based exam administered by a U.S. regulator. When referring to the dollar, we mean the U.S. dollar; so does FINRA.

When the value of the dollar declines against another currency, the prices of U.S. products cost less in terms of the foreign currency. Exports will tend to increase and imports decrease.

When the value of the dollar strengthens against another currency, the price of U.S. products increases in terms of the foreign currency. Exports will tend to decrease and imports increase.

EXAMPLE

Ford, an auto manufacturer based in the United States builds the Focus, a small passenger sedan. Toyota, a car manufacturer based in Japan builds the Corolla, a small passenger sedan.

The Focus is priced in dollars, and the Corolla is priced in yen.

- If the dollar strengthens against the yen, the following will occur:
  - It will cost more yen to get a dollar and fewer dollars to buy Yen.
  - The price of the Focus rises in Yen, and so sales of the Focus drop in Japan.
  - Conversely, the price of the Corolla decreases in dollars, so sales of the Corolla increase in the United States.

- If the dollar weakens against the yen, the following will occur:
  - It will cost more dollars to get yen and fewer yen to buy dollars.
  - The price of the Focus decreases in yen, and so sales of the Focus increase in Japan.
  - Conversely, the price of the Corolla increases in dollars, so sales of the Corolla decrease in the United States.

TAKE NOTE

A strong dollar means imports are less expensive here in the United States. U.S. companies must still compete on price and so will need to also keep their prices down. The net effect is that a strong dollar helps keep inflation in check in the United States.

A weak dollar has the opposite effect and will tend to increase the rate of inflation.

LO 14.d Define the balance of trade.

The flow of money between the United States and other countries is known as the **balance of payments**. The balance of payments may be a **surplus** (more money flowing into the United States than out) or a **deficit** (more money flowing out of the United States than in). A deficit may occur when interest rates in another country are high because money flows to where it earns the highest return.

The largest component of the balance of payments is the **balance of trade**—the export and import of merchandise.

On the U.S. credit side (money flowing in) are sales of American products to foreign countries (U.S. exports). On the U.S. debit side (money flowing out) are American purchases of foreign goods (U.S. imports). This will cause American dollars to flow out of the country. When debits exceed credits, a deficit in the balance of payments occurs; when credits exceed debits, a surplus exists. See Figure 14.1.

Figure 14.1: Balance of Trade

Debit Items	Credit Items
Imports	Exports
U.S. investments abroad	Foreign spending in the U.S.
U.S. bank loans abroad	
U.S. foreign aid	

KNOWLEDGE CHECK

These questions apply to material covered in Lesson 14.1 and Lesson 14.2.

1. All of the following situations could cause a fall in the value of the U.S. dollar in relation to the Japanese yen **except**
    A. Japanese investors buying U.S. Treasury securities.
    B. U.S. investors buying Japanese securities.
    C. an increase in Japan's trade surplus over that of the United States.
    D. a general decrease in U.S. interest rates.

2. Which organization or governmental unit sets fiscal policy?
    A. Federal Reserve Board (FRB)
    B. Government Economic Board
    C. Congress and the president
    D. Secretary of the Treasury

3. Which of the following economists is considered a supporter of demand-side economics?
    A. Adam Smith
    B. John Maynard Keynes
    C. Arthur Laffer
    D. Milton Friedman

Answers

1. **A** Increased foreign investment in the United States would raise the U.S. dollar's relative value. A decrease in U.S. interest rates would chase money out of the United States and increase the foreign currency's relative value. In choice B, the value of the yen should increase, meaning the dollar will fall in comparison. In choice C, U.S. consumers are buying more Japanese goods than the Japanese are buying U.S. goods. Therefore, the value of the dollar should fall relative to the yen. LO 14.c

2. **C** Congress and the president set fiscal policy, whereas the FRB sets monetary policy. LO 14.b

3. **B** John Maynard Keynes was the first demand-side economist; he believed that by increasing the income available for spending and saving, a government could increase demand and improve the country's economic well-being. Higher taxes and higher government spending are key tenets of this theory. LO 14.b

UNIT 15

Industries and Companies

LEARNING OBJECTIVES

When you have completed this unit, you will be able to accomplish the following.

> LO 15.a Classify industries by type (cyclical, noncyclical, countercyclical, growth).
> LO 15.b Indicate the impact of the business cycle on different industries.
> LO 15.c Recognize the components and uses of a balance sheet.
> LO 15.d Recognize the components and uses of an income statement.

INTRODUCTION

Fundamental analysis is the study of industries and companies to identify the best places to invest. Different industries perform better or worse depending on the business cycle. Once a promising industry has been chosen, the individual companies are examined to determine their financial strength and likelihood for growth. The process of examining the economy to identify industries that will do well in the near future and then the companies within those industries that are financially strong is fundamental analysis. It is sometimes called top-down analysis because you start at the top (the economy) and work your way down to the company.

LESSON 15.1: TYPES OF INDUSTRIES

LO 15.a Classify industries by type (e.g., cyclical, noncyclical, countercyclical, growth).

Some industries perform better, or worse, depending on the business cycle. Industries are divided for this purpose into four broad classes: cyclical, noncyclical, countercyclical, and growth.

Cyclical industries

Cyclical industries are highly sensitive to business cycles and inflation trends. Most cyclical industries produce durable goods, such as heavy machinery, and raw materials, such as steel and automobiles. During recessions, the demand for such products declines as manufacturers postpone investments in new capital goods and consumers postpone purchases of these goods, such as automobiles.

Examples of cyclical industries are these:

- Steel
- Autos
- Heavy equipment
- Capital goods (washers and dryers, etc.)

If the company produces industrial metals such as steel or aluminum or makes stuff from steel or aluminum, it is probably cyclical.

Noncyclical (defensive) industries

Defensive industries are least affected by normal business cycles. Companies in defensive industries generally produce nondurable consumer goods (sometimes called consumables), such as food, pharmaceuticals, and tobacco. Public consumption of such goods remains fairly steady throughout the business cycle. During recessions and bear markets, stocks in defensive industries generally decline less than stocks in other industries, but during expansions and bull markets, defensive stocks may advance less. Investments in defensive industries tend to involve less risk and, consequently, lower investment returns.

Examples of noncyclical or defensive industries are these:

- Food
- Utilities—highest dividend payout ratio
- Clothing
- Drugs
- Tobacco
- Liquor

If the company makes a product that is used once and consumed in the process, it is probably defensive.

Countercyclical

Countercyclical industries tend to turn down as the economy heats up and to rise when the economy turns down. They are producers of a product that people by when they are scared and looking for safety. The primary example would be gold mining and refinement, though any precious metal will do. People tend to flock to gold when the economy is weak and move away from gold as the economy improves and investors move into investments with better return potential (and more risk).

Growth or special situation

A **growth** industry is one that seems to be disconnected from the business cycle, doing well regardless of the economy. This may apply to an individual stock, as well as to a specific company.

A special situation is normally applied to a specific company, but it could apply to an industry as a whole. A special situation might be anything from a hostile takeover to a cultural shift that moves the consumer away from the product. Unlike growth, special situation may not be a positive condition.

 EXAMPLE

In the late 1990s and into the first decade or so of the 2000s, mobile information companies (smartphones and apps) grew at a tremendous pace. Even during the Great Recession, consumers still shoveled out money to buy the newest smartphones. A growth industry.

At the same time, companies that had historically done well producing public telephone equipment (phone booths) saw that business decrease dramatically. Also, makers of street maps are not enjoying the information revolution much either. A special situation, and not a good one.

LO 15.b Indicate the impact of the business cycle on different industries.

Here is a summary of some of the information in noted in the previous paragraphs:

Cyclical Industries tend to do well in expansions and poorly in contractions.

Defensive Industries tend to be less impacted by the business cycle, maintaining sales throughout the cycle. Defensive industries do not drop as much as cyclical industries do in poor economies, and they do not grow as fast as cyclical industries do in expanding economies.

Countercyclical industries do better when the economy is weak and lose value when the economy strengthens.

Growth Industries don't care about the economy: they just keep growing (until they don't).

Special situations are situational; some specific circumstance is affecting them.

LESSON 15.2: FINANCIALS

LO 15.c Recognize the components and uses of a balance sheet.

Corporate financial reports

A corporation's financial reports provide fundamental analysts the data they need to understand the financial strengths and weaknesses of a company. From the information on these statements, we can calculate ratios that allow us to compare a company's financials with those of a competitor. Financial reports are released on quarterly and annual bases. The two primary reports are the **balance sheet** and the **income statement**.

The balance sheet

The **balance sheet** provides a snapshot of a company's financial position at a specific time. It identifies the value of the company's assets (what it owns) and its liabilities (what it owes). The difference between these two figures is the corporation's **equity**, or **net worth**.

A corporation can be compared to a homeowner who borrows money to buy a home. The homeowner's equity is the difference between the mortgage balance (liability) and the home's market value (asset value). A corporation can buy assets using borrowed money (liabilities) and equity raised by selling stock. The value of its assets must equal (balance with) the value of its liabilities and equity.

Although it is useful in determining a company's current value, the balance sheet cannot tell the analyst whether the company's business is improving or deteriorating. The balance sheet also does not measure the profitability of a business. That can be found in the income statement, which will be detailed shortly.

 EXAMPLE

JimCo Inc. Balance Sheet
December 31st, 2019

ASSETS			LIABILITIES		
Current Assets			Current Liabilities		
Cash and Equivalents	4,000,000		Accounts Payable	1,000,000	
Securities Portfolio	1,000,000		Accrued Wages	4,000,000	
Accounts Receivable	15,000,000		Interest	4,000,000	
Inventory	20,000,000		Accrued Taxes	1,000,000	
Total Current Assets		40,000,000	Total Current Liabilities		10,000,000
			Long Term Liabilities		
			8% Convertible ($100) Debentures of 2032		50,000,000
Fixed Assets					
Building, Furniture, and Fixtures	40,000,000		**TOTAL LIABILITIES**		**60,000,000**
Land Values	15,000,000				
Total Fixed Assets		55,000,000	NET WORTH		
			Preferred Stock (Par $100)		
			$5 Straight convertible ($50)	20,000,000	
			Common Stock		
			1 million ($5 par)	5,000,000	
Other Assets, Intangibles, Goodwill		5,000,000	Retained Earnings	15,000,000	
			TOTAL NET WORTH		**40,000,000**
TOTAL ASSETS		**100,000,000**	**TOTAL LIABILITIES and NET WORTH**		**100,000,000**

The basic balance sheet equation can be expressed in two ways:

assets – liabilities = net worth (100MM – 60MM = 40MM)

assets = liabilities + net worth (100MM = 60MM + 40MM)

 TAKE NOTE

Why do they call it a balance sheet? First, it reflects the balances of the different accounts. Second, it was traditionally set up in two columns (as above) and the figures at the bottom of the two columns should be equal. If they're not equal, your balance sheet doesn't balance; try again.

The components of the balance sheet

Assets

Assets are divided into three categories: current assets, fixed assets, and other.

- **Current assets** are cash and assets that may be easily converted to cash. Securities, accounts receivable, and the company's inventory are examples of current assets.

- **Fixed assets** are assets that are difficult to liquidate. Real estate, furniture, and equipment are all examples of fixed assets.

- **Other assets** may also be called **intangibles** or **goodwill**. This category represents things that are difficult to value. Trademarks, copyrights, reputation, and intellectual property are examples of this category.

Liabilities

Liabilities are divided into two categories: current and long-term liabilities.

Current liabilities are those liabilities that are due now or in the near future (within 12 months). Current liabilities would include accrued wages, accrued taxes, accounts payable, or interest payments.

Long-term liabilities are debt that will not be paid off in the near future. For a corporation, this will normally be notes and bonds. The interest that is due in the next 12 months will be reflected in the current liabilities, but the principal is a long-term liability.

Net Worth (also called Shareholder's Equity)

The net worth section has several components.

- **Preferred stock**—any funds received from the sale of preferred stock

- **Common stock**—the par value of the common stock

- **Capital in excess of par**—moneys received from the sale of common stock in excess of the par value

- **Retained earnings**—the earnings the company has made that have not been paid out as dividends

Balance sheet analysis

There is a tremendous amount of information available from the balance sheet. Fortunately, there are only four ratios or numbers that are tested.

Short-term liquidity

Working capital: This figure is the amount of money that a company can spend (or lose) and remain operational. The formula for working capital is:

current assets – current liabilities = working capital (expressed as a dollar amount)

Current ratio: This figure is a better figure to use when comparing the liquidity of a company. The formula for current ratio is:

current assets:current liabilities = current ratio (expressed as a ratio (2:1, 1.25:1)).

Acid ratio: Also called the **quick ratio**, this ratio is the test of a company's liquidity if everything really goes bad. The formula for acid ratio is:

(current assets – inventory):current liabilities = acid ratio (expressed as a ratio (0.7:1, 1.1:1)).

Long-term solvency

The most common measure of long-term solvency is the **debt ratio** (or **debt-to-equity ratio**). It is a measure of how much of a corporation's net worth is derived from long-term debt. A corporation with a debt ratio that is higher than the industry average is said to be **highly leveraged**. The formula for debt ratio is:

long-term debt / (long-term debt + net worth) = debt ratio (expressed as a percentage (56%. 12%)).

LO 15.d Recognize the components and uses of an income statement.

The **income statement** (also called a profit and loss, or P&L) summarizes a corporation's revenues and expenses for a fiscal period—usually quarterly, year-to-date, or the full year. It compares revenue with costs and expenses during the period. It reflects the business activity in cash flow over a specific time period. Fundamental analysts use the income statement to judge the efficiency of a company's operation and its profitability.

 EXAMPLE

JimCo Income Statement	Profit and loss or P&L
January 1 through December 31, 2019	
Net sales	60,000,000
Cost of goods sold	10,000,000
General operating expenses	30,000,000
Operating Income	20,000,000
Interest expense (8% debentures)	4,000,000
Pretax Income	16,000,000
Taxes	6,000,000
Net Income After Taxes	10,000,000
Preferred dividends	1,000,000
Earnings Available to Common	9,000,000

Components of the income statement

Figure 15.1: Components of the Income Statement

Net Sales
-     cost of goods sold (COGS)
-     <u>operating costs (including depreciation)</u>
=   operating profit
+   <u>nonoperating income</u>
=   operating income (earnings before interest and taxes)
-     <u>interest expenses</u>
=   taxable income (pretax income)
-     <u>taxes</u>
=   net income after taxes
-     <u>preferred dividends</u>
=   earnings available to common
-     <u>common dividends</u>
=   retained earnings

There are two calculations you may see from the income statement earnings per share (EPS) and the price/earnings ratio (PE ratio).

Earnings per share (EPS) is calculated by dividing the earnings available to the common shareholder (earnings) by the number of outstanding shares.

The PE ratio is a measure of the amount of earnings a company makes compared with its current market value (CMV, or the stock's price). The formula for PE ratio is: CMV / EPS = PE ratio (expressed as a number).

EXAMPLE

The ABC Corporation has earnings of $20,000,000 and has 10,000,000 outstanding shares. It has a current market value of $32.00.

- Calculate EPS
  - EPS = earnings / outstanding shares
  - EPS = 20,000,000 / 10,000,000
  - EPS = $2
- Calculate P/E ratio
  - P/E = CMV/EPS
  - P/E = 32 / 2
  - P/E = 16

KNOWLEDGE CHECK

These questions apply to material covered in Lesson 15.1 and Lesson 15.2.

1. All of the following ratios are measures of the liquidity of a corporation **except**
    A. acid ratio.
    B. debt-to-equity ratio.
    C. current ratio.
    D. quick ratio.

2. Profits that are not distributed to shareholders are called
    A. capital surplus.
    B. dividends.
    C. retained earnings.
    D. Interest.

3. ABC, with 3 million shares outstanding, reports after-tax earnings of $7.5 million. ABC stock is trading at $50 a share. The P/E ratio is
    A. 20.
    B. 25.
    C. 33.
    D. 40.

4. Which of the following stocks is regarded as a defensive stock?
    A. Aerospace stock
    B. Stock selling close to its support level
    C. Stock with a strong cash position and a low ratio of debt
    D. Electric utility stock

5. The economy appears to be moving into recession. Which of the following companies will likely deliver the best returns if the recession fears prove accurate?
    A. Southern Utah Gas and Electric
    B. Seabird Airlines
    C. Hinckley Gold and Silver Mining
    D. Butterfly Heavy Equipment

Answers

1. **B** Debt-to-equity ratio is a measure of a corporation's long-term solvency. All the others listed here are used to measure short-term liquidity LO 15.c

2. **C** Earnings that are available to the common shareholder but not distributed to them are retained by the company: retained earnings. LO 15.c

3. **A** When calculating PE ratio, you first must know the earnings per share. ABC has 7.5 million in earnings and 3 million shares, so EPS of $2.50. PE ratio is CMV / EPS. For ABC, it is 50/2.5 = 20. LO 15.d

4. **D** Defensive stocks are less susceptible to the business cycle: dropping less in contractions and growing less in expansions than cyclical industries. Another term for defensive stocks is noncyclical. LO 15.a

5. **C** Countercyclical stocks tend to go up when the economy is struggling. The most common type of countercyclical stocks are those tied to precious metals. An electric utility is defensive, it does not move as much as a cyclical stock like an airline or an equipment manufacturer, but it still goes up or down with the economy. LO 15.b

PART

3

Understanding Trading, Customer Accounts, and Prohibited Activities

Your exam will include 23 questions on the topics covered in Part 3

There are 14 units in Part 3: Understanding Trading, Customer Accounts, and Prohibited Activities

UNIT 16

Placing a Trade

LEARNING OBJECTIVES

When you have completed this unit, you will be able to accomplish the following.

› LO 16.a Define bullish and bearish sentiment.
› LO 16.b Differentiate market and limit orders.
› LO 16.c Define a stop order.
› LO 16.d Identify specialized, day, and GTC instructions.

INTRODUCTION

In Unit 16, we discuss the basics of how to place a trade and the types of trades normal for the secondary markets. We also take a look at different qualifiers and time limits allowed for most trades.

LESSON 16.1: MARKET ATTITUDE AND TRADE TYPES

LO 16.a Define bullish and bearish sentiment.

They terms *bull* and *bear* (not to mention *bullish* and *bearish*) are used widely in the securities business. You probably already have a good idea what they mean. However, let's take a closer look at the bulls and the bears.

These terms refer to an investor's attitude toward a market or a specific security.

Bull: If a person believes that a given market or stock is likely to go up in value rather than down, that person is bullish or "a bull." In a hybrid position like an options hedge (covered call, for example), you always look at the larger position (meaning the one with more value when the position was established). Whatever leg of the position represents the largest amount of money invested determines the attitude. If you are long a stock, you want it to go up; you are a bull.

Bear: If a person believes that a given market or stock is going to go down in value rather than up, that person is bearish or "a bear." If you are short a stock, you are a bear.

As noted previously, the larger position in a hedge determines the market attitude. If the customer holds a short stock position and a long call as a hedge, that person is bearish. Why? The short stock position represents more money, so that position determines the attitude.

TEST TOPIC ALERT

Still having trouble with the bull/bear concept? When a bull is trotting across a field, its horns point up. Bulls think it is going up. When a bear walks through the forest, its claws point down. Bears think it is going down. (Whatever "it" is.)

EXAMPLE

Dr. Chiang owns 500 shares of BuyStuff, Inc., a big box retailer. He believes that the company has solid long-term prospects, and he is bullish on BuyStuff's future prospects. However, he notices that the stock has weakened a bit and is concerned there may be a short-term drop. In order to protect his current position (which he prefers to keep), he buys puts. Does buying the put mean the good doctor is now a bear? No, it does not. He still owns (and has more money in) the long stock position. He is just getting some insurance should he be wrong and the stock drops significantly.

LO 16.b Differentiate market and limit orders.

We can begin our discussion of orders with simple order instructions taken from investors to buy or sell securities. An investor will enter an order with a BD to execute a buy or sell transaction, and the order will be entered by the BD on the appropriate exchange or trading venue. In the following paragraphs, we will discuss the different types of orders.

Market and limit orders

Most orders entered are either market orders or limit orders:

- *Market order*—Buy or sell, it is executed immediately at the best available market price.
- *Limit order*—buy or sell; the limit price is the maximum purchase price if buying, or the minimum selling price if selling.

While market orders are always executed immediately at the current market price, limit orders can only be executed at the limit price designated by the customer or better. For a buy limit order, *or better* means at the limit price *or lower*. For a sell limit order, *or better* means at the limit price *or higher*.

EXAMPLE

Buy market order: **Buy 1,000 shares XYZ at MKT.**

(This order would be executed immediately to buy at the best available market price.)

Sell market order: **Sell 1,000 shares XYZ at MKT.**

(This order would be executed immediately to sell at the best available market price.)

Buy limit order: **Buy 1,000 shares of XYZ at 32.**

(This order could only be executed to purchase XYZ at 32 or better. Because this is an instruction to buy, *or better* would be lower. Therefore, it would need to be executed at 32 or lower.)

Sell limit order: **Sell 1,000 shares of XYZ at 32.**

(This order could only be executed to sell XYZ at 32 or better. Because this is an instruction to sell, *or better* would be higher. Therefore, it would need to be executed at 32 or higher.)

Limit orders to either buy or sell come with a built-in risk. The risk is that the market may never go as low as the buy limit designated on the order or as high as the sell limit designated on the order. It is possible that the order will never be executed. In this light, customers who enter limit orders risk missing the market—that is, the opportunity to buy or sell because of the limit they've imposed on the buy or sell order.

TAKE NOTE

Market orders always take precedence over limit orders and are executed when entered in time priority. Limit orders also stand in time priority, but behind market orders. There may be multiple orders to buy stock at a particular price. Once the stock begins trading at that price, those limit orders that were entered first will be filled first.

LO 16.c Define a stop order.

In conjunction with market and limit orders, there are unique order types known as **stop orders** and **stop limit** orders.

TAKE NOTE

A stop order is *not* an order, but a trigger price that, when reached, will trigger an order. Stop orders have no standing as to time priority.

Stop order—Buy or sell, a stop order does not become a "live" working order in the marketplace until the stock trades at or through a specified price (the stop price). Once the order is "triggered" by the stock reaching the specified stop price, the order becomes a market order, and like any other market order, it should be executed immediately at the best available market price.

EXAMPLE

BigCo., Inc. (Ticker BCO), common stock is trading at a CMV = $12.

Order: Buy 2,000 shares BCO at 15 stop.

As soon as XYZ trades at or through the stop price of 15, this order will become a live working market order, and like all market orders, it will be executed immediately at the next available price. Note that this stop order triggers if the CMV of BigCo rises to (or above) 15. The resulting market order may execute at any price (it is a market order).

Stop limit order—Buy or sell, this order type also has a stop price and does not become a "live" working order until the stock trades at or through the stop price. However, it also has a limit price, so once the order is "triggered" by the stock reaching the specified stop price, the order becomes a limit order to buy or sell at the specified limit. Like any other limit order, it may or may not be executed depending on where the price of the stock is.

EXAMPLE

BigCo., Inc., common stock is trading at a CMV = $12.

Order: Buy 2,000 shares BCO at 15 stop limit 16.

As soon as XYZ trades at or through the stop price of 15, this order will become a live working limit order, and like all limit orders, it will only be executed if the stock can be purchased for $16 (the limit price) or less.

LO 16.d Identify specialized, day, and GTC instructions.

Finally, in addition to an order being either a market order, limit order, stop order, or stop limit order, there are numerous restrictions that can be applied to an order. In other words, additional instructions are attached to the order that a customer would like adhered to. Though not all of these designations are accepted on every exchange or trading venue, the following are the most common. They are divided into time restrictions: day order, good 'til canceled (GTC), or market-on-open/close. The second set are the fill restrictions: fill-or-kill (FOK), immediate or cancel (IOC), or all-or-none (AON).

Time restrictions

Day order—An order is assumed to be a day order; this is the default time limit. A day order is valid only until the close of trading on the day it is entered. If the order has not been filled, it is canceled at the close of the day's trading. Keep in mind that while market orders should be filled immediately, this is of more importance with limit orders. If the order is partially filled, then any unexecuted portion of the order is canceled at the end of the trading day.

Good 'til canceled (GTC) order—GTC orders are valid until executed or canceled. However, all GTC orders are automatically canceled if unexecuted on the last business day of April and the last business day of October. If the customer wishes to have the order remain working beyond those specific days, the customer must request that the order continue for the next cycle.

Market-at-open or market-on-close order—These are market orders designated to be executed at the opening of the day or at the close of the day. Depending on the market (exchange or OTC) the order is being sent to, the customer is not guaranteed the exact opening or closing price but instead a price at, or close to, the first or last price of the day.

Fill restrictions

Fill-or-kill (FOK) order—This is an instruction to fill (execute in its entirety) the order immediately or kill (cancel) the order completely. With a FOK order, there can't be a partial execution.

Immediate-or-cancel (IOC) order—IOC orders are like FOK orders except that a partial execution is acceptable. In other words, if only a portion of the order can be filled, it is, and the remaining unexecuted portion is canceled.

All-or-none (AON) order—AON orders must be executed in their entirety or not at all. AON orders can be day orders or GTC orders. They differ from the FOKs in that they do not have to be filled immediately. In other words, they can be held until the end of the day (for day orders) or beyond (for GTC orders) until they can be filled in their entirety.

Note that the three above fill restrictions are only for limit orders. A market order is always filled at the best available price and immediately.

KNOWLEDGE CHECK

1. ABC stock is currently trading at $63. Julia Miller would like to purchase ABC stock, but not at $63. If the price of ABC stock were to fall to $58 or less, then Miller wants to buy the stock. Which type of order should Miller place considering her objective?
    A. Market order
    B. Buy limit
    C. Buy stop
    D. Buy stop limit

2. When an investor is long a stock,
    A. the investor is bearish.
    B. buying the stock in the secondary market will close the position.
    C. there is limited gain potential.
    D. the investor is bullish.

3. Your customer places a trade to buy 1,000 shares of Seabird Airlines at a limit of 32 FOK. When the order reaches the floor of the exchange, there are 500 shares available to buy at 32. What is the likely outcome of the trade?
    A. 500 shares filled, 500 share order remains until filled of canceled at the end of the day.
    B. 500 shares filled, the rest of the order is canceled.
    C. 500 shares filled at 32, 500 at the market.
    D. Order canceled, nothing done.

Answers

1. **B**   While market orders are always executed immediately at the current market price, limit orders can only be executed at the limit price designated by the customer or better. For a buy limit order, *or better* means at the limit price *or lower*. Miller should place a buy limit order at $58. LO 16.b

2. **D**   When an investor is long stock, the stock was purchased and the stock is owned. When an investor owns stock, he is bullish—anticipating the stock will rise in value. If the stock rises in value, the position can be closed by selling it in the secondary market for a profit. Because there is no limit to how high the price can go, profit is unlimited. LO 16.a

3. **D**   In a fill-or-kill order, the entire order must be filled immediately or canceled. In this example, there are not 1,000 shares available to buy at 32, so the order is canceled entirely. LO 16.d

UNIT
17

Quotes

LEARNING OBJECTIVES

When you have completed this unit, you will be able to accomplish the following.

> LO 17.a Define bid, ask, and size.
> LO 17.b Calculate the bid/ask spread.

INTRODUCTION

In Unit 17, we take a look at the quote. The quote is what most investors want to hear before they place a trade. Often in the securities industry, you will hear expressions like "the current quote is" or the "stock is being quoted at." What do these mean? What is a **quote**?

How we get the quote and what exactly it means is the topic of this unit.

TAKE NOTE

All quotes maintained in active markets, such as a stock exchange, are dynamic and change constantly throughout the trading day.

LESSON 17.1: QUOTES

LO 17.a Define bid, ask, and size.

A quote on a given security is usually two-sided, consisting of a *bid* and an *ask* (sometimes called *offer*). Most quotes will also provide *size*, which is the number of shares currently available at the bid and at the ask. Size for a stock quote is expressed in round lots (units of 100 shares).

TEST TOPIC ALERT

A bid is always less than the ask price.

Bid

The bid price is the highest amount someone is currently willing to pay for the security. The size is the number of shares that someone is will to buy at the bid. The bid is, essentially, someone standing up and saying, "I will buy this stock at this price." If an investor wants to sell, she is selling to the bidder, so the *bid price is the price a seller receives*.

EXAMPLE

BCO stock is bid 42, size 10.

This means that there is a buyer (maybe multiple buyers) willing to buy up to 1,000 shares of BCO at $42/share. If your customer wants to sell some BCO stock, he knows that he could *sell as much as 1,000 shares at $42 a share.*

Ask (or Offer)

The ask price is the lowest amount someone is currently willing to sell the security for. The size is the number of shares that someone is willing to sell at the ask. The ask is, essentially, someone standing up and saying, "I will sell this stock at this price." If an investor wants to buy, she is buying from the person making the offer, so the ask *price is the price a buyer pays*.

EXAMPLE

BCO stock is ask 42.5, size 12.

This means that there is someone (maybe multiple persons) willing to sell as many as 1,200 shares of BCO at $42.5/share. If your customer wants to buy some BCO stock, he knows he can *buy as many as 1,200 shares at 42.50 a share.*

TEST TOPIC ALERT

The quote on BCO stock from the information in the example would read like this:

BCO bid 42 ask 42.5 size 10 × 12

Where we get the bid and the ask

How the quote is generated depends on where it trades.

Quotes for listed stocks

On an exchange, the DMM maintains an order book. In the book are all the open limit orders for the assigned stock.

The highest buy limit is the most that someone will pay for the stock and establishes the bid. The size of the limit order (or orders if several are at the same limit) establishes the size.

The lowest sell limit is the least someone will sell their stock at and establishes the ask. The size of the limit order (or orders if several are at the same limit) establishes the size.

EXAMPLE

DMM Book for BCO

Shares	Sell Limits	Buy Limits
200	43	
100	42.75	
400	42.5	
800	42.5	
1,000		42
300		41.75
1,500		41.5

The bid and size is based on the highest open buy limit. The ask and size is based on the lowest sell limits (two orders in this example). A customer placing a market order to buy would pay $42.5; a market order to sell would execute at $42.

Quotes for OTC stocks and bonds

The OTC market is made up of BDs—some acting as market makers (dealers) and some acting as brokers. The trading is between these BDs. Here the bid is the highest bid from a market maker, and the ask is the lowest ask from a market maker. Remember, your customer will sell to the dealer at the bid, or buy from the dealer at the ask.

EXAMPLE

There are three dealers for MegaGig Storage, Inc. (Ticker MGS).

Market maker quotes are as follows:

Gold Coast Stocks	Bid 15	Ask 15.25	Size 15 × 20
Great Plains Equities	Bid 15.20	Ask 15.27	Size 5 × 8
Seaboard Securities	Bid 15.15	Ask 15.22	Size 10 × 12
The quote on MGS will be	Bid 15.2	Ask 15.22	Size 5 × 12

LO 17.b Calculate the bid/ask spread.

The spread is simply the difference between the bid and the ask prices. Really, it is just that. It is the difference between what the security may be bought for and what it sells for.

Remember: A **market maker is buying at the bid and selling at the ask.** That's how they make money.

EXAMPLE

From the examples above:

BCO bid 42 ask 42.5—The spread is 50 cents.

MGS bid 15.20 ask 15.22 – The spread is 2 cents.

KNOWLEDGE CHECK

1. The current quote for DEF stock is 49.50 bid—ask 49.75. If an investor wanted to buy or sell DEF stock, we can conclude which of the following?
    I.   The best price anyone in the secondary market is willing to sell at is 49.50.
    II.   The best price anyone in the secondary market is willing to sell at is 49.75.
    III. The best price anyone in the secondary market is willing to buy at is 49.50.
    IV.   The best price anyone in the secondary market is willing to buy at is 49.75.
    A. I and III
    B. I and IV
    C. II and III
    D. II and IV

2. BCO is currently quoted bid 42 ask 42.5 10 × 12. Your customer may be able to buy
    A. 1,000 shares at $42/share.
    B. 1,200 shares at $42/share.
    C. 1,200 shares at $42.5/share.
    D. 1,000 shares at $42.5/share.

3. MGS stock is quoted at 15.20 bid—ask 15.22 5 × 12. The spread is
    A. $ 0.02.
    B. $ 0.25.
    C. $ 0.2.
    D. 2.

Answers

1. **C**   II and III. The bid is the best price someone will pay for, and the ask is the lowest price someone will sell the stock.

2. **C**   Customers buy at the ask (42.5), and there are 1,200 shares available at that price (12 × 100).

3. **A**   The difference between the bid and the ask is 2 cents ($0.02).

UNIT 18

Position, Strategies, and Trade Authority

LEARNING OBJECTIVES

When you have completed this unit, you will be able to accomplish the following.

› LO 18.a Associate buying and selling long.
› LO 18.b Associate selling short and buying to close and cover.
› LO 18.c Define short against the box.
› LO 18.d Recall the locate requirement.
› LO 18.e Recognize a solicited or unsolicited trade.
› LO 18.f Identify what is or is not a discretionary trade.
› LO 18.g Name the authorizations required for a discretionary trading.
› LO 18.h Name the features and requirements of a wrap account.

INTRODUCTION

Your customer has placed a trade, but to what purpose? Are they establishing a stock position, or closing an existing one? The first part of Unit 18 will discuss the long and short positions and the opening and closing of securities positions. The second part of Unit 18 will take a look at the granting of trade authorizations for persons other than the account owners.

LESSON 18.1: POSITIONS AND STRATEGIES

LO 18.a Associate buying and selling long.

When an investor buys a security, he has taken a **long** position in that security. Meaning he now owns the security. Someone who is long the security hopes that the security will rise in value and he will be able to sell it later for a profit. This is a *bullish* position (anticipating that the security will rise in value).

The risk associated with a long position is if the price of the security falls. Maximum loss for the investor occurs if the security becomes worthless.

Investors open a long position by buying a security and then may later close the position by selling the security, hopefully at a higher price and for a profit. The amount they paid for the position is called the "**cost basis.**" When they close the position, the money they receive is their **sales proceeds.**

TEST TOPIC ALERT

Long: Buy to open, sell to close.

EXAMPLE

Three customer accounts are as follows:

Bill Smith: Long 3,000 shares of XYZ

Sarah Mills: Long 30 XYZ warrants

Jill Burns: Long 20 XYZ call options

Someone who owns shares of stock (Smith) is considered bullish. Owning securities convertible into the shares of stock such as rights, warrants (Mills), or long call options (Burns) would also be a considered a bullish market attitude.

EXAMPLE

Your customer, Bill Smith, purchased 3,000 shares of XYZ at $24 a share, establishing a long position in XYZ. Later, Bill sells the 3,000 shares at $30 a share, closing the long position. He also made a profit of $6 a share.

LO 18.b Associate selling short and buying to close/cover.

An investor can also sell a security to **open** a position. To do this, an investor is actually selling a security he does not own. This is done by borrowing stock from a stock lender and selling (shorting) the borrowed shares. Selling a security one does not own is known as being *short* or having a short position in the security. Just the opposite of being long, a short customer is taking the view that the stock will decline in price, enabling the customer to buy the shares back later at a lower price. Buying back the shares enables the investor to return them to the party they were initially borrowed from. In this scenario, the customer profits by the difference between the short sale price and the price at which the shares are bought back. This is known as being *bearish* (anticipating the security will fall in value).

The risk to a short seller is that the price of the borrowed shares increases, forcing the seller to buy back at a higher price instead of a lower price as anticipated. Because there is no limit on how high a security's price may rise, a short seller has unlimited loss potential.

Just as investors can open a position by buying a security, so too can they open a position (a short position) by selling a security. Later, to close the position, hopefully at a lower price for a profit, they would buy back the security, this is also called "covering" the position.

TEST TOPIC ALERT

Short: Sell to open, buy to close.

EXAMPLE

Three customer accounts are as follows:

Bill Smith: short 3,000 shares of XYZ

Jill Burns: long 20 XYZ put options

Someone who sold shares of stock they did not own (Smith) is considered bearish. Someone who own put options (Burns) would also be a considered a bearish market attitude.

EXAMPLE

Your customer, Bill Smith, sold short 3,000 shares of XYZ at $30 a share, establishing a short position in XYZ. Later, Bill buys the 3,000 shares at $24 a share, closing (covering) the short position. He also made a profit of $6 a share.

LO 18.c Define short against the box.

An investor may sell a stock short that she owns. This is a very different thing than closing a long position. In a "short against the box," an investor borrows and sells short stock that she owns. Note that she does not sell the stock she owns but borrows the shares and sells. Why would an investor do that? They very rarely do. It was used to delay the realization of a capital gain until a later time, usually the following tax year. However, this rule was changed in 1997, more than 20 years ago. But the Taxpayer Relief Act took away the delaying of capital gains this way, and there is now little reason to do a "short against the box." Unfortunately, though rarely done in the real world, the concept is still tested.

LO 18.d Recall the locate requirement.

 When an investor wants to enter a short sale, the broker-dealer taking the trade must first locate the shares that will be borrowed for the short sale. If the BD does not have the shares available within its accounts, it can arrange to borrow the shares from another BD. No matter where the shares are borrowed from, they must be located and secured before a short sale may be executed. The locate requirement is part of Regulation SHO. A BD that executes a short sale before locating the shares is in violation of Regulation SHO. The term for this is an "uncovered short."

TAKE NOTE

Do not confuse **going short on an option** (writing) with an **uncovered short**. Selling an uncovered option is perfectly legal. *It is selling a stock short without locating the source of the shares that is a rules violation.*

KNOWLEDGE CHECK

1. Three years ago your client, Lucy Jones, purchased 200 shares of Tremor Corporation. The shares have appreciated and she wants to take her profits. She would do this by entering
    A. an opening sale.
    B. a short sale.
    C. a closing sale.
    D. a covering purchase.

Unit 18

2. Your client, Dan Brown, believes that the Seabird Coffee Company's shares are significantly overvalued and will soon drop sharply in value. In order to profit from this drop, he could
    A. buy calls on Seabird common stock.
    B. sell Seabird shares short.
    C. sell Seabird shares long.
    D. sell puts on Seabird common stock.

3. Entering a sale of stock short without locating the shares first is an uncovered short and is a violation of
    A. Regulation SHO.
    B. Regulation SHRT.
    C. the uptick rule.
    D. short against the box.

Answers

1. **C** A long position is closed by selling the position, a closing sale. LO 18.a

2. **B** If a client thinks a stock is going to drop, he may make a profit by selling the stock short. Buying calls and selling puts are both bullish positions and will not be profitable if the shares drop in value. Selling the shares just takes the customer out of the position. LO 18.b

3. **A** The locate requirement is part of Regulation SHO. LO 18.d

LESSON 18.2: TRADE AUTHORITY

LO 18.e Recognize a solicited or unsolicited trade.

Solicited trade

If a representative or a communication from a BD introduces the purchase of a specific security to a customer, the trade is solicited. If something the BD or the representative did led to the customer placing a trade for a specific security, it's probably a solicited trade. Solicited trades must be marked as solicited on the trade ticket (order form). Marking a solicited trade as unsolicited is a regulatory violation.

EXAMPLE

Registered representative Jones called his customer and suggested that the customer purchase the Windmill Growth Fund. Two weeks later the customer calls and places a trade for the fund. That is a solicited trade.

Unsolicited trade

If a client places a trade that has not been suggested by the BD or a representative, it will be considered unsolicited. The trade ticket or order form for an unsolicited trade should be marked "unsolicited."

EXAMPLE

Your customer, Dr. Jones, calls and instructs you to buy $5,000 of the Tanis Growth Fund for his account. You have not discussed buying the Tanis Fund with Dr. Jones. This is an unsolicited trade.

Discretionary trades

LO 18.f Identify what is or is not a discretionary trade.

A customer may grant trading authority to a registered representative (RR) to place trades in their account without preauthorization from the customer. This is a discretionary trade. Exercising discretion requires specific authorization to place such trades. This is a type of power of attorney granted by the customer to the RR. These trades must be marked as discretionary; failure to do so is a serious violation.

What constitutes a discretionary trade?

All trades have three key elements:

1. An **action** (buy or sell)
2. The **amount** of the trade (shares or dollars)
3. The specific **asset** to be traded (what you are buying or selling)

These three elements are called the three As of discretion. In addition to these three, there is also an element of time and price.

If a representative chooses on his own discretion one or more of the three As, the trade is a discretionary trade. A customer must agree to all three of the "A" elements in a way that it may be objectively identified.

TAKE NOTE

Allowing the representative to choose the time or the price at which a trade is executed is not considered discretion. This is called time and price authority.

EXAMPLE

Customer Sam Spade calls you and places an order to buy 100 shares of Falcon Studios stock. He further instructs that you may choose the time and price at which to place the trade. Spade has provided you all three of the "A" elements: the action (buy), the amount (100 shares), and the asset (Falcon stock). This trade is *not* discretion.

Ms. Francis calls you and says, "I have $10,000 sitting in my account. I want you to take that money and purchase a great technology company into my account." Here, Francis identified the action (buy) and the amount ($10,000), but the asset was not clearly identified. If the representative decided on the stock to buy and placed the trade without further information from the customer, this would be a discretionary trade.

TAKE NOTE

If the representative chooses *one or more* of the three "A" elements without the client's specific agreement, it is a discretionary trade.

LO 18.g Name the authorizations required for a discretionary trading.

It is important to note that discretionary trading is allowed so long as proper authorizations have been received. In order for a discretionary trade to be properly entered, the

■ client must agree, in writing, to grant a representative discretionary trading authority, and

■ a principal of the firm must, in writing, approve the discretionary trading authority.

A client who chooses to revoke the discretion must do so in writing. Accounts that allow discretionary trades will be supervised more closely than accounts that do not. Principals will want to make sure the authority is being used in a manner that benefits the customer.

TAKE NOTE

Discretion is granted to the representative, not the *BD*. If the representative should pass away or leave the firm, that authority ends.

LO 18.h Name the features and requirements of a wrap account.

Wrap accounts are accounts for which firms provide a group of services, such as asset allocation, portfolio management, executions, and administration, for a single fee.

The fee may be a set monthly or quarterly amount but is most often a percentage of assets under management (AUM).

Wrap accounts are generally investment advisory accounts. This means that the BD must meet the fiduciary requirements under the Investment Advisers Act of 1940. Among the required disclosures is that the client may be able to get all of the same services on a separate basis for less cost.

KNOWLEDGE CHECK

1. Your customer calls and requests that you purchase 300 shares of Seabird Coffee Company. He recently read an article online about the company's new collaboration with Sorag coffee makers and likes the prospects of Seabird. This is an example of
   A. a solicited trade.
   B. an unsolicited trade.
   C. a discretionary trade.
   D. a suggested trade.

2. Your customer, Cleveland Brown, would like you to be able to place trades in his account as and when you think best. In order to trade on a discretionary basis in Mr. Brown's account, you will need authorization from which of these?
   I.   FINRA
   II. A principal
   III. The customer
   IV. State administrator
   A. I and II
   B. II and III
   C. I and III
   D. I and IV

3. The customer must agree to three specific elements of a trade before the trade's execution for the trade to be nondiscretionary. Which of the following is not required?
    A. Action
    B. Asset
    C. Allowance
    D. Amount

Answers

1. **B** The customer chose this trade and placed it without prompting from the firm or a representative, an unsolicited trade. LO 18.e

2. **B** Adding discretion to an account requires written authorization from the customer and a firm principal. LO 18.g

3. **C** Action, asset, and amount are the three elements. Allowance has no meaning in this context. It was just a good, distracting word that starts with A. LO 18.f

UNIT 19

Settlement

LEARNING OBJECTIVES

When you have completed this unit, you will be able to accomplish the following.

- › LO 19.a Recall regular way settlement for corporate, municipal, and treasury issues.
- › LO 19.b Define cash settlement trade.
- › LO 19.c Recall settlement for option trades and option exercises.
- › LO 19.d Define good delivery.
- › LO 19.e Differentiate delivery of physical certs and electronic holdings.

INTRODUCTION

When a customer's trade is executed, it begins a process called settlement. Settlement is the process that ensures that both parties to a transaction receive what they are supposed to receive: money to the seller and securities to the buyer. Settlement is also designed to ensure that the trade is completed in a timely manner. Depending on the type of transaction, trades must be completed (settled) by the end of the day on the settlement date.

LESSON 19.1: SETTLEMENT DATES AND GOOD DELIVERY

LO 19.a Recall regular way settlement for corporate, municipal, and treasury issues.

Settlement occurs by the end of the business day either one or two business days following the trade date. You will see this expressed as "T+1" for those trades that settle the next business day, or "T+2" for those trades that settle in two business days. Which (one day or two days) depends on the type of security. This is called *regular way* settlement.

TAKE NOTE

Settlement rules are for secondary market trades.

What settles in one business day?

- All Treasury securities: T-Bills, T-Notes, and T-bonds in regular way settlement is T+1

What settles in two business days? (T+2)

- Corporate issues (stocks and bonds)
- Municipal debt
- Agency securities such as GNMA
- GSE securities such as FNMA and FHLMC

What has to happen by the end of the settlement day? The BD representing the seller receives the cash due the seller and the BD representing the buyer receives the securities due the buyer in good order.

LO 19.b Define cash settlement trade.

Cash settlement, or same-day settlement, requires delivery of securities from the seller and payment from the buyer on the same day a trade is executed. Stocks or bonds sold for cash settlement must be available on the spot for delivery to the buyer. Both parties to the transaction would have to agree for cash settlement to occur. Cash settlements are rare but still occur.

TAKE NOTE

Both parties (buyer and seller) to a cash settlement must agree before the trade takes place.

TAKE NOTE

A cash settlement trade is a trade that settles on the trade date. *Do not* confuse this with a cash trade, which is simply a trade that does not involve any margin borrowing; the buyer paid for the trade "cash."

LO 19.c Recall settlement for option trades and option exercises.

When an option **trades,** settlement is next business day (T+1). This applies to all option trades.

When an option is **exercised** by the owner (long), there is a required time for completion. This is often referred to as "settlement"; though it is not a settlement of a trade, the mechanics are similar.

In an **equity option exercise**, the transaction must be completed by the second business day (T+2) after the exercise. This two-day delay allows the person delivering the stock time to acquire the stock to be delivered. The settlement process is essentially the same: one side receives stock and the other is paid.

In the exercise of an **index option**, there is no underlying security to deliver. The writer pays the owner cash equal to the in-the-money amount. This payment is the next business day (T+1).

LO 19.d Define good delivery.

Good delivery rules govern the delivery of physical stock and bond certificates in a trade. When a certificate is delivered, it must be endorsed (signed)

- by all owners whose name appears on the face of the certificate and
- signed exactly as the name appears.

By "exactly," it means just that. If the name on the face of the certificate read James T. Kirk, the signature must be James T. Kirk. If the middle name was written out instead of an initial, then the signature must match. If the name is James Tiberius Kirk, then the signature must match. Writing in "T" instead of the full name would not be good delivery.

The rules do allow the "&" symbol in place of "and."

Instead of signing the back of the certificate, the customer could sign a separate document called a stock power (or, in the case of a bond, "bond power"). It is common to use a stock power when certificates will be mailed. A signed certificate is like an endorsed check, it is easier to negotiate. When mailing a certificate, a customer would send the certificate and the signed power under separate cover. Note that the stock power identifies the specific certificate (issuer, number of shares, certificate number).

 EXAMPLE

Mr. Jones lives several hundred miles from the closest branch of his broker-dealer, Underwood Financial. He plans to sell 400 shares of Sierra Verde Coffee Company stock that he owns in certificate form. He mails the unsigned certificate to his broker. Three days later he completes a stock power and send that to his broker. When his BD receives both documents, he can deposit the shares into Jones's account.

LO 19.e Differentiate delivery of physical certificates and electronic holdings.

When securities are issued with physical paper certificates (bonds or shares), it is those certificates that would be required for physical delivery. However, most securities are sold without a physical certificate. In those instances, evidence of ownership is kept on record at a central agency. For example, earlier, we noted that government securities issued by the U.S. Treasury are all issued in book-entry form, meaning that no physical securities (paper certificates) exist. Transfer of ownership is recorded by entering the change on the books or electronic files and is more efficient and faster than paper certificates.

KNOWLEDGE CHECK

1. Ms. Chiang executes a trade to purchase 100 shares of ABC Corporation common in her cash account on Thursday, June 30. Cash must be in her account sufficient to pay for the trade by the close of business on
   A. July 1.
   B. July 2.
   C. July 4.
   D. July 5.

2. The purchase of an equity option settles ___, the exercise of an equity option settles ___.
   A. T+1, T+2
   B. T+2, T+1
   C. same day, T+1
   D. T+2, T+3

3. A stock power may be used to
   A. authorize discretionary trading.
   B. place an unsolicited trade.
   C. replace the owner's signature on the back of a certificate.
   D. pay for a trade.

Answers

1. **D** Regular way settlement for corporate securities is two business days. The second business day following Thursday, June 30, is Tuesday, July 5. Saturday and Sunday are not business days. July 4 is Independence Day, a national holiday. LO 19.a

2. **A** All option trades settle next day. The exercise of an equity option must complete two days after exercise instructions are issued. LO 19.c

3. **C** A signed stock or bond power replaces the client's signature on the back of a certificate. LO 19.e

LEARNING OBJECTIVES

When you have completed this unit, you will be able to accomplish the following.

› LO 20.a Differentiate cash dividends from stocks and mutual funds.
› LO 20.b Calculate current yield.
› LO 20.c Calculate capital gains and losses.
› LO 20.d Identify long-term gains.
› LO 20.e Calculate total return.
› LO 20.f Relate ordinary income, investment income, and capital gains.
› LO 20.g Identify security benchmarks and indices.

INTRODUCTION

We have spent a great deal of time learning how securities are created and how customers invest in different products. In this unit, we will work on how investment returns are measured and the different ways your customers will pay taxes on those returns.

LESSON 20.1: INVESTMENT RETURNS

LO 20.a Differentiate cash dividends from stocks and mutual funds.

Dividends from stocks are covered in Unit 1, including the dates involved in the process (D*E*RP should sound familiar). The process for distribution of dividends from mutual funds is somewhat different, and it is important to understand the differences.

The dates involved in a cash dividend from a stock are in the DERP order to account for trading on the secondary market where settlement creates a delay between the day the trade takes place and the day the customer is an owner of record. You will likely recall that mutual funds do not trade in the secondary markets. When a customer purchases or redeems mutual fund shares the transaction is directly with the fund, so the trade is completed (settled) the day it is executed.

Purchasers of mutual fund shares become owners of record on the day the buy takes place. Sellers of mutual funds cease to be owners on the day the trade takes place.

The result of the trade and settlement date on the same day is that you may buy the fund and receive the dividend as an owner of record on the same day. So when is the dividend no longer available to new owners? The day *after* the record date. The ex-dividend date for a mutual fund is the day after the record date.

TAKE NOTE

For mutual funds, the order is declaration date – (record and payable date) – ex-dividend date.

Also note that the ex-dividend for a mutual fund is set by the fund's board of directors, not FINRA or an exchange.

LO 20.b Calculate current yield.

Yield is a measurement of the amount on income an investor will receive as a percentage of the cost of the investment. The term *current yield* may apply to both stocks and bonds. If the income is from a stock dividend, it is also called dividend yield.

The formula:

annual income (in dollars) / current market value = current yield

Pay attention to the question on yield. The question may provide you with the quarterly dividend. Current yield is an annual figure. You will need to get to the annual amount of the dividend before you divide.

EXAMPLE

ABC Corporation pays a $0.25 quarterly dividend. ABC stock is trading at $20 a share. What is the current yield of ABC stock?

0.25 × 4 (four quarters in a year) / 20 = 1/20 = 0.05 (5%)

LO 20.c Calculate capital gains and losses

Capital gains are generated from closing an open position at a profit. If you close an open position for a loss you have capital losses. The formula is:

sales proceeds – adjusted cost basis = (capital gains if a positive number, capital losses if a negative number)

Adjusted cost basis is the amount paid for a position modified by any adjustments. The effect of a stock dividend (Part 1) is an example of adjusting a cost basis.

EXAMPLE

Your customer purchased 100 shares of ABC Corporation for $22 a share three years ago. Last week they sold the 100 shares for $25 a share.

sales proceeds (2,500) – cost basis (2,200) = $300 gain

LO 20.d Identify long-term gains.

A long-term gain is taxed differently than a short-term gain. In order to receive long-term capital gains treatment, a position must have been held for *more* than one year. This means that any position that was held for *one year* or *less* is short term.

There is a difference in how long-term gains and short-term gains are taxed, so the determination that a position has been held long enough to receive long-term capital gains treatment is important.

LO 20.e Calculate total return.

Total return is a measure of the return an investor receives from an investment that includes both income and any gain or loss realized. This is expressed as a percentage of the cost basis of the investment.

The formula for calculating capital gains is:

income received + gains (or – losses) / cost basis = total return

EXAMPLE

Mr. Ross purchased 100 shares of Glengarry Real Estate, Inc., for $20 a share. After holding the stock for one year, he sold the shares for $21 a share. Over the year, the company paid a $0.25 quarterly dividend. What is Mr. Ross's total return?

Four 25-cent dividends is $1 in income.

He sold the stock for a $1 gain ($21 – $20).

$1 income + $1 gain = $2.

Divide the $2 / $20 (cost basis) = 0.1 (10%)

TAKE NOTE

A total return calculation may use realized capital gains or losses for closed positions, but it may also be used for open positions using unrealized capital gains or losses.

KNOWLEDGE CHECK

1. The Windmill Growth Fund declares a 15-cent dividend that will be shareholders on the record date of Wednesday, November 12. The most likely ex-dividend date is
    A. Monday, November 10.
    B. Tuesday, November 11.
    C. Wednesday, November 12.
    D. Thursday, November 13.

2. Seabird Airlines, Inc., pays a $0.40 a share quarterly dividend, and shares are currently trading at $32 a share. The current yield for Seabird is
   A. 1¼%.
   B. 2½%.
   C. 5%.
   D. 10%.

3. Your client, Mrs. Watt, sold her investment in Ohm Electric Company on June 10 for $22 a share. She purchased the stock on July 10 of the previous year for $18 a share. She has realized
   A. a long-term capital loss.
   B. a long-term capital gain.
   C. a short-term capital loss.
   D. a short-term capital gain.

Answers

1. **D** With a mutual fund dividend, the ex-date is normally the day *after* the record date. This is due to the nature of a mutual fund purchase (or redemption) settling on the same day as the trade. LO 20.a

2. **C** Remember that it is a quarterly dividend, while current yield is an annualized figure. This problem required you to multiply the quarterly dividend times four to get to the annual income figure. 0.40 × 4 = 1.60. Then divide 1.60 by 32 (current market value), which gives you a result of 0.05 (or 5%). LO 20.b

3. **D** A holding period starting on July 10 and ending on June 10 of the following year is a period of 11 months, less than a year. The stock was purchased for $18 and sold for $22, so she has a gain with a holding period of less than a year—a short-term capital gain. LO 20.d

LESSON 20.2: TAXATION AND BENCHMARKS

LO 20.f Relate ordinary income, investment income, and capital gains.

Ordinary income

Ordinary income consists of several different types of income that are added together to determine ordinary income. It is ordinary income that is used to determine the income tax rate that an investor will pay. The three primary components of ordinary income are earned income, investment income, and passive income.

Earned income

Earned income includes salary, wages, bonuses, tips, and other income that is derived from active participation in a trade or business. For most people, the majority (often all) of their taxable income is derived from earned income.

TAKE NOTE

Eligibility for IRA contributions is based on earned income, not ordinary income.

Investment income

Investment income is that which is earned from one's investments. Sometimes called *portfolio income*, it would include dividends and interest payments. Investment Income is income derived from an asset the investor holds.

Passive income

Passive income is a type of investment income that is derived from certain investments, primarily direct participation programs such as limited partnerships and many real estate investments. These types of investments may produce passive losses, as well as passive income. A taxpayer who has passive losses in a given year may use those losses to offset any passive income received that tax year.

TAKE NOTE

Passive losses may only be used to offset passive income. Passive losses may not offset any other types of income.

Capital gains and capital losses

Capital gains and capital losses, and what qualifies as long term versus short term, were covered in the previous unit. The taxation of capital gains deserves some more detail, as does the use of capital losses.

These gains and losses are generated from the buying and selling of a security. Gains and losses are generated when an investment position is closed and the investor no longer holds the asset.

Long-term capital gains

Long-term capital gains are taxed at an advantages rate. The actual rate is not tested because the rate changes regularly. The long-term rate is almost always lower than the investor's ordinary income tax rate.

Short-term capital gains

Capital gains made from assets held for a period of one year or less are taxed as ordinary income. In almost all circumstances, the ordinary income tax rate will exceed the long-term capital gains tax rate.

Long- and short-term capital losses

The difference in how long- and short-term capital losses are handled for taxes is not a testable point. However, what could be tested is the use of capital losses.

Capital losses may be used to offset capital gains on a dollar-for-dollar basis. Further, if an investor has losses that exceed gains in a given year, she may use up to $3,000 of those losses to reduce ordinary income. If an investor still has losses in excess of gains and the $3,000, she may carry those losses into the next tax year. These are called carryforward losses, and they may be carried forward until used with no time limit (indefinitely).

EXAMPLE

In the previous tax year the investor has the following:

Capital gains	$24,000
Capital losses	$32,000
Net losses	$ 8,000

The investor may reduce their ordinary income by $3,000 and may carry the remaining $5,000 of losses into the new tax year.

TAKE NOTE

Unrealized gains and losses are found on open positions. Unrealized gains and losses have no tax impact. If you buy a stock for $20 a share and the stock rises to $25 a share, you have a gain of $5 a share. The *gain is unrealized* and has no tax implications, but it likely pleases you. From a tax perspective, nothing has happened. If you were to then sell the stock (**closing the position**), the $5 would become a **realized capital gain** and taxes would be due.

Wash sale

Consider that an investor can use capital loses to offset capital gains. A **wash sale** is an attempt to create a loss for tax purposes (sell at a loss) when one's intent is to still maintain ownership of the securities. Any repurchase of the same within 30 days before or after the date establishing the loss would be recognized as one's intent to maintain ownership. If this occurs, the loss established at the time of the sale is disallowed.

TAKE NOTE

A wash sale is not illegal. Attempting to use the losses from the wash sale in order to reduce taxes is illegal.

EXAMPLE

October 21, 2013, buy 1,000 XYZ at 30

November 17, 2014, sell 1,000 XYZ at 28

Note that a loss has been established.

November 23, 2014, buy 1,000 XYZ at 27

Note that the long position in XYZ stock has been reestablished a few days after the sale that had created the loss. The sale is now considered a *prohibited wash sale*, and the loss is disallowed for tax purposes.

Two additional points on wash sale rules should be noted.

■ First, the rule applies to re-creating long positions, as in the previous example, and to re-creating short positions.

■ Second, the rule applies for attempts to recreate the same position using not only the exact same security but also substantially identical securities. For instance, a long stock position in XYZ stock is closed with a sale for a loss. Not only do the wash sale rules prohibit reestablishing the positon by repurchasing XYZ stock, but they would also recognize the purchase of XYZ call options or rights that can be exercised to purchase shares of XYZ stock as a way of reestablishing the position if the options or rights are exercised. In this light, the XYZ call options or rights would be considered substantially identical to the XYZ stock. Also, the purchase of a convertible bond or preferred stock from the same issuer.

TAKE NOTE

Any position that may be converted or exercised into the same security as the one that was sold for a loss may be "substantial identical."

LO 20.g Identify security benchmarks and indices.

For investors to set reasonable return expectations, they need to understand how the broader market is performing. If markets are strongly bullish, a specific investment may be providing a positive return but still be lagging the market as a whole. A security in a bear market may have a negative return but still be outperforming the market as a whole. While there's no single unwavering standard or benchmark, there are performance standards an investor can watch. An investment should be judged within the context of the portfolio's strategy, and performance can be compared against an appropriate standard or benchmark.

The following are a few of the more frequently cited indices and averages:

- **Dow Jones Industrial Average (DJIA)**—The most widely cited measure of the market's performance in the popular press, the DJIA tracks the performance of 30 stocks of large, well-known companies.

- **Standard & Poor's (S&P) 500 Index**—The S&P 500 Index tracks 500 stocks of large U.S. companies and is the basis for several index mutual funds and exchange-traded funds (ETFs). The S&P 500 is the benchmark most professionals use when speaking about overall market performance.

- **Russell 2000 Index**—This index tracks 2,000 small-company stocks and serves as the benchmark for smaller companies in the overall market.

- **Wilshire 5000**—Tracking over 5,000 stocks, the Wilshire 5000 covers all the companies listed on the major stock markets, including companies of all sizes across all industries. The Wilshire is considered the broadest measure of overall stock market performance. The 5,000 is a bit of an understatement, this index has closer to 6,700 components. The index was created in 1974 by Wilshire Associates.

- **Barclays Capital U.S. Aggregate Bond Index**—This is a composite index that combines several bond indexes to give a picture of the entire bond market.

- **MSCI EAFE Index**—This index is designed to measure the equity market performance of developed (first world) markets outside of the United States and Canada. It is maintained by MSCI, Inc. EAFE stands for **Europe, Australasia,** and **Far East.** This is the most widely recognized index for foreign equities.

KNOWLEDGE CHECK

1. All of the following are components of ordinary income **except**
   A. A bonus from their employer
   B. Interest payments from a bond portfolio
   C. Profit made from the sale of a long-held security
   D. Consultation fees received from a client

2. Your customer had $120,000 in ordinary income in the prior tax year. This customer also sold two stock positions—the first for a gain of $47,000, and the second for a loss of $50,000. For that tax year, the customer will pay tax on
   A. $117,000 in ordinary income and zero net gains.
   B. $117,000 in ordinary income and $3,000 in gains.
   C. $120,000 in ordinary income and zero net gains.
   D. $120,000 in ordinary income and $3,000 in net gains.

3. A customer owns a diversified portfolio of domestic large-cap stocks. This customer would like to compare her portfolio's performance to the overall market. The best index to use as a benchmark is which of the following?
   A. EAFE Index
   B. S&P 500 Index
   C. Barclay's Aggregate Bond Index
   D. Russell 2000 index

Answers

1. **C** Profits made from the sale of a long-held (more than one year) investment are long-term capital gains and are not part of ordinary income. Bonuses and consulting fees are earned income, and interest payments are portfolio income. Both are components of ordinary income. LO 20.d

2. **A** The $47,000 in gains is completely offset by the $50,000 in losses. The remaining losses may be used to reduce ordinary income (up to $3,000 a year). LO 20.f

3. **B** The S&P 500 is an index of large U.S. companies and is the closest of these to the portfolio's makeup. The Russell 2000 is an index of small companies. The Barclay's is a bond index and the EAFE is non-US companies. LO 20.g

EXAMPLE   Even forward split

An investor owns 100 shares at $60 per share. Therefore, the total position value is $6,000 (100 × $60 = $6,000).

Assume a 2:1 split. To find the new number of shares, multiply the original number by 2 (the first number of the split) and then divide by 1 (the second number of the split) (100 × 2 = 200; 200 ÷ 1 = 200). We now know that the investor will receive an additional 100 shares from the split for a total of 200 shares. Because the total position value of the shares is the same before and after the split, determine the new per share value as follows:

$6,000 (the total value of the position) ÷ 200 (the total post-split shares) = 30. The new per share value is $30.

After the adjustment for the 2:1 corporate split action, the investor now owns 200 shares at $30 per share.

EXAMPLE   Forward uneven split

An investor owns 100 shares at $60 per share. Therefore, the total position value is $6,000 (100 × $60 = $6,000).

Assume a 5:4 split. To find the new number of shares, multiply the original number by 5 (the first number of the split) and then divide by 4 (the second number of the split) (100 × 5 = 500; 500 ÷ 4 = 125). Determine the new per share value as follows:

$6,000 ÷ 125 = 48. The new per share value is $48.

After the adjustment for the 5:4 corporate split action, the investor now owns 125 shares at $48 per share.

Reverse split

Sometimes, a stock price becomes so low that it attains an undesirable aura about it. In some cases, a low stock price might not meet the listing criteria of a stock exchange that it is listed on and delisting can occur. To combat these issues, a corporation can do a reverse stock split. Unlike a forward split where the number of shares is increased and the price per share is decreased, a reverse split has the opposite effect on the number and price of shares. After a reverse split, investors own fewer shares at more worth per share.

TAKE NOTE

In a reverse split, the number of shares decreases while the price per share increases. The cost basis per share will likewise increase. As in a forward split, the total value of the position is unchanged by the split.

A reverse split can also be characterized as either an even split or an uneven split. In an even split, the investor will always be given one share for a certain number of shares owned: 1 for 2, or 1 for 3, for example. In an uneven split, the split can be designated in any ratio: 2 for 3, or 4 for 5, for example. Let's look at the math involved for an even reverse split. As with forward splits, always keep in mind that the total position value for the investor is always the same before and after the split.

EXAMPLE   Reverse even split

An investor owns 100 shares at $5. Therefore, the total position value is $500 (100 × $5 = $500).

Assume a 1:4 reverse split. What is the new number and value of shares?

100 × 1 = 100; 100 ÷ 4 = 25. The new number of shares is 25.

$500 ÷ 25 = $20. The new per share value is $20.

After the adjustment for the 1:4 corporate split action, the investor now owns 25 shares at $20 per share.

An uneven reverse split follows the same pattern; however, that is not something that is tested.

TEST TOPIC ALERT

Not all questions on splits involve calculations. If you remember that there are more or fewer shares at lower or greater value as a result of the corporate action (split) depending on whether it is a forward or a reverse split, you might be able to answer the question without using math.

LO 21.b Recall the tax implications of stock dividends and stock splits.

At the time of the split, there is no tax event, there are no tax implications. The cost basis per share will change, and this may have an effect when the shares are sold, but not until then. It may seem odd to have a learning objective with so little to know, but this is important and needs to be emphasized; there are no tax implications at the time of the split.

LO 21.c Define M&A and spin-off.

M&A is short for mergers and acquisitions.

Merger

In a merger, two (or more) companies combine operations and assets. In a typical merger, the shareholders of both companies receive new shares of the combined company and their shares of the old company are canceled.

Acquisition

In an acquisition, one company takes over the operations and assets of another firm. In a typical acquisition, the shareholders of the company that was acquired will receive shares of the company that did the acquiring, and their old shares are canceled.

Spin-off

In a spin-off, a corporation forms a subsidiary company out of some of the corporation's assets and operations. It then issues shares of the newly formed corporation to the shareholders of the original company.

EXAMPLE

Several years ago. Sea/Air Services (a small airline) merged with Bird Flights (another small airline) and formed a new company: Seabird Airlines. Shareholders in Sea/Air and Bird Flights received shares of Seabird Airlines and the shares of Sea/Air and Bird were canceled.

Five years later, Seabird Airlines has grown substantially and acquires Short Hop Air, a small regional carrier in the Pacific Northwest. Short Hop's shareholders receive shares of Seabird Airlines, and Short Hop shares are canceled.

Another 10 years goes by and Seabird Airlines becomes a major airline. In order to provide better services overall, Seabird forms a new corporation that will service smaller airports and provide connecting services to major hubs. This new company is called Seagull Air. Seabird's shareholders will receive shares of the new company. Their existing shares in Seabird are still theirs. Seagull Air is a spin-off from Seabird.

LO 21.d Differentiate a buy back and a tender offer.

Buyback

A buyback is when a company buys its own outstanding shares in the open market from existing shareholders. Companies might buy back shares for numerous reasons. For example, doing so reduces the number of shares available (supply) and therefore can increase the value of shares still available. This approach to increasing shareholder value is becoming more popular as corporations prefer share buybacks to paying dividends.

Tender offer

An offer to buy a security directly from the owners of the security (and not through secondary markets) is called a tender offer. Corporations may make a tender offer on their own debt as a way to retire the debt early. Company's looking to acquire another company (either friendly or hostile) may make a tender offer to buy the target company's shares. A company making a bid to take over another company might also make a tender offer on the target's convertible securities.

TAKE NOTE

Buybacks and tender offers are normally cash offers.

LO 21.e Recognize the tax consequences of different corporate actions.

If the corporate action results in the existing shareholders receiving shares of stock, there is generally no tax event at the time of the action.

If the corporate action results in the stockholder receiving cash, it will generally result in a tax event because it is a sale of the security.

- Stock splits and stock dividends are never taxable events because they result in the receipt of additional shares.

- Mergers, acquisitions, and spin-offs are generally not taxable events because shareholders receive stock. However, these offers may be a mix of stocks and cash payments. The cash portion is taxable as a capital gain or loss.

- Buybacks and tender offers are almost always all cash offers and are treated as a sale of the security resulting in a capital gain or loss.

LO 21.f Recall notification requirements for corporate actions.

Issuers are required by the Securities and Exchange Commission (SEC) to give notice of corporate actions to shareholders for such actions as cash dividends, stock dividends, a forward or reverse split, or a rights or warrants offering.

The following should be included in the notice:

- Title of the security
- Date of declaration
- Date of record for determining holders entitled to receive the distribution or to participate in the split
- Date of payment or distribution
- For a cash dividend—the amount to be paid
- For a stock dividend—the rate of the dividend (e.g., 10%)
- For a split (forward or reverse)—the rate of the distribution (e.g., 2:1, 3:2)

Notice should be given no later than 10 days before the record involved or, in case of a rights subscription or other offering if giving 10 days advance notice is not practical, on or before the record date and in no event later than the effective date.

LO 21.g Define proxy voting.

Every publicly traded company must have an annual general shareholder meeting where management presents any decisions that would require shareholder approval. The approval (or disapproval) is given by means of voting for each decision. Shareholders may attend the meeting in person to vote or they may vote by proxy either electronically or by mail.

Rather than attend meetings in person, most corporate stockholders usually vote by means of a proxy, which is like an absentee ballot. A proxy is a limited power of attorney that a stockholder gives to another person, transferring the right to vote on the stockholder's behalf.

A proxy is automatically revoked if the stockholder attends the shareholder meeting or if the proxy is replaced by another proxy that the stockholder executes at a later date.

Proxy solicitation

Stockholders may receive multiple proxy solicitations (offers to let a third party vote the shares) for controversial company proposals. If proxies are solicited, the SEC requires a company to give stockholders information about the items to be voted on and allow the SEC to review this information before it sends the proxies to stockholders. In a proxy contest, everyone who participates must register with the SEC. Also, anyone who is not a direct participant but who provides stockholders with unsolicited advice must register as a participant.

Forwarding proxies and related material

Member BD firms must cooperate with issuers by ensuring that customers whose stock is held in the BD's name (street name) are alerted to all financial matters concerning issuers (e.g., quarterly reports and proxy statements). To do so, members act as forwarding agents for all proxies and other corporate materials received from an issuer for street name stock.

Member firms that are nominal owners of record (the stock is held in street name) must vote street name stock in accordance with the wishes of the beneficial owners (the BD's customers who purchased the shares). If a customer signs and returns a proxy statement and fails to indicate how the shares are to be voted, the member must vote the shares as recommended by the issuer's management.

If a customer does not return the proxy by the 10th day before the annual shareholder meeting, the member may vote the shares as it sees fit as long as the matters to be voted on are of minor importance. If the matters to be voted on are of major importance (e.g., merger or issuance of additional securities), the member may never vote the shares as it sees fit. In this case, if the proxy is not returned, the shares are not voted.

TAKE NOTE

Member BD firms are reimbursed by issuers for all costs relating to the forwarding of proxy materials. Such costs include postage and related clerical expenses.

KNOWLEDGE CHECK

1. Which of the following is a taxable event for an investor when it occurs?
    A. Stock dividend distribution
    B. Cash dividend distribution
    C. Forward split
    D. Reverse split

2. In a stock buyback, the shares are purchased by which of the following?
    A. Owner
    B. Board of directors
    C. Issuer of the shares
    D. Investment trust

3. A customer has returned a signed proxy statement for stock held in street name by a member firm. He did not indicate how he wanted to vote for any issues listed on his ballot. What action, if any, is required of the member firm?
    A. No action is required and no votes are cast.
    B. The firm must contact the beneficial owner of the stock and ask for direction on how to vote on the proposals listed.
    C. The firm may vote on the ballot as it sees fit for the benefit of the customer.
    D. The firm must vote in accordance with the recommendations made by the issuer of the stock.

Answers

1. **B** There is no economic benefit for investors when a stock splits or when a stock dividend occurs. In each of these cases, the investor's cost basis in the investment is adjusted based on the resulting stock the investor owns after the split or additional stock received from a stock dividend. Only cash dividends are taxable (in the year they are distributed). LO 21.b

2. **C** In a stock buyback, the issuer of the stock buys the shares from the secondary markets. LO 21.d

3. **D** If a customer signs and returns a proxy statement for shares held in street name and fails to indicate how the shares are to be voted, the member must vote the shares as recommended by the issuer's management. LO 21.g

UNIT 22

Nonqualified Accounts

LEARNING OBJECTIVES

When you have completed this unit, you will be able to accomplish the following.

> LO 22.a   Differentiate individual and joint registrations.
> LO 22.b   Define transfer on death and power of attorney instructions.
> LO 22.c   Define the different types of business accounts.
> LO 22.d   Differentiate living, revocable, and irrevocable trusts.
> LO 22.e   Define custodial accounts.
> LO 22.f   Differentiate ESAs and 529 plans.

INTRODUCTION

Customers open accounts; that is the context for our interactions with customers. The kind of account a customer has opened is important in understanding both what the customer is trying to accomplish as well as any limitations based on the account's registration type.

Nonqualified accounts are those that not part of a retirement plan. Though some of these accounts are tax-deferred accounts, most are not. Let's take a look at the most common nonqualified account registrations.

LESSON 22.1: NONQUALIFIED ACCOUNTS

LO 22.a Differentiate individual and joint registrations.

Individual accounts

An **individual** account has one beneficial owner. The account holder is the only person who can control the investments within the account and request distributions of cash or securities from the account. An individual account is straightforward; one owner, one authorized trader unless there are additional appointments. Those appointments may only be made by the owner or a court.

When the individual owner dies, the account assets are distributed through the owner's estate unless other arrangements have been made ahead of time.

Joint accounts

In a **joint** account, *two or more adults* are named on the account as co-owners, with each allowed some form of control over the account. The account forms for joint accounts require the signatures of all owners.

Joint account agreements provide that any or all tenants may transact business in the account. Checks must be made payable to the names in which the account is registered and endorsed for deposit by all tenants, although mail only needs to be sent to a single address.

In addition to the new account form, a joint account must be designated as either tenants in common (TIC) or joint tenants with right of survivorship (JTWROS). These designations determine how the account ownership will be handled if any party to the account dies.

Though there are other types of joint accounts these two (TIC and JTWROS) are the most common.

Joint tenants with rights of survivorship (JTWROS)

Joint tenants with right of survivorship (JTWROS) ownership stipulates that a deceased tenant's interest in the account passes to the surviving tenant(s). All tenants in the account have an undivided interest in the account. Effectively, all tenants own all of the account equally. If one tenant dies, then the account remains the property of all the surviving tenants. This type of registration is very common for married couples. If one dies, the surviving spouse may continue managing the account with little difficulty.

Tenants in common (TIC)

Tenants in common (TIC) ownership provides that a deceased tenant's fractional interest in the account is retained by that tenant's estate and is not passed to the surviving tenant(s). Tenants in a TIC should have an agreement as to what percentage of the account is owned by each tenant. If no such agreement has been executed, it is assumed that the account is owned equally. When a tenant dies, the decedent's portion of the account is identified and must be distributed through the decedent's estate. The account will remain frozen (no trading or withdrawals) until the required estate paperwork has been received and processed.

TEST TOPIC ALERT

JTWROS—All parties have an undivided interest in the account.

TIC—Each party must specify a percentage interest in the account.

LO 22.b Define transfer on death and power of attorney instructions.

Transfer on death (TOD)

Transfer on death (TOD) is a designation that an owner(s) may add to an account that allows the owner to pass all or a portion of the account to a named beneficiary or beneficiaries at death. This account avoids probate (i.e., having the decedent's will declared genuine by a court of law) because the estate is bypassed. However, the assets in the account do not avoid estate tax, if applicable. A TOD may be added to individual accounts and JTWROS accounts. In the case of a joint account, the TOD becomes effective after the death of the last surviving tenant.

EXAMPLE

Uncle Buck has an individual account that he desires to give to his favorite niece upon his death, but he does not want her to have access to it before that. He adds TOD instructions to the account.

Mr. & Mrs. Heisman have designed their estate to go to charity upon the second death. However, they want certain assets to pass directly to their nephews. They establish a joint tenants with rights of survivorship account and add transfer on death instruction to the account. The account will be transferred to the nephews after the second person passes away.

Power of attorney (POA)

If a person who is not an owner is given any authority over the account, the customer must file written authorization with the BD giving that person access to the account. This trading authorization usually takes the form of a power of attorney. Two basic types of trading authorizations are full powers of attorney and limited powers of attorney. The power of attorney is granted to a natural person such as a representative or an attorney, not a firm (such as a BD or a law firm). All POAs are canceled upon the death of either party. All persons so appointed have a fiduciary duty to the account's owners.

TAKE NOTE

Granting a POA does not take away the account owner's authority to manage the account.

Full power of attorney (FPOA)

A full power of attorney grants the appointed person the power to deposit or withdraw cash or securities and make investment decisions for the account. The POA has much the same power over the account as the owner of the account. A RR having FPOA on a customer account that is not a family member would be highly unusual. Most firms would not approve the appointment.

Limited power of attorney (LPOA)

A limited power of attorney allows the appointed person to have some, but not total, control over an account. The document specifies the level of access the person may exercise. Limited power of attorney, also called limited trading authorization, allows the entering of buy and sell orders but no withdrawal of assets. These are more common. A common use of an LPOA would be a spouse granting LPOA for an IRA account.

Durable power of attorney

A POA ends with the death of either party. In addition to death, a POA ends with the incapacity of the grantor of the power (the account owner). Many POAs have language that allows the power to continue if the owner is incapacitated. If a POA has this language it is called a **durable** POA.

> **TEST TOPIC ALERT**
>
> For the third time, all POAs end with the death of either the person who granted the power (account owner) or the person so appointed (the "attorney"). This includes durable powers.

LO 22.c Define the different types of business accounts.

Business accounts are opened to hold the assets of a business. In many ways, they are the same as the nonqualified accounts discussed previously, except the owner may be natural persons or a business entity.

Sole proprietor account

An account opened for a sole proprietor is effectively the property of the business owner. The account may have a business name associated with it, in addition to the owner's name. Most firms will have an additional form to add a fictitious business name to the account. These are sometime called d/b/a accounts, which stands for "doing business as." Checks deposited into the account could be made payable to the account owner or the business name.

> **EXAMPLE**
>
> The account is registered as: John Baker d/b/a The Baker's Corner Confection Store. Checks deposited to the account may be payable to John or The Baker's Corner.

Partnership accounts

A partnership is an unincorporated association of two or more individuals. Partnerships frequently open accounts necessary for business purposes.

The partnership must have a written partnership agreement **and an authorization from the partners** stating which of the partners can make transactions for the account. If the partnership desires a margin account, the partnership agreement must *not* have language prohibiting margin.

An amended partnership agreement (similar to a corporate resolution) must be obtained each year if any changes have been made.

Corporate accounts

Corporations, like individuals, may desire to open a brokerage account. When opening an account for a corporation, a firm must obtain a copy of the corporate charter, as well as a corporate resolution. The charter is proof that the corporation does exist, and the resolution authorizes both the opening of the account and the officers designated to enter orders. The corporate resolution is a resolution of the board of directors.

A resolution must contain

- the business's legal right to open an investment account;

- an indication of any limitations that the owners, stockholders, a court, or any other entity has placed on the securities in which the business can invest; and

- the individual who will represent the business in transactions involving the account.

If the corporation desires a margin account, the corporation's charter must not prohibit this activity.

KNOWLEDGE CHECK

1. An individual opens an account with your firm. She tells you that upon her death, she wants any assets in the account to be divided equally among her three children. She also wants the ability to change the allocation in the event that conditions change and one of the children is in greater need than the others, but she does not want to incur any significant legal expense. You would suggest that the account be opened
    A. as a joint account with right of survivorship.
    B. as a joint account with tenants in common.
    C. as an individual transfer on death (TOD) account.
    D. under a discretionary power.

2. If three individuals have a tenants in common (TIC) account with your firm and one individual dies, then
    A. the two survivors continue as cotenants, along with the decedent's estate.
    B. the account must be liquidated and the proceeds split evenly between the two survivors and the decedent's estate.
    C. trading is discontinued until the executor names a replacement for the deceased.
    D. the account is converted to joint tenants with rights of survivorship.

3. A corporation opening a brokerage account must present all of the following documents except
    A. a new account form.
    B. an authorization from the state department of corporations.
    C. a copy of the corporate charter.
    D. a resolution of the board of directors.

Answers

1. **C** An individual account with a TOD designation would be best for this customer. A joint account would make the children owners of the account, and a discretionary power does not accomplish the owner's desire to transfer the account on her death. LO 22.b

2. **A** In a TIC, the estate replaces the decedent tenant. Eventually the decedent's portion of the account will be distributed to the estate's beneficiaries. LO 22.a

3. **B** A corporation does not (normally) need authorization from the state to open an account. LO 22.c

LESSON 22.2: TRUST, CUSTODIAL, AND EDUCATION ACCOUNTS

Trust accounts

A trust is a way to hold assets that allows for greater flexibility in assigning the different aspects of ownership. What are the aspects of ownership? If you own something, you legally possess it and have certain rights in regard to the asset. You can choose how the assets will be used and who benefits from the use of the asset.

Assets that are held in trust belong to the trust. Assets are placed into the trust by a grantor (or settlor): the person who owns the asset. The settlor may appoint a trustee, whose job is to manage the assets for the benefit of a beneficiary. The beneficiary is selected by the grantor, and the assets of the trust are to be managed for their benefit. These three roles can each be different people, breaking up the three aspects of ownership for the assets held in the trust.

LO 22.d Differentiate living, revocable, and irrevocable trusts.

Living trust

A trust that is created and funded by the grantor during the grantor's lifetime is called a living trust. Questions about a living trust are much more common than questions about decedent's trusts. The same is true of trusts: living trusts are much more common than decedent's trusts.

Decedent's trust

A trust that is funded by a will or some other estate process where the assets are placed in the trust after the owner has passed away is called a decedent's trust.

Revocable trust

Most living trusts may be modified or even completely revoked by the grantor. As long as the grantor is alive, the trust may be modified as the grantor (or grantors) sees fit. So long as the grantor has this level of control, the assets in the trust are still considered part of the grantor's assets and will be included in the estate. In a revocable living trust, it is common for the grantor to also be the trustee and the beneficiary.

Irrevocable trust

When a grantor forms a trust that cannot be modified, it is an irrevocable trust. Assets placed in an irrevocable trust may be removed from the grantors estate. The grantor gives up control of the assets in an irrevocable trust. In order for an asset to be removed from an estate, the grantor may not serve as the trustee or be the beneficiary of the trust.

An irrevocable life insurance trust is an estate planning strategy that is often used to help pay estate taxes when an estate holds a large illiquid asset such as a family business. Details on how the strategy functions is beyond the scope of this exam.

 TAKE NOTE

The trustee of a trust has a fiduciary duty to manage the trust for the benefit of the beneficiary of the trust.

LO 22.e Define custodial accounts.

Custodial accounts

Accounts set up for minors can be established under either the **Uniform Gift to Minors Act** (UGMA) or the Uniform Transfers to Minors Act (UTMA). These accounts require an adult to act as **custodian** for a minor (the beneficial owner). Any kind of security or cash may be given to the account without limitation.

Any assets given to a minor through an UGMA or UTMA account are managed by a custodian until the minor reaches the age of majority.

The custodian has full control over the minor's account and can

- buy or sell securities;
- exercise rights or warrants; or
- liquidate, trade, or hold securities.

The custodian may also use the property in the account in any way deemed proper for the minor's support, education, maintenance, general use, or benefit. However, the account is not normally used to pay expenses associated with raising a child (normal parental responsibilities).

RRs must know the following rules of custodial accounts.

- An account may have only one custodian and one minor or beneficial owner.
- Only an individual can be a custodian for a minor's account.
- A minor can be the beneficiary of more than one account, and a person may serve as custodian for more than one account, as long as each account benefits only one minor.
- The donor of securities can act as custodian or can appoint someone else to do so.
- Unless they are acting as custodians, parents have no legal control over a custodial account or the securities in it.

When opening a custodial account, a representative must ensure that the account application contains the custodian's name, the minor's name and Social Security number, and the state in which the account is registered. Unlike opening a trust account where documentation of the trustee's authority is required, no documentation of custodial rights or court certification is required for an individual acting as the custodian for a minor.

Any securities in a custodial account are registered in custodial name for the benefit of the minor. Securities bought in a custodial account must be registered in such a way that the custodial relationship is evident.

 EXAMPLE

Marilyn Johnson, the donor, has appointed her daughter's aunt, Barbara Wood, as custodian for the account of her minor daughter, Alexis. The account and the certificates would read "Barbara Wood as custodian for Alexis Johnson."

Because the minor is the **beneficial owner** (the account contains the minor's Social Security number), any tax liability is that of the minor. Though the minor is responsible for any and all taxes on the account, it is the parent's or legal guardian's responsibility to see that the taxes are paid.

Remember that a custodial account is a type of fiduciary account, and as such, the fiduciary is charged with fiduciary responsibilities in managing the minor's account. Certain restrictions have been placed on what is deemed to be proper handling of the investments in these accounts. The most important limitations follow.

- Custodial accounts may be opened and managed as cash accounts only.

- A custodian may not purchase securities in an account on margin or pledge them as collateral for a loan.

- A custodian must reinvest all cash proceeds, dividends, and interest within a reasonable time. Cash proceeds from sales or dividends may be held in a non-interest-bearing custodial account for a reasonable period, but should not remain idle for long.

- Investment decisions must take into account a minor's age and the custodial relationship. Commodities futures, naked options, and other high-risk securities are examples of inappropriate investments. Options may not be bought in a custodial account; however, covered call writing is normally allowed.

- Stock subscription rights or warrants must be either exercised or sold.

- A custodian cannot delegate away fiduciary responsibility but can grant trading authority and investment decisions to a qualified third party.

- A custodian may loan money to an account but cannot borrow from it.

- A custodian may be reimbursed for any reasonable expenses incurred in managing the account, as well as compensation for doing so. However, if the custodian is also the donor, only reimbursement of expenses is permitted and not compensation.

- Custodial accounts are under the minor's Social Security number and taxed at the minor's tax rate.

If the beneficiary of a custodial account (minor) dies, the securities in the account pass to the minor's estate, not to the parents' or custodian's estate.

In the event of the custodian's death or resignation, either a court of law or the donor of the securities in the account must appoint a new custodian.

UTMA vs. UGMA

The two types of custodial account are very similar, but there are a few differences. The individual states choose which type of custodial account is available in their state.

UTMA accounts allow for real estate to be titled in custodial name; UGMA accounts do not.

UTMA accounts may be held in custodial name until the beneficiary turns 25 (21 in some states); UGMA accounts are available to the minor at age of majority for the state.

Accounts with a fiduciary

A fiduciary is any person legally appointed and authorized to represent another person, act on her behalf, and make whatever decisions are necessary to the prudent management of her account. Fiduciaries include

- a trustee designated to administer a trust;

- an executor designated in a decedent's will to manage the affairs of the estate;

- an administrator appointed by the courts to liquidate the estate of a person who died intestate (without a will);

- a guardian designated by the courts to handle a minor's affairs until the minor reaches the age of majority or to handle an incompetent person's affairs;

- a custodian for a minor;

- a receiver in a bankruptcy; and

- a conservator for an incompetent person.

Any trades that the fiduciary enters must be compatible with the investment objectives of the underlying entity.

Opening a fiduciary account may require a court certification of the individual's appointment and authority. An account for a trustee must include a trust agreement detailing the limitations placed on the fiduciary.

The RR for a fiduciary account must be aware of the following rules.

- Proper authorization must be given, because the necessary court documents must be filed with and verified by the BD.

- Speculative transactions are generally not permitted.

- Margin accounts are only permitted if authorized by the legal documents establishing the fiduciary accounts.

- The prudent investor rule requires fiduciaries to make wise and safe investments.

- Many states publish a legal list of securities approved for fiduciary accounts.

- A fiduciary may not share in an account's profits but may charge a reasonable fee for services.

 TAKE NOTE

A trust must specifically allow for margin in order to open an account with margin.

LO 22.f Differentiate ESAs and 529 plans.

Both ESA and 529 plans are accounts for education savings. The two accounts are otherwise very different.

Coverdell Education Savings Account (Education IRA)

Coverdell Education IRAs allow after-tax contributions of up to $2,000 per student per year for children younger than age 18. Contribution limits may be reduced or eliminated for higher-income taxpayers. Growth and income within the portfolio is deferred. There is no tax deduction for these contributions.

- Distributions are tax free as long as the funds are used for qualified education expenses. These expenses include those for college, secondary, or elementary school.

- Nonqualified distributions are subject to income tax plus a 10% penalty for amounts that are in excess of principal.

- If a student's account is not depleted by age 30, the funds must be distributed to the individual subject to income tax and a 10% penalty or rolled into an education IRA for another beneficiary.

The Coverdell ESA is not as popular as the 529 plans due to the rather small contribution limit, as well the limits on a contributor's income.

529 plans

A Section 529 plan is a specific type of education savings account available to investors. The plans allow money saved to be used for qualified expenses for K-12 and postsecondary education. Qualified expenses include tuition at an elementary or secondary public, private, or religious school for up to $10,000 per year. This distribution limit does not apply to postsecondary (college and graduate school) costs.

Because they are state sponsored, they are defined as a *municipal fund security*. As such, the sale of these plans must be accompanied or preceded by an official statement or offering circular (similar to a prospectus) in the same way that other municipal securities sales would be.

There are two basic types of 529 plans: prepaid tuition plans for state residents and savings plans for residents and nonresidents. Prepaid plans allow resident donors to lock in current tuition rates by paying now for future education costs. The prepaid plan provides protection against inflation in the costs of education. Education inflation rates have historically been significantly higher than the general rate of inflation.

The more popular option is the college savings plan, which allows donors to save money to be used later for education expenses. Money contributed to a 529 college savings plan is then invested in one or more separate accounts, purchasing units, not shares.

TAKE NOTE

Money placed in a 529 college savings plan is invested into units of a separate account, not shares of a mutual fund. The terminology is important.

Any adult can open a 529 plan for a future college student. The donor does not have to be related to the student. (Adult students may also contribute to their own 529 plan.) With a 529 plan, the donor can invest a lump sum or make periodic payments. When the student is ready for college, the donor withdraws the amount needed to pay for qualified education expenses (e.g., tuition, room and board, and books). In the case of a prepaid tuition plan, the tuition credits are applied.

Contributions, which are considered gifts under federal tax law, are made with after-tax dollars, and earnings accumulate on a tax-deferred basis. Withdrawals are tax free at the federal level if they are used for qualified education expenses. Most states permit tax-free withdrawals as well. In addition, some states allow contributions into in-state plans to be tax deductible. Therefore, if one of your customers wishes to open an out-of-state plan, you must advise the customer that certain tax advantages, such as the one just noted, may not be available to out-of-state donors.

If a beneficiary does not need the funds for school, there are no tax consequences if the donor changes the designated beneficiary to another member of the family. For example, if one child gets a full scholarship, a parental donor can roll funds from that child's 529 plan into a sibling's plan without penalty.

Other relevant points regarding Section 529 plans are as follows.

■ Overall total contribution levels can vary from state to state. There are no annual contribution limits.

■ Assets in the account remain under the donor's control, even after the student becomes of legal age.

■ There are no income limitations on making contributions to a 529 plan.

■ Account balances left unused may be transferred to a related beneficiary.

■ There is no age limit to the 529 accounts, either contributions or distributions.

■ Rollovers are permitted from one state's plan to another state's plan, but no more than once every 12 months.

 KNOWLEDGE CHECK

1. A trust formed during the grantors lifetime that may be modified only by the original grantor(s) is normally called
   A. an irrevocable living trust.
   B. a revocable living trust.
   C. an A-B trust.
   D. a life insurance trust.

2. Which of the following investments would **not** be allowed in a custodial account?
   A. Covered call options
   B. Small-company stocks from an emerging market
   C. Blue-chip stocks
   D. Uncovered call options

3. All of the following are true of a 529 college savings plan **except**
   A. distribution must be complete by the beneficiary's 30th birthday.
   B. there are no taxes due for distributions used for qualified education expenses.
   C. there is no income limit for the person making a contribution.
   D. there is no annual contribution limit.

Answers

1. **B** If a grantor forms and funds a trust in his lifetime, it is a living trust. If anyone has the power to modify the trust, it is a revocable trust. An A-B trust is a type of revocable living trust used for estate planning purposes and not expected to appear on the test except, as you see here, a distraction. LO 22.d

2. **D** Uncovered call options with their inherent (unlimited) risk are not appropriate for a custodial account. Covered calls are allowed, as are most common stocks. LO 22.e

3. **A** There is no beneficiary age limit for 529 plans, either for contributions or distributions. LO 22.f

UNIT 23

Qualified Plans

LEARNING OBJECTIVES

When you have completed this unit, you will be able to accomplish the following.

> › LO 23.a   Recall contribution and distribution rules for traditional and Roth IRA accounts.
> › LO 23.b   Differentiate defined benefit and defined contribution plans.

INTRODUCTION

Most people invest to prepare for retirement. The government has established several special account types designed for retirement savings. These qualified accounts allow for tax-deferred savings for retirement. Some require sponsorship by an employer and others do not, but all are designed to encourage people to save money for their retirement.

LESSON 23.1: INDIVIDUAL RETIREMENT ACCOUNTS AND EMPLOYER-SPONSORED PLANS

LO 23.a Recall contribution and distribution rules for traditional and Roth IRA accounts.

Individual retirement accounts

Individual retirement accounts (IRAs) were created as a way of encouraging people to save for retirement. All employed individuals, regardless of whether they are covered by a qualified corporate retirement plan, may open and contribute to an IRA. IRAs are considered qualified plans by the IRS.

Qualified plans allow the earnings in the account to grow tax deferred. Additionally, individuals making a contribution to an IRA can take a tax deduction for the amount of the contribution if certain criteria are met. If an individual is not actively participating in other qualified plans, such as an employer's 401(k) plan, the full amount of the contribution to the IRA is deductible. For an individual covered by another qualified plan, the portion deductible is determined by that person's income level. The tax deduction gradually phases out as the taxpayer's adjusted gross income (AGI) climbs. The exact income levels above which tax-deductible contributions are prohibited is not critical for testing purposes because these levels are, by law, raised each year. *However, contributions may still be made* because the earnings on these amounts are still tax deferred.

TAKE NOTE

Contributions to IRAs are made out of earned income, not ordinary income.

TEST TOPIC ALERT

The concepts around contributions are tested, but the annual dollar limit is not. This number may change annually, so is not included as a test point.

Traditional IRAs

Contributions—An eligible individual may make contributions up to a maximum dollar amount (this amount can change from year to year as determined by the tax code), provided that the contribution does not exceed earned income for the year. The dollar cap is increased by a catch-up amount for individuals age 50 and older. Currently the catch-up amount is $1,000.00

No contributions are allowed starting with the year the account holder turns 70½.

Investments—Within an IRA, investments can be made in stocks, bonds, investment company securities, U.S.-minted gold and silver coins, and many other securities.

There are, however, certain investments that are considered ineligible for use in an IRA. Collectibles (e.g., antiques, gems, rare coins, works of art, stamps) are not acceptable IRA investments. Life insurance contracts may not be purchased in an IRA.

TAKE NOTE

Although life insurance is not allowed within IRAs, annuities are allowed. However, FINRA has expressed concern about the suitability of a tax-favored product (like an annuity) within a tax-favored account.

The following is a partial list of investments generally considered appropriate for IRAs:

- Stocks
- Bonds
- Mutual funds
- Unit investment trusts (UITs)
- Government securities
- U.S. government-issued gold and silver coins

Certain investment practices are also considered inappropriate for IRAs or any other retirement plan:

- Short sales of stock
- Speculative option strategies
- Tax-exempt municipal securities
- Margin account trading

However, covered call writing is permissible because it is a conservative way to generate investment income.

Rollover—A rollover is when a customer withdraws and takes possession of IRA assets and then returns the assets back to an IRA (or other qualified account) within 60 calendar days. As long as the customer successfully completes the rollover, there are no tax implications for the withdrawal. A person is allowed to perform one rollover per rolling year, not per IRA and not per calendar year.

TEST TOPIC ALERT

Rollovers have a time limit of 60 calendar days, not 2 months.

Transfer – A customer may transfer IRA assets from one IRA account to another IRA account. This is sometimes called a custodian-to-custodian transfer. There is no limit to the number of times a customer may do a transfer. If a customer moves money from an employer plan—such as a 401(k)—to an IRA, this is sometimes called a **direct rollover**. Be careful; this activity is actually a transfer and not a rollover.

Withdrawals—Distributions may begin without penalty after age 59½ and are generally added to ordinary income for tax purposes. Distributions before age 59½ are subject to a 10% penalty, as well as regular income tax. There are exceptions to the penalty (but not the taxes) if the distribution is due to

- death of the owner;
- disability of the owner;
- first-time homebuyer for purchase of a principal residence (up to $10,000);
- education expenses for the taxpayer, spouse, child, or grandchild;
- medical premiums for unemployed individuals; and
- medical expenses in excess of defined adjusted gross income (AGI) limits.

Required minimum distributions—Called RMDs, these distributions are required beginning in the year the account owner turns 72 and annually by December 31 thereafter. The amount of the RMD is based on the account values as of the end of the previous year. If an investor has more than one account that requires RMDs, the total of all the accounts is used to determine the amount. The account holder may choose which account (or accounts) to take the distribution from.

EXAMPLE

A taxpayer is 75 years of age and has three traditional IRAs. One is at a bank, one at an insurance company, and the third at a broker-dealer. The total of the RMDs from each of the accounts is $20,000. The taxpayer could take all $20,000 from one of the accounts or could take from all three accounts in any combination desired as long as the total withdrawn is $20,000.

TAKE NOTE

The **first** RMD may be delayed to April 1 of the year after the account holder turns 70½. If the RMD is delayed this way, there will need to be a second distribution in that year by December 31.

If an account holder fails to take an RMD by the required date, any amount below the RMD amount will be subject to a 50% penalty (called an excise tax).

Roth IRAs

Introduced in 1997 as part of the Taxpayer Relief Act, the Roth IRA (named after its principal sponsor, Senator William Roth) is a variation on the traditional IRA. In this section, we will highlight the differences and similarities of traditional and Roth IRAs.

■   *Contributions*—Contributions rules for Roth IRAs are the same as traditional IRAs. It might be better to say that the two types have a combined limit. The limit to IRA contributions is for all contributions to all IRAs in a year. A customer *cannot* contribute the maximum in both a traditional and a Roth IRA. As with traditional IRAs, the contribution must come from earned income.

EXAMPLE

If the annual maximum contribution for IRAs is $6,000, an investor could contribute $4,000 to a traditional IRA and $2,000 to a Roth IRA, for a total contribution to all IRAs of $6,000.

However, it is important to note that *contributions to a Roth IRA are not deductible* from current income.

An additional limitation is that an investor's eligibility to contribute to a Roth IRA is phased out at higher income limits, eventually falling to zero. The income figure is not tested, but the concept may be.

There is no age limit for contributions to a Roth IRA, though remember that contributions must be from earned income.

■   *Investments*—The investment limitations for a Roth IRA are essentially the same as for a traditional IRA.

■   *Rollover*—The rollover rules are the same for traditional and Roth IRAs. Remember that only one is allowed per rolling year per person. You cannot do a rollover in a traditional and another in a Roth.

■   *Transfer*—The rules are the same as for traditional IRAs, but the transfer from a Roth account must be to a Roth account.

■   *Withdrawals*—Distributions is where the Roth shines. Distributions of the cost basis are always tax free. Qualified distribution of income or gains in the account are also **tax free**. Nonqualified distribution of income or gains from the account are taxed as ordinary income and subject to a 10% penalty.

For a distribution to be qualified

The account holder must have held a Roth IRA for at least five years before the distribution and the account holder must be age 59½ or older.

Exceptions to the age limit are as follows:

- Death (no penalty for the beneficiary)
- Disability of the account owner
- A first-time home purchase (up to $10,000)

There is no RMD rule for Roth IRAs. Account holders can leave the money in their accounts until they die.

Suitability—Roth IRAs are considered a good way to save for retirement for those who are younger (more years of growth that may be tax free) and those in lower income tax brackets (for whom the current deduction has little value). Anyone who may not deduct a contribution to a traditional IRA would be better off putting money in a Roth IRA.

LO 23.b Differentiate defined benefit and defined contribution plans.

There are a number of qualified retirement savings plans that require sponsorship by an employer, and so are only available to employees. They are broadly divided into two types: defined benefit plans and defined contribution plans.

Defined benefit plans (traditional pension plans)

As is evident in the name, a defined benefit plan defines within the plan document the benefit it will pay to retirees. These are often called pension plans. The plan will determine a benefit that retirees receive based on years of service, age, and salary at the time of retirement. The plan will replace a portion of the preretirement income.

 EXAMPLE

Rick & Ty's Furniture Stores have a pension plan that pays a benefit calculated as follows:

Employees may begin collecting as early as age 60.

Employees will receive an income equal to 2% per year of service of the average salary of the last five years of service. The maximum benefit is 70%.

Joe, a truck driver for the company, retires at age 65. Joe has worked for R&T since he was 25 years old, a total of 40 years. His average annual salary over the last five years was $60,000.

40 years × 2% = 80% (this exceeds the maximum benefit, so his number will be 70%)

70% of $60K is $42,000 a year. He will receive monthly payments equal to $42,000 a year for the rest of his life.

Employers will use the services of an outside firm to determine how much the company needs to contribute to the plan to have sufficient assets to meet the defined benefit payments. Employers are required to make the payments as defined in the plan. This places the investment risk on the company, and many companies are moving away from these types of plans.

TAKE NOTE

Pension plans from private employers pay a fixed benefit. Once the employee begins to collect benefits, the amount will not change. The beneficiary takes on purchasing power risk. Pensions from government agencies often include a cost-of-living adjustment (COLA)

Defined contribution plans

As the name would indicate, these plans define the amount that may be contributed to the plan. Employees in these plans will normally have a balance that they may invest in a mix of securities as defined within the plan. At retirement, employees may take possession of the assets in their account, often transferring the assets to an IRA for distribution during retirement. Employers may be required to contribute to the plan depending on the type of plan and the specifics of a particular plan.

Here is a partial list of defined contribution plans:

- 401(k) plans
- 403(b) plans
- Profit-sharing plans
- Money purchase plans
- SIMPLE plans

These, among other DC plans, are more popular today because the investing risk is carried by the employee. The liability for the employer is much smaller. Also, the assets in these plans are transportable between employer plans, making them a better choice for a mobile work force that changes employers several times over an active career.

KNOWLEDGE CHECK

1. In order to contribute to both a traditional IRA and a Roth IRA in the same year, a customer must have sufficient
   A. ordinary income.
   B. passive income.
   C. earned income.
   D. portfolio income.

2. Mr. Perez began contributing $3,000 a year to a Roth IRA account 10 years ago when he was 50 years old. The account value today has grown to $60,000. He withdraws $5,000 from the account. Mr. Perez will owe taxes on
   A. the entire amount.
   B. none of the withdrawal.
   C. the principal portion of the withdrawal.
   D. the gains plus a 10% penalty for premature distribution.

3. A retirement plan that requires a formula-based payment for the retiree's life is
   A. a pension plan.
   B. a defined contribution plan.
   C. a money purchase plan.
   D. 401(k) plan.

Answers

1. **C**   An IRA contribution must come from earned income. LO 23.a

2. **B**   Perez meets the requirements of a qualified distribution from his Roth IRA. He is over 59½ (he started 10 years ago at the age of 50, so he is now 60), He has had the account for more than 5 years (about 10 years). There are no taxes for this distribution. LO 23.a

3. **A**   *Pension plan* is another name for a defined benefit plan. A defined benefit plan pays a benefit to the retiree for life. The payment is based on a formula that defines the amount of the benefit. LO 23.b

UNIT 24

Account Features

LEARNING OBJECTIVES

When you have completed this unit, you will be able to accomplish the following.

> LO 24.a Define cash account.
> LO 24.b Define margin account.
> LO 24.c Calculate initial deposit requirements.
> LO 24.d Define maintenance call.
> LO 24.e Differentiate fee-based and commission-based trading accounts.

INTRODUCTION

In Unit 24, we cover brokerage accounts, both cash and margin, as well as a few other types. Margin is an account feature that allows the customer to purchase securities without all the cash, borrowing some money to pay for the purchase. We will also look at what the exam means by "fee-based" account.

LESSON 24.1: CASH ACCOUNTS, FEE-BASED ACCOUNTS, AND MARGIN ACCOUNTS

LO 24.a Define cash account.

A **cash account** is the basic type of investment account. Anyone eligible to open an investment account can open a cash account. In a cash account, a customer pays in full for any securities purchased. Payment is expected by the end of the day on the settlement date. With most corporate and municipal securities, this is the second business day (T+2). Regular way settlement is an industry standard enforced by the self-regulatory organizations (primarily FINRA). However, the federal government also has an expectation for payment under Federal Reserve Regulation T. Under Regulation T, payment must occur not later than two business days after the standard settlement period. Note that few BDs will tolerate customers that do not respect regular way settlement rules, much less a failure to pay that results in a government regulator asking "where's the money?"

EXAMPLE

Corporate stock is purchased in a cash account, and it will settle regular way T+2. In a cash account, full payment would be required no later than two business days after T+2—in other words, T+4.

Certain accounts must be opened as cash accounts—accounts that have contribution limits (IRAs and other retirement plans) and custodial accounts under UTMA and UGMA.

LO 24.b Define margin account.

Margin buying

Trading **on margin** is a common practice in the securities industry. It allows customers to increase their trading capital by borrowing either cash or securities through their BDs.

There are two types of margin accounts: long and short. In a long margin account, customers purchase securities and pay interest on the money borrowed until the loan is repaid. In a short margin account, stock is borrowed and then sold short, enabling the customer to profit if its value declines. All short sales must be executed through, and accounted for, in a margin account.

Stock can be borrowed from several sources for short sales in a margin account: the member firm executing a short sale on behalf of the customer, margin customers of that member firm, other member firms, specialized companies known as *stock lending firms*, and institutional investors. The most common source is another customer's margin account, but permission must be given by signing a consent to loan agreement, which we'll discuss later in this unit.

Margin accounts offer some advantages for customers. Consider that, in a margin account, a customer can

- purchase more securities with a lower initial cash outlay and
- leverage the investment by borrowing a portion of the purchase price.

Leveraging magnifies the customer's rate of return or rate of loss in adverse market conditions. Figure 24.1 demonstrates this, but it does not account for trading costs (commissions) or for interest costs applied for the funds borrowed.

Figure 24.1: Cash Purchase vs. Margin Purchase

	Cash Purchase	**Margin Purchase**
Purchase of 1,000 shares of ABC for $20	Customer pays $20,000 for purchase	Customer borrows 50% ($10,000) from BD, deposits equity of $10,000
Return after increase from $20 to $30 per share	Customer experiences 50% return (gain/initial investment: $10,000 ÷ $20,000 = 50%)	Customer experiences 100% return (gain/initial investment: $10,000 ÷ $10,000 = 100%)
Return after decrease from $20 to $15 per share	Customer experiences 25% loss (loss/initial investment: –$5,000 ÷ $20,000 = –25%)	Customer experiences 50% loss (loss/initial investment: –$5,000 ÷ $10,000 = –50%)

The advantages of margin accounts for BDs are that

- margin account loans generate interest income for the firm; and

- margin customers typically trade larger positions because of increased trading capital, generating higher commissions for the firm.

Hypothecation and rehypothecation

Hypothecation is the pledging of customer securities as collateral for margin loans. A hypothecation agreement must be signed by a customer who wants to open a margin account. This agreement is generally contained within the margin agreement, so customers are giving permission for this process to occur when they sign the margin agreement.

Typically, a BD will not use its own cash to lend for margin purchases; the BD borrows the money from the bank. The loan from the bank to the broker for this purpose is also secured by a portion of the stocks purchased on margin. After a customer pledges securities to the BD by signing the margin agreement, the BD **rehypothecates** (repledges) the securities as collateral for a loan from a bank. Federal Reserve Regulation U oversees the process of a bank lending money to BDs based on customer securities having been pledged as collateral for the loan.

Firms cannot commingle customer securities with securities owned by the firm. However, firms can commingle one customer's securities with another customer's securities for hypothecation if customers have given specific permission by signing the hypothecation agreement.

Accounts that may have a margin feature

Most **individual and joint accounts** may be margin accounts once all the required forms are submitted and a principal approves. This would also apply to sole proprietor business accounts.

Corporate and partnership accounts may have margin. However, before margin may be added to one of these account types, the corporate charter or bylaws (partnership agreement in the case of a partnership) must be checked to see if a prohibition against margin exists in the document. If the document is silent, then margin is allowed.

Trust and other fiduciary accounts require that the trust or similar document be checked. For this type of account to have margin, the document must specifically allow it. If the trust is silent, then margin is not allowed.

As written earlier, accounts that have contribution limits (IRAs and other retirement plans) and custodial accounts under UTMA and UGMA may not be margin accounts.

Like all accounts, margin accounts would need to be approved by a principal of the firm before the first trade. The approval would need to be in accordance with whether or not margin is permissible for the type of account being set up, as outlined in the previous section.

Forms for a margin account

There are three forms associated with adding margin borrowing to an account:

Credit agreement

The credit agreement discloses the terms of the credit extended by the BD, including the method of interest computation and situations under which interest rates may change.

Hypothecation agreement

As noted earlier in this unit, the hypothecation agreement allows the securities to be pledged for the loan and gives permission to the BD to repledge customer margin securities as collateral. The firm rehypothecates customer securities to the bank, and the bank loans money to the BD on the basis of the loan value of these securities. All customer securities must be held in street name (registered in the name of the BD) to facilitate this process. When customer securities are held in street name, the BD is known as the nominal, or named, owner. The customer is the beneficial owner because he retains all rights of ownership.

Consent to loan agreement

If signed, the loan consent form gives permission to the firm to loan the customers margin securities to other customers or BDs, usually to facilitate short sales where securities need to be borrowed.

> **TAKE NOTE**
>
> To open a margin account, it is mandatory that the customer sign the credit agreement and hypothecation agreement. The loan consent form is optional. A further note: a BD may make the consent to loan agreement mandatory for its margin customers, but this form is not a regulatory requirement.

Additionally, before opening a margin account, you must provide customers with a risk disclosure document. This information must also be provided to margin customers on an annual basis. The document discusses the risks associated with margin trading, some of which are listed here.

- Customers are not entitled to choose which securities can be sold if a maintenance call is not met.
- Customers can lose more money than initially deposited.
- Customers are not entitled to an extension of time to meet a margin call.
- Firms can increase their in-house margin requirements without advance notice.

Securities eligible for margin borrowing

Regulation T also identifies which securities are eligible for purchase on margin and which may be used as collateral for loans for other purchases.

The following may be purchased on margin and used as collateral:

- Exchange-listed stocks, bonds
- Nasdaq stocks
- OTC issues approved by the FRB for margin
- Warrants

The following cannot be purchased on margin and cannot be used as collateral for a margin loan:

- Options (both calls and puts)
- Rights
- Non-National Market Securities (NMS) OTC issues not approved by the Federal Reserve Board (FRB)
- Insurance contracts

The following cannot be bought on margin, but can be used as collateral after being held for 30 days:

- Mutual funds
- New issues if they meet the requirements listed above

Last, certain securities are exempt from the FRB's Regulation T margin requirements. Securities exempt from Regulation T include

- U.S. Treasury bills, notes, and bonds;
- government agency issues; and
- municipal securities.

If these exempt securities are bought or sold in a margin account, they are subject to the firm's determination of an initial deposit requirement. Firms may impose stricter requirements, but at a minimum, must follow maintenance requirements established by FINRA. These requirements are covered later.

TEST TOPIC ALERT

Differentiate between the use of the terms *margin* and *marginable*.

- Margin is the amount of equity that must be deposited to buy securities in a margin account.
- *Marginable* refers to securities that can be used as collateral in a margin account.

TAKE NOTE

The FRB can change Regulation T at any time, but the current requirement (50%) has been in place since 1974. Assume Regulation T equals 50% in test questions unless it is specified differently.

LO 24.c Calculate initial deposit requirements.

Regulation T and FINRA initial margin deposit requirements

Customers are required to deposit a minimum amount of equity for their first purchase in a margin account. Regulation T states that a deposit of 50% of the market value of the purchase is required. FINRA also has an initial requirement of $2,000 or 100%, whichever is less.

The customer is required to deposit the greater of the Regulation T requirement or the FINRA minimum.

Figure 24.2 depicts the required initial deposit.

Figure 24.2: Required Initial Deposits Example

Customer Purchase	Regulation T Requirement	FINRA Minimum Rule	Customer Deposit Required
Buy 100 shares at $50/share	$2,500	$2,000	$2,500
Buy 100 shares at $30/share	$1,500	$2,000	$2,000
Buy 100 shares at $15/share	$750	$1,500	$1,500

Here is another way to approach this.

■ If the customer's first purchase in a margin account is greater than $4,000, deposit 50%. (Regulation T requirement)

■ If it is between $2,000 and $4,000, deposit $2,000. (FINRA minimum)

■ If it is less than $2,000, deposit 100% of the purchase price (FINRA minimum)

LO 24.d Define maintenance call

Just as margin trading can accelerate gains, it can also accelerate losses. If a stock's value drops, the customer's equity in the account will also drop. If the customer's equity drops below 25% of the account's market value, the customer receives a maintenance call (also called a margin maintenance call). The customer is required to deposit additional assets to bring the equity in the account up to the 25% minimum. If a customer fails to make the required deposit (normally required by the end of the day), the BD may liquidate assets from the account to bring the account's equity up to 25%.

The minimum maintenance requirement is a FINRA rule. A BD is allowed to have higher minimums, called a house call.

The calculation of a maintenance call is not expected to be on the SIE Exam, but the concept of a maintenance call is a possible test point.

LO 24.e Differentiate fee-based and commission-based trading accounts

Most customer accounts are **commission based,** meaning that a commission is charged for each transaction. An alternate way of charging for trading is a "fee-based" account.

In a fee-based account, the customer pays a set fee, either monthly or quarterly, for all trading in the account. The fee may be a set fee for every account, but a fee based on a percentage of the account's value is most common.

A fee-based account would be appropriate for customers that trade frequently. This sort of account would not be appropriate for a customer that buys and holds securities with little trading.

KNOWLEDGE CHECK

1. Your customer purchases 200 shares ABC stock at $9 a share in a cash account. The customer is expected to deposit how much to pay for the trade?
    A. $900
    B. $1,800
    C. $2.000
    D. $450

2. Your customer purchases 200 shares of ABC stock at $9 a share in a margin cash account. The customer is expected to deposit how much to pay for the trade?
    A. $900
    B. $1,800
    C. $2.000
    D. $450

3. When opening a new brokerage account that will allow for margin trading, all of the following forms are required **except**
    A. account application.
    B. credit agreement.
    C. consent to loan agreement.
    D. hypothecation agreement.

Answers

1. **B** This is a cash account—100% of the trade must be paid for by the customer. LO 24.a

2. **B** In a margin account, the minimum deposit is the higher of 50% of the purchase price (Regulation T) or the FINRA requirement of $2,000 or 100% of the purchase if less than $2,000. In this case, the 200 shares at $9 is $1,800, below $2,000, so no borrowing is allowed. LO 24.c

3. **C** The consent to loan agreement is not a regulatory requirement. LO 24.b

UNIT 25

AML/BSA

LEARNING OBJECTIVES

When you have completed this unit, you will be able to accomplish the following.

> LO 25.a Define money laundering.
> LO 25.b Identify the three stages of money laundering.
> LO 25.c Recall the purpose of FinCEN.
> LO 25.d Recognize when to use Currency Transaction and Suspicious Activity reports.
> LO 25.e Recall the requirement for an AML officer under the BSA.
> LO 25.f Recall the purpose of OFAC .
> LO 25.g Determine when to consult the SDN list.

INTRODUCTION

As financial services professionals, we have an important role to play in assisting law enforcement and in fighting terrorism. Our firms, and we ourselves, are tasked with being aware of and reporting suspicious behavior. The penalties for failing to follow the steps necessary for detecting and preventing money laundering can be serious, and participating in it is a serious crime.

LESSON 25.1: ANTI-MONEY LAUNDERING RULES

LO 25.a Define money laundering.

The **Bank Secrecy Act** establishes the U.S. Treasury Department as the lead agency for developing regulations in connection with **anti-money laundering** (AML) programs. Before September 11, 2001, money laundering rules were concerned mostly with the origin of the cash. *Money laundering* was defined as the process of creating the appearance that money originally obtained from criminal activity, such as drug trafficking or terrorist activity, came from a legitimate source.

After September 11, 2001, and with the passage of the USA PATRIOT Act of 2001, regulators became just as focused and concerned with where the funds are going. The idea is to prevent "clean" money (money that has been laundered) from being used for "dirty" purposes (such as funding terrorist activities).

LO 25.b Identify the three stages of money laundering.

The three basic stages of money laundering are as follows.

1. **Placement**—This first stage of laundering is when funds or assets are moved into the laundering system. This stage is recognized as the time when illegal funds are the most susceptible to detection.

2. **Layering**—The goal of money launderers during this stage is to conceal the source of the funds or assets. This is done through a series of layers of transactions that are generally numerous and can vary in form and complexity. Often the transactions do not make business or investing sense, but they make perfect sense if you are trying to obscure the original source of the funds.

3. **Integration**—In the final stage, illegal funds are commingled with legitimate funds in what appear to be viable legitimate business concerns. This can be accomplished using front companies operating on a cash basis, import and export companies, and many other types of businesses. At this point, the funds make their way back to the criminals in a way that appears to be a legitimate source of income.

LO 25.c Recall the purpose of FinCEN.

The Financial Crimes Enforcement Network (FinCEN) is a bureau of the U.S. Treasury Department that collects and analyzes information about financial transactions to combat money laundering, domestic and international terrorist financing, and other financial crimes.

As part of the Treasury (and not the Department of Justice), FinCEN does not have an enforcement branch. It is better understood as an intelligence agency using the information available in the financial system to detect illegal activity.

LO 25.d Recognize when to use Currency Transaction and Suspicious Activity reports.

Currency Transaction Reports (CTRs)

The Bank Secrecy Act requires BDs to report any **currency** received in the amount of more than $10,000 on a single day. Though paying for purchased securities with currency is not prohibited, many firms do not permit this. Failure to report can result in fines of up to $500,000, 10 years in prison, or both. Records relating to filed reports must be retained for 5 years.

The report must be filed within 15 days of receipt of the currency. This rule is part of the regulatory effort to deal with money laundering. The two federal agencies empowered to deal with this abuse are the Federal Reserve and the U.S. Treasury Department.

Designing deposits to fall under the $10,000 radar is a prohibited activity known as *structuring*. Financial institutions should have systems in place to monitor for and recognize such attempts.

EXAMPLE

A customer makes 25 $500 cash deposits to pay for a $12,500 transaction. This should be recognized as an attempt to structure payments to fall under the $10,000 limit to avoid the filing of a CTR.

TAKE NOTE

CTRs involve deposits of **currency**, not checks or wire transfers, and not necessarily U.S. dollars.

Suspicious Activities Reports (SARs)

The USA PATRIOT Act requires firms to report to the **Financial Crimes Enforcement Network** (FinCEN) when there is an event, transaction, or series of events or transactions that appear to be questionable.

The act requires firms to report to FinCEN any transaction that alone or in the aggregate involves at least $5,000 in funds or other assets if the firm suspects that it falls within one of the following four classes.

- The transaction involves funds derived from illegal activity.
- The transaction is designed to evade the requirements of the Bank Secrecy Act.
- The transaction appears to serve no business or lawful purpose.
- The transaction involves the use of the firm to facilitate criminal activity.

Firms must file a suspicious activity report (SAR) within 30 days of becoming aware of the suspicious transaction(s). Copies of each SAR filing and the related documentation must be retained for five years from the date of the filing.

The act also requires that the filing of a SAR remain confidential. The person involved in the transaction who is the subject of the report must not be notified. If subpoenaed, the firm must refuse to provide the information and must notify FinCEN of the request unless the disclosure is required by FinCEN, the SEC, an industry self-regulatory organization (SRO), or other law enforcement authority.

In addition, the USA PATRIOT Act requires firms to make and retain records relating to wire transfers of $3,000 or more. Information to be collected includes the name and address of both sender and recipient, the amount of the transfer, the name of the recipient's financial institution, and the account number of the recipient.

EXAMPLE

A pattern of cash deposits over time could trigger a SAR filing. For example, if a customer were to deposit $1,000 each week for many weeks in a row, this might constitute suspicious activity, and the filing of a SAR would be appropriate.

LO 25.e Recall the requirement for an AML officer under the BSA.

Firms are required to designate a chief anti-money laundering (AML) officer. There is no requirement for this person to be registered as a representative or a principal.

The AML officer will establish internal compliance procedures to detect abuses. There are signs or red flags that might suggest the possibility of money laundering. If a red flag is detected, it should be reported to the principal designated to receive such reports immediately. Examples of red flags are

- a customer exhibiting a lack of concern regarding risks, commissions, or other transaction costs;
- a customer attempting to make frequent or large deposits of currency or cashier's checks;
- a customer making a large number of wire transfers to unrelated third parties;
- a customer engaging in excessive journal entries between unrelated accounts; and
- a customer who designs currency deposits or withdrawals to fall under the $10,000 cash transaction report (CTR) filing threshold, a practice known as *structuring*.

LO 25.f Recall the purpose of OFAC.

The **USA PATRIOT Act** requires financial institutions to maintain customer identification programs (CIPs) to prevent financing of terrorist operations and money laundering. Financial institutions, such as banks and BDs, must keep records of identification information and check customer names against the Specially Designated Nationals (SDN) list maintained by the Office of Foreign Assets Control (OFAC).

Office of Foreign Asset Control (OFAC)

The **Office of Foreign Assets Control** (OFAC) publishes and maintains a list of individuals and companies owned or controlled by, or who are acting for or on behalf of, targeted countries, individuals, groups, or entities that are designated under programs that are not country specific, such as terrorists and those trafficking in narcotics. When individuals or groups appear on the Specially Designated Nationals (SDN) list, their assets are blocked, and U.S. persons and businesses, which include RRs and BDs, are generally prohibited from dealing with or conducting business with them.

New customers must be advised, before the account is opened, that the firm is requesting information to verify their identities. This notification may be placed on the firm's website, delivered verbally, or placed on the new account form.

LO 25.g Determine when to consult the SDN list.

U.S. persons (U.S. citizens and permanent resident aliens regardless of location, U.S. incorporated entities and their foreign branches, and in some circumstances their subsidiaries) are prohibited from doing business with anyone on the OFAC SDN list—and should check the list to ensure they are not in breach of the law if there is any uncertainty. Businesses should conduct checks before establishing a relationship with the person or entity, or conducting transactions with them, and periodically throughout the relationship.

OFAC maintains the SDN list in a searchable format on the Treasury website. Several SROs maintain a copy of the list for their members, including FINRA.

KNOWLEDGE CHECK

1. Which of the following is **not** a step in the money laundering process?
   A. Placement
   B. Layering
   C. Insertion
   D. Integration

2. Which of the following transactions done in a single day would **not** cause a firm to file a Currency Transaction Report (CTR)?
   A. Deposits of a series of four checks of $3,000 each
   B. Twenty-two deposits of $500 cash
   C. Four deposits of $3,000 cash and an outbound wired funds transaction for $10,000
   D. A withdrawal of $12,000 from an account followed by a deposit of $11,000 cash into a third-party account

3. The Office of Foreign Asset Control is a division of
   A. the State Department.
   B. the Justice Department.
   C. the Treasury Department.
   D. the Federal Reserve Bank.

Answers

1. **C** The three steps of money laundering are placement, layering, and integration. Insertion is not one of the steps. LO 25.b

2. **A** Checks are not currency. All the others include cash deposits in excess of $10,000. LO 25.b

3. **C** OFAC is part of the Treasury Department. LO 25.f

UNIT 26

General Suitability

LEARNING OBJECTIVES

When you have completed this unit, you will be able to accomplish the following.

> LO 26.a Use the know your customer rule.
> LO 26.b Define an investment recommendation.
> LO 26.c Relate customer objectives with investment characteristics.

INTRODUCTION

Whether or not an investment strategy or security is suitable for a customer is a determination made by an RR as to whether the strategy or security matches the customer's investment objectives and financial capability. The representative must have enough information about the customer to make this judgment.

LESSON 26.1: MAKING SUITABLE RECOMMENDATIONS

LO 26.a Use the know your customer rule.

FINRA and other SROs require brokers to know their customers. This implies understanding a customer's financial status (net worth and net income), investment objectives, and all facts essential in making suitable recommendations. It is an RR's responsibility to perform due diligence to determine the validity of a customer's information.

Based on that information, RRs must have a reasonable basis to believe that a recommended transaction or investment strategy involving a security or securities is suitable for the customer.

Recommendations can be advice to invest in, or employ investment strategies to hold, or sell specific securities, as well as suggestions pertaining to market sectors, day trading, or divesting of an asset or other investments to make funds available to purchase securities.

Regarding the term *customer*, FINRA defines it to exclude other brokers and certain potential investors (someone who is not your client at the time the advice is given). Therefore, the rule would not apply if the recipient of the advice is not currently a client and neither the representative nor the firm receives direct or indirect compensation as a result of giving the advice.

Financial considerations

Your customers' financial circumstances are an important part of understanding what is or is not a suitable investment for them. If a circumstance may be easily quantified as an amount of money (either a lump sum or a stream of payments) it is likely a financial circumstance.

Examples of financial circumstances are as follows:

- Income
- Value of their home
- Liquid net worth
- Debt payments
- Total debt

Nonfinancial circumstances

A customer's nonfinancial considerations are often as important as his financial concerns. Therefore, an RR or an investment adviser should know

- the customer's age;
- the customer's marital status;
- the number and ages of customer's dependents;
- the customer's employment status;
- the employment of customer's immediate family members.

Tolerance for risk and investment goals

A customer's risk tolerance and investment goals are other important considerations that will shape his portfolio. To understand a customer's attitude about investment alternatives, the representative or adviser should ask the customer the following questions to complete the customer profile and know the customer.

- What kind of risks can you afford to take?
- How liquid must your investments be?
- How important are tax considerations?
- Are you seeking long-term or short-term investments (investment time horizon)?
- What is your investment experience?
- What types of investments do you currently hold?

LO 26.b Define an investment recommendation.

When a registered representative (or other associated person) provides information that a reasonable person would view as suggesting a course of action regarding a security, a class of investment, or an investment strategy, that person is making a recommendation.

A person making a recommendation should consider the circumstances of the communication, the knowledge and sophistication of the recipient, and their circumstances. Lack of an intent to provide a recommendation does not prevent a communication that meets the above criteria from being considered as such.

LO 26.c Relate customer objectives with investment characteristics.

As a first rule, an investment's primary purpose should align with the customer's primary objective.

EXAMPLE

■ A security that produces current income for a client seeking income

■ A security that has a good probability of growth for customer's seeking capital appreciation

■ A security that is very stable for investors seeking safety

The next step is to consider the customer's tolerance for risk, with more conservative investments more appropriate for those with a low tolerance for risk and more aggressive investments for those with a higher tolerance for risk.

Finally, any other circumstance (time frame) that impacts the investment decision.

Figure 26.1 is a chart that matches many of the more common investment types with customer objectives.

Figure 26.1: Investment Types and Customer Objectives

Investor Objective	Recommendations
Preservation of capital/safety	CDs, money market mutual funds, fixed annuities, government securities and funds, agency issues, investment-grade corporate bonds, and corporate bond funds
Growth	Common stock, common stock mutual funds
(Balanced, moderate growth)	Blue-chip stocks, defensive stocks
(Aggressive growth)	Technology stocks, sector funds
Income	Bonds (but not zero coupons), REITs, CMOs
(Tax-free income)	Municipal bonds, municipal bond funds, Roth IRAs
(High-yield income)	Below investment-grade corporate bonds, corporate bond funds
(From stock portfolio)	Preferred stocks, utility stocks, blue-chip stocks
Liquidity	Securities listed on an exchange, unlisted Nasdaq stocks or bonds, mutual funds, publicly traded REITs
Portfolio diversification	Mutual funds, in general: more specifically, asset allocation funds and balanced funds
	For equity portfolios, add some debt and vice versa
	For domestic portfolios, add some foreign securities
	For bond portfolios, diversify by region/rating
Speculation	Option contracts, DPPs, high-yield bonds, unlisted/non-Nasdaq stocks or bonds, sector funds, precious metals, commodities, futures

KNOWLEDGE CHECK

1. Which of the following is a nonfinancial consideration or circumstance?
   A. Has the customer ever been divorced?
   B. What is the customer's current income?
   C. How much is the customer's mortgage balance?
   D. What is the balance of the customer's 401(k)?

2. Which of the following is an investment recommendation?
   A. A recommendation to read the business press to develop an understanding of the economy
   B. A suggestion that the Windmill Family of Funds would be a good basis for a portfolio
   C. A discussion about the inverse relationship between bond values and interest rates
   D. Sharing an opinion about the amusement parks run by a particular company

3. Mr. Johnson is a 77-year-old retiree. He would like to invest cash to generate some additional income. He also says that he is very nervous about losing money in the markets. Which of the following is the most suitable recommendation for Mr. Johnson?
   A. The Windmill Growth Fund
   B. The EAFE Emerging Markets Fund
   C. The Washington Treasury Bond Fund
   D. Jim's Really Great Technology Fund

Answers

1. **A** Debt and asset account balances, as well as income, are all financial considerations. A person's current or former marital status may be useful but is not, in itself, a financial consideration. LO 26.a

2. **B** Only the reference to the Windmill Funds directs a customer to a security. The others are only educational resources or a suggestion that the representative likes amusement parks. LO 26.b

3. **C** The Washington Treasury Bond Fund is a portfolio of very safe bonds meeting the customer's desire for safe income. The others are all equity funds likely oriented toward long-term growth. LO 26.c

UNIT 27

Communications With the Public

LEARNING OBJECTIVES

When you have completed this unit, you will be able to accomplish the following.

- › LO 27.a Recall general rules for communication with the public.
- › LO 27.b Classify communications as institutional, retail, or correspondence.
- › LO 27.c Recall the cold call rules of the TCPA of 1991.
- › LO 27.d Name the two types of do-not-call lists and when to consult them.
- › LO 27.e Recall the rules for holding customer mail and statement frequency.
- › LO 27.f Identify the expectations under Regulation S-P.
- › LO 27.g Relate the expectations of a firm's business continuity plan.

INTRODUCTION

The rules about communications with our customers are designed to protect investors and to remind us of our duty to them. The purpose is to ensure that the information we provide is fair, balanced, and complete. Your principal is a significant part of helping you to understand the rules about communication with the public.

LESSON 27.1: COMMUNICATIONS WITH THE PUBLIC

LO 27.a Recall general rules for communication with the public.

FINRA holds BDs to general standards regarding all member firm communications. All member communications must be based on principles of fair dealing and good faith. Statements must be clear and not misleading within the context that they are made, and they must be fair and balanced regarding potential risks and benefits. Omission of material facts is not permitted, nor is making false, exaggerated, or misleading statements or claims. No communication should ever imply that past performance will be repeated. Finally, FINRA mandates that members must consider the nature of the audience to which the communication will be directed and should provide details and explanations appropriate to the audience.

LO 27.b Classify communications as institutional, retail, or correspondence.

In accordance with FINRA, there are three categories of communications:

- Institutional communications
- Retail communications
- Correspondence

Institutional communication

Institutional communication means any written (including electronic) communication that is distributed or made available only to institutional investors, but it does not include a member's internal communications (e.g., internal memos). Examples of institutional investors are

- another member firm or RR;
- a bank;
- a savings and loan association (S&L);
- an insurance company;
- a registered investment company (mutual fund);
- an employee benefit plan;
- a governmental entity or subdivision;
- a person acting solely on behalf of an institutional investor; and
- any entity with $50 million or more of total assets, including natural persons.

FINRA mandates that no member may treat a communication as having been distributed to an institutional investor if the member firm *has reason to believe* that the communication or any part of it will be forwarded or made available to any retail investor.

Each firm must establish if they will require principal approval of institutional communication before use or allow for post-use approval. If a BD does not require prior principal approval, it must provide for (and document) education and training of associated persons regarding institutional communication.

Retail communication

Retail communication means any written (including electronic) communication that is distributed or made available to *more than 25 retail investors within any 30-calendar-day period.* A retail investor is any person other than an institutional investor, regardless of whether the person has an account with the member.

A copy of all retail communication must be filed with FINRA. For a new member firm (firms in the first year of FINRA membership), the filing must occur at least 10 days before use. For established member firms, the filing must happen within 10 days of first use.

TAKE NOTE

The requirement is that a firm send a copy to FINRA for filing. This is not an approval process, just a file copy of the communication

The rules require that all retail communication receive principal approval before use or filing with FINRA.

Correspondence

Correspondence means any written (including electronic) communication that is distributed or made available to *25 or fewer retail investors within any 30-calendar-day period.*

As with institutional communication, each firm must establish if it will require principal approval of correspondence before use or allow for post-use approval. If a BD does not require prior principal approval, it must provide for (and document) education and training of associated persons regarding correspondence.

Social media use

Regarding the use of social media and online activities, firms are required to monitor the business-related social media presence of all representatives. Most static content, such as a website or a blog, typically must be approved by a registered principal before use—and sometimes may be required to be filed with FINRA. There is no requirement to preapprove individual posts in interactive online forums, but firms must have policies and procedures in their written supervisory procedures concerning these activities. Representatives may use social media platforms to engage with both existing customers and prospective clients.

TEST TOPIC ALERT

If they are not institutional customers, they are retail customers.

LO 27.c Recall the cold call rules of the TCPA of 1991.

The Telephone Consumer Protection Act of 1991 (TCPA), administered by the Federal Communications Commission (FCC), was enacted to protect consumers from unwanted telephone solicitations (telemarketing).

A *telephone solicitation* is defined as a telephone call initiated for the purpose of encouraging the purchase of or investment in property, goods, or services. The act governs commercial calls, recorded solicitations from auto-dialers, and solicitations and advertisements to fax machines and modems.

The basic rules under the TCPA are as follows:

■ Ensure that anyone making cold calls informs prospects of their name, the company's name, and the company's telephone number or address

■ Ensure that solicitation occurs only between 8:00 am and 9:00 pm based on the prospect's time zone

■ No calls to numbers on the company or federal do-not-call list

The act exempts calls

- made to parties with whom the caller has an established business relationship or from whom the caller has prior express permission or invitation;

- made on behalf of a tax-exempt nonprofit organization;

- not made for a commercial purpose; and

- made for legitimate debt collection purposes.

LO 27.d Name the two types of do-not-call lists and when to consult them.

The TCPA requires an organization that does telemarketing (cold-calling in particular) to

- maintain a do-not-call list of prospects who do not want to be called, and keep a prospect's name on the list until the prospect requests its removal;

- institute a written policy on maintenance procedures for the do-not-call list;

- train representatives on using the list;

- ensure that representatives acknowledge and immediately record the names and telephone numbers of prospects who ask not to be called again;

- ensure that telemarketers do not call a prospect from the time of the prospect's do-not-call request; and

- ensure that the company's do-not-call list is no more than 30 days old.

The Federal Trade Commission maintains the National Do Not Call Registry. Telemarketers are also required to check numbers against this list. Like a company list, the national list being used may not be more than 30 days old.

TEST TOPIC ALERT

Before making a telephone solicitation, a representative must check the number against both the company's and the National Do Not Call Registry. If the number appears on one or both of these lists, *don't call it.*

LO 27.e Recall the rules for holding customer mail and statement frequency.

Your firm is permitted to hold mail for a customer (e.g., statements and confirmations) provided that

- the member firm receives written instructions that include the time period the request is being made for up to three months (requests may be granted for periods longer than three months for an acceptable reason, such as safety or security concerns but not merely for the sake of convenience);

- the member firm informs the customer of any alternate methods the customer may use to receive or monitor account activity, such as email or through the member firm's website (the member must obtain customer confirmation that this information regarding alternate methods was received); and

- the member firm verifies at reasonable intervals that the customer's instructions still apply.

Additionally, during the time that a member firm is holding mail for a customer, the firm must be able to communicate with the customer in a timely manner to provide important account information. The firm must take actions reasonably designed to ensure that a customer's mail is not tampered with or used in a manner that would violate FINRA rules or federal securities laws.

While holding mail is a courtesy that firms are permitted to extend to customers, the rule does not require them to. If extending the courtesy is consistent with the BD's in-house rules, the written request by the customer to do so implies that the customer is also giving the BD permission to do so.

LO 27.f Identify the expectations under Regulation S-P.

This regulation was enacted by the SEC to protect the privacy of customer information. In particular, the regulation deals with nonpublic personal information.

Nonpublic personal information

The SEC, in Regulation SP, notes examples of nonpublic personal information. This type of information would include a customer's Social Security number, account balances, transaction history, and any information collected through an internet cookie.

Confidentiality of information

If your firm reserves the right to disclose to unaffiliated third parties nonpublic personal information, the notice must provide customers a reasonable means to opt out of this disclosure. Reasonable opt out means providing customers with a form with check-off boxes, along with a prepaid return envelope, providing an electronic means to opt out for customers who have agreed to the electronic delivery of information, and providing a toll-free telephone number. Asking customers to write a letter to express their disclosure preferences or to opt out would not be considered reasonable under Regulation SP.

Regulation SP privacy notifications

Regarding *privacy of consumer financial information*, Regulation SP is designed to protect a customer's nonpublic, personal information. Under Regulation SP, firms must provide their customers with a description of their privacy policies (a privacy notice). The notice must state the types of personal information that the firm collects and who the firm shares this information with. Firms must initially provide every customer with a privacy notice at the *time the relationship is first established*. Once the relationship is established, the firm must provide with an *updated version of this notice annually*.

Safeguard requirements

In addition, the regulation embodies the obligation of financial institutions to safeguard customer information as it related to all forms of existing and developing technology. For example, this would include, but not be limited to, securing desktop and laptop computers and encrypting email.

LO 27.g Relate the expectations of a firm's business continuity plan.

FINRA requires member firms to create and maintain a **business continuity plan** (BCP) to deal with the possibility of a significant business disruption. The plan must address certain points having to do with the consequences of the event, including but not limited to the following:

■ Data backup and recovery (hard copy and electronic)

■ Alternate communications between the firm and its customers

■ Alternate communications between the firm and its employees

■ Alternate physical location of employees

■ Communications with regulators

■ Prompt customer access to funds and securities in the event the firm is unable to continue its business

Firms must designate a member of senior management who is also a principal to approve, update, and conduct an annual review of the plan. Additionally, FINRA requires firms to provide them with the names of two emergency contact persons who may be contacted by FINRA in the event of a significant business disruption. Each contact person must be a principal and a member of senior management, and firms must update this contact information promptly, in no case later than 30 days following any change.

Regarding communicating this information to customers, a firm must disclose to its customers how it will respond to significant events of varying scope. This disclosure must be made, in writing, to customers at the time of account opening, posted on the firm's website, and mailed to customers on request.

 KNOWLEDGE CHECK

1. Which of the following is **not** one of the three general classes of communication with the public?
    A. Institutional
    B. Retail
    C. Correspondence
    D. Educational

2. Which of the following is **not** a rule under the TCPA of 1991?
    A. Calls must be made between 8:00 am and 9:00 pm in the prospect's time.
    B. Solicitors must identify themselves and their company.
    C. Calls must be made between 9:00 am and 8:00 am in the prospect's time.
    D. All telemarketing firms must maintain a do-not-call list.

3. Seacoast Securities is a new FINRA member firm. It is preparing a new marketing campaign, including a mass mail advertisement. The advertisement must
    A. be filed with FINRA within 10 days of first use.
    B. be filed with the SEC within 10 days of first use.
    C. be Filed with FINRA at least 10 days before use.
    D. be approved by a FINRA before use.

Answers

1. **D** Though communication may be educational, the three classes of communication are institutional, retail, and correspondence. LO 27.b

2. **C** Calls must be between 8:00 am and 9:00 pm. LO 27.c

3. **D** A new member firm is required to file a copy of all retail communication with FINRA at least 10 days before use. The filing with FINRA is just a record; no approval from FINRA is required. LO 27.b

UNIT 28

Record Keeping Requirements under SEC 17a-3 & 4

LEARNING OBJECTIVES

When you have completed this unit, you will be able to accomplish the following.

> LO 28.a Identify what records are kept for the life of the firm.
> LO 28.b Identify records maintained for six years.
> LO 28.c Identify records maintained for four years.
> LO 28.d Identify records maintained for three years.

INTRODUCTION

Among the most important rules that protect both the customer and broker-dealers are the recordkeeping rules. Keeping good, accurate records is vital to maintaining the public's trust in our firms and in us as their representatives.

SEC rules mandate which records must be prepared by members, when those records must be prepared, and for how long the records must be retained. In lieu of maintaining paper records, firms may use digital storage media. Such storage media must have the capability to maintain records in nonrewriteable and nonerasable format.

LESSON 28.1: RECORD KEEPING REQUIREMENTS

LO 28.a Identify what records are kept for the life of the firm

Records that are part of the life of the firm are retained for as long as the firm exists. The term seen most often is "indefinitely." These records are the following:

- **Partnership agreement**—The foundational document of a partnership. If there is no written partnership agreement, there is no partnership.

- **Corporate charter or articles of incorporation**—The name varies depending on the laws of the state of incorporation. This is the foundational document of a corporation. If there is no charter, there is no corporation.

- **Stock certificate books**—For closely held corporations, this is an actual book where the certificates are held until they are issued. A record of who the certificates are issued to is also found in the book.

- **Minutes**—A record of the meetings of the board of directors (corporation) or the partners (partnership).

- **Amendments**—Any amendments to any of these records are kept with the original record.

- **Organizational records**—These are other records related to the foundations of the firm. An example would be Form BD, the registration application for a broker-dealer.

LO 28.b Identify records maintained for six years.

Six-year records are generally those having to do with the BD's holdings and assets it holds for customers. A BD's financial records are also six-year retention records.

A partial list of those records that must be retained for six years from last use are listed here:

- **Blotters**—A blotter is a record of original entry. A member generally maintains blotters relating to the purchase and sale of securities, the receipt and delivery of securities, and the receipt and disbursement of cash. Blotters must reflect transactions as of trade date (or event date) and must be prepared no later than the following business day.

- **General ledger**—The general ledger contains accounting records of the firm's assets, liabilities, and net worth accounts. From the general ledger, a firm prepares its financial statements. The general ledger must be prepared as frequently as necessary to determine compliance with the net capital rule, but in no event less frequently than monthly.

- **Stock record**—The stock record shows all securities held by the firm, the ownership of those securities, and where the securities are held. The stock record must be posted no later than the business day after the settlement date.

- **Customer ledgers**—Customer ledgers are customer statements. Cash accounts and margin accounts are shown on separate ledgers. These ledgers must be posted no later than the settlement date.

- **Customer account records**—Customer account records might include the new account form and margin agreement, if appropriate.

- **Designation of principals**—When an associate is appointed to a principal position and what areas the will oversee.

LO 28.c Identify records maintained for four years.

Written complaints must be retained for four years after resolution. These records are normally maintained at the office of supervisory jurisdiction for the office where the complaint originated. If a complaint was delivered directly to the firm's headquarters, the record may be retained there.

TAKE NOTE

FINRA and SEC regulations apply to written complaints. Written extends to almost any communication that has letters organized into words; paper, email, text, instant message, tweet, social media post, and the list goes on. Most firms have procedures for verbal complaints, but only written complaints have regulatory standing.

LO 28.d Identify records maintained for three years.

Almost everything else must be retained for three years after last use. Some examples include these:

- Advertising
- Trial balances (monthly financial report)
- Form U-4, U-5, and fingerprint cards for terminated personnel
- Customer confirmations
- Order tickets
- Other ledgers, such as securities borrowed and securities loaned, monies borrowed and monies loaned, and dividends and interest received
- A list of every office where each associated person regularly conducts business
- Associated persons' compensation records
- The firm's compliance and procedures manual

TAKE NOTE

For three- and six-year records, the most recent two years must be kept "readily accessible," meaning at the branch office, OSJ, or headquarters where the document would normally be stored. After two years, they may be stored at an offsite location so long as the records may be retrieved.

KNOWLEDGE CHECK

1. All of the following records must be retained indefinitely except
    A. stock certificate books.
    B. articles of incorporation.
    C. customer ledgers.
    D. board meeting minutes.

2. A written customer complaint is retained
    A. for four years.
    B. for six years.
    C. for three years.
    D. until resolved.

3. Which of the following records has a three-year retention requirement?
    A. Amendments to the partnership agreement
    B. Trade blotters
    C. Customer statements
    D. Order tickets

Answers

1. **C**   Customers' ledgers (statements) must be retained for six years. Stock books, articles of incorporation, and meeting minutes are related to the life of the firm and are retained indefinitely. LO 28.a

2. **A**   Written customer complaints are retained for four years. LO 28.c

3. **D**   An order ticket must be retained for three years. An amendment to a founding document is retained indefinitely. Customer ledgers (statements) and trade blotters are held for at least six years. LO 28.d

UNIT 29

Prohibited Activities

LEARNING OBJECTIVES

When you have completed this unit, you will be able to accomplish the following.

> LO 29.a Define insider trading.
> LO 29.b Recall the penalties for insider trading.
> LO 29.c Identify types of market manipulation.
> LO 29.d Identify restricted persons under Rule 5130.
> LO 29.e Define improper use of customer assets.
> LO 29.f Name the special concerns and expectations when serving senior clients.
> LO 29.g Recall document handling rules.

INTRODUCTION

We are charged with providing our clients with the information they need to make informed investment decisions. If making a recommendation, it must be suitable. Additionally, we have access to tools and information that may be abused in a way that benefits us but harms our customers or the reputation of the industry. Unit 29 covers several of the rules that govern how we interact with our customers and the markets as a whole.

LESSON 29.1: INSIDER TRADING, MARKET MANIPULATION, AND RESTRICTED PERSONS

LO 29.a Define insider trading.

Although the Securities Exchange Act of 1934 prohibited the use of insider information in making trades. Under the Act, the penalties for insider trading were up to $5,000 in fines. As we entered the 1980s, people with inside information were in a position to make millions of dollars, and the fines were seen as a cost of doing business. The Insider Trading and Securities

Fraud Enforcement Act of 1988 (or Insider Trading Act) amended its provisions and specified significant penalties for insider trading and securities fraud, giving some real "teeth" to the prohibitions against using inside information.

All BDs must establish written supervisory procedures specifically prohibiting the misuse of inside information. Additionally, they must establish policies that restrict the passing of potentially material nonpublic information between a firm's departments. This barrier against the free flow of sensitive information is known as a *firewall* or an *information barrier*.

The Insider Trading Act defines an insider as *any person who has access to material nonpublic information* about a company. Material information is information that would most likely influence the price of the company's stock. *Utilizing that information* for the purpose of gain, or to avoid a loss, constitutes *insider trading*.

TAKE NOTE

The possession of inside information is not illegal. It is the use of such information to make a gain or avoid a loss that constitutes insider trading.

TEST TOPIC ALERT

Inside information, by definition, is any material nonpublic information—that is, any information that has not been disseminated to, or is not readily available to, the general public.

The Insider Trading Act prohibits insiders from trading on or communicating nonpublic information. Both the **tipper** (the person who relays the information) and the **tippee** (the person who receives the information) are liable, as is anyone who trades on information that they know or should know is not public or who has control over the misuse of this information.

The key elements of tipper and tippee liability under insider trading rules are as follows.

- Is the information material and nonpublic?

- Does the tipper owe a fiduciary duty to a company or its stockholders? Has he breached it?

- Does the tipper meet the personal benefits test (even something as simple as enhancing a friendship or reputation)?

- Does the tippee know or should the tippee have known that the information was inside or confidential?

LO 29.b Recall the penalties for insider trading.

The SEC can investigate any person suspected of violating any of the provisions of the Insider Trading Act. If the SEC determines that a violation has occurred, civil penalties of up to three times the profits made or losses avoided may be levied. A controlling person, such as an RR or BD, could be fined $1 million or three times the profit made or loss avoided, whichever is greater.

Violators may also face criminal penalties of up to $5 million and up to 20 years in jail. If the violator is an employee of a BD, the firm (which is supposed to have procedures in place to prevent this) could be fined up to three times damages or $25 million, whichever is greater.

TAKE NOTE

Persons who enter trades at or near the same time (but on the other side of the market) in the same security as a person who has inside information are known as **contemporaneous traders**. Contemporaneous traders may sue persons that have violated insider trading regulations, and suits may be initiated up to five years after the violation has occurred.

Bounties

The Insider Trading Act specifically allowed for payment to informers. However, amended under the Dodd-Frank legislation, awards may now be paid in connection with original information concerning any violation of securities law, including insider trading. The information bounty or award can range from 10% to 30% of amounts recovered, based on the information received.

LO 29.c Identify types of market manipulation.

No security is exempt from the industry's antifraud provisions. This means that fraud or **market manipulation** cannot be involved in the trading of any security. The following are a number of prohibited trading practices, because they are all meant to manipulate the markets and deceive market participants.

Market rumors

Misleading information or rumors can be used for the sole purpose of manipulating the price of a stock up or down. The spreading of false information and market rumors by industry personnel is expressly prohibited.

Additionally, regulators have issued alerts to warn investors about fraudsters who may or may not be securities industry persons, attempting to manipulate share prices by spreading false or misleading information about stocks. For example, while social media can provide many benefits for investors who want to research potential investments, it also presents opportunities for fraudsters. Through social media, fraudsters can spread false or misleading information about a stock to large numbers of people with minimal effort and at a relatively low cost. They can also conceal their identities or even impersonate credible sources of market information. Social media platforms that might be used in this way would include online bulletin boards, email blasts, and internet chat rooms.

Pump and dump

A form of securities fraud commonly known as **pump and dump** is the act of inflating (pumping) the price of an owned stock by perpetrating false and misleading positive rumors, in order to sell the stock at a higher price later. Generally, the shares owned are first accumulated at lower prices before the misleading information is doled out to the investing public. After the stock price rises due to the frenzied buying caused by the rumors, the operators of the scheme then sell (dump) their overvalued shares in the open market. The fraudsters profit while the selling pressure associated with dumping drives the price downward, causing investors who purchased based on the rumors to lose their money.

Front running

Front running is the act of placing orders for one's own account ahead of other orders that are known to be entering the market in an attempt to gain from the price movement that is likely to occur.

EXAMPLE

A mutual fund company enters an order to purchase 300,000 shares of AABB stock with your firm for execution at the market. Before entering the order to be executed in the open market, an RR (who is aware of the large pending order to buy) places an order for his own personal account to buy 500 shares. This is front running.

Excessive trading (churning)

Excessive trading in a customer's account to generate commissions rather than to help achieve the customer's stated investment objectives is an abuse of fiduciary responsibility known as **churning**. Excessive frequency or excessive size of transactions not in keeping with the client's trading history or financial ability are often signs of churning.

To prevent such abuses, SROs require that a principal of the member firm review all accounts, especially those for which an RR or an investment adviser has discretionary authority.

EXAMPLE

A principal, while reviewing transactions done by the firm, notices that a client who had previously done a trade or two per quarter recently has been doing one or two per week. At a minimum, this should generate a red flag for churning. A discussion with the RR assigned to the account should occur to determine if any further monitoring or actions should take place.

Marking the close and marking the open

Entering trades before the opening (or at or near the close) solely to manipulate the reported price of where a stock will open or close is prohibited.

- **Marking the open**—Entering orders before the opening for a stock or falsely reporting trades that never occurred to influence the opening price of a stock is called marking the open.

- **Marking the close**—Effecting trades at or near the close of the trading day or falsely reporting trades that never occurred to influence the closing price of a stock is called marking the close. For example, putting in buy orders at the close for the purpose of pushing up the price of a stock so that it is valued higher in one's portfolio or account at the end of the day is marking the close.

Freeriding

Freeriding is a term used when securities are purchased and then sold before making payment for the purchase. Freeriding is generally prohibited in both cash and margin accounts. As a penalty, the account will be frozen for 90 days, and no new transactions can occur unless there is cash or marginable securities in the account before the purchase is made.

Matched Orders

Matching orders is a manipulation that involves one party selling stock to another with the understanding that the stock will be repurchased later (usually the same day) at virtually the same price. The intent of such transactions is to make it appear that far more activity in a stock (share volume) exists than actually does. This is sometimes called ***painting the tape***.

LO 29.d Identify restricted persons under Rule 5130.

Designed to protect the integrity of the public offering process and public investors, Rule 5130 ensures that

- members make a bona fide public offering of securities at the public offering price (POP);

- members do not withhold securities in a public offering for their own benefit or use such securities to reward persons who are in a position to direct future business to the member; and

- industry insiders, such as members and their associated persons, do not take advantage of their insider status to gain access to new issues for their own benefit at the expense of public customers.

Essentially, the rules apply to IPOs of common stock. The rules prohibit member firms from selling a new issue to any account where restricted persons are beneficial owners. Before selling an IPO to any account, representatives are required to obtain a written representation from the account owner(s) that the account is eligible to purchase a new common stock issue at the POP. Restricted persons, those not allowed to purchase shares at the POP, are defined as follows:

- Member firms (whether or not they are involved in the IPO)

- Employees of member firms

- Finders and fiduciaries acting on behalf of the managing underwriter, including attorneys, accountants, financial consultants, and so on.

- Portfolio managers, including any person who has the authority to buy or sell securities for a bank, savings and loan association, insurance company, or investment company

- Any person owning 10% or more of a member firm

Further, any immediate family member of any natural person of those listed above are also restricted. Immediate family includes parents, in-laws, spouses, siblings, children, or any other individual to whom the person provides material support.

TAKE NOTE

Aunts and uncles, as well as grandparents, are not considered immediate family. If, however, one of these individuals lives in the same household as a restricted person, that individual would be a restricted person.

Finally, there is a de minimis exemption. If the beneficial interests of restricted persons do not exceed 10% of an account, the account may purchase a new equity issue. In other words, restricted persons will be able to have an interest in an account that purchases new equity issues as long as no more than 10% of the account's beneficial owners are restricted persons.

EXAMPLE

Daryl Miller is a restricted person. He is a member of an investment club and has a 5% interest in the investment club account. Because his interest in the club account does not exceed 10%, *the investment club account is not considered a restricted account.*

KNOWLEDGE CHECK

1. Penalties for insider trading may include all of the following **except**
    A. up to $5,000,000 for a person.
    B. up to 20 years in prison for a person.
    C. up to $25,000,000 for a firm.
    D. up to 20 years in prison for a firm.

2. All of the following are types of prohibited activities **except**
    A. wash sales.
    B. pump and dump.
    C. churning.
    D. front running.

3. Jim is a restricted person under Rule 5130. Which of the following members of Jim's family may buy a new issue at the IPO?
    A. Jim's brother Robert
    B. Jim's grandfather Farris
    C. Jim's sister DeAnn
    D. Jim's daughter April

Answers

1. **D** You can't put a firm in prison. Entities don't go to jail, natural persons do. LO 29.b

2. **A** A wash sale is not prohibited. Using the losses from a wash sale to lower your taxes is. Pump and dump, churning, and front running are all prohibited practices. LO 29.c

3. **B** Grandfathers, aunts, and uncles are not immediate family under Rule 5130. LO 29.d

LESSON 29.2: OTHER CUSTOMER CARE RULES

LO 29.e Define improper use of customer assets.

Problematic activities

Anytime that funds or securities of a customer are used in any way other than was intended by the customer, improper use has occurred. All such uses are prohibited.

FINRA expects member firms to detect or investigate "red flags" that alert the firm to improper use of customer funds. Exception reports may be generated to indicate red flags, such as conflicting information in new account applications and suspicious transfers of funds between unrelated accounts. The BD is expected to implement reasonable systems and controls regarding the supervisory review of customer accounts to thwart, among other things, the falsification of new account applications and other records to take advantage of vulnerable customers.

There is no end to the number of red flags and combinations of red flags, but a very small sampling might include

- suspicious activity involving transfers and disbursements in customer accounts;

- activity in the account of a deceased person;

- excessive customer complaints; and

- exception reports showing discrepancies regarding more than one address or a street address not matching a city or a ZIP code provided or a telephone area code not matching an address provided.

Borrowing from or lending to customers

The most common examples of misuse might be in the form of borrowing or lending even with consent. Note that borrowing without consent is indistinguishable from stealing. Taking (borrowing) a customer's funds for either the firm's or the representative's own use is prohibited. Lending a customer's securities for the purpose of short sales when no loan consent agreement has been signed by the customer is another way in which improper use might occur.

However, borrowing and lending arrangements can be permitted under certain circumstances. Firms that permit lending arrangements between representatives and customers must have written procedures in place to monitor such activity. Registered persons who wish to borrow from or lend money to customers are, in most cases, required to provide prior written notice of the proposed arrangement to the firm, and the firm must approve the arrangement in writing.

The Conduct Rules permit the following five types of lending arrangements.

1. There is an immediate family relationship between the representative and the customer (no notice or approval is needed).

2. The customer is in the business of lending money (e.g., a bank, and no approval is needed).

3. The customer and the representatives are both registered persons with the same firm (firm approval required).

4. The customer and the representative have a personal relationship outside the broker-customer relationship (firm approval required).

5. The customer and the representative have a business relationship outside the broker-customer relationship (firm approval required).

 TAKE NOTE

A representative's BD must have procedures in place allowing for borrowing or lending arrangements with customers. If the firm does not allow for such arrangements, then a representative may not enter into such an arrangement.

Guarantees and sharing in customer accounts

BDs, investment advisers, and RRs may not guarantee any customer against a loss or guarantee a gain. All such guarantees or anything intended to convey a guarantee is prohibited.

Member firms and representatives are also prohibited from sharing in profits or losses in a customer's account. An exception is made if a joint account has received the member firm's prior written approval and the RR shares in the profits and losses only to the extent of his proportionate financial contribution to the joint account. Contribution to the account cannot be measured in knowledge or expertise, but only in dollars. The firm, however, may share in a loss if the loss was due to an error made by the firm.

Exceptions to the proportion rule are made when sharing in a joint account with immediate family members. In these instances, directly proportionate sharing of profits and losses is not mandatory. Immediate family members include parents, mother-in-law or father-in-law, spouses, children, and any relative to whom the officer or employee in question contributes financial support. Financial support is broadly defined to include anyone who is living in the same residence.

TAKE NOTE

Firms cannot have joint accounts with customers.

LO 29.f Name the special concerns and expectations when serving senior clients.

FINRA, along with other regulators, specifically addresses the financial exploitation of seniors and other specified adult customers. FINRA defines the impacted accounts as those for individuals

- age 65 and older, or
- age 18 and older, whom the member reasonably believes has a mental or physical impairment that renders the individual unable to protect her own interests.

FINRA notes financial exploitation to be

- the wrongful or unauthorized taking, withholding, appropriation, or use of funds or securities; or
- any act or omission of an act taken by a person to obtain control, through deception, intimidation or undue influence, over the specified adult's money, assets or property; or convert the specified adult's money, assets, or property.

This includes any act aligning with the previous, done through the use of a power of attorney, guardianship, or any other authority.

Essentially, to prevent potential exploitation, the rules regarding the accounts of seniors and other specified adult customers do two things.

1. Member firms and associated persons must make "reasonable efforts" to obtain the name and contact information for a trusted contact person.

2. Member firms will be permitted to, but not required to, place temporary holds on customer accounts when there is a reasonable belief of financial exploitation.

Trusted contact person

A reasonable effort to obtain the name and contact information for a trusted contact person must be made when

- opening a customer's account, or
- updating the account information for an existing account.

Importantly, it should be noted that the member firm is not prohibited from opening an account when the customer fails or refuses to provide the information, so long as the member firm took reasonable efforts to obtain such information. Asking the customer to provide the name and contact information for a trusted contact person constitutes a reasonable effort.

When the customer has provided the name and contact information for a trusted contact person, the member firm must disclose in writing to the customer that the member or an associated person is authorized to contact the trusted contact person and disclose certain information about the customer's account.

FINRA notes that the trusted contact person is intended to be a resource for the member firm in administering the customer's account, protecting assets, and responding to possible financial exploitation.

EXAMPLES

- A member is unable to contact a customer after multiple attempts. The member could contact a trusted contact person to inquire about the customer's current contact information.

- A member firm suspects that the customer may be suffering from Alzheimer's disease, dementia, or other forms of diminished capacity. The member could reach out to the trusted contact person.

- A member believes possible financial exploitation of the customer is occurring. Before placing a temporary hold on a disbursement, the member could contact a trusted contact person to discuss the facts.

Temporary holds on disbursements and review

If the member firm reasonably believes that financial exploitation has occurred, is occurring, has been attempted, or will be attempted, it can place a temporary hold on disbursements of funds or securities. Note that the rule does not require the member firm to take this action, but allows it to do so at its discretion.

The hold can be no longer than 15 business days under the rule. A state regulator or agency of jurisdiction, however, can terminate the hold sooner, or extend the hold longer.

If a member firm places a temporary hold on disbursements, it must immediately initiate an internal review of the facts and circumstances that caused the member to initiate the temporary hold on the disbursements. In addition, the rule requires the member to provide notification of the hold and the reason for the hold to the trusted contact person and all parties authorized to transact business in the account, no later than two business days after the date the hold was initiated.

However, a member firm is not required to provide notification to the trusted contact person or a party authorized to transact business in the account, if the trusted contact person or party is unavailable or the member reasonably believes that the trusted contact person or party is the perpetrator of the financial exploitation.

LO 29.g Recall document handling rules.

Account statements and trade confirmations

BDs communicate and verify activity in a customer's account via account statements and trade confirmations. While they may appear different from one BD to the next, there is uniformity required regarding the information provided and the time frames for delivery.

Electronic delivery

FINRA allows members to electronically send documents, such as confirmations and account statements, to customers as long as certain conditions are met. To do so, the firm must have procedures in place to show that the information sent has been delivered as intended and that the confidentiality and security of personal information are protected. Further, customers must provide written consent to electronic delivery.

In addition, a customer who consents to receive information and documents electronically must be provided with the information in paper form, upon request.

Updating customer account records

To ensure that the information obtained from each new customer is accurate, firms must furnish to each customer, within 30 days of opening the account, a copy of the account record. The firm must include a statement that the customer should mark any corrections on the record and return it along with a statement that the customer should notify the firm of any future changes to information in the account record so that accurate and current records can be maintained.

If the customer should ever contact the firm with any changes, the firm must furnish the customer with an updated account record within 30 days of receipt of the notice of change. Further, this account updating must occur at least every 36 months thereafter

EXAMPLE

Changes in employment and financial status are two common amendments needed to be made to an account record. Changes in investment objective should also be expected and are likely over time.

Account statements and delivery requirements

Account statements provided to customers give a general accounting of securities and cash held in the account.

A statement shows

- all activity in the account since the previous statement;
- securities positions, long or short; and
- account balances, debit or credit.

If a customer's account has a cash balance (known as a *free credit balance*), the firm may hold it in the account. However, the statement must advise the customer that these funds are available on request.

Under FINRA rules, members are required to send statements to customers at least quarterly. If there is activity in the account in any given month, or penny stocks are held in the account, a statement must be sent that month.

TAKE NOTE

Activity is defined as purchases, sales, interest, or dividends received, or any funds flowing in or out of the account. *Penny stocks* are defined as those priced under $5 per share.

Finally, account statements must include a statement advising customers to promptly report any discrepancy or inaccuracy to their brokerage firms and clearing firms.

Trade confirmations and delivery requirements

A **trade confirmation** is a printed document that confirms a trade, its settlement date, and the amount of money due from or owed to the customer. For each transaction, a customer must be sent or given a written confirmation of the trade at or before the completion of the transaction—the settlement date.

The trade confirmation includes the following information:

- Trade date—day on which the transaction is executed (the settlement date is usually the second business day after the trade date)

- Account number—branch office number followed by an account number

- RR internal ID number (or AE number)— account executive's identification number

- BOT (bought) or SLD (sold)—indicates a customer's role in a trade

- Number (or quantity)—number of shares of stock or the par value of bonds bought or sold for the customer

- Description—specific security bought or sold for the customer

- Yield—indicates that the yield for callable bonds may be affected by the exercise of a call provision

- CUSIP number—applicable Committee on Uniform Securities Identification Procedures (CUSIP) number, if any

- Price—price per share for stock or bonds before a charge or deduction

- Amount—price paid or received before commissions and other charges; also called extended principal for municipal securities transactions

- Commission—added to buy transactions; subtracted from sell transactions completed on an agency basis. Note: Commission will not appear on the confirmation if a markup (or markdown) has been charged in a principal transaction.

- Net amount—obtained on purchases by adding expenses (commissions and postage) to the principal amount

- Whether the transaction is a purchase or sale, interest is always added whenever bonds are traded with accrued interest (interest that hasn't been paid yet but will be owed to the seller up the settlement date)

Finally, the confirmation must also show the capacity in which the BD acts (agency or principal) and the commission in cases where the BD acts as an agent.

Nontrade confirmations/third-party activity notices

Firms are required to send confirmations of activity in accounts even when the activity is not trade related or initiated by a third party. The following are three examples of such instances where a confirmation of third-party activity would be generated.

EXAMPLE

Customers with a foreign bank account may from time to time wire money from the foreign country back to a brokerage account in the United States (or the reverse). When the funds are credited (or debited) to and from the account, a confirmation of the deposit/withdrawal is sent.

EXAMPLE

When a deposit (or withdrawal) of a stock certificate is made, this is an activity that is not trade related. The customer receives a confirmation of the activity.

EXAMPLE

A customer with an outside money manager handling some of the customer's money may execute through a BD where the customer has an account and the manager withdraws his fee quarterly in advance. Each time a fee is taken, a confirmation is sent from the BD indicating that specific "third-party activity" occurred and was logged.

KNOWLEDGE CHECK

1. Seabird Securities does not have any firm policies regarding borrowing or lending arrangements between associated persons and customers. Under which of the following circumstances would a registered representative be allowed to borrow from a customer?
    A. Borrowing from his Uncle Joe
    B. Borrowing from Dustin, his college buddy
    C. Under no circumstance
    D. Borrowing from Dr. DuVall, his optometrist

2. Which of the following statements concerning the delivery of statements is **not** correct.
    A. Statements must be sent monthly.
    B. Statements must be sent at least quarterly.
    C. Statements must be sent for any month in which there is activity.
    D. Statements must be sent monthly if the account holds penny stocks.

3. Which of the following customers are of special concern for potential exploitation?
    A. Mr. Johansen, age 70
    B. Mrs. Roberts, age 60
    C. Mr. Gating, age 30, and known to be irresponsible
    D. Mr. Henning, age 55, going through a mid-life crises

Answers

1. **C**   If a firm has no policy regarding loans to and from customers, then the activity is not allowed. LO 29.e

2. **A**   Statements are only required to be sent monthly if there is activity in the account or the account holds penny stocks. LO 29.g

3. **A**   Special concern is for customers 65 and older, or other adults that are unable to protect their own interest due to illness, injury, or disability. Just being irresponsible or stupid is not enough. LO 29.f

PART

4

Overview of the Regulatory Framework

Your exam will include seven questions on the topics covered in Part 4.

There are three units in Part 4: Overview of the Regulatory Framework.

UNIT
30

Associating With a Broker-Dealer

LEARNING OBJECTIVES

When you have completed this unit, you will be able to accomplish the following.

> LO 30.a Identify the information found on Form U-4.
> LO 30.b Recall the filing requirements for Form U-4.
> LO 30.c Recall fingerprint requirements for associated people.
> LO 30.d Identify disqualifying events.
> LO 30.e Recall limitations on nonregistered personnel.
> LO 30.f Recall the role of a principal.
> LO 30.g Identify testing requirements.

INTRODUCTION

Unit 30 dives into the process of becoming associated with a broker-dealer. In addition to Form U-4, this unit will cover fingerprinting, nonregistered personnel, and the role of a principal.

LESSON 30.1: ASSOCIATING WITH A BROKER-DEALER

The process to becoming a registered representative starts with the SIE, and then goes to top-off exams, but to sit for a top-off exam, you must be sponsored by a broker-dealer. One of the most important steps for associating with a broker-dealer is to file FINRA Form U-4.

___

LO 30.a Identify the information found on Form U-4.

___

To register an associated person of a member firm with FINRA, the member fills out and submits **Form U-4**, but registration is not effective until the person passes the appropriate qualification exam(s). If a person fails the exam, 30 days must elapse before a second attempt can be made. If a person fails an exam three straight times, the person must wait six months (180 days) before making a fourth attempt.

Information required on Form U-4 is extensive and includes

- name, address, and any aliases;
- 5-year residency history;
- 10-year employment history;
- information on any charges, arrests, or convictions relating to the investment business; and
- a required detailed explanation for an affirmative answer (yes) to any of the questions regarding charges, arrests, or convictions. This information must be provided on the Disclosure Reporting Pages (DRP) on Form U-4.

In addition to registering with FINRA, a representative must satisfy the registration requirements of each state she does business in. The Form U-4 must be checkmarked for each state, and the accompanying fee and qualification exam, if any, must be satisfied. If a representative's firm is also a member of an exchange, such as the NYSE or the CBOE, this must be noted on the Form U-4, and once again, applicable fees must be paid and qualification exams passed, if required.

TAKE NOTE

Information on marital status or educational background (e.g., degrees obtained) is not required on Form U-4. However, within the 10-year employment history required on Form U-4, full-time education would be included.

LO 30.b Recall the filing requirements for Form U-4.

When a U-4 is filed requesting an exam, it will open a window of 120 days for the exam to be completed. Though a new U-4 would not be required if the 120 days elapses, there is a cost for reopening a window.

The U-4 is not a one-time filing. If a registered person separates from one firm and joins a different firm, the U-4 must be completed. Also while a person is associated with a member firm, any changes to the U-4 information require filing an amended form with the CRD no later than 30 days after the member becomes aware of these changes. The associated person does have a responsibility to inform his employer of these changes. The 30-day requirement is for standard events (moving, new certifications, etc.). If the amendment involves a statutory disqualification, an amended form must be filed within 10 business days.

LO 30.c Recall fingerprint requirements for associated people.

Registered BDs must have **fingerprint records** made for most of their employees, and all directors, officers, and partners must submit those fingerprint cards to the U.S. attorney general (Justice Department) for identification and processing. Persons who must be fingerprinted are those involved in sales and those who handle cash or customer securities. Clerical persons (sometimes called ministerial persons) need not be fingerprinted. However, any associated person put in a position that would have them handle cash or securities would be required to be fingerprinted.

EXAMPLE

A receptionist who handles incoming mail would need to be fingerprinted due to the likelihood of having access to cash or securities. A receptionist who does not handle incoming mail, and therefore would not be in a position to have access to cash or securities, would not need to be fingerprinted.

TAKE NOTE

Those selling only mutual funds, variable annuities, or direct participation programs (DPPs) are exempt from fingerprinting. Certain BD employees (typically clerical) are exempt from the fingerprinting requirement as well, if they

- are not involved in securities sales;

- do not handle or have access to cash or securities or to the books and records of original entry relating to money and securities; and

- do not supervise other employees engaged in these activities.

LO 30.d Identify disqualifying events.

A person may not act as an RR or principal unless FINRA's eligibility standards regarding training, experience, and competence are met.

Statutory disqualification—Disciplinary sanctions by the SEC, another SRO, a foreign financial regulator, or a foreign equivalent of an SRO may be cause for statutory disqualification of FINRA membership.

An individual applying for registration as an associated person will be rejected if he

- has been or is expelled or suspended from membership or participation in any other SRO or from the foreign equivalent of an SRO;

- is under an SEC order or an order of a foreign financial regulator denying, suspending, or revoking his registration or barring him from association with a BD; or

- has been found to be the cause of another BD or associated person being expelled or suspended by another SRO, the SEC, or a foreign equivalent of an SRO.

The following also can automatically disqualify an applicant for registration:

- Misstatements willfully made in an application for membership or registration as an associated person

- A felony conviction, either domestic or foreign, or a misdemeanor conviction involving securities or money within the past 10 years

- Court injunctions prohibiting the individual from acting as an investment adviser, an underwriter, or a BD or in other capacities aligned with the securities and financial services industry

EXAMPLE

An applicant applying for registration lists a conviction for a Ponzi scheme whereby he accepted investments from individuals promising high returns. Returns paid to them subsequently came from investments received from new investors. It should be recognized that this conviction would statutorily disqualify the individual from registering as an associated person in the securities industry because the conviction involves money and fraud.

TAKE NOTE

The Central Registration Depository (CRD) maintains information on the disciplinary history of all persons currently registered. A customer can access this information toll free through the CRD's **BrokerCheck**. A hyperlink to BrokerCheck is required on all FINRA member firm websites.

TAKE NOTE

While a bankruptcy or unsatisfied lien does not disqualify one from registering, failure to disclose the facts would.

LESSON 30.2: OTHER PERSONNEL RULES

LO 30.e Recall limitations on nonregistered personnel.

Nonregistered employees of broker-dealers have a limited scope of activities.

Some of the activities permitted for a nonregistered employee of a BD are as follows:

- Responding to general, noninvestment questions (What are your hours of operation? May I leave a message for . . .? Where is the restroom?)

- Providing literature on request, setting appointments, inviting prospects to a seminar, and similar activities

Nonregistered (or nonlicensed) persons may *not* engage in investment banking or other securities business (opening an account, soliciting trades, etc.).

TEST TOPIC ALERT

Upon successfully passing the SIE, you are *not* registered. You are limited to the activities allowed a nonlicensed person. Performing functions of a representative before licensing is a good way to be barred from the industry.

LO 30.f Recall the role of a principal.

Anyone who manages or supervises any part of a member's investment banking or securities business must be registered as a **principal** with FINRA (including people involved solely in training associated persons). Unless the member firm is a sole proprietorship, it must employ at least two registered principals.

Principals supervise representatives and are responsible for seeing that the member firm's policies and all regulations are followed. Among the duties of a principal are the following:

- Accepting new accounts (approving)

- Approving accounts for margin or options trading

- Approving or reviewing communications

- Reviewing trading activity

- Hiring and training new representatives

- Responding to written complaints (all written complaints go to a principal for action)

Before being appointed as a principal, a registered representative must pass one of the principal's exams. There are several principals' exams covering specific areas of securities and investment banking.

LO 30.g Identify testing requirements.

There are very few requirements for filling out Form U-4. There is no education requirement, not even a requirement that a representative be a U.S. citizen. There are two requirements to remember:

- Sponsorship by a broker-dealer member firm is required.
- Complete and truthful disclosure is required on all required forms.

Disclosure is very important to FINRA. A willful misstatement on the U-4 may result in being barred from the industry for life. Lying on the U-4 is a good way to end a career before it starts.

KNOWLEDGE CHECK

These questions apply to material covered in Lesson 30.1 and Lesson 30.2.

1. An individual applying for registration as an associated person will be rejected if he
    A. submitted an application for registration that omitted mention of a minor traffic violation that occurred two years ago.
    B. failed to include the ZIP code on his home address.
    C. is under a court injunction regarding a domestic issue.
    D. is under an order of a foreign financial regulator denying, suspending, or revoking his registration or barring him from association with a BD.

2. As a means of protecting the integrity of the industry and protecting the investing public, associated persons of FINRA member firms must submit fingerprint records to
    A. the U.S. attorney general.
    B. the attorney general for the state in which they reside.
    C. the Securities and Exchange Commission (SEC).
    D. the FBI.

3. The receptionist at a BD opens all incoming mail and forwards it to various departments and people of the firm. Which of the following statements is **true**?
    I.   The receptionist must be fingerprinted.
    II. The receptionist need not be fingerprinted.
    III. The receptionist must be registered with FINRA.
    IV. The receptionist need not be registered with FINRA.
    A. I and III
    B. I and IV
    C. II and III
    D. II and IV

Answers

1. **D**   There are a number of reasons why application for registration as an associated person might be rejected. Among them are if the applicant is under an SEC order or an order of a foreign financial regulator denying, suspending, or revoking his registration or barring him from association with a BD. Non-securities-related misdemeanors, such as traffic violations, do not have to be reported. The ZIP code being left out is not a cause for rejection, and only a court injunction enjoining him from entering the securities business would be cause for rejection, not a domestic issue. LO 30.d

2. **A**   Registered BDs must have **fingerprint records** made for most of their employees, and all directors, officers, and partners must submit those fingerprint cards to the U.S. attorney general for identification and processing. LO 30.c

3. **B**   When opening mail for the BD, it is inevitable that the receptionist will handle monies and securities from customers and, as such, will need to be fingerprinted. Registration is not required. LO 30.e

UNIT 31

Terminating Association With a Broker-Dealer

LEARNING OBJECTIVES

When you have completed this unit, you will be able to accomplish the following.

> LO 31.a Recall the information on Form U-5.
> LO 31.b Recall the filing requirements for Form U-5.
> LO 31.c Identify the time limit before retesting is required.

INTRODUCTION

Just as a form is filed when you associate with a member firm, a form is filed when that association ends. FINRA wants to know when you are working, and when you stop for any reason. FINRA would also like to know the reason.

LESSON 31.1: THE U-5 FORM AND RETESTING

LO 31.a Recall the information on Form U-5.

Should a person registered with a member resign or be terminated, the member must file Form U-5 with the CRD within 30 days of the termination date. Members must also provide a copy of the form to their former employee within the same time frame. Failure to do so within 30 days will result in a late filing fee being assessed against the member. The form requires the member to indicate the reason for termination and provide an explanation where appropriate. Failure to provide accurate information could lead to severe disciplinary action. There are five reasons listed for termination on the form:

- Discharged
- Permitted to resign
- Deceased

- Voluntary

- Other

If the member checks the discharged, other, or permitted to resign box, all the details surrounding the termination must be disclosed. A voluntary resignation is assumed to be under circumstances that will not affect future eligibility for employment within the industry. Deceased is self-explanatory.

LO 31.b Recall the filing requirements for Form U-5.

As mentioned in the previous section, a U-5 must be filed by the member within 30 calendar days of termination. A failure to file on time or a misrepresentation on the form may result in significant fines and other penalties up to termination of a member firm from FINRA.

The form also includes any state registrations of the terminating person. Those registrations will end at the same time.

Additionally, the form allows for a partial termination. This occurs when a person ends some, but not all, of her registrations.

 EXAMPLE

A principal desires to step away from supervision and work as a representative with no principal designations. A partial termination is selected on the U-5, indicating which registrations are ending.

LO 31.c Identify the time limit before retesting is required.

After a form U-5 for a full termination is filed, FINRA and other regulators retain jurisdiction for two years. The regulators may still require a terminated person to provide evidence and answer questions during this period.

Within the two years, a person may associate with another (or the same) member firm without requalifying (retaking the exams). If that person does not re-affiliate with a member firm within the two years, he will need to successfully pass the qualifying exams again.

 TAKE NOTE

Passing the SIE allows for a person to take a top-off exam and affiliate with a member firm for up to **four years** without retaking the SIE. If more than four years elapses after taking the SIE before passing a top-off, an affiliating a person would need to take the Securities Industry Essentials Exam again.

Military service

If a representative leaves the industry for regular military service, that person's license is placed in a special inactive status. This status continues until 90 days after leaving military service. The two-year time frame begins at the end of the 90-day period. This allows a registered person to serve in the military for an extended period without having to retest to return to the industry.

TAKE NOTE

After representatives terminate employment, they no longer receive commissions from the BD. However, continuing commissions may be allowed under a contract that exists before termination. This is normally done for retirees and may allow for payments to heirs. These payments are for existing business relationships only, not new business.

KNOWLEDGE CHECK

1. Which of the reasons for termination from Form U-5 do **not** require a detailed explanation?
   I. Discharged
   II. Permitted to resign
   III. Deceased
   IV. Voluntary
   V. Other
   A. I and II
   B. II and III
   C. III and IV
   D. I, II, and V

2. How soon after termination must Form U-5 be filed with CRD?
   A. 60 days
   B. 90 days
   C. 30 days
   D. 120 days

3. FINRA retains regulatory jurisdiction for how long after a registered person terminates association with a member firm?
   A. 2 years
   B. 120 days
   C. 1 year
   D. 90 days

Answers

1. **C**   If the representative leaves voluntarily or dies, no further information is required from FINRA. A reason of discharged, permitted to resign, or other requires that those reasons be detailed. LO 31.a

2. **C**   Form U-5 must be filed within 30 days of termination to avoid possible penalties. LO 31.b

3. **A**   FINRA and other regulators retain jurisdiction to investigate possible violations for two years after a representative leaves the industry. LO 31.c

UNIT
32

Ongoing Expectations of Associated Persons

LEARNING OBJECTIVES

When you have completed this unit, you will be able to accomplish the following.

> LO 32.a. Define Firm Element Continuing Education.
> LO 32.b. Recall the time frame for Regulatory Element Continuing Education.
> LO 32.c. Recall the steps for handling written complaints.
> LO 32.d. Indicate the rules associated with outside business activities.
> LO 32.e. Define selling away.
> LO 32.f. Recall rules on gifts and gratuities to employees of other member firms.
> LO 32.g. Recall limitations and rules regarding political contribution.
> LO 32.h. Recall rules for home-based offices.

INTRODUCTION

In addition to disqualifying events discussed in earlier units, there are several ongoing expectations for registered representatives. Several, but not all, are detailed here in Unit 32.

LESSON 32.1: ONGOING EXPECTATIONS OF ASSOCIATED PERSONS

Registered persons are required to participate in **continuing education** (CE) programs. The CE requirement has two components: a firm element and a regulatory element.

LO 32.a Define Firm Element Continuing Education.

The **firm element** requires member firms to prepare an annual training plan, taking into account such factors as recent regulatory developments, the scope of the member's business activities, the performance of its personnel in the regulatory element, and its supervisory needs. This annual in-house training must be given to all registered persons who have direct contact with the public.

The firm element CE requirements must be completed by December 31, but a member firm may require an earlier date. Failure to complete the firm element may result in suspension of a representative's license.

A significant portion of the firm element CE should be related to the firm's normal business activities and relevant to the representative's duties.

LO 32.b Recall the time frame for Regulatory Element Continuing Education.

The **regulatory element** requires that all registered persons complete a computer-based training session within 120 days of the person's second registration anniversary and every three years thereafter (i.e., within 120 days of the person's 5th, 8th, 11th registration anniversary, and so on). The content of the regulatory element is determined by FINRA and is appropriate to either the RR or principal status of the person.

If a person fails to complete the regulatory element within the prescribed period, FINRA will deactivate that person's registration until the requirements of the program are met.

LO 32.c Recall the steps for handling written complaints.

Though written complaints have been discussed previously, here are a few additional points on how these complaints should be handled.

Whenever a customer complaint is received or a potential red flag for a customer or account is identified, it is essential that the proper personnel be notified. Persons who should be notified may include the account's representative, the account's principal, the branch manager, or a member of the compliance department. *A principal will need to address the complaint.*

A complaint is defined as a written statement by a customer (or a person acting on behalf of a customer) alleging a grievance arising out of, or in connection with, a securities transaction.

If a complaint is resolved to the satisfaction of both the member firm and the customer, no further action is needed.

A report listing all written complaints is filed with FINRA within 15 days of the end of each calendar quarter. Copies of complaints must be held for four years after resolution.

LO 32.d Indicate the rules associated with outside business activities.

An associated person cannot work for any business other than his member firm (independent activity) without his employing BD's knowledge. If a registered person wants to be employed by or accept compensation from an entity other than the member firm, that person must provide prior written notice to the member. *Note that the employing member's permission is not a regulatory requirement.* The firm, however, does have the right to reject or restrict any outside affiliation if it feels a conflict of interest exists. These affiliations would also include serving as an officer or director of a company or owning any interest in another financial services company.

A **passive investment**, such as the purchase of a limited partnership unit or investment company share or unit, is not considered an outside business activity. An associated person may make a passive investment for his own account without providing written notice to the employing BD.

EXAMPLE

An RR currently working full time with a BD wants to teach night classes in business and finance at a local community college to earn extra income while building her securities practice. Under the rules governing outside business activity, prior written notice to the employing member BD would need to be made.

The same RR wants to volunteer for her son's little league association, serving in any way she can be of help (coaching, committees, etc.). *As long as no compensation* was involved, notice to the employing member would *not* need to be made for participation in this activity.

LO 32.e Define selling away

The Conduct Rules define a **private securities transaction** as any sale of securities outside an associated person's regular business and her employing member. Private securities transactions are also known as **selling away**.

If an associated person wishes to enter into a private securities transaction, that person must

- provide prior written notice to her employer;

- describe in detail the proposed transaction;

- describe in detail her proposed role in the transaction; and

- disclose whether she has or may receive compensation for the transaction.

With compensation

If the transaction involves compensation, the employing member may approve or disapprove the associated person's participation. If the member approves the participation, it must treat the transaction as if it is being done on its own behalf by entering the transaction on its own books and supervising the associated person during the transaction. If the member disapproves the transaction, the associated person may not participate in it.

Without compensation

If the associated person has not received or will not receive compensation for the private securities transaction, the employing member must acknowledge that it has received written notification and may require the associated person to adhere to specified conditions during participation.

Transactions that the associated person enters into on behalf of immediate family members and for which the associated person receives no compensation are excluded from the definition of private securities transactions.

TAKE NOTE

Supervision, and thus the responsibility for all that is associated with the transaction, is that of the employing member firm, *not* the BD, who is accommodating the private securities transaction.

TEST TOPIC ALERT

Selling away without your firm's knowledge is a serious violation of the Conduct Rules.

LO 32.f Recall rules on gifts and gratuities to employees of other member firms.

BDs may not distribute business-related compensation (cash or noncash gifts or gratuities) to the employees of other member firms except as provided in the exceptions listed here:

- The compensation is not conditional on sales or promises of sales.

- It has the employing member's prior approval.

- The compensation's total value does not exceed the annual limit set by the regulatory bodies (currently $100 per year).

The $100 limit may be exceeded under the following exceptions:

- Occasional noncash expenditures, such as dinners, seminars, or tickets to entertainment events

- Reminder advertising items, such as pens, mouse pads, and similar items that carry the firm's logo

- Items given for a life event (weddings, birth of a child, retirement, etc.)

Note that all such gifts must be reasonable. Placing your logo on the side of a new car does not make it reminder advertising.

If a representative of the firm that is providing the tickets to an event or paying for a meal accompanies the recipient, that activity is allowed as a normal business entertainment event.

EXAMPLE

Twice each year, a mutual funds sales associate likes to sit down at a nice restaurant with a few BD representatives to discuss new funds that his company is offering and explore possible suitable recommendations for their clients. These dinners can sometimes cost $400–$500. This would be permitted because it is occasional and business is being discussed with the mutual fund sales associate present (a.k.a. an allowable business entertainment expense).

EXAMPLE

A mutual fund sales associate sends an RR two tickets for all of the home games of the RR's favorite sports team. The value of the two tickets is approximately $4,500. This would be considered a violation because it is not occasional—and further, there can be no assumption that the sales associate would be present at each game to discuss business, nor would there be a reasonable need to do so that often.

LO 32.g Recall limitations and rules regarding political contribution.

Political contributions should never be used to procure business. All business should be awarded on the basis of merit only and not political favor acquired via contributions to political parties, elected individuals candidates, or third parties with connections to those with political affiliations. Industry rules regarding political contributions are intended to preserve investor confidence and market integrity.

MSRB Rule G-37

Recalling that the **Municipal Securities Rulemaking Board** (MSRB) was established as an SRO to enact and interpret rules relating to the underwriting and trading of municipal securities as well as advising municipal issuers, it should be noted that it also has rules to prevent *pay to play*—MSRB Rule G-37. Because the MSRB has no enforcement capability, these rules would be enforced by FINRA.

The MSRB play-for-pay rule deals with the influence of political contributions on the selection of underwriters. The rule focuses on

- negotiated underwritings in which a municipal issuer selects an underwriter and negotiates a deal (not underwritings in which underwriters bid on a proposed new issue); and

- financial advisory work in which a municipal issuer selects a municipal firm to help it structure a new issue.

Rule G-37 prohibits municipal firms from engaging in the municipal securities business noted here (negotiated underwritings/financial advisory work) with an issuer for two years after a contribution is made to an official of that issuer by

- the municipal firm;

- a municipal finance professional (MFP) associated with the firm; or

- any political action committee (PAC) controlled by the firm.

An MFP is an associated person of a FINRA member firm engaged in municipal securities underwriting, trading, sales, financial advisory, research, investment advice, or any other activities that involve communication with public investors. Associated persons whose activities are limited solely to sales or have only clerical or ministerial functions are not MFPs.

Contributions of up to $250 per election are permitted to be made by MFPs (registered persons) *eligible to vote for that official.* The $250 de minimis exemption does not apply to contributions made by municipal firms (a firm is not a voter).

EXAMPLE

A municipal securities firm routinely makes political contributions to candidates in local municipalities. Later, it wants to take part in the underwriting of a new issue of municipal bonds in one of those municipalities. The municipality is requiring that bids be made by member firms in order for the municipality to select the underwriters. Because this isn't a negotiated underwriting, the municipality would be allowed to submit a bid to participate in underwriting the issue of new bonds. Had it been a negotiated underwriting, the member firm would have been unable to negotiate with the municipality for a period of two years after the last contribution was made.

LO 32.h Recall rules for home-based offices.

It is not unusual for a BD to allow RRs to operate out of a home or residence, commonly referred to as working from a **home office**. In these instances, approval of the member firm's SRO is required because it would be for any office associated with the BD. All normal business activities, including taking customer orders for the purchase and sale of securities, would be permitted. Given all normal business activities are permitted at a home office, it would be subject to a premise visit and review by principals of the firm and FINRA examiners, as any BD office would be. Additionally, the home office address and telephone number may be advertised in any normal manner, such as on business cards or through various public media venues such as newspapers and websites.

TAKE NOTE

A member firm's principals, compliance officers, and regulators may visit, inspect, and audit an office that resides in a residence the same way they can a normal office.

KNOWLEDGE CHECK

1. Which of the following is *correct* regarding the continuing education regulatory element requirements?
    A. Training must be completed within 120 days of the person's second registration anniversary and every 5 years thereafter.
    B. Training must be completed within 120 days of the person's first registration anniversary and then annually thereafter.
    C. Training must be completed within 120 days of the person's second registration anniversary and every 3 years thereafter.
    D. Training must be completed annually.

2. A BD may give other firms' employees gratuities without violating the rules, provided the compensation's total value does not exceed
    A. $50.
    B. $100.
    C. $250.
    D. $500.

3. You overhear a discussion about a registered representative (RR) being disciplined because of selling away. Which of FINRA's Conduct Rules was violated?
    A. Outside business activity
    B. Accepting excessive noncash compensation
    C. Private securities transactions
    D. Failure to direct the client's trade to the best available market

Answers

1. **C** The regulatory element requires that all registered persons complete a computer-based training session within 120 days of the person's second registration anniversary and every 3 years thereafter. LO 32.b

2. **B** Under the current rules, the cash gift that may be made without raising concern is $100 per person per year. LO 32.f

3. **C** The Conduct Rules define a private securities transaction as any sale of securities outside an associated person's regular business and his employing member. Private securities transactions are also known as *selling away*. LO 32.e

COMMON ABBREVIATIONS

ADR/ADS   American depositary receipt (share)

AIR   assumed interest rate

BA   banker's acceptance

BD   broker-dealer

BDC   business development (growth) company

CD   certificate of deposit

CDO   collateralized debt obligation

CEO   chief executive officer

CMO   collateralized mortgage obligation

CMV   current market value

COP   Code of Procedure

CPI   Consumer Price Index

CY   current yield

DBCC   District Business Conduct Committee

DEA   designated examining authority

DJIA   Dow Jones Industrial Average

DMM   Designated Market Maker

EE   Series EE savings bonds

EPS   earnings per share

ERISA   Employee Retirement Income Security Act of 1974

ETF   exchange-traded fund

FAC   face-amount certificate

Fed   Federal Reserve System

FDIC   Federal Deposit Insurance Corporation

FGIC   Financial Guaranty Insurance Company

FIFO   first-in, first-out

FINRA   Financial Industry Regulatory Authority

FNMA   Federal National Mortgage Association

FOMC   Federal Open Market Committee

FRB   Federal Reserve Board

GNMA   Government National Mortgage Association

GDP   gross domestic product

GO   general obligation bond

HH   Series HH savings bond

HSA   health savings account

IDR/IDB   industrial development revenue bond

IPO   initial public offering

IRA   individual retirement account

IRC   Internal Revenue Code

IRS   Internal Revenue Service

JTIC   joint tenants in common

JTWROS   joint tenants with right of survivorship

LIFO   last-in, first-out

MSRB   Municipal Securities Rulemaking Board

Nasdaq   National Association of Securities Dealers Automated Quotation system

NAV   net asset value

NHA   New Housing Authority

NL   no load

NYSE   New York Stock Exchange

OSJ   office of supervisory jurisdiction

OTC   over the counter

PE   price-to-earnings ratio

PHA   Public Housing Authority

POP   public offering price

REIT   real estate investment trust

RR   registered representative

SAI   statement of additional information

SEC   Securities and Exchange Commission

SEP   simplified employee pension plan

SIPC   Securities Investor Protection Corporation

SRO   self-regulatory organization

T+2   trade date plus two business days' settlement

TCPA   Telephone Consumer Protection Act

TSA   tax-sheltered annuity

UGMA/UTMA   Uniform Gift (Transfers) to Minors Act

UIT   unit investment trust

UPC   Uniform Practice Code

YLD   yield

YTC   yield to call

YTM   yield to maturity

ZR   zero-coupon

GLOSSARY

1035 exchange   A tax-free exchange between like contracts. This provision applies to transfers from annuity to annuity, life to life, and life to annuity. It cannot be used for transfers from an annuity to a life insurance policy.

12b-1 fee   A section of the Investment Company Act of 1940 that permits an open-end investment company (mutual fund) to levy an ongoing charge for advertising and sales promotional expenses. This fee may not exceed .75% and, if above .25%, the fund may not describe itself as no-load.

401(k) plan   A tax-deferred defined contribution retirement plan offered by a private-sector employer.

403(b) plan   A tax-deferred retirement plan available to employees of public schools and certain nonprofit organizations.

529 savings plans   Plans designed by states to provide tax-advantaged means of saving for eligible education expenses.

75-5-10 test   The standard for judging whether an investment company qualifies as diversified under the Investment Company Act of 1940. Seventy-five percent of a fund's assets must be invested in such a way that no more than 5% of its total assets are invested in any one company's voting securities, and no single investment may represent ownership of more than 10% of any one company's outstanding voting securities. There are no restrictions on the remaining 25% of the funds' assets.

acceptance, waiver, and consent   A form of plea bargaining under the Code of Procedure. FINRA's Enforcement Department brings disciplinary actions against a respondent and, if the respondent agrees, the proposed settlement is accepted, all rights to a hearing are waived, and the respondent consents to the penalty submitted.

account executive   *See* registered representative.

accredited investor   Any institution or individual meeting minimum requirements for the purchase of securities qualifying under the Regulation D registration exemption.

accrued interest   The interest that has accumulated since the last interest payment, up to but not including the settlement date, and that is added to the contract price of a bond transaction. *See also* flat.

accumulation stage   The period during which contributions are made to an annuity contract. *See also* accumulation unit.

accumulation unit   An accounting measure used to determine an annuitant's proportionate interest in the insurer's separate account during a variable annuity's accumulation (deposit) stage. *See also* accumulation stage, annuity unit, separate account.

acid-test ratio   A measure of a corporation's liquidity, calculated by adding cash, cash equivalents, and accounts and notes receivable, but not inventory, and dividing the result by total current liabilities. It is a more stringent test of liquidity than current ratio. *See also* current ratio.

ad valorem tax   A tax based on the value of real or personal property.

adjusted (cost) basis   Adjusted basis is used to compute the gain or loss on the sale or other disposition of the asset or security.

adjusted gross income (AGI)   Gross income from all sources minus certain adjustments to income, such as deductible contributions to an IRA and net capital losses. It is the amount of income that will be subject to tax. *See* tax liability.

administrator   (1) The official or agency administering the securities laws of a state. (2) A person authorized by a court of law to liquidate an intestate decedent's estate.

ADR   *See* American Depositary Receipt.

ADS   *See* American Depositary Receipt.

advertisement   Any promotional material where the firm has little control over the type of individuals being exposed to the material.

advisory account   An account through which a registered investment adviser (RIA) or investment adviser representative (IAR) of the RIA provides investment advice to her clients for a fee.

affiliated person   Anyone in a position to influence decisions made in a corporation, including officers, directors, principal stockholders, and members of their immediate families. Their shares are often referred to as *control stock*.

agency basis   *See* agency transaction.

agency issue   A debt security issued by an authorized agency of the federal government. Such issues are backed by the issuing agencies themselves, not by the full faith and credit of the U.S. government (except GNMA and Federal Import Export Bank issues). *See* government security.

agency transaction   A transaction in which a broker-dealer acts for the accounts of others by buying or selling securities on behalf of customers. *Syn.* agency basis. *See also* agent; broker; principal transaction.

agent   (1) An individual or firm that effects securities transactions for the accounts of others. (2) A securities salesperson who represents a broker-dealer or issuer when selling or trying to sell securities to the investing public; this individual is considered an agent whether he actually receives or simply solicits orders. *See* broker; broker-dealer; dealer; principal.

aggregate exercise price   The strike price expressed in total dollars. The aggregate exercise price for a standard July 40 call contract is $4,000 (100 shares at $40 per share).

aggressive investment strategy   A method of portfolio allocation and management aimed at achieving maximum return. Aggressive investors pursue aggressive policies, including margin trading, arbitrage, and option trading. *See also* balanced investment strategy, defensive investment strategy.

agreement among underwriters (AAU)   The agreement that sets forth the terms under which each member of an underwriting syndicate will participate in a new issue offering and states the duties and responsibilities of the underwriting manager. *See* syndicate; underwriting manager.

agreement of limited partnership   The contract that establishes guidelines for the operation of a direct participation program, including the roles of the general and limited partners.

AIR   *See* assumed interest rate.

all-or-none order (AON)   An order that instructs the firm to execute the entire order. Firm does not have to execute immediately.

all-or-none underwriting (AON)   A form of best efforts underwriting in which the underwriter agrees that, if it is unable to sell all the shares (or a prescribed minimum), the issuer will cancel the offering.

alternative minimum tax (AMT)   An alternative tax computation that adds certain tax preference items back into adjusted gross income. If the AMT is higher than the regular tax liability for the year, the regular tax and the amount by which the AMT exceeds the regular tax are paid. *See* tax preference item.

American Depositary Receipt (ADR)   Facilitate trading in foreign securities in the U.S. domestic markets. Sometimes these are shown as ADS (American Depositary Shares) and are similar to a GDR (Global Depositary Receipt), which is traded outside the United States.

American Depositary Shares   *See* American Depositary Receipt.

American Stock Exchange   Former name of the NYSE American Stock Exchange. This exchange should not be confused with the NYSE Amex Options Exchange.

American-style option   An option contract that may be exercised at any time between the date of purchase and the expiration date. Most exchange-traded options are American-style.

AML   *See* anti-money laundering.

amortization   (1) The paying off of debt in regular installments over a period of time. (2) The ratable deduction of certain capitalized expenditures over a specified period of time.

amortization of bond premium   An accounting process whereby the initial cost of a bond purchased at a premium is decreased to reflect the basis of the bond as it approaches maturity. *See also* accretion of bond discount.

annual compliance review   An annual meeting that all registered representatives and principals must attend, the purpose being to review compliance issues.

annual report   A formal statement issued yearly by a corporation to its shareowners. It is a reflection of the corporation's financial and operational wellbeing at the close of the business year (balance sheet) and earnings performance (income statement).

annual return on investment (ROI)   For example, the annual return on a bond investment, which equals the annual interest and either plus the prorated discount or minus the prorated premium.

annuitant   A person who receives an annuity contract's distribution.

annuitize   To change an annuity contract from the accumulation (pay-in) stage to the distribution (pay-out) stage.

annuity   A contract between an insurance company and an individual. Upon annuitization, it guarantees lifetime income to the individual on whose life the contract is based in return for either a lump sum or a periodic payment to the insurance company.

annuity unit   An accounting measure used to determine the amount of each payment during an annuity's distribution stage. *See also* accumulation unit; annuity; distribution stage.

anti-money laundering   A program required to be instituted by all FINRA member firms under NASD Rule 3011. All personnel are to be trained to identify the different stages of money laundering and how to combat it.

AON   *See* all or none order; all or none underwriting.

AP   *See* associated person of a member.

appreciation   The increase in value of an asset.

arbitration The arrangement whereby FINRA's Board of Arbitration or a designated arbitration association hears and settles disputes between members, allied members, member organizations, and their employees. Nonmembers in dispute with members or employees may submit voluntarily to arbitration. Once both parties agree to the process, there is no appeal. *See also* simplified arbitration.

ask An indication by a trader or dealer of a willingness to sell a security or a commodity; the price at which an investor can buy a security. *Syn.* offer; POP.

assessed value The value of a property, as appraised by a taxing authority, for the purpose of levying taxes. Assessed value may equal market value or a stipulated percentage of market value. *See also* ad valorem tax.

assessment An additional amount of capital that a participant in a direct participation program may be called upon to furnish beyond the subscription amount. Assessments may be mandatory or optional and must be called within 12 months.

asset A balance sheet item expressing what a corporation owns.

asset allocation fund A mutual fund that splits its investment assets among stocks, bonds, and other vehicles, with a view to provide a consistent return for the investor.

asset class allocation Dividing an investment portfolio among different asset categories such as stocks, bonds, cash, and tangible assets, such as real estate, precious metals, and other commodities. *Syn.* asset allocation.

asset-backed security (ABS) One whose value and income payments are backed by the expected cash flow from a specific pool of underlying assets. Pooling the assets into financial instruments allows them to be sold to investors more easily than selling them individually. This process is called securitization.

assignment (1) A document accompanying, or part of a stock certificate signed by the person named on the certificate for the purpose of transferring the certificate's title to another person's name. (2) The act of identifying and notifying an account holder that an option held short in that account has been exercised by the option owner. *See also* stock power. (3) Transferring an investment advisory contract to another firm. This may not be done without written consent of the customer. A change in the majority interest in an investment advisory firm organized as a partnership is also considered assignment.

associated person Any employee, manager, director, officer, or partner of a member broker-dealer or another entity (e.g., issuer or bank), or any person controlling, controlled by, or in common control with that member, is considered an associated person of that member.

associated person of a member (AP) An individual who solicits customers, orders, or funds on behalf of a futures commission merchant (FCM) and is controlled by that member or an introducing broker (IB).

assumed interest rate (AIR) (1) The net rate of investment return that must be credited to a variable life insurance policy to ensure that at all times, the variable death benefit equals the amount of the death benefit. The AIR forms the basis for projecting payments, but it is not guaranteed. (2) The rate that a variable annuity separate account must earn to keep annuity payments level. If the account earns more than the AIR, the next payment will increase; if it earns less, the next payment will decrease.

at the money The term used to describe an option when the underlying stock is trading precisely at the exercise price of the option. *See also* in the money; out of the money.

auction market A market in which buyers enter competitive bids and sellers enter competitive offers simultaneously. The NYSE is an auction market. *Syn.* double auction market.

authorized stock The number of shares of stock that a corporation may legally issue. This number is stipulated in the corporation's state-approved charter and may be changed by a vote of the corporation's stockholders.

Automated Quotation System (Nasdaq) The Nasdaq Stock Market is a U.S.-registered stock exchange providing an automatic execution venue. Trade reporting for Nasdaq trades goes through the FINRA/Nasdaq Trade Reporting Facility (TRF).

automatic exercise A procedure initiated by Options Clearing Corporation (OCC) to automatically exercise in-the-money options upon their expiration.

automatic reinvestment A feature available to shareholders whereby dividend distributions are automatically reinvested.

average A price at a midpoint among a number of prices. Technical analysts frequently use averages as market indicators. *See also* index.

AWC *See* acceptance, waiver, and consent.

BA *See* banker's acceptance.

back-end load A fee that is charged when mutual fund shares or variable annuity contracts are redeemed. It is typically found with Class B shares (and for one year with Class C shares). It declines annually, decreasing to zero over an extended holding period—up to eight years—as described in the prospectus. *Syn.* contingent-deferred sales load.

backdating The predating of a letter of intent (LOI) by as many as 90 days to allow an investor to incorporate recent deposits for the purpose of qualifying for a sales load discount (breakpoint) on a purchase of open-end investment company shares.

balance of payments (BOP) An international accounting record of all transactions made by one particular country with others during a certain time period; it compares the amount of foreign currency the country has taken in with the amount of its own currency it has paid out. *See also* balance of trade.

balance of trade The largest component of a country's balance of payments; it concerns the export and import of merchandise (not services). Debit items include imports, foreign aid, domestic spending abroad, and domestic investments abroad. Credit items include exports, foreign spending in the domestic economy, and foreign investments in the domestic economy. *See* balance of payments.

balance sheet A financial statement showing the assets, liabilities, and shareholder's equity at a particular moment.

balance sheet equation A formula stating that a corporation's assets equal the sum of its liabilities plus shareholders' equity.

balanced fund A mutual fund whose stated investment policy is to have, at all times, some portion of its investment assets in bonds and preferred stock, as well as in-common stock, in an attempt to provide both growth and income. *See also* mutual fund.

balloon maturity A balloon maturity refers to a large number of an issuer's bonds that become due at the same time. Compare term bonds.

BAN *See* bond anticipation note.

bank holding company A holding company whose primary asset is a commercial bank. *See* holding company.

Bank Secrecy Act (BSA) The Bank Secrecy Act authorizes the Treasury Department to require financial institutions to maintain records of personal financial transactions that involve the movement of currency in excess of $10,000 in and out of accounts. It also authorizes the Treasury Department to require any financial institution to report any suspicious transaction. These reports, called suspicious activity reports (SARs), are filed with the Treasury Department's Financial Crimes Enforcement Network (FinCEN).

banker's acceptance (BA) A money market instrument used to finance international trade. A banker's acceptance is a time draft drawn on a bank by an importer or exporter of goods, and it represents the bank's conditional promise to pay the face amount of the note at maturity (normally less than three months).

basis (1) The cost of an asset or security. (2) Another term for yield to maturity (e.g., this bond is selling at a 5.78 basis).

basis point A measure of a bond's yield, equal to 1/100 of 1% of a yield. A bond whose yield increases from 5.0% to 5.5% is said to increase by 50 basis points. A basis point is equal to 10 cents.

BD *See* broker-dealer.

bear An investor who acts on the belief that a security or the market is falling or is expected to fall. *See* bull.

bear market A market in which prices of a certain group of securities are falling or are expected to fall. *See* bull market.

benchmark portfolio A model portfolio of a large number of assets, such as the S&P 500, against which the performance of a fund or portfolio is measured.

best efforts underwriting A securities underwriting in which the underwriter acts as an agent for the issuer and puts forth its best efforts to sell as many shares as possible of those available. The underwriter has no liability for unsold shares, unlike in a firm commitment underwriting. *See also* underwriting, *see* firm commitment.

bid (1) An indication by an investor, a trader, or a dealer of a willingness to buy a security or commodity; the price at which an investor can sell to a broker-dealer. (2) The price at which an investor can redeem shares of a mutual fund. *See* also offer; public offering price; quotation.

blotter A book of original entry in which a broker-dealer records on a daily basis every transaction, movement of securities, and cash receipt and disbursement. *Syn.* daily journal; diary; day book.

blue-chip stock The equity issues of financially stable, well-established companies that have demonstrated their ability to pay dividends in both good and bad times.

blue-sky To register a securities offering in a particular state.

blue-sky laws The nickname for state regulations governing the securities industry.

board of directors Individuals elected by stockholders to establish corporate management policies. A board of directors decides, among other issues, if and when dividends will be paid to stockholders.

bona fide From the Latin "good faith," something that is bona fide is genuine, authentic, and real. An example would be a bona fide quote.

bona fide quote An offer from a broker-dealer to buy or sell securities; it indicates a willingness to execute a trade under the terms and conditions accompanying the quote. *See* firm quote; nominal quote; subject quote; workout quote.

bond A legal obligation of an issuing company or government to repay the principal of a loan to bond investors at a specified future date. Corporate bonds are usually issued with a par or face value of $1,000, and municipal bonds with a par of $5,000, representing the amount of money borrowed. The issuer promises to pay a percentage of the par value as interest on the borrowed funds. The interest payment is stated on the face of the bond or its description at issue.

bond anticipation note (BAN) A short-term municipal debt security to be paid from the proceeds of long-term debt when it is issued.

bond fund A mutual fund whose investment objective is to provide stable income with a minimal capital risk. It invests in income-producing instruments that may include corporate, government, or municipal bonds.

bond power A document that is used in lieu of an assignment form to authorize the transfer of the debt securities. *See* stock power.

bond quote Quotes for corporate, municipal, and government bonds are percentages of the bonds' face values (usually $1,000). Corporate bonds are quoted in increments of 1/8. Government bonds are quoted in increments of 1/32. Municipal bonds may be quoted on a dollar basis or on a yield-to-maturity basis. *See* quotation; stock quote.

bond rating An evaluation of the possibility of a bond issuer's default, based on an analysis of the issuer's financial condition and likelihood of meeting all obligations. Standard & Poor's, Moody's Investors Service, and Fitch Investors Service, among others, provide bond rating services. Ratings of municipal bonds may be found on the EMMA System operated by the Municipal Securities Rulemaking Board.

bond yield The annual rate of return on a bond investment. Types of yield include nominal yield, current yield, yield to maturity, and yield to call. *See* current yield, nominal yield.

book value per share A measure of the net worth of each share of common stock. It is calculated by subtracting intangible assets and preferred stock from total net worth, then dividing the result by the number of shares of common outstanding. *Syn.* net tangible assets per share.

book-entry *See* street name.

book-entry security A security sold without a certificate. Evidence of ownership is maintained on records kept by a centralized service such as the Depository Trust Corporation. For example, the U.S. Treasury Department keeps records of purchasers of Treasury bills. Transfer of ownership is recorded by entering the change on the books or electronic files. *See also* coupon bond, registered, registered as to principal only.

bounty An award paid in connection for original information concerning any violation of securities law. Under Dodd-Frank legislation, awards may range from 10%–30% of amounts recovered.

branch office Any location identified to the public, by any means, as a place where a registered broker-dealer conducts business. *See* office of supervisory jurisdiction (OSJ); satellite office.

branch office manager (BOM) An individual designated by a member firm to manage a branch office location. *See also* branch office.

breakeven long hedge Long option hedge in which the investor neither gains nor loses. The breakeven point is reached when the market price of the stock equals its purchase price plus the premium paid for the put.

breakeven point The point at which gains equal losses.

breakeven short hedge A short option hedge in which the investor neither gains nor loses. The breakeven point is reached when the market price of the stock equals the sale price of the short position minus the premium paid.

breaking the buck (or break the buck) An expression used to describe the net asset value (NAV) of a money market fund falling below $1. Breaking the buck may happen if a fund leverages assets.

breakpoint The schedule of sales charge discounts a mutual fund offers for lump-sum or cumulative investments. Breakpoints are available to any person. Investment clubs or associations formed for the purpose of investing do not qualify for breakpoints.

breakpoint sale The sale of mutual fund shares in an amount just below the level at which the purchaser would qualify for reduced sales charges. This violates the Conduct Rules.

broad-based index An index designed to reflect the movement of the market as a whole. Examples include the S&P 100, the S&P 500, the AMEX Major Market Index, and the Value Line Composite Index.

broker (1) An individual or firm that charges a fee or commission for executing buy and sell orders submitted by a customer. (2) The role of a firm when it acts as an agent for a customer and charges the customer a commission for its services. *See also* agent; broker-dealer; dealer.

broker-dealer Person or firm in the business of buying and selling securities. A firm may act as both broker (agent) or dealer (principal) but not in the same transaction. Broker-dealers normally must register with the SEC, the appropriate SROs, and any state in which they do business.

bull An investor who believes that a security, a commodity, or the market overall is likely to rise. *See also* bear.

bull market A market where prices of a certain group of commodities or securities are rising or are expected to rise. *See also* bear market.

bulletin board *See* OTC Bulletin Board.

business continuity plan A plan required by regulators for broker-dealers to identify procedures relating to an emergency or significant business disruption, which allows the member to meet all existing obligations.

business cycle   A predictable long-term pattern of alternating periods of economic growth and decline. The cycle passes through four stages: expansion, peak, contraction, and trough.

business day   A day on which financial markets are open for trading. Saturdays, Sundays, and most legal holidays are not considered business days.

business risk   The risk inherent in equity securities that poor management decisions will have a negative impact on the stock's performance. Can be reduced through diversification. *Syn.* unsystematic risk.

buy stop order   An order to buy a security that is entered at a price above the current offering price and that is triggered when the market price touches or goes through the buy stop price.

buy-in   A procedure that the buyer of a security follows when the seller fails to complete the contract (fails to deliver the security). The buyer closes the contract by buying the security in the open market (buy-in) and charges the account of the seller for transaction fees and any loss caused by changes in the markets (if any). *See* sell-out.

buy-write   *See* covered call writer.

calendar year   For accounting purposes, a year that ends on December 31. *See* fiscal year.

call   (1) An option contract giving the owner the right to buy a specified amount of an underlying security at a specified price within a specified time. (2) The act of exercising a call option. *See also* put.

call date   The date, specified in the prospectus of every callable security, after which the security's issuer has the option to redeem the issue at par or at par plus a premium.

call feature   *See* call provision.

call loan rate   The rate of interest a brokerage firm charges its margin account clients on their debit balances.

call option   A contract giving the owner the right to buy a specified amount of an underlying security at a specified price within a specified time.

call price   The price, usually a premium over par value, at which a bond or preferred stock may be redeemed at the discretion of the issuer.

call protection   A provision in a bond indenture stating that the issue is noncallable for a certain period (e.g., 5 or 10 years) after the original issue date. *See* call provision.

call provision   The written agreement between an issuer and its bondholders or preferred stockholders giving the issuer the option to redeem the securities at a specified price before maturity and under certain conditions. *Syn.* call feature.

call risk   The potential for a bond to be called before maturity, leaving the investor without the bond's current income. Because this is more likely to occur during times of falling interest rates, the investor may not be able to reinvest the principal at a comparable rate of return. This risk applies to callable preferred shares, as well.

callable bond   A type of bond issued with a provision allowing the issuer to redeem the bond before maturity at a predetermined price. *See also* call price.

callable preferred stock   A type of preferred stock issued with a provision allowing the corporation to call in the stock at a certain price and retire it. *See* call price; preferred stock.

capital   Accumulated money or goods available for use in producing more money or goods.

capital appreciation   A rise in the market price of an asset.

capital asset   All tangible property, including securities, real estate, and other property, held for the long term.

capital gain   The profit realized when a capital asset is sold for a price higher than the purchase price. *See also* capital loss; long-term gain.

capital gains distributions   Payments made to mutual fund shareholders of gains realized on the sale of the fund's portfolio securities. These amounts, if any, are paid once a year.

capital loss   The loss incurred when a capital asset is sold for a price lower than the purchase price. *See* capital gain; long-term loss.

capital market   The segment of the securities market that deals in instruments with more than one year to maturity—that is, long-term debt and equity securities.

capital risk   The potential for an investor to lose all money invested owing to circumstances unrelated to the financial strength of the issuer. For example, derivative instruments such as options carry risk independent of the changing value of the underlying securities.

capitalization   (1) The sum of a corporation's long-term debt, stock, and surpluses. *Syn.* invested capital. *See* capital structure. (2) The number of outstanding shares multiplied by share price. (3) The costs to acquire an asset expensed over the life of the asset.

capping   An illegal form of market manipulation that attempts to keep the price of a subject security from rising. It is generally used by those with a short position. *See* pegging.

carrying broker   *See* clearing broker-dealer.

cash account   An account in which the customer is required by the Fed's Regulation T to pay, in full, for securities purchased no later than two days after the standard payment period set by the Uniform Practice Code. *Syn.* special cash account. *See also* margin account; Regulation T.

cash compensation FINRA's list of cash compensation includes any discount, concession, fee, service fee, commission, asset-based sales charge, loan, override, or cash employee benefit received in connection with the sale and distribution of investment company securities. *See also* noncash compensation.

cash dividend Money paid to a corporation's stockholders out of the corporation's current earnings or accumulated profits. The board of directors must declare all dividends.

cash equivalent A security that can be readily converted into cash. Examples include Treasury bills, certificates of deposit, and money market instruments and funds.

cash flow The money received by a business minus the money paid out. Cash flow is also equal to net income plus depreciation or depletion.

cash settlement Requires delivery of securities from the seller and payment from the buyer on the same day the trade is executed.

cash trade *See* cash transaction.

cash transaction A settlement contract that calls for delivery and payment on the same day the trade is executed; payment is due by 2:30 p.m. EST (or within 30 minutes of the trade if made after 2:00 p.m. EST). *Syn.* cash trad; cash settlement. *See also* regular way; settlement date.

catch-up provision A tax-code stipulation that permits individuals over age 50 to make additional annual contributions to their individual retirement accounts (IRAs) and/or their 401(k) accounts. Economic Growth and Tax Relief Reconciliation Act of 2001.

CBOE *See* Chicago Board Options Exchange.

CD *See* negotiable certificate of deposit.

CDSC Conditional deferred sales charge. Sometimes called a back-end load (conditional deferred sales load, or CDSL) to differentiate between it and a front-end load. Instead of charging a load on each purchase, there is no sales charge unless the investor redeems shares too early. These charges begin reducing after the first year and generally decline to zero between the sixth and eighth year after purchase. *See* front-end load.

CE *See* continuing education.

Central Registration Depository An automated database containing detailed records, information, and forms regarding licensing status, employment status, employment history, fingerprint results, disciplinary disclosures for all registered securities individuals, and all firms in the U.S. securities industry.

certificate The physical document representing a security engraved with information concerning the issuer and details of the specific issue.

certificate of deposit (CD) A debt instrument issued by a bank that pays a fixed interest rate over a specific time period. CDs are insured up to $250,000 by the FDIC. *See* negotiable certificate of deposit.

CHB *See* commission house broker.

Chicago Board Options Exchange (CBOE) The first nationally recognized securities exchange listing and trading options. The self-regulatory organization with jurisdiction over all writing and trading of standardized options and related contracts listed on that exchange.

churning Excessive trading in a customer's account with the view to generate commissions. *Syn.* overtrading.

claimant Party initiating a demand for arbitration to FINRA or the NFA.

class Options of the same type (i.e., all calls or all puts) on the same underlying security. *See also* series; type.

Class A share (1) A class of mutual fund shares issued with a front-end sales load. (2) Shares of a company that have differing characteristics from other classes of stock (e.g., Class A shares in a company offering multiple share classes may offer super voting privileges of many times the number of votes Class B shares may offer).

Class B share A class of mutual fund shares issued with a back-end load. A mutual fund offers different classes of shares to allow investors to choose the type of sales charge they will pay. *See* also back-end load; Class A share; Class C share.

Class C share A class of mutual fund shares issued with a level load. A mutual fund offers different classes of shares to allow investors to choose the type of sales charge they will pay. *See* also Class A share; Class B share.

classical economics The theory that maximum economic benefit will be achieved if government does not attempt to influence the economy (i.e., if businesses are allowed to seek profitable opportunities as they see fit).

clearing agency An intermediary between the buy and sell sides in a securities transaction that receives and delivers payments and securities. Any organization that fills this function, including a securities depository [such as the National Securities Clearing Corporation (NSCC)] but not including a Federal Reserve Bank, is considered a clearing agency.

clearing broker-dealer A broker-dealer that clears its own trades as well as those of introducing (correspondent) brokers. A clearing broker-dealer can hold customers' securities and cash. *Syn.* carrying broker.

clearing corporation An organization associated with an exchange to promptly and efficiently handle the confirmation, settlement, and delivery of securities transactions. Clearing corporations are also referred to as *clearing firms* or *clearinghouses*. *See* clearinghouse.

client profile   Information generated on a client that identifies capital and discretionary income available for appropriate investment, according to the investor's investment objectives, financial and tax status, and monetary needs.

close   (1) The price of the last transaction for a particular commodity or commodity option on a particular day. (2) The midprice of a closing trading range. *See also* closing range.

close out   A procedure provided under MSRB rules that permits a broker, dealer, or dealer bank that has purchased securities from another broker, dealer, or dealer bank but has not yet received them (or which, as a seller of securities, has tendered a good delivery of the securities but has had such delivery improperly rejected) to take action to complete the transaction.

closed-end management company   An investment company that issues a fixed number of shares in an actively managed portfolio of securities. The shares may be of several classes, and they are traded in the secondary marketplace, either on an exchange or over the counter. The market price of the shares is determined by supply and demand. *Syn.* publicly traded fund.

closing purchase   An options (or futures) transaction in which the seller buys back an option in the same series; the two transactions effectively cancel each other out, and the position is liquidated. *See* opening purchase.

closing sale   An options transaction in which the buyer sells an option in the same series; the two transactions effectively cancel each other out, and the position is liquidated. *See also* closing purchase; opening sale.

CMO   *See* collateralized mortgage obligation.

CMV   *See* current market value.

Code of Arbitration Procedure   FINRA's formal method of handling securities-related disputes or clearing controversies between members, public customers, clearing corporations, or clearing banks. Any claim, dispute, or controversy between member firms or associated persons is required to be submitted to arbitration. The MSRB has no arbitration rules except to say its members are subject to FINRA's Code of Arbitration.

Code of Procedure (COP)   FINRA's formal procedure for handling trade practice complaints involving violations of the Member Conduct Rules. FINRA's Department of Enforcement is the first body to hear and judge complaints. Appeals and review of Department of Enforcement decisions are handled by the National Adjudicatory Council.

coincident indicator   A measurable economic factor that varies directly and simultaneously with the business cycle, thus indicating the current state of the economy. Examples include nonagricultural employment, personal income, and industrial production. *See* lagging indicator; leading indicator.

collateral   Certain assets set aside and pledged to a lender for the duration of a loan. If the borrower fails to meet obligations to pay principal or interest, the lender has claim to the assets.

collateral trust bond   A secured bond backed by stocks or bonds of another issuer. The collateral is held by a trustee for safekeeping. *Syn.* collateral trust certificate.

collateral trust certificate   *See* collateral trust bond.

collateralized mortgage obligation (CMO)   A mortgage-backed corporate security. Unlike pass-through obligations issued by FNMA and GNMA, its yield is not guaranteed, and it does not have the federal government's backing. These issues attempt to return interest and principal at a predetermined rate.

college savings plan   College savings plans allow contributors to invest after-tax dollars in professionally managed accounts that contain a mix of stocks, bonds, and other investments selected to reflect a child's age or a family's investment preference. *Syn.* qualified tuition plan.

combination fund   An equity mutual fund that attempts to combine the objectives of growth and current yield by dividing its portfolio between companies that show long-term growth potential and companies that pay high dividends.

combination privilege   A benefit offered by a mutual fund whereby the investor may qualify for a sales charge breakpoint by combining separate investments in two or more mutual funds in the same family of funds.

combined account   A customer account that has long and short margin positions in different securities. *Syn.* mixed account.

commercial paper (CP)   A short-term, unsecured debt instrument primarily issued by corporations and banks, typically for the funding of short-term liabilities such as payrolls, accounts payable, and inventories and normally priced at a discount and redeemed at face value. Maturities are 270 days or less.

commingling   (1) The combining by a brokerage firm of one customer's securities with another customer's securities and pledging them as joint collateral for a bank loan; unless authorized by the customers, this violates SEC Rule 15c2-1. (2) The combining by a brokerage firm of customer securities with firm securities and pledging them as joint collateral for a bank loan; this practice is prohibited. *See also* cross lien; segregation.

commission A service charge assessed by an agent in return for arranging the purchase or sale of a security. A commission must be fair and reasonable, considering all the relevant factors of the transaction. *Syn.* sales charge.

Commission Shortened term for the Securities and Exchange Commission, which was created by Congress to regulate the securities markets and protect investors. Composed of five commissioners appointed by the President of the United States and approved by the Senate. The SEC enforces, among others, the Securities Act of 1933, Securities Exchange Act of 1934, Trust Indenture Act of 1939, Investment Company Act of 1940, and Investment Advisers Act of 1940. If in context the subject is commodity futures, the word refers to the CFTC.

commission house broker (CHB) A member of an exchange who is eligible to execute orders for customers of a member firm on the floor of the exchange. *Syn.* floor broker.

commodity Any bulk good traded on an exchange or in the cash market, including metals, grains, and meats.

common stock A security that represents ownership in a corporation. Holders of common stock exercise control by electing a board of directors and voting on corporate policy. *See also* equity; preferred stock.

common stock fund A mutual fund portfolio that consists primarily of common stocks. The emphasis of these portfolios is usually on growth.

communications with the public As defined by FINRA, there are three categories of communications: retail communications, correspondence, and institutional communications. *See* retail communications, correspondence, and institutional communications.

community property A marital property classification recognized by some, but not all, states. In these jurisdictions, most property acquired during the marriage is considered to be owned jointly by both spouses and would be divided at the time of divorce, annulment, or death.

comparison (1) The process of matching the data concerning an interdealer transaction specified by each party to the transaction in order to determine that both parties agree on the details of the transaction. (2) A term used to refer to an interdealer confirmation.

competitive bid underwriting A firm commitment underwriting in which rival syndicates submit sealed bids for underwriting the issue. Competitive bidding is often used to select the underwriters for issues of general obligation municipal bonds and may be required by law in some states. *See also* negotiated underwriting.

completion of the transaction As defined by FINRA, the point at which a customer pays any part of the purchase price to the broker-dealer for a security he has purchased or for delivering a security that he has sold. If the customer makes payment to the broker-dealer before the payment is due, the completion of the transaction occurs when the broker-dealer delivers the security.

compliance department The department within a brokerage firm that oversees the firm's compliance with all applicable laws, rules, and regulations of federal and state regulators and its designated examining authority such as FINRA, NFA, MSRB, et cetera.

Composite Average *See* Dow Jones Composite Average.

concession The amount of payment the selling broker-dealer retains from the sale of a newly issued security.

Conduct Rules Rules written to ensure that FINRA member firms and their representatives follow just and equitable principles of trade. The rules complement and support the Securities Act of 1933, the Securities Exchange Act of 1934, and all other securities laws.

conduit theory A means for an investment company to avoid taxation on net investment income distributed to shareholders. If a mutual fund acts as a conduit for the distribution of net investment income, it may qualify as a regulated investment company and be taxed only on the income the fund retains. *Syn.* pipeline theory.

confirmation (securities trade) Written notification disclosing details of a customer securities transaction. It is used to verify that trades were carried out according to instructions. It may be mailed or paperless, as the customer wishes. It must be sent on or before the completion of the transaction.

conflict of interest Circumstances or conditions that oppose the client's best interest, thus enabling a member or AP to benefit from a relationship with a client.

consent to lend agreement *See* loan consent agreement.

constructive receipt (1) The date on which the Internal Revenue Service considers a taxpayer to have received dividends or other income. (2) Determined by when the recipient, company, or individual of the income has control over it.

Consumer Price Index (CPI) A measure of price changes in a "market basket" of consumer goods and services used to identify periods of inflation or deflation.

consumption A term used by Keynesian economists to refer to the purchase by household units of newly produced goods and services.

contemporaneous trader   A person who enters a trade at or near the same time and in the same security as a person who has inside information. The contemporaneous trader may bring suit against the inside trader. *See also* Insider Trading and Securities Fraud Enforcement Act of 1988.

contingent deferred sales load   *See* back-end load.

continuing commissions policy   FINRA rules permit payment of commissions to retired registered representatives or their beneficiaries that accrue from certain ongoing investments, as long as such compensation is called for in a bona fide contract.

continuing education   A securities industry requirement that has two components: the regulatory element, which is taken by all registered persons on a schedule based on their date of association, and the firm element, which is unique to each firm and applies to those with public contact or those who are their supervisors. *See also* regulatory element; firm element.

contra broker   The broker on the buy side of a sell order or on the sell side of a buy order.

contraction   A period of general economic decline, which is one of the business cycle's four stages. *See* business cycle.

contractionary policy   A monetary policy that decreases the money supply, usually with the intention of raising interest rates and combating inflation.

contributory plan   A retirement plan to which both the employee and the employer make contributions. *See* noncontributory plan.

control (controlling, controlled by, under common control with)   The power to direct or affect the direction of the management and policies of a company, whether through the ownership of voting securities, by contract, or otherwise. Control is presumed to exist if a person, directly or indirectly, owns, controls, holds with the power to vote, or holds proxies representing more than 10% of a company's voting securities.

control person   (1) A director, officer, or other affiliate of an issuer. (2) A stockholder who owns at least 10% of any class of a corporation's outstanding voting securities. *See also* affiliate; insider.

control relationship   A control relationship exists with respect to a security if a broker-dealer controls, is controlled by, or is under common control with the issuer or another person obligated with respect to the debt service of the issue.

control security   Any security owned by a director, officer, or other affiliate of the issuer or by a stockholder who owns at least 10% of any class of a corporation's voting securities. Who owns a security, not the security itself, determines whether it is a control security. *See also* Rule 144.

conversion parity   Two securities—one of which can be converted into the other—of equal dollar value. A convertible security holder can calculate parity to help decide whether converting would lead to gain or loss.

conversion price   The dollar amount of a convertible security's par value that is exchangeable for one share of the issuer's common stock.

conversion privilege   A feature the issuer adds to a corporate debt security that allows the holder to change the security into shares of the issuer's common stock. This makes the security attractive to investors and, therefore, more marketable. *See also* convertible bond; convertible preferred stock.

conversion rate   *See* conversion ratio.

conversion ratio   The number of shares of common stock per par value amount that a holder would receive following a conversion of a convertible bond or preferred share. *Syn.* conversion rate.

conversion value   The total market value of common stock into which a corporate debt instrument is convertible.

convertible bond   A corporate debt security, such as a bond or debenture, that is exchangeable for the equity securities of the issuing corporation at a specified price or rate.

convertible preferred stock   An equity security that may be exchanged for common stock at specified prices or rates. Dividends may be cumulative or noncumulative. *See also* cumulative preferred stock; noncumulative preferred stock; preferred stock.

cooling-off period   A waiting period between a registration statement's filing date with the SEC and the registration effective date. In practice, the period varies in length. *Syn.* Waiting period.

COP   *See* Code of Procedure.

corporate account   An account held in a corporation's name specifying which officers are authorized to trade in the account. A corporation must provide a copy of its charter and bylaws authorizing a margin account.

corporate bond   A long-term debt security issued by a corporation to finance its capital improvements and operations.

corporation   A form of business organization in which its total worth is divided into shares of common stock, with each share representing a unit of ownership. A corporation is characterized by a continuous life span and its owners' limited liability.

correspondence FINRA defines this category of communications with the public as any written (including electronic) communication that is distributed or made available to 25 or fewer retail investors within any 30-calendar-day period.

cost basis The price paid for an asset, including any commissions or fees, used to calculate capital gains or losses when the asset is sold. Also includes any reinvested distributions.

coterminous A term used to describe municipal entities that share the same boundaries. For example, a municipality's school district and fire district may issue debt separately, although the debt is backed by revenues from the same taxpayers. *See also* overlapping debt.

coupon bond A debt obligation with coupons representing semiannual interest payments attached; the coupons are submitted to the trustee by the holder to receive the interest payments. No record of the purchaser is kept by the issuer, and the purchaser's name is not printed on the certificate. Since 1983, federally tax-advantaged bonds may not be issued in bearer form, with the exception of obligations maturing in a year or less. *Syn.* bearer bond. *See also* book-entry security; registered; registered as to principal only.

coupon yield *See* nominal yield.

covenant A promise made to bondholders found in a debt issue's trust indenture that identifies bondholders' rights and other provisions. Examples include rate covenants that establish a minimum revenue coverage for a bond; insurance covenants that require insurance on a project; and maintenance covenants that require maintenance on a facility constructed by the proceeds of a bond issue.

Coverdell ESA Formerly known as the Education IRA, this offers tax-deferred growth and tax-free withdrawal of funds used to pay for education. Subject to certain earnings limits, after-tax contributions up to a certain amount per year may be made for a beneficiary up until the beneficiary's 18th birthday. The account may be used for qualifying educational expenses at any grade level, from elementary school through graduate school.

covered call writer An investor who sells a call option while owning the underlying security or some other asset that guarantees the ability to deliver if the call is exercised.

covered put writer An investor who sells a put option while owning an asset that guarantees the ability to pay if the put is exercised (e.g., cash in the account).

covered security *See* federal covered security.

CPI *See* Consumer Price Index.

CR Credit record. *See* credit balance.

credit agreement A component of a customer's margin account agreement, outlining the conditions of the credit arrangement between the brokerage firm and customer.

credit balance (CR) The amount of money remaining in a customer's account after all commitments have been paid in full. *Syn.* credit record; credit register. *See also* debit balance.

credit record *See* credit balance.

credit risk The degree of probability that the issuer of a debt security will default in the payment of either principal or interest. Securities issued by the U.S. government are considered to have little credit risk. *Syn.* default risk; financial risk. *See* Moody's; Standard & Poor's; Fitch Ratings.

CTR *See* currency transaction report.

cumulative preferred stock An equity security that offers the holder any unpaid dividends in arrears. These dividends accumulate and must be paid to the cumulative preferred stockholder before any dividends may be paid to the common stockholders.

cumulative voting A voting procedure that permits stockholders to either cast all of their votes for any one candidate or to cast their total number of votes in any proportion they choose. This results in greater representation for minority stockholders.

currency transaction report (CTR) A report filed by financial institutions to the IRS for deposits of any currency of more than $10,000 on a single day.

current assets Cash and other assets that may be converted into cash within the next 12 months. Examples include such liquid items as cash and equivalents (T-bills), accounts receivable, inventory, and prepaid expenses.

current liabilities A corporation's debt obligations due for payment within the next 12 months. Examples include accounts payable, accrued wages payable, and current long-term debt.

current market value (CMV) The worth of the securities in an account. The market value of listed securities is based on the closing prices on the previous business day. *Syn.* long market value.

current ratio A measure of a corporation's liquidity—that is, its ability to transfer assets into cash to meet current short-term obligations. It is calculated by dividing total current assets by total current liabilities. *Syn.* working capital ratio.

current report *See* Form 8K.

current yield The annual rate of return on a security, calculated by dividing the interest or dividends paid by the security's current market price. *See also* bond yield.

CUSIP   Committee on Uniform Securities Identification Procedures. A CUSIP number is a unique alphanumeric code assigned to that specific security by the CUSIP Global Services. The CUSIP number is used to expedite and reduce the risks associated with timely clearance and settlement.

CUSIP number   A CUSIP number is a unique nine-character alphanumeric code assigned to that specific security by Standard & Poor's. The CUSIP number is used to expedite clearance and settlement.

custodial account   An account in which a custodian enters trades on behalf of the beneficial owner, who is often a minor. A custodian cannot delegate away fiduciary responsibility but can grant trading authority and investment decisions to a qualified third party.

custodian   An institution or person responsible for making all investment, management, and distribution decisions in an account maintained in the best interests of another. For example, mutual funds have custodians responsible for safeguarding certificates and performing clerical duties.

custody   Maintaining possession of a customer's money and/or securities.

customer   Any person who opens an account with a broker-dealer. A customer may be classified in terms of account ownership, trading authorization, payment method, or types of securities traded.

customer agreement (margin agreement)   A document that a customer must sign when opening a margin account with a broker-dealer. It allows the firm to liquidate all or a portion of the account if the customer fails to meet a margin call.

customer complaint   A complaint is only a complaint when it is made in writing. All firms must maintain procedures for handling customer complaints and keep records of their disposition.

customer confirmation   Printed document stating the trade date, settlement date, and money due from or owed to a customer. It is sent or given to the customer on or before the settlement date. *See also* dealer confirmation; duplicate confirmation.

customer identification program (CIP)   The measures taken by a broker-dealer firm to verify the identity of each customer. Measures include obtaining unexpired photo identification, such as a valid driver's license or passport, and determining whether the customer's name appears on the U.S. Treasury's lists of known or suspected terrorists.

customer ledger   The accounting record that lists separately all customer cash and margin accounts carried by a firm. *See also* general ledger; stock record.

customer statement   A document showing a customer's trading activity, positions, and account balance. The SEC requires that customer statements be sent at least quarterly.

cycle   Options expire on a hybrid cycle that involves a total of four option series: the two nearest-term calendar months and the next two months from the traditional cycle to which that class of options has been assigned. For example, on January 1, a stock in the January cycle will be trading options expiring in these months: January, February, April, and July. After the January expiration, the months outstanding will be February, March, April, and July.

cyclical industry   A fundamental analysis term for an industry that is sensitive to the business cycle and price changes. Most cyclical industries produce durable goods, such as raw materials and heavy equipment.

daily journal   Day book or diary. *See* blotter.

dark pool   This term refers to an alternative trading system (ATS) where a supply of shares exists that is not displayed for all to *See*. Dark pools are akin to members-only trading platforms for those wishing to execute larger trades without their interest being made known through an open book. A dark pool provides anonymity to investors and sensitivity of share prices to movement when any sizeable demand appears.

DEA   *See* Designated Examining Authority.

dealer   (1) An individual or firm engaged in the business of buying and selling securities for its own account, either directly or through a broker. (2) The role of a firm when it acts as a principal and charges the customer a markup or markdown. *Syn.* principal. *See also* broker; broker-dealer.

dealer confirmation   Unlike customer confirmations, dealers exchange confirmations no later than the business day following the trade. However, in the case of a cash trade, confirmations are exchanged the day of the trade.

debenture   A debt obligation backed by the issuing corporation's general credit. *Syn.* unsecured bond.

debit balance (DR)   The amount of money a customer owes a brokerage firm. *Syn.* debit record; debit register. *See* credit balance.

debit record   *See* debit balance.

debt security   A security representing a loan by an investor to an issuer such as a corporation, municipality, the federal government, or a federal agency.

debt service   The schedule for repayment of interest and principal (or the scheduled sinking fund contribution) on an outstanding debt. *See also* sinking fund.

declaration date   The date on which a corporation announces an upcoming dividend's amount, payment date, and record date.

deduction   An item or expenditure subtracted from adjusted gross income to reduce the amount of income subject to tax.

default   (1) The failure to pay interest or principal promptly when due. (2) The failure to perform on a futures contract as required by an exchange.

default risk   *See* credit risk.

defeasance   The termination of a debt obligation. A corporation or municipality removes debt from its balance sheet by issuing a new debt issue and setting funds aside to call in the older debt in government securities by creating a trust that generates enough cash flow to provide for the payment of interest and principal. *See also* advance refunding; SLGS.

defensive industry   A fundamental analysis term for an industry that is relatively unaffected by the business cycle. Most defensive industries produce nondurable goods for which demand remains steady throughout the business cycle. Examples of this include the food industry and utilities.

deferred annuity   An annuity contract that delays payment of income, installments, or a lump sum until the investor elects to receive it. *See also* annuity.

deferred compensation plan   A nonqualified retirement plan whereby the employee defers receiving current compensation in favor of a larger payout at retirement (or in the case of disability or death).

deficiency letter   The SEC's notification of additions or corrections that a prospective issuer must make to a registration statement before the SEC will clear the offering for distribution. *Syn.* bedbug letter.

defined benefit plan   A qualified retirement plan that specifies the total amount of money that the employee will receive at retirement.

defined contribution plan   A qualified retirement plan that specifies the amount of money that the employer will contribute annually to the plan.

deflation   A persistent and measurable fall in the general level of prices. *See also* inflation.

delivery   A change in ownership or control of a security in exchange for cash. Delivery takes place on the settlement date.

demand   A consumer's desire and willingness to pay for a good or service. *See also* supply.

demand bonds   Long-term debt with demand "put" provision requiring the issuer to repurchase the bonds on notice from the bondholder at a price equal to the principal and accrued interest.

demand deposit   A sum of money left with a bank (or borrowed from a bank and left on deposit) that the depositing customer has the right to withdraw at any time.

Department of Enforcement   *See* FINRA Department of Enforcement. Also known as the Enforcement Department.

depletion   A tax deduction that compensates a business for the decreasing supply of the natural resource that provides its income (oil, gas, coal, gold, or other nonrenewable resource). *See also* cost depletion; percentage depletion.

depreciation   (1) A tax deduction that compensates a business for the cost of certain tangible assets. (2) A decrease in the value of a particular currency relative to other currencies.

depreciation expense   A bookkeeping entry of a noncash expense charged against earnings to recover the cost of an asset over its useful life.

depression   A prolonged period of general economic decline. Specifically, the GDP declines for at least six quarters in a row and is accompanied by high unemployment.

derivative   An investment vehicle, the value of which is based on the value of another security. Futures, forwards, swaps, and options are among the most common types of derivatives. Derivatives are generally used by institutional investors to increase overall portfolio return or hedge portfolio risk.

Designated Examining Authority (DEA)   A broker-dealer registered with the SEC or the CFTC is assigned a designated examining authority (DEA), such as FINRA, CBOE, NYSE, NFA, or another self-regulatory organization (SRO) to examine the firm's compliance, sales practices, financial responsibilities, books, and records. A broker-dealer may have more than one DEA.

designated market maker (DMM)   A registered trader that is obligated to maintain a fair and orderly market for specific securities assigned to the firm. Formerly known as specialists, they provide NBBO quotes, facilitate liquidity, open and close securities and furnish trading feedback to brokers.

designated primary market maker (DPM)   A firm's designated proprietary trader on the Chicago Board Options Exchange (CBOE) who is required to maintain continuous two-sided bid and ask quotes in all the option series in all of the allocated option classes.

developmental drilling program   A limited partnership that drills for oil, gas, or minerals in areas of proven reserves or near existing fields. *See also* exploratory drilling program; income program; step-out well.

direct participation program (DPP)   A business organized so as to pass through all income, gains, losses, and tax benefits to its owners (partners), the investors; the business may be structured as a limited partnership. Examples include oil and gas programs, real estate programs, agricultural programs, motion pictures, and cattle programs. An interest in a DPP is a security. *Syn.* program.

disclosure statement   A document provided by a member firm or CPO/CTA that fully discloses all material facts related to the firm and investing in commodities or commodity pools.

discount   The difference between the lower price paid for a security and the security's face amount at issue. *See also* premium.

discount bond   A bond that sells at a lower price than its face value. *See also* par value; premium bond.

discount rate   The interest rate charged by the 12 Federal Reserve Banks for short-term loans made to member banks.

discretion   The authority given to someone other than an account's beneficial owner to make investment decisions for the account. *See also* limited power of attorney.

discretionary account   An account in which the principal (beneficial owner) has given the registered representative authority to enter transactions at the representative's discretion. The registered representative may, if so directed by the customer, use the discretion about price (buy or sell), time, and choice of securities (bought or sold).

discretionary order   An order entered by a registered representative for a discretionary account allowing use of the representative's judgment on the customer's behalf, with respect to the choice of security, quantity of security, and/or whether the transaction should be a purchase or sale.

disgorge(ment)   In legal usage, the forced giving up of profits made through illegal activity (e.g., insider trading).

disposable income   The sum that people divide between spending and personal savings. *See also* personal income.

distribution   Any cash or other property distributed to shareholders or general partners that arises from their interests in the business, investment company, or partnership.

diversification   A risk management technique that mixes a wide variety of investments within a portfolio, thus minimizing the impact of any one security on overall portfolio performance.

diversified common stock fund   A mutual fund that invests its assets in a wide range of common stocks. The fund's objectives may be growth, income, or a combination of both. *See also* growth fund; mutual fund.

diversified management company   As defined by the Investment Company Act of 1940, a management company that meets certain standards for percentage of assets invested. These companies use diversification to manage risk. *See also* management company; nondiversified management company; 75-5-10 test.

dividend   A distribution of the earnings of a corporation. Dividends may be in the form of cash, stock, or property. All dividends must be declared by the board of directors. *See also* cash dividend; stock dividend

dividend yield   The annual rate of return on a common or preferred stock investment. The yield is calculated by dividing the annual dividend by the stock's purchase price. *See also* current yield; dividend.

DJIA   *See* Dow Jones Industrial Average.

DJTA   *See* Dow Jones Transportation Average.

DJUA   *See* Dow Jones Utilities Average.

DMM   *See* designated market maker.

Do Not Call List   List of prospects requesting no further contact from soliciting broker-dealers and their associated persons. Contacting customers on the Do Not Call List is a violation.

Dodd-Frank Act   The term by which the Wall Street Reform and Consumer Protection Act of 2010 is known. Considered to be the most significant legislation impacting the securities industry since the 1930s.

dollar cost averaging   A system of buying mutual fund shares in fixed dollar amounts at regular fixed intervals, regardless of the share's price. The investor purchases more shares when prices are low and fewer shares when prices are high, thus lowering the average cost per share over time.

donor   A person who makes a gift of money or securities to another. Once the gift is donated, the donor gives up all rights to it. Gifts of securities to minors under the Uniform Gifts to Minors Act provide tax advantages to the donor. *See also* Uniform Gifts to Minors Act.

double auction market   A market where buyers compete against other buyers and sellers compete against other sellers. The New York Stock Exchange uses this trading model. *See* auction market.

double-barreled bond   A municipal security backed by the full faith and credit of the issuing municipality as well as by pledged revenues. *See also* general obligation bond; revenue bond.

Dow Jones averages   The most widely quoted and oldest measures of change in stock prices. There are four averages, each based on the prices of a limited number of stocks in a particular category.

Dow Jones Composite Average (DJCA)   A market indicator composed of the 65 stocks that make up the Dow Jones Industrial, Transportation, and Utilities averages. *See also* average; Dow Jones Industrial Average; Dow Jones Transportation Average; Dow Jones Utilities Average.

Dow Jones Industrial Average (DJIA)   The most widely used stock market indicator, composed of 30 large, actively traded issues of industrial stocks. Futures contracts and futures option contracts trade on the Chicago Board of Trade.

Dow Jones Transportation Average (DJTA) A market indicator composed of 20 transportation stocks. *See also* average; Dow Jones Composite Average; Dow Jones Industrial Average; Dow Jones Utilities Average.

Dow Jones Utilities Average (DJUA) A market indicator composed of 15 utilities stocks. *See also* average; Dow Jones Composite Average; Dow Jones Industrial Average; Dow Jones Transportation Average.

Dow Theory A technical market theory that long-term trends in the stock market may be confirmed by analyzing the movements of the Dow Jones Industrial Average and the Dow Jones Transportation Average.

DPP *See* direct participation program.

DR Debit register. *See* debit balance.

due diligence The careful investigation by the underwriting participants necessary to ensure that all material information pertinent to an issue has been disclosed to prospective investors.

due diligence meeting A meeting at which an issuing corporation's officials and representatives of the underwriting group present information on, and answer questions about, a pending issue of securities.

duplicate confirmation A copy of a customer's confirmation that a brokerage firm sends to a party other than the customer.

durable power of attorney A document giving either full or limited authority to a third party who survives the mental or physical incompetence (but not death) of the grantor. *See* full power of attorney; limited power of attorney.

earned income Income derived from active participation in a trade or business, including wages, salary, tips, commissions, and bonuses. *See* portfolio income; unearned income.

ECN *See* Electronic Communications Network.

Education IRA *See* Coverdell ESA.

Education Savings Account *See* Coverdell ESA.

effective date The date the registration of an issue of securities becomes effective, allowing the underwriters to sell the newly issued securities to the public and confirm sales to investors who have given indications of interest.

effective tax rate The overall rate paid on a taxpayer's total taxable income. It will always be less than the marginal tax rate. *See* marginal tax rate.

electronic bulletin board Also known as a message board, it is an online discussion site. It originated as the modern equivalent of a traditional bulletin board.

Electronic Communications Network (ECN) Any electronic trading system that widely disseminates to third parties orders entered by market makers, institutional investors, and so forth. ECNs are agency broker-dealers.

electronic storage An acceptable method of recordkeeping, generally on computer disc. Among the requirements is that it cannot be altered and can be used to generate a paper copy upon request.

eligible security *See* margin security.

endorsement The signature on the back of a stock or bond certificate by the person named on the certificate as the owner. Owners must endorse certificates when transferring them to another person. *See also* assignment.

EPS *See* earnings per share.

EQ *See* equity.

equipment bond *See* equipment trust certificate.

equipment leasing limited partnership A direct participation program that purchases equipment for leasing to other businesses on a long-term basis. Tax-sheltered income is the primary objective of such a partnership.

equipment trust certificate A debt obligation, generally issued by transportation companies such as railroads, that is backed by equipment (rolling stock). *Syn.* equipment bond; equipment note.

equity (1) The ownership interest of common and preferred stockholders in a corporation. (2) In a margin account, equity equals what is owned less what is owed. *See also* common stock; margin account.

equity index annuity *See* index annuity.

equity option A security representing the right to buy or sell common stock at a specified price within a specified time. *See also* nonequity option; option.

equity security A financial instrument representing proportional ownership interest held in a corporation, company, or other enterprise recognized in the form of shares (e.g., common stock, preferred stock, convertible bonds, rights, warrants, and options).

ESA *See* Coverdell ESA.

estate tax A tax imposed by a state or the federal government on the assets a person possesses at the time of death.

ETF *See* exchange-traded fund (ETF).

ethics training Training in ethical responsibilities required every three years for APs and other NFA/CFTC registrants.

ex-date The first date on which a security is traded without entitling the buyer to receive distributions previously declared. *Syn.* ex-dividend date; ex-warrants; ex-rights; ex-distribution.

ex-dividend date *See* ex-date.

exchange Any organization, association, or group of persons that maintains or provides a marketplace in which securities can be bought and sold. An exchange does not have to be a physical place, as several strictly electronic exchanges do business around the world.

Exchange Act *See* Securities Exchange Act of 1934.

exchange market All of the exchanges on which listed securities are traded.

exchange privilege A feature offered by a mutual fund allowing an individual to transfer an investment in one fund to another fund under the same sponsor without incurring an additional sales charge.

exchange traded fund (ETF) An investment company legally classified as an open-end company or unit investment trust (UIT), but differing from traditional open-end companies (mutual funds) and UITs. An ETF issues shares in large blocks that are known as *creation units.* Those who purchase creation units are frequently large institutional traders or investors. The creation units can then be split up and sold as individual shares in the secondary markets, allowing individual investors to purchase shares.

exchange-listed security A security that has met certain requirements and has been admitted to full trading privileges on an exchange. The NYSE, NYSE American, Nasdaq, and all other exchanges set their listing requirements for volume of shares outstanding, corporate earnings, and other characteristics. Exchange-listed securities can also be traded in the third market.

executor/executrix A person given fiduciary authorization through a valid will to manage the affairs of a decedent's estate.

exempt Not being required to do something that others are required to do.

exempt security A security that need not be in formal compliance with a given piece of legislation, such as the Securities Act of 1933 or the Uniform Securities Act as adopted by a state. Examples include U.S. government and municipal securities. No security is exempt from the antifraud provisions of any securities legislation.

exempt transaction (federal) Transactions that do not trigger a federal registration. Examples include Regulation A+ offerings, Regulation S offerings, Regulation D offerings, and Rule 147/147A offerings.

exempt transaction (state) Transactions that do not trigger a state's registration and advertising requirements under the Uniform Securities Act. Examples of exempt transactions include transactions with financial institutions, unsolicited transactions, and private placement transactions.

exercise To effect the transaction offered by an option, right, or warrant. For example, an equity call holder exercises a call by buying 100 shares of the underlying stock at the agreed-upon price within the agreed-upon time period, or the use of a right granted under a contract. For example, a futures call holder exercises by buying the underlying futures at the agreed-upon ("exercise") price within the agreed-upon time period.

exercise price The cost per share at which the holder of an option or warrant may buy or sell the underlying security. *Syn.* strike price.

expense ratio A ratio for comparing a mutual fund's efficiency by dividing the fund's expenses by its net assets.

expiration date The specified date on which an option buyer no longer has the rights specified in the option contract.

exploratory drilling program A limited partnership that aims to locate and recover undiscovered reserves of oil, gas, or minerals. *Syn.* wildcatting. *See also* developmental drilling program; income program.

exploratory well A well drilled in search of either an undiscovered pool of oil or gas, or with the hope of substantially extending the limits of an existing pool of oil or gas.

FAC *See* face-amount certificate company.

face value *See* par value.

face-amount certificate company (FAC) An investment company that issues certificates obligating it to pay an investor a stated amount of money (the face amount) on a specific future date. The investor pays into the certificate in periodic payments or in a lump sum.

factors affecting option pricing This includes current stock price, the strike price, the time of expiration, the volatility of the stock price, the risk-free interest rate, and dividends expected during the life of the option.

Fannie Mae *See* Federal National Mortgage Association.

Farm Credit Administration (FCA) The government agency that coordinates the activities of the banks in the Farm Credit System. *See also* Farm Credit System.

Farm Credit System (FCS) An organization of 73 customer-owned lending institutions that provide credit services to farmers and mortgages on farm property. Included in the system are the Federal Land Banks, Federal Intermediate Credit Banks, and Banks for Cooperatives. *See also* Federal Intermediate Credit Bank.

FCA *See* Farm Credit Administration.

FCO *See* foreign currency option.

FCS *See* Farm Credit System.

FDIC *See* Federal Deposit Insurance Corporation.

Fed *See* Federal Reserve System.

Fed call   *See* margin call.

Federal Deposit Insurance Corporation (FDIC)   A federal government agency that insures deposits in banks and thrifts for up to $250,000 per depositor.

federal funds   Known as *fed funds*, these are immediately available funds representing excess reserves of commercial banks held at Federal Reserve banks. Federal funds are the primary payment mode for government securities and are often used to pay for new issues of municipal securities and secondary market transactions in certain types of securities.

federal funds rate   The interest rate charged by one institution lending federal funds to another.

federal margin   *See* margin.

Federal National Mortgage Association (FNMA)   A publicly held corporation that purchases conventional mortgages and mortgages from government agencies, including the Federal Housing Administration, Department of Veterans Affairs, and Farmers Home Administration. *Syn.* Fannie Mae.

Federal Open Market Committee (FOMC)   A committee that makes decisions concerning the Fed's operations to control the money supply.

Federal Reserve (The Fed)   The central bank of the United States that regulates the monetary system. It strives for price stability and economic growth.

Federal Reserve Board (FRB)   A seven-member group that directs the operations of the Federal Reserve System. Board members are appointed by the president, subject to approval by Congress.

Federal Reserve System   The central banking system of the United States that regulates flow of money and credit. The system includes 12 regional banks, 24 branch banks, and hundreds of national and state banks. *Syn.* Fed.

fee-based account   A method of managing a customer account that involves charging an annual or quarterly fee for services rather than a commission for each trade. Member firms must use fee-based accounts solely in the interest of the customer and place a customer into such an account only if it does not result in higher charges for the customer.

FHLMC   *See* Federal Home Loan Mortgage Corporation.

fiduciary   A person authorized, in good faith, to hold assets for another person and manage those assets for the benefit of that person.

FIFO   *See* first in, first out.

fill or kill order (FOK)   An order that instructs the broker to fill the entire order immediately. If the entire order cannot be executed immediately, it is canceled.

final prospectus   The legal document that states a new issue security's price, delivery date, and underwriting spread, as well as other material information. It must be given to every investor who purchases a new issue of registered securities. *Syn.* prospectus. *See* preliminary prospectus; red herring.

Financial Crimes Enforcement Network (FinCEN)   A part of the U.S. Department of the Treasury that collects information from financial institutions and coordinates with law enforcement to combat money laundering.

Financial Industry Regulatory Authority (FINRA)   The largest regulator for securities firms doing business in the United States. It oversees approximately 635,000 registered representatives. Overseen by the SEC, its primary role is to maintain the fairness of U.S. capital markets. FINRA was preceded by NASD, which merged with most of NYSE Regulation in 2007 to form a new regulatory authority.

financial risk   An unsystematic risk. Generally, the concern is that an issuer will be unable to meet its debt obligations as they come due. *See* credit risk.

FinCEN   *See* Financial Crimes Enforcement Network

FinCEN Form 112   Currency transactions in excess of $10,000 must be reported within 15 days on this form. Also known as a Currency Transaction Report (CTR).

FINRA   The acronym for the Financial Industry Regulatory Authority and the result of the cooperative effort of NASD and the NYSE to harmonize regulation in the securities industry.

FINRA 5% markup policy   A guideline for reasonable markups, markdowns, and commissions for secondary over-the-counter transactions. According to the policy, all commissions on broker transactions and all markups or markdowns on principal transactions should be fair and reasonable for that particular transaction. In the past, 5% has been used as a guideline. *Syn.* markup policy.

FINRA bylaws   The body of rules that describes how FINRA functions, defines its powers, and determines the qualifications and registration requirements for brokers.

FINRA Conduct Rules   Regulations designed to ensure that FINRA member firms and their representatives follow fair and ethical trade practices when dealing with the public. The rules complement and serve as extensions of the Securities Act of 1933, the Securities Exchange Act of 1934, and the Investment Company Act of 1940.

FINRA Enforcement Department   A department within FINRA that determines disciplinary action for violations of its rules and the securities laws. It will file a complaint with FINRA's Office of Hearing Officers (OHO).

FINRA Manual A publication of FINRA policies for regulating its member firms; it includes the Conduct Rules, the Uniform Practice Code, and the codes of Procedure and Arbitration Procedure.

FINRA Rules The Code of Procedure, Code of Arbitration Procedure, and Uniform Practice Code by which FINRA regulates its member firms.

firm commitment underwriting A type of underwriting commitment in which the underwriter agrees to sell an entire new issue of securities. The underwriter acts as a dealer, pays the issuer a lump sum for the securities, and assumes all financial responsibility for any unsold shares. *See also* underwriting.

firm element The portion of the industry continuing education program that requires each firm to annually survey its needs and provide training relevant to those needs to all registered persons who have contact with the public. Those who supervise the aforementioned are covered as well. Any medium may be used to deliver the training, so long as it can be reasonably demonstrated to have been delivered.

firm quote The sure price at which a trading unit of a security may be bought or sold. All quotes are firm quotes unless otherwise indicated.

first in, first out (FIFO) An accounting method, used to assess a company's inventory, in which it is assumed that the first goods acquired are the first to be sold. The same method is used by the IRS to determine cost basis for tax purposes. *See also* average basis; last in, first out; share identification.

fiscal policy The federal tax and spending policies set by Congress or the president. These policies affect tax rates, interest rates, and government spending in an effort to control the economy. *See also* monetary policy.

fiscal year An accounting year that ends on a day other than December 31 (calendar year accounting). *See* calendar year.

Fitch Ratings A rating service for corporate bonds, municipal bonds, commercial paper, and other debt obligations. *See* bond rating; Moody's Investors Service; Standard & Poor's Corporation.

fixed annuity An insurance contract in which the insurance company makes fixed-dollar payments to the annuitant for the term of the contract, usually until the annuitant dies. The insurance company guarantees both earnings and principal.

fixed asset A tangible, physical property used in the course of a corporation's everyday operations. It includes buildings, equipment, and land.

fixed-index annuity *See* index annuity.

fixed-premium variable life Variable life is a permanent insurance policy sold by prospectus that directs premiums to one or more separate account investment funds as the policy owner wishes.

flat A term used to describe bonds traded without accrued interest. They are traded at the agreed-upon market price only. *See also* accrued interest.

floor broker A member of an exchange who executes transactions only on an agent-only basis for the member's firm's customers and the customers of other members firms.

floor trader An exchange member who executes transactions from the floor of the exchange only for his own account.

FNMA *See* Federal National Mortgage Association.

FOK *See* fill-or-kill order.

follow-on offering An offering of securities following a company's initial public offering (IPO). May be primary or secondary. *See* add-on financing.

FOMC *See* Federal Open Market Committee.

foreign currency Money issued by a country other than the one in which the investor resides. Options and futures contracts on numerous foreign currencies are traded on U.S. exchanges.

foreign exchange rate The price of one country's currency in terms of another currency. *Syn.* exchange rate.

foreign fund *See* sector fund; specialized fund.

foreign government securities Financial instruments which are issued by a sovereign government of a country other than the United States. The purchasers of these securities become the foreign government's lender or creditor. There are several additional risk factors to consider (e.g., currency risk, political risk, and liquidity risk).

Form 10-K An annual audited report that must be submitted by reporting companies to the SEC. The form is due within 90 days of year end.

Form 10-Q A quarterly report containing a corporation's unaudited financial data and certain nonrecurring events that arise during the quarterly period, such as significant litigation, must be reported. A Form 10-Q must be submitted to the SEC no later than 45 days after the end of each of the first three fiscal quarters.

Form 1040 The IRS form used to file individual income tax. Schedule C of the Form 1040 is used to report business income for sole proprietorships.

Form 1041 The IRS form used by estates and trusts to report their income for tax purposes.

Form 1065 The information return filed by a partnership or LLC. Because income and losses flow through to owners, the entity pays no tax.

Form 112 (CTR)   The form filed with FinCEN when transactions or aggregated transactions total more than $10,000.

Form 1120 and 1120S   The tax returns filed by corporations. The *S* is for an S corporation.

Form 8-K   A form submitted to the SEC to report events of consequence that occur in a corporation, including changes in control of the corporation or in its name, address, financial standing, board of directors, or auditors. *Syn.* current report.

Form U4   The standardized application form for registration as an associated person.

Form U5   The standardized application form for termination of an associated person.

fourth market   The direct trading of large blocks of securities between institutional investors through a computer network.

fractional share   A portion of a whole share of stock most commonly found with mutual funds.

fraud   The deliberate concealment, misrepresentation, or omission of material information or the truth, so as to deceive or manipulate another party for unlawful or unfair gain.

FRB   *See* Federal Reserve Board.

Freddie Mac   *See* Federal Home Loan Mortgage Corporation.

free credit balance   The unencumbered cash funds in customer accounts.

freeriding   Buying and selling securities prior to the payment due date without making payment. This practice violates the SEC's Regulation T.

freeriding and withholding   The failure of a member participating in the distribution of a hot issue to make a bona fide public offering at the public offering price. *See* hot issue.

front running   The prohibited practice of entering an order for the benefit of a securities firm or professional before entering a customer order received.

front-end fee   The expenses paid for services rendered during a direct participation program's organization or acquisition phase, including front-end organization and offering expenses, acquisition fees and expenses, and any other similar fees designated by the sponsor.

front-end load   A mutual fund commission or sales charge that is included in the purchase price. *See also* back-end load; Class A share

frontier fund   A foreign stock fund that invests in preemerging economies.

frozen account   An account requiring cash in advance before a buy order is executed and securities in hand before a sell order is executed. The account holder has violated Regulation T.

full faith and credit bond   A bond based on the full faith and credit of an issuer who has the ability to levy taxes. Syn general obligation bond.

full power of attorney   A written authorization for someone other than the beneficial owner of an account to make deposits and withdrawals and execute trades in the account. *See also* limited power of attorney

full trading authorization   A legal power given to a third party to trade an account and add or withdraw funds.

fully disclosed broker   *See* introducing broker.

fully registered bond   A debt issue having the bondholder's name on the certificate. Principal and interest are paid directly to the investor. *See also* registered; registered as to principal only.

fund manager   *See* portfolio manager.

fundamental analysis   The study of the business prospects of an individual company within the context of its industry and the overall economy. *See also* technical analysis.

fungibility   Interchangeability resulting from standardization. Options listed on national exchanges are fungible. Nonstandardized OTC options are not.

fungible   A term referring to the interchangeability of financial instruments having effectively identical features. Cash is fungible, as are most securities.

GAAP   *See* Generally Accepted Accounting Principles.

GAN   *See* grant anticipation note.

GDP   *See* gross domestic product.

general account   The account that holds all of an insurer's assets other than those in separate accounts. The general account holds the contributions paid for traditional life insurance contracts. *See also* separate account.

general ledger   The records to which all of a brokerage firm's assets, liabilities, capital accounts, and income and expense accounts are posted. *See also* customer ledger; stock record.

general obligation bond (GO)   A municipal debt issue backed by the full faith, credit, and taxing power of the issuer for payment of interest and principal. *Syn.* full faith and credit bond. *See also* revenue bond.

general partner (GP)   An active party in a direct participation program who is personally liable for all debts of the program and who manages the business of the program. *See also* limited partner.

general partnership An association of two or more parties formed to conduct a business jointly. The general partners are jointly and severally liable for the partnership's liabilities. *See also* limited partnership.

general securities principal *See* Series 24.

general securities representative *See* Series 7.

general securities sales supervisor *See* Series 9; Series 10.

generally accepted accounting principles The accounting standards set forth by the Financial Accounting Standards Board for all publicly traded companies in the United States. Normally shown as GAAP.

generic advertising Communications with the public that promote securities as investments but do not refer to particular securities.

Ginnie Mae *See* Government National Mortgage Association.

GNMA *See* Government National Mortgage Association.

GNP *See* gross national product.

GO *See* general obligation bond.

good delivery (form) A term describing a security that is negotiable, in compliance with the contract of the sale, and ready to be transferred from seller to purchaser. *See also* uniform delivery ticket.

good delivery (time) Delivery of the certificate by the seller and payment by the buyer on settlement date—currently T+2 for the regular way.

good-til-canceled order (GTC) An order that is left on the specialist's book until it is either executed or canceled. *Syn.* open order.

goodwill An intangible asset that represents the value that a firm's business reputation adds to its perceived value.

Government National Mortgage Association (GNMA) A wholly government-owned corporation that issues pass-through mortgage debt certificates backed by the full faith and credit of the U.S. government. *Syn.* Ginnie Mae.

government security A debt obligation of the U.S. government, backed by its full faith, credit, and taxing power, and regarded as having no risk of default.

government-sponsored enterprises (GSEs) Corporations created by Congress to foster a public purpose such as affordable housing. Examples include the Federal National Mortgage Association (Fannie Mae) and the Federal Home Loan Mortgage (Freddie Mac).

GP *See* general partner; general partnership.

grant anticipation note (GAN) A short-term municipal debt security issued in anticipation of receiving a funding grant, typically from a government agency.

grantor The creator of the trust relationship and generally the owner of the assets initially contributed to the trust. *Syn.* settlor; trustor.

grantor trust A term used in the Internal Revenue Code to describe any trust over which the grantor or other owner retains the power to control or direct the trust's income or assets.

green shoe option A provision of an issue's registration statement that allows an underwriter to buy extra shares from the issuer (thus increasing the size of the offering) if public demand proves exceptionally strong. The term derives from the Green Shoe Manufacturing Company, which first used the technique.

gross domestic product (GDP) The total value of goods and services produced in a country during one year. It includes consumption, government purchases, investments, and exports minus imports.

gross income All income of a taxpayer derived from whatever source.

gross national product (GNP) A measure of the value of all goods and services produced by a country's residents and businesses. It estimates the value of the final products and services manufactured by a country's residents, regardless of the production location.

gross revenues All money received by a business from its operations. The term typically does not include interest income or income from the sale, refinancing, or other disposition of properties.

growth and income fund A mutual fund whose aim is to provide for a degree of both income and long-term growth.

growth fund A diversified common stock fund that has capital appreciation as its primary goal. It invests in companies that reinvest most of their earnings for expansion, research, or development.

growth industry An industry that is growing faster than the economy as a whole as a result of technological changes, new products, or changing consumer tastes.

growth stock A relatively speculative issue that is believed to offer significant potential for capital gains. It often pays low dividends and sells at a high price/earnings ratio.

growth-style investing A management style that attempts to find stocks with positive earnings momentum. *See* value style investing.

GTC *See* good-till-canceled order.

guaranteed bond A debt obligation issued with a promise from a corporation other than the issuing corporation to maintain payments of principal and interest.

guaranteed security The term guaranteed means guaranteed by a third party as to the payment of principal, interest, or dividends.

guardian A fiduciary, generally appointed by a court, who manages the assets of a minor or incompetent for the benefit of that person. *See also* fiduciary.

hedge An investment made to reduce the risk of adverse price movements in a security. Derivatives are a common way to hedge.

hedge fund A form of investment company that, as a regular policy, hedges its market commitments. It does this by holding securities it believes are likely to increase in value, and at the same time, is short other securities it believes are likely to decrease in value. The sole objective is capital appreciation. This type of fund is highly aggressive and generally available to sophisticated investors.

high The highest price a security or commodity reaches during a specified period of time. *See also* low.

high-yield bond A bond with a less-than-investment grade rating. *Syn.* junk bond

high-yield security A debt security of lower-than-investment grade offering higher yields with greater risk.

holding company A company organized to invest in and manage other corporations that is not considered an investment company.

house maintenance call *See* margin maintenance call.

house maintenance requirement *See* margin maintenance requirement.

hypothecation The practice of pledging securities as collateral for a loan. This is most commonly done when purchasing on margin. *See* margin account.

IAR *See* investment adviser representative.

IB *See* introducing broker.

IDB *See* industrial development bond.

identity theft A fraud committed or attempted using the identifying information of another person without authority.

IDR *See* industrial development bond.

immediate annuity An annuity contract that provides for monthly payments to begin immediately (generally in no more than 60 days) after deposit of the invested funds. *See also* deferred annuity.

immediate family A person who is supported financially by a person associated with the securities industry, including a parent, mother- or father-in-law, husband or wife, child, and any other individual to whom the person provides material support.

immediate-or-cancel order (IOC) An order that instructs the floor broker to execute immediately, in full or in part. Any portion of the order that remains unexecuted is canceled.

in-the-money The term used to describe an option that has intrinsic value, such as a call option, when the stock is selling above the exercise price, or a put option, when the stock is selling below the exercise price. *See also* at-the-money; intrinsic value; out-of-the-money.

income bond A debt obligation where the coupon interest is paid only if the corporation's earnings are sufficient to meet the interest payment. *Syn.* adjustment bond. *See also* flat.

income fund A mutual fund that seeks to provide stable current income by investing in securities that pay interest and/or dividends.

income statement A financial statement spanning a period showing the accounting profit or loss for the period.

indenture A contract between the issuer of debt securities and a trustee for the benefit of the bondholders.

independently prepared reprint (IPR) Any article reprint that meets certain standards designed to ensure that the reprint was issued by an independent publisher and was not materially altered by the member.

index *See* security market index.

index annuity An annuity product issued by an insurance company that provides for potential growth by tracking a specified index. It is not considered a security. *Syn.* equity index annuity; fixed index annuity.

index fund Investors who wish to invest passively can invest in an index mutual fund or ETF, which seeks to replicate the performance of a security market index such as the Standard & Poor's 500. Index funds have low operating expenses and low portfolio turnover.

index option A security representing the right to receive, in cash, the difference between the underlying value of a market index and the strike price of the option. *See also* capped index option.

indication of interest (IOI) An investor's expression of potential interest in buying a security currently in registration.

individual retirement account (IRA) A retirement investing tool for employed individuals that allows an annual contribution of 100% of earned income up to an indexed dollar maximum.

industrial development (revenue) bond (IDB) In general, securities issued by a state, local government, or development agency used to finance the construction or purchase of industrial, commercial, or manufacturing facilities that are to be purchased by or leased to a private user.

industrial revenue bond (IDR)   *See* industrial development bond.

industry fund   *See* sector fund.

inflation   A persistent and measurable rise in the general level of prices. *See* deflation.

inflation risk   *See* purchasing power risk.

initial margin   The initial monies or securities that are deposited as a good-faith deposit when a securities or futures position is initially opened. *See* Regulation T.

initial margin requirement   The amount of equity a customer must deposit when making a new purchase in a margin account. *See also* margin; margin call.

initial public offering (IPO)   The first sale of common stock by a corporation to the public. *See also* new issue market; public offering.

inside information   Material nonpublic information (MNPI) a person obtained or used for the purpose of trading in securities. *See also* material fact.

inside market   The best price at which a stock can be bought and sold. The best ask price is the lowest. The best bid price is the highest. The difference between the two prices is also called the *spread*.

insider   Any person who possesses or has access to material nonpublic information about a corporation. An insider includes directors, officers, and stockholders who own at least 10% of any class of equity security of a corporation.

Insider Trading Act   *See* Insider Trading and Securities Fraud Enforcement Act of 1988.

Insider Trading and Securities Fraud Enforcement Act of 1988   Legislation that defines what constitutes the illicit use of nonpublic information in making securities trades and the liabilities and penalties that apply. *Syn.* Insider Trading Act. *See also* contemporaneous trader; insider.

institutional account   Any account opened by a bank, savings and loan, insurance company, or registered investment company; an investment adviser registered either with the SEC or with a state; or any corporation, trust, natural person, et cetera, with total assets of at least $50 million.

institutional communication   FINRA-defined category of communications, written or electronic, distributed or made available to institutional investors only. It does not include a member's internal communications (i.e., internal memos).

institutional investor   A person or organization that trades securities in larger share quantities or dollar amounts. Institutional investors are covered by fewer protective regulations because it is assumed that they are more knowledgeable and better able to protect themselves. Examples would be member firms, banks and savings and loan associations, insurance companies, mutual funds, government entities, any entity with $50 million or more in total assets, or any person acting solely on behalf of an institutional investor.

institutional sales material   A form of public communication that does not require prior principal approval. Does not have to be filed with FINRA.

intangible asset   A property owned that is not physical, such as a formula, a copyright, or goodwill. *See also* goodwill.

intangible drilling cost (IDC)   In an oil and gas limited partnership, a tax-deductible cost. Usually this is for a nonphysical asset, such as labor or fuel, that does not depreciate. *Syn.* intangible drilling development expense.

interactive content   Content published in a way that allows for other users to comment on, reuse, or "like" it.

interest   The charge for the privilege of borrowing money, usually expressed as an annual percentage rate.

interest rate option   A security representing the right to buy or sell government debt securities.

interest rate risk   The systematic risk associated with investments, relating to the sensitivity of price or value, to fluctuations at the current level of interest rates.

Internal Revenue Code (IRC)   The legislation that defines tax liabilities and deductions for U.S. taxpayers.

Internal Revenue Service (IRS)   The U.S. government agency responsible for collecting most federal taxes and for administering tax rules and regulations.

intrinsic value   The potential profit to be made from exercising an option. A call option is said to have intrinsic value when the underlying stock is trading above the exercise price. *See also* time value.

introduced account   An account opened by a nonclearing (introducing) commodity firm. The firm carrying the account often receives full disclosure of the individual customer's account information, maintains records of statements, and confirms for individual customers. *See also* fully disclosed account; omnibus account.

introducing broker (IB)   A broker-dealer that does not hold customers' money or securities. Instead, it introduces customer accounts to a clearing broker-dealer, which handles all cash and securities for those accounts. *Syn.* fully disclosed broker. *See* clearing broker-dealer.

investment adviser   A person in the business of giving advice on securities for compensation.

investment adviser representative Any partner, officer, director, or other individual associated with an investment adviser who gives investment advice, manages client portfolios, determines which investment recommendations should be given, sells investment advisory services, or supervises employees involved in any of these activities.

Investment Advisers Act of 1940 Federal legislation requiring certain investment advisers to register as such with the SEC.

investment banker An institution in the business of raising capital for corporations and municipalities. An investment banker may not accept deposits or make commercial loans. *Syn.* investment bank.

investment banking business A broker, dealer, or municipal or government securities dealer that underwrites or distributes new issues of securities as a dealer or that buys and sells securities for the accounts of others as a broker. *Syn.* investment securities business.

investment company A company engaged in the business of pooling investors' money and investing and reinvesting in securities. Examples include face-amount certificate companies, unit investment trusts, and management companies.

Investment Company Act Amendments of 1970 Amendments to the Investment Company Act of 1940 requiring, in particular, that sales charges relate to the services a fund provides its shareholders. *See* Investment Company Act of 1940.

Investment Company Act of 1940 Federal legislation setting forth the regulatory requirements for investment companies.

Investment Company/Variable Contract Products Limited Principal *See* Series 26.

Investment Company/Variable Contract Products Limited Representative *See* Series 6.

investment grade The broad credit designation given to bonds that have a high probability of being paid and minor, if any, speculative features. Bonds rated BBB or higher by Standard and Poor's or Baa or higher by Moody's Investors Service are deemed by those agencies to be investment grade.

investment objective Any goal a client hopes to achieve through investing. Examples include current income, capital growth, and preservation of capital.

IOC *See* immediate-or-cancel order.

IOI *See* indication of interest.

IPO *See* initial public offering.

IRA *See* individual retirement account.

IRA rollover The reinvestment of assets that an individual receives as a distribution from a qualified tax-deferred retirement plan into an individual retirement account.

IRA transfer The direct reinvestment of retirement assets from one qualified tax-deferred retirement plan to another, or to an individual retirement, without ever passing through the investor's hands.

IRB *See* industrial revenue bond.

IRC *See* Internal Revenue Code.

irrevocable stock power *See* stock power.

irrevocable trust A trust that cannot be altered or canceled by the grantor at any time.

IRS *See* Internal Revenue Service.

issue Can be any of a company's class of securities (n) or the act of distributing them (v).

issued stock Equity securities authorized by the issuer's registration statement and distributed to the public. *See also* outstanding stock; treasury stock.

issuer (1) The entity, such as a corporation or municipality, that offers or proposes to offer its securities for sale. (2) The creator of an option. The issuer of an over-the-counter option is the option writer, and the issuer of a listed option is the Options Clearing Corporation.

ITSFEA *See* Insider Trading and Securities Fraud Enforcement Act of 1988.

joint account An account in which two or more individuals possess some form of control over the account and may transact business in the account.

joint life with last survivor An annuity payout option that covers two or more people, with annuity payments continuing as long as one of the annuitants remains alive.

joint tenants with right of survivorship (JTWROS) A form of joint ownership of an account whereby a deceased tenant's fractional interest in the account passes to the surviving tenant(s). *See also* tenants in common.

joint venture The cooperation of two or more individuals or enterprises in a specific business enterprise, rather than in a continuing relationship such as a partnership.

JTWROS *See* joint tenants with right of survivorship.

junior lien debt A bond backed by the same collateral backing a previous issue and having a subordinate claim to the collateral in the event of default. *See also* closed-end covenant; open-end covenant.

junk bond *See* high-yield bond.

Keogh plan A qualified tax-deferred retirement plan for persons who are self-employed. *Syn.* HR-10 plan. *See also* individual retirement account; nonqualified retirement plan; qualified retirement plan.

Keynesian economics The theory that active government intervention in the marketplace is the best way to ensure economic growth and stability.

kiddie tax Any unearned income in excess of a designated amount ($2,100 in 2019) received by a minor under age 19 (or 24 if full-time student) that is taxed to that minor, but at trust rates

Know Your Customer Rule Regulation requires that every member must use reasonable diligence, in regard to the opening and maintenance of every account, to know (and retain) the essential facts concerning every customer and concerning the authority of each person acting on behalf of such customer.

lagging indicator A measurable economic factor that changes after the economy has started to follow a particular pattern or trend. Lagging indicators are believed to confirm long-term trends. Examples include average duration of unemployment, corporate profits, and labor cost per unit of output. *See also* coincident indicator; leading indicator.

large-cap A measurement of a stock's market capitalization. These stocks have a market cap in excess of $10 billion.

last in, first out (LIFO) An accounting method used to assess a corporation's inventory in which it is assumed that the last goods acquired are the first to be sold. The method is used to determine cost basis for tax purposes. The IRS designates last in, first out as the order in which sales or withdrawals from an investment are made.

leading indicator A measurable economic factor that changes before the economy starts to follow a particular pattern or trend. Leading indicators are believed to predict changes in the economy. Examples include new orders for durable goods, slowdowns in deliveries by vendors, and numbers of building permits issued. *See also* coincident indicator; lagging indicator.

leg A term describing one side of a position with two or more sides. For example, a short straddle with a leg in the stock.

legend stock Private placement stock. Stock certificates are issued with a stamped notification that requires the fulfillment of a holding period before transfer. *Syn.* lettered stock; restricted security; Regulation D.

legislative risk The potential for an investor to be adversely affected by changes in investment or tax laws.

letter of intent (LOI) A nonbinding agreement between a purchaser of mutual funds and the fund underwriter that allows the investor up to 13 months to reach a specified dollar purchase. *See* breakpoint.

lettered stock Private placement stock. *See* legend stock; restricted security.

Level 1 The basic level of Nasdaq service. Through a desktop quotation service, it provides registered representatives and public subscribers with up-to-the-minute inside bid and ask quotations on over-the-counter stocks.

Level 2 The second level of Nasdaq service. Through a desktop quotation service, it provides up-to-the-minute inside bid and ask quotations and the bids and asks of each market maker for a security. *See also* National Association of Securities Dealers Automated Quotation System.

Level 3 The broadest level of Nasdaq service. It provides real time inside bid and ask quotations, supplies the bids and asks of each market maker for a security, and allows each market maker to enter new and updated quotations. *Syn.* market maker level.

level load A mutual fund sales fee charged annually based on the net asset value of a share. A 12b-1 asset-based fee is an example of a level load. *See also* back-end load; Class C share; front-end load.

leverage Using borrowed capital to increase investment return.

liability A legal obligation to pay a debt. Current liabilities are debts payable within 12 months. Long-term liabilities are debts payable over a period of more than 12 months.

LIBOR *See* London Interbank Offered Rate.

life annuity/straight annuity An annuity payout option that pays over the annuitant's lifetime.

life annuity with period certain An annuity payout option that guarantees the annuitant a monthly check for the longer of a certain period or the annuitant's death. If the annuitant dies before the period expires, the payments go to the annuitant's named beneficiary for the duration of the certain period.

LIFO *See* last in, first out.

limit order An order that instructs the trader to buy a specified security below a certain price or to sell a specified security above a certain price (e.g., "Buy 100 IBM at 120 or better [lower]"). *Syn.* or better order. *See also* stop limit order; stop order.

limited liability An investor's right to limit potential losses to no more than the amount invested. Equity shareholders, such as corporate stockholders and limited partners, have limited liability.

limited liability company (LLC) A hybrid between a partnership and a corporation, in that it combines the pass-through treatment of a partnership with the limited liability accorded to corporate shareholders.

limited partner (LP)   An investor in a direct participation program who does not participate in the management or control of the program and whose liability for partnership debts is limited to the amount invested in the program. *See also* general partner; participant; passive investor.

limited partnership (LP)   A business, formed by filing a partnership agreement with a state, that consists of a general partner and one or more limited partners.

limited partnership agreement   The contract between a partnership's limited and general partners that provides the guidelines for partnership operation and states the rights and responsibilities of each partner.

limited power of attorney   A legal authorization for someone other than the beneficial owner of an account to make investment decisions in the account.

limited principal   A person who has passed an examination evidencing the knowledge necessary to supervise the business of a broker-dealer in a limited area of expertise such as investment company shares (e.g., Series 26).

limited representative   A person who has passed an examination evidencing the knowledge and qualifications necessary to sell certain specified investment products (e.g., Series 6).

limited trading authorization   *See* limited power of attorney.

liquidation priority   In the case of a corporation's liquidation, the order that is followed for paying off creditors and stockholders.

liquidity   The ease with which an asset can be converted to cash in the marketplace.

liquidity ratio   A measure of a corporation's ability to meet its current obligations. The ratio compares current assets to current liabilities. *See also* acid-test ratio; current ratio.

liquidity risk   The potential that an investor might not be able to sell an investment when desired without adverse price disruption. *Syn.* marketability risk.

listed option   An option contract that may be bought and sold on a national securities exchange in a continuous secondary market. Listed options carry standardized strike prices and expiration dates. *Syn.* standardized option. *See also* OTC option.

listed security   A stock, bond, or other security that satisfies certain minimum requirements and is traded on a regional or national securities exchange such as the New York Stock Exchange. *See also* over-the-counter.

living trust   A trust created during the lifetime of the grantor; also known as an inter vivos trust.

LLC   *See* limited liability company.

LMV   *See* current market value.

loan consent agreement   An optional contract between a brokerage firm and a margin customer that permits the firm to lend margin securities to other brokers. The contract is part of the margin agreement. *Syn.* consent to lend agreement.

local government investment pools (LGIPs)   Designed by states or local governments to provide investment vehicles for public funds collected by local government entities.

locate requirement   SEC rule requiring firms to locate securities for borrowing prior to the short sale of any equity security. *See* Regulation SHO.

LOI   *See* letter of intent.

long   The term used to describe the owning of a security, contract, or commodity. For example, an owner of common stock is said to have a long position in the stock. *See also* short; short against the box.

long market value (LMV)   *See* current market value.

long-term capital gain   The profit earned on the sale of a capital asset that has been owned for more than 12 months. *See also* capital gain; capital loss; long-term capital loss; short-term capital gain.

long-term capital loss   The loss realized on the sale of a capital asset that has been owned for more than 12 months. *See also* capital gain; capital loss; long-term capital gain; short-term capital loss.

loss carryover   A capital loss incurred in one tax year that is carried over to the next or later years for use as a capital loss deduction. *See also* capital loss.

low   The lowest price a security or commodity reaches during a specified time period. *See also* high.

LP   *See* limited partner; limited partnership.

M1   A category of the money supply that includes all coins, currency, and demand deposits (i.e., checking accounts and NOW accounts). *See also* M2; M3; money supply.

M2   A category of the money supply that includes M1, in addition to all time deposits, savings deposits, and noninstitutional money market funds. *See also* M1; M3; money supply.

M3   A category of the money supply that includes M2, in addition to all large time deposits, institutional money market funds, short-term repurchase agreements, and certain other large liquid assets. *See also* M1; M2; money supply.

MA   *See* municipal advisor.

maintenance call   *See* margin maintenance call.

maintenance requirement   *See* margin maintenance requirement.

make a market   To stand ready to buy or sell a particular security as a dealer for its own account. *See also* market maker.

Maloney Act   An amendment enacted in 1938 to broaden Section 15 of the Securities Exchange Act of 1934. Named for its sponsor, the late Sen. Francis Maloney of Connecticut, the amendment provided for the creation of a self-regulatory organization for the specific purpose of supervising the over-the-counter securities market. *See also* National Association of Securities Dealers, Inc., precursor to FINRA.

management company   An investment company, either open-end or closed-end, that trades various types of securities under the direction of its portfolio manager, in accordance with specific objectives stated in the prospectus. *See* investment company.

management fee   (1) The payment to the sponsor of a direct participation program for managing and administering the program. (2) Fees that are paid out of fund assets to its investment adviser for investment portfolio management. (3) The portion of the underwriting spread paid to the managing underwriter.

managing underwriter   The brokerage firm responsible for organizing a syndicate, preparing the issue, negotiating with the issuer and underwriters, and allocating stock to the selling group. *Syn.* manager of the syndicate; managing underwriter; syndicate manager, book running manager. *Related items* agreement among underwriters; syndicate.

margin   The amount of equity contributed by a customer as a percentage of the current market value of the securities held in a margin account. *See also* equity; initial margin requirement; margin call; Regulation T.

margin account   An account with a broker-dealer where the firm lends money to the client to purchase securities. *See* cash account; hypothecation.

margin call   The Federal Reserve Board's demand that a customer deposit a specified amount of money or securities when a purchase is made in a margin account; the amount is expressed as a percentage of the market value of the securities at the time of purchase. The deposit must be made within one payment period. *Syn.* Fed call; federal call; federal margin; Reg T call; T call. *See also* initial margin requirement; margin.

margin deficiency   *See* margin maintenance requirement.

margin excess   *See* excess equity.

margin maintenance call   A demand that a margin customer deposit money or securities when the customer's equity falls below the margin maintenance requirement set by the broker-dealer or FINRA. *Syn.* house maintenance call; maintenance call; FINRA maintenance call; minimum maintenance call.

margin maintenance requirement   The minimum equity that must be held in a margin account, determined by the broker-dealer and FINRA. The amount of equity required varies with the type of security bought on margin, and the broker-dealer's house requirement is usually higher than that set by FINRA. *Syn.* house maintenance requirement; maintenance requirement; FINRA maintenance requirement.

margin security   A security that is eligible for purchase on margin. A firm is permitted to lend money to help customers purchase securities, using them as collateral for margin purchases. *Syn.* eligible security. *See also* nonmargin security; OTC margin security.

marginal tax rate   The rate of taxation on any additional taxable income received. It is sometimes referred to as the tax on the "next" dollar or the "last" dollar of income. *See* effective tax rate.

market capitalization   Computed by multiplying the number of outstanding common shares by the market price per share.

market maker   A dealer willing to accept the risk of holding a particular security in its own account to facilitate trading in that security. *See also* make a market.

market NH   *See* not held order.

market not held order   *See* not held order.

market order   An order that is to be executed immediately at the best available price. A market order is the only order that guarantees execution. *Syn.* unrestricted order.

market risk   The potential for an investor to experience losses owing to day-to-day fluctuations in the prices at which securities can be bought or sold. *See* systematic risk.

market value   The price at which investors buy or sell a share of common stock or a bond at a given time. *See also* current market value.

marketability   The ease with which a security can be bought or sold; having a readily available market for trading.

marketability risk   *See* liquidity risk.

married put   The simultaneous purchase of a stock and a put on that stock specifically identified as a hedge.

matched order   The fraudulent practice of simultaneously entering identical or nearly identical buy and sell orders for a security to create the appearance of active trading in that security.

material fact   Information that a knowledgeable investor would deem significant in making an investment determination. *See also* inside information.

maturity date   The date on which a bond's principal is repaid to the investor and interest payments cease. *See* balloon maturity; principal; serial bond; term maturity.

mean When referring to a series of values, such as portfolio returns, the average. A measure of central tendency known as the arithmetic mean.

median When viewing a series of values, such as portfolio returns, the number that has as many occurrences above as below. A measure of central tendency.

member (1) Of the NYSE: a person leasing a license to operate on the trading floor. (2) Of FINRA: any broker or dealer admitted to membership.

Member Conduct Rules FINRA rules that outline ethical trade practices to be followed by member firms in their dealings with the public.

member firm A broker-dealer registered with a self-regulatory organization such as the New York Stock Exchange, the Chicago Board of Exchange, FINRA, Municipal Securities Ruling Board, et cetera.

membership Members of FINRA, one of the exchanges, another SRO, or a clearing corporation.

merger Combining two or more companies by offering the stockholders of one company cash and/or securities in another company in exchange for the surrender of their stock. *See also* SEC Rule 145.

MFP *See* municipal finance professional.

mid-cap Stocks with a market capitalization of $2 billion to $10 billion.

minimum margin requirement *See* margin maintenance requirement.

minor rule violation (MRV) In instances where FINRA's Enforcement Department considers a violation minor and the respondent does not dispute the allegation, the department may prepare and request that the respondent sign an MRV letter, accepting a finding of violation. Once the respondent signs an MRV letter, the settlement is final with no appeal possible.

mode When viewing a series of values, the one that occurs the most frequently. A measure of central tendency.

modifier *See* trade modifiers.

monetarist theory An economic theory holding that the money supply is the major determinant of price levels and that, therefore, a well-controlled money supply will have the most beneficial impact on the economy.

monetary policy The Federal Reserve Board's actions that determine the size and rate of the money supply's growth, which, in turn, affect interest rates. *See also* fiscal policy.

money laundering The act of cleaning money from illegitimate enterprises through three stages known as placement, layering, and integration for the purpose of hiding the money's origin in anticipation of its later use for legitimate and illegitimate purposes.

money market The securities market that deals in short-term debt, such as debt maturing in less than one year (e.g. Treasury bills, commercial paper).

money market fund A mutual fund that invests in short-term debt instruments. The fund's objective is to earn interest while maintaining a stable net asset value of $1 per share. Usually sold with no load, the fund may also offer draft-writing privileges and low opening investments. *See also* mutual fund.

money market instruments Debt obligations that are traded in the money market and mature in a year or less.

money supply The total stock of bills, coins, loans, credit, and other liquid instruments in the economy. It is divided into four categories—L, M1, M2, and M3—according to the type of account in which the instrument is kept. *See also* M1; M2; M3.

moral obligation bond A municipal revenue bond for which a state legislature has the authority, but no legal obligation, to appropriate money in the event the municipal issuer defaults.

mortality guarantee The insurance company guarantee that an annuitant will receive payments for life. There is a charge made against the account as an operating expense to cover the cost of this guarantee. Mutual funds do not have a mortality guarantee.

mortgage bond A debt obligation secured by a property pledge. It represents a lien or mortgage against the issuing corporation's properties and real estate assets.

MRD Minimum required distribution. *See* required minimum distribution.

MRV *See* minor rules violation.

MSRB *See* Municipal Securities Rulemaking Board.

municipal advisor An individual or entity acting as a fiduciary, providing advice to a municipal entity regarding municipal financial products or the issuance of municipal securities with respect to the structure, timing, and terms. They also can solicit municipalities for compensation on behalf of an unaffiliated municipal securities dealer or investment adviser to engage the municipality regarding municipal financial products, the issuance of municipal securities, or investment advisory services.

municipal bond A debt security issued by a state, municipality, or other subdivision (such as a school, park, sanitation, or other local taxing district) to finance its capital expenditures. Such expenditures might include the construction of highways, public works, or school buildings. *Syn.* municipal security.

municipal bond fund A mutual fund that invests in municipal bonds and operates as either a unit investment trust or an open-end fund, with the view to maximize federally tax-exempt income. *See also* mutual fund; unit investment trust.

municipal broker's broker   A broker acting as an agent for another broker or dealer in trading municipal securities providing liquidity and anonymity. The broker's broker does not take positions in a security or transact orders for the public. *See also* broker's broker.

municipal finance professional (MFP)   An associated person (AP) of a FINRA member firm engaged in municipal securities underwriting, trading, sales, financial advisory, research, investment advice, or any other activities that involve communication with public investors. APs whose activities are limited solely to sales with natural persons and clerical or ministerial functions are not MFPs.

municipal fund security   A municipal security that, but for the application of Section 2(b) of the Investment Company Act of 1940, would constitute an investment company within the meaning of Section 3 of the Investment Company Act of 1940.

municipal note   A short-term municipal security issued in anticipation of funds from another source. *See also* municipal bond.

Municipal Securities Rulemaking Board (MSRB)   A self-regulatory organization that adopts rules with regard to the unique municipal bond market covering professional qualifications, fair practices, uniform practice, and market transparency and places administrative burdens on brokers and dealers.

municipal security   Debt security issued by a state or local government, or an authority other than the federal government, to raise money for a public project. Interest payable on these instruments may be free of federal income tax.

mutual fund   An investment company that continuously offers new equity shares in an actively managed portfolio of securities. *Syn.* open-end investment company; open-end management company.

mutual fund broker-dealer   A broker-dealer dealing exclusively in mutual funds and variable contracts.

mutual fund custodian   A national bank, stock exchange member firm, trust company, or other qualified institution that physically safeguards the securities a mutual fund holds. It does not manage the fund's investments; its function is solely clerical.

NAC   *See* National Adjudicatory Council.

naked   *See* uncovered.

naked call writer   *See* uncovered call writer

naked short selling   Selling a stock short without first borrowing the stock or confirming that the stock can be borrowed. Sellers who cannot deliver the shares sold by settlement will cause a fail-to-deliver transaction.

NASAA   *See* North American Securities Administrators Association.

NASD   *See* National Association of Securities Dealers, Inc.

Nasdaq   *See* National Association of Securities Dealers Automated Quotations, a stock exchange.

Nasdaq Capital Market   Of the three Nasdaq market tiers, has the least stringent listing requirements.

Nasdaq Composite Index (IXIC)   Measures thousands of domestic and non-U.S.-based common stocks and ADRs listed on the Nasdaq.

Nasdaq Execution Services   Nasdaq's broker-dealer.

Nasdaq Global Market   One of three Nasdaq market tiers. Global Market is mid cap, second in hierarchy behind the Global Select Market, and higher than Nasdaq Capital Market.

Nasdaq Global Market Companies   Companies that are listed on the Nasdaq Global Market that meet financial and liquidity requirements and agree to specific corporate governance standards.

Nasdaq Global Select Market   Market tier with initial listing standards that rank among the highest of any market.

Nasdaq Global Select Market Companies   The Nasdaq Global Select Market demands the highest initial listing standards. Issuers of Global Select securities are well-known, seasoned issuers with a high degree of transparency, liquidity, and strict corporate governance. Considered the top tier of Nasdaq-listed securities.

Nasdaq-100   An index of the largest 100 nonfinancial stocks on Nasdaq, weighted according to capitalization.

National Adjudicatory Council (NAC)   Authorized to act for FINRA with respect to an appeal or review of any proceeding.

National Association of Securities Dealers Automated Quotations (Nasdaq)   A U.S.-based cash equities stock exchange.

National Association of Securities Dealers, Inc. (NASD)   A now defunct self-regulatory organization for the over-the-counter market. The NASD was organized under the provisions of the 1938 Maloney Act. *See also* Maloney Act. NASD was dissolved in 2007 with the formation of FINRA.

National Market System (Regulation NMS)   A broad, sweeping SEC regulation designed to bring trading and reporting uniformity to U.S. securities markets. *See also* order protection rule; minimum increment price rule.

National Public Finance Guarantee   A public corporation offering insurance as to the timely payment of principal and interest on qualified municipal issues. Nonrated issues with insurance are implied to be rated AAA.

National Securities Clearing Corporation (NSCC) An organization that acts as a medium through which member brokerage firms, banks, and exchanges reconcile accounts with each other. Provides clearance and settlement functions as well as ACATS. *See* qualified service representative.

National Securities Markets Improvement Act of 1996 (NSMIA) Federal legislation designed to clarify the demarcation between federal and state securities law, as well as improve the efficiency of the securities markets in the United States by elimination of duplicate federal and state regulatory efforts.

NAV *See* net asset value.

NAV of fund The net total of a mutual fund's assets and liabilities. It is used to calculate the price of new fund shares.

NAV per share The value of a mutual fund share, calculated by dividing the fund's total net asset value by the number of shares outstanding.

negotiable certificate of deposit (CD) An unsecured promissory note issued with a minimum face value of $100,000. It evidences a time deposit of funds with the issuing bank and is guaranteed by the bank. *Syn.* Jumbo CD.

negotiable security A characteristic that permits the owner to assign, give, transfer, or sell it to another person without a third party's permission.

net asset value (NAV) The daily computation of the value of a mutual fund that is reached by deducting the fund's liabilities from the closing market value of all of its shares and then dividing by the number of outstanding shares.

net change The difference between a security's closing price on the trading day reported and the previous day's closing price. In over-the-counter transactions, the term refers to the difference between the closing bids.

net investment income (NII) The source of an investment company's dividend payments.

net investment return Pretax income received from investment assets (e.g., bonds, stocks, mutual funds, and other investments less related expenses).

net proceeds The amount of money received from the sale an asset, less expenses incurred, such as selling commissions.

net worth The amount by which assets exceed liabilities. *Syn.* owners' equity; shareholders' equity; stockholders' equity.

new account form The form that must be filled out for each new account opened with a brokerage firm. The form specifies, at a minimum, the account owner, trading authorization, payment and delivery method, and types of securities appropriate for the customer.

New York Stock Exchange Composite Index An index of the common stocks, ADRs, REITs, and tracking stock listed on the NYSE.

NFA Rule 2-30 *See* "Know Your Customer".

NMS *See* National Market System.

NNM *See* Nasdaq National Market.

no-load The term used to describe a mutual fund whose shares are offered without a sales charge.

no-load fund A mutual fund whose shares are sold without a commission or sales charge. The investment company distributes the shares directly. *See also* mutual fund; net asset value; sales load.

nominal yield The interest rate stated on the face of a bond that represents the percentage of interest the issuer pays on the bond's face value. *Syn.* coupon rate; stated yield. *See also* bond yield.

nonaffiliate A person, who is not an executive officer, a director, or large shareholder, in a relationship of control with an issuer.

noncash compensation Payments that are not cash on offers of compensation in connection with the sale of securities (e.g. meals, sports tickets, merchandise, and travel). FINRA rules prohibit members and their associated persons from directly or indirectly accepting or making payments, with few exceptions.

noncash compensation (investment companies) Items received in connection with the sale of investment company securities that are not considered cash compensation. This would include seminars, reminder advertising with the fund's name, meals, and other reasonable entertainment expenses.

non-Nasdaq registration In accordance with SEC 15c2-11, firms that wish to make market in Pink Open Market or OTC Bulletin Board securities must file Form 211 with FINRA. *See* OTC Bulletin Board; piggyback exception.

nonqualified annuity An annuity that does not qualify for tax deductibility of contributions under IRS codes.

nonaccredited investor An investor not meeting the income or net worth requirements of Regulation D. Nonaccredited investors are counted for purposes of the 35-investor limitation for Regulation D private placements.

noncumulative preferred stock An equity security that does not pay any dividends in arrears to the holder. *See also* convertible preferred stock; cumulative preferred stock; preferred stock.

nondiscrimination In a qualified retirement plan, a formula for calculating contributions and benefits that must be applied uniformly so as to ensure that all employees receive the same treatment. *See also* qualified retirement plan.

noneligible security   *See* nonmargin security.

nonequity option   A security representing the right to buy or sell an investment instrument other than a common stock at a specified price within a specified period. Examples include foreign currencies, indexes, and interest rates. *See also* equity option; foreign currency option; index option; interest rate option; option.

nonexempt security   A security whose issue and sale must be in compliance with the Uniform Securities Act and/or the various federal securities acts, most notably the Securities Act of 1933. *See* exempt security.

nonissuer transaction   A securities trade where the proceeds do not accrue to the issuer.

nonmargin security   A security that does not have loan value that must be paid for in full and that may not be used as collateral for a loan. *See also* margin security.

nonqualified retirement plan   A corporate retirement plan that does not meet the standards set by the Employee Retirement Income Security Act of 1974.

nonsytematic risk   Company-specific risk that can be reduced through diversification. *Syn.* unsystematic risk. *See* systematic risk.

North American Securities Administrators Association (NASAA)   The body responsible for the Series 63, 65, and 66 exams, a voluntary association whose membership consists of 67 state, provincial, and territorial securities administrators in the 50 states, the District of Columbia, Puerto Rico, the U.S. Virgin Islands, Canada, and Mexico.

note   A short-term debt security, usually maturing in five years or less. *See* municipal note; Treasury note.

NSCC   *See* National Securities Clearing Corporation.

NSMIA   *See* National Securities Markets Improvement Act of 1996.

NYSE   *See* New York Stock Exchange.

NYSE Composite Index   *See* New York Stock Exchange Composite Index.

OB   Or better. *See* limit order.

OCC   *See* (1) Options Clearing Corporation or (2) Office of the Comptroller of the Currency.

OCC Disclosure Document   *See* options disclosure document.

ODD   *See* options disclosure document.

odd lot   An amount of a security that is less than the normal unit of trading for that security. Generally, an odd lot is fewer than 100 shares of stock or five bonds. *See also* round lot.

odd-lot theory   In technical analysis, a theory that assumes small investors are nearly always wrong. Therefore, if odd-lot sales are up, signifying that small investors are selling, it is a good time to buy.

offer   (1) Under the Uniform Securities Act, any attempt to solicit a purchase or sale in a security for value. (2) An indication by an investor, trader, or dealer of a willingness to sell a security; the price at which an investor can buy from a broker-dealer. *See* bid.

offering circular   Similar to a prospectus used by corporations issuing securities under a safe harbor from the Securities Act of 1933 (e.g., small offerings, such as a Regulation A, that offer no more than $50 million).

Office of Supervisory Jurisdiction (OSJ)   A so-designated branch office of a broker-dealer where, for example, structuring an offering, order execution, market making, maintaining custody of funds or securities, final approval of new accounts, and retail communication takes place. See also branch office; satellite office.

Office of the Comptroller of the Currency (OCC)   (1) The bureau of the U.S. Department of the Treasury that is responsible for issuing and enforcing regulations governing the investing and lending practices of the nation's banks. The regulator of national banks that are registered with the MSRB to underwrite municipal bonds. (2) The Options Clearing Corporation.

official notice of sale   The invitation to bid on a municipal bond issue. The invitation is sent to prospective underwriters and specifies, among other things, the date, time, and place of sale; description of the issue; maturities; and call provisions, as well as the amount of good faith deposit required.

official statement (OS)   A disclosure document distributed to purchasers of municipal securities. The OS is the responsibility of the issuer and must be prepared for issues greater than $1 million. *See* SEC Rule 15c2-12.

OID   *See* original issue discount bond.

oil and gas direct participation program   A direct participation program formed to locate new oil and gas reserves, develop existing reserves, or generate income from producing wells. *Syn.* oil and gas limited partnership.

oil depletion allowance   An accounting procedure that reduces the taxable portion of revenues from the sale of oil to compensate for the decreased supply of oil in the ground. Depletion is the natural resource counterpart of depreciation.

omitting prospectus   SEC Rule 482 provides for a mutual fund to advertise performance figures but without providing the full disclosure of material facts found in a statutory prospectus.

open order   *See* good-till-canceled order.

open-end investment company   *See* mutual fund.

open-market operations The buying and selling of government or agency debt securities by the Federal Reserve Board's Federal Open Market Committee to control the money supply.

operating expenses The day-to-day costs incurred in running a business, such as out-of-pocket expenses for labor, materials, supplies, and so forth.

option A contract that represents the right to buy or sell a security or futures contract at a specified price within a specified time. The purchaser acquires a right, and the seller assumes an obligation.

option agreement The document a customer must sign within 15 calendar days of being approved for options trading. In it, the customer agrees to abide by the rules of the options exchanges and not to exceed position or exercise limits.

option income fund A fund that invests in securities and writes options against these positions (known as covered calls). Income is earned from writing (selling) the options.

Options Clearing Corporation (OCC) The organization that issues options, standardizes option contracts, and guarantees their performance.

options disclosure document A publication of the Options Clearing Corporation that outlines the risks and rewards of investing in options. The document must be given to each customer at the time of opening an options account and must accompany any options sales literature sent to a customer. *Syn.* OCC Disclosure Document.

or better order (OB) *See* limit order.

ordinary income Mainly wages, salaries, commissions, and interest income (as from bonds) taxed at the individual's marginal rate tax bracket.

original issue discount bond (OID) A debt security issued at a discount from face value. The discount on an OID bond is accreted annually for the purpose of calculating cost basis. *See also* zero-coupon bond.

OS *See* official statement.

OSJ *See* Office of Supervisory Jurisdiction.

OTC *See* over the counter.

OTC Bulletin Board (OTCBB) A regulated interdealer quotation system that displays real-time quotes, last-sale prices, and volume information for OTC equity securities not listed or traded on an exchange.

OTC equity security A non-NMS stock.

OTC margin security A security that is not traded on a national exchange but has been designated by the Federal Reserve Board as eligible for trading on margin.

OTC market A negotiated market in which broker-dealers deal directly with one another rather than through an auction on an exchange floor. *Syn.* second market.

OTC Market Group, Inc. The publisher of compiled quotes from market makers in over-the-counter stocks and bonds.

out-of-the-money The term used to describe an option that has no intrinsic value (e.g., a call option when the stock is selling below the exercise price, or a put option when the stock is selling above the exercise price). *See also* at-the-money; in-the-money; intrinsic value.

outside business activity (OBA) Employment by, or compensation from, any person as a result of any business activity—other than a passive investment—outside the scope of their employment with a securities broker-dealer.

outstanding stock Equity securities issued by a corporation and in the hands of the public. Issued stock that the issuer has not reacquired. *See also* treasury stock.

over the counter (OTC) *See* OTC market.

overallotment Occurs when the public interest is especially strong and the underwriter sells more than the number of shares available. *See also* green shoe option.

owners' equity *See* net worth.

P/E ratio *See* price-earnings ratio.

par value The dollar amount assigned to a security by the issuer. Par for common stock usually bears no relationship to the market price. Par for debt security is usually $1,000, while par for preferred is usually $100. *Syn.* face value; principal; stated value.

parity (convertible securities) When a convertible security (bond or preferred stock) is selling at the same price as the value of the converted common stock.

parity (options) Describes an in-the-money option trading at its intrinsic value (i.e., an option trading at parity with the underlying security). *See* intrinsic value.

parity (trading priority) In an exchange market, a situation in which all brokers bidding have equal standing, and the winning bid is awarded by a random drawing. *See also* precedence; priority.

parking (1) A violation of securities industry rules by selling securities and simultaneously agreeing to repurchase the securities in the future in an unbooked transaction. (2) The prohibited practice of maintaining the registration of an associated person who has left the securities business.

partial call The redemption by an issuer of a portion of an outstanding bond issue before the maturity date. *See also* catastrophe call; in-whole call; mandatory call.

partially registered *See* registered as to principal only.

participating preferred stock   Preferred stock offering the owner a share of corporate earnings remaining after all senior securities to it have been paid. The payment is made in addition to the fixed dividend stated on the certificate and may be cumulative or noncumulative. *See also* convertible preferred stock; cumulative preferred stock; noncumulative preferred stock; preferred stock.

partnership   A form of business organization requiring a minimum of two participants.

partnership account   Empowers individual members to act on behalf of the partnership as a whole.

pass-through certificate   A security representing an interest in a pool of conventional, Veterans Administration, Farmers Home Administration, or other agency mortgages. The pool receives the principal and interest payments, which it passes through to each certificate holder. *See* Federal National Mortgage Association; Government National Mortgage Association.

passive investment   An interest in, for example, rental property, limited partnership, or other enterprise in which the individual is not actively involved. Passive income, therefore, does not include earnings from wages or active business participation, nor does it include income from dividends, interest, and capital gains. *See also* passive loss; unearned income.

passive loss   A loss incurred through a rental property, limited partnership, or other enterprise in which the individual is not actively involved. These losses may be used to offset passive income only, not wage or portfolio income. *See also* passive income.

passive management style   A cost-efficient management style based on buying a broad market index of stocks and holding it. See active management style.

payment date   The day on which a declared dividend is paid to all stockholders owning shares on the record date. *See* record date; ex-date.

PE ratio   *See* price-earnings ratio.

peak   The stage of the business cycle that signals the end of a period of increasing business activity throughout the economy. *Syn.* prosperity. *See also* business cycle.

penny stock   An OTC equity security trading at less than $5 per share. A penny stock is a low-priced OTCBB or OTC Pink Open Market stock. *See* OTC equity security.

pension plan   A contract between an individual and an employer, labor union, government entity, or other institution that provides for the distribution of pension benefits at retirement.

Pension Reform Act   *See* Employee Retirement Income Security Act of 1974.

person   As defined in securities law, an individual, corporation, partnership, association, fund, joint stock company, unincorporated organization, trust, government, or political subdivision of a government.

personal income (PI)   An individual's total earnings derived from wages, passive business enterprises, and investments. *See also* disposable income.

phantom income   Taxable income that is not constructively received but taxed as if it were. *See also* crossover point.

Pink Open Market   An electronic publication compiled by the OTC Market Group, Inc., that contains interdealer wholesale quotations for over-the-counter stocks.

Pink Sheets   Obsolete term for Pink Open Market.

pipeline theory   *See* conduit theory.

point   A measure of a securities price. (For example, a bond's price of 1 point is equal to 1% of the par value of $1,000, or $10. In stock, 1 point is $1 per share.) *See also* basis point.

political risk   The risk that an investment's returns could suffer as a result of political changes or instability in a country, such as from a change in government, nationalization of industries, military control, or tax codes.

pool (asset-backed securities)   A specified collection of underlying assets that backs the income and/or principal payments of an asset-backed security (ABS). The pool of assets may be made up of mortgages, credit card receivables, leases, royalties, auto loans, or other receivables.

POP   *See* public offering price.

portfolio income   Earnings from interest, dividends, and all nonbusiness investments. *See* earned income; passive income; unearned income.

portfolio manager   The entity (i.e., the adviser) responsible for investing a mutual fund's assets, implementing its investment strategy, and managing day-to-day portfolio trading. *Syn.* fund manager.

position   The amount of a security either owned (a long position) or owed (a short position) by an individual or a dealer.

power of attorney (POA)   A written authorization to represent or act on another's behalf.

power of substitution   *See* power of attorney.

precedence   In an exchange market, the hierarchy of bid and offer ranking according to the number of shares involved. *See also* parity; priority.

predispute arbitration agreement   A clause in a broker-dealer's customer account agreement in which the customer agrees to resolve disputes by arbitration.

preemptive right   A stockholder's legal right to maintain a proportionate ownership by purchasing newly issued shares before the new stock is offered to the public. *See also* right.

preferred stock   An equity security that represents nonvoting ownership in a corporation. Preferred stock is senior to common and junior to debt. *See also* callable preferred stock; convertible preferred stock; cumulative preferred stock.

preferred stock fund   A mutual fund whose investment objective is to provide stable income with minimal capital risk by investing in income-producing instruments such as preferred stock. *See also* bond fund.

preliminary official statement   An offering statement created by issuers for their municipal securities. It does not contain pricing or the effective date.

preliminary prospectus   An abbreviated prospectus that is distributed while the SEC is reviewing an issuer's registration statement. It contains all of the essential facts, but it does not contain pricing or the effective date.

premium   (1) The amount of cash that an option buyer pays to an option seller. (2) The difference between the higher price paid for a debt security and the security's face amount at issue. *See also* discount.

premium bond   A bond that sells at a higher price than its face value. *See* discount bond; par value.

prepaid tuition plans   A type of 529 plan that allows contributors to purchase tuition credits or certificates at today's prices. Contributors bear no investment or inflation risk because the accounts are generally guaranteed to grow at a rate equal to college tuition increases.

price-earnings (P/E) ratio   A tool for comparing the prices of different common stocks by dividing the current market price of the stock by the earnings per share.

primary dealer   Large bank or brokerage firm designated by the Federal Reserve Board to bid at Treasury auctions.

primary distribution   *See* primary offering.

primary offering   An offering in which the proceeds of the underwriting go to the issuing corporation, agency, or municipality. The issuer seeks to increase its capitalization either by selling shares of stock, representing ownership, or by selling bonds, representing loans to the issuer.

prime brokerage account   An account where a customer selects a member firm (the prime broker) to provide custody and other services, while other firms (the executing brokers) handle all trades placed by the customer.

prime rate   The interest rate that commercial banks charge their prime or most creditworthy customers—generally large corporations.

principal   (1) A supervisory employee at a broker-dealer. (2) A party in a transaction who is trading for the party's own account.

principal transaction   A transaction in which a broker-dealer either buys securities from customers and takes them into its own inventory or sells securities to customers from its inventory. *See also* agency transaction; agent; broker-dealer; principal.

priority   In an exchange market, the ranking of bids and offers according to the first person to bid or offer at a given price.

private placement   An offering of new issue securities under Regulation D that is not available to the public as a whole, but rather, select investors. *See also* Regulation D.

probity   Being morally and ethically above reproach; having integrity. A necessary trait for someone in this business.

profit-sharing plan   An employee benefit plan established and maintained by an employer whereby the employees receive a share of the business's profits.

profitability   The ability to generate a level of income and gain in excess of expenses.

progressive tax   A tax that takes a larger percentage of income from high-income earners than that of low-income earners (e.g., the graduated income tax). *See* regressive tax.

promissory note   A financial instrument, which is included in the definition of a security, that contains a written promise by one party to pay another party a definite sum of money, either on demand or at a specified future date. The most common form on the exam is commercial paper.

promotional material   Broadly defined under NFA Rule 2-29 to include advertising, sales literature, prepared sales presentations, seminars, internet, and other communications that may induce the public to trade futures or futures options. Promotional material must be balanced and fair.

proscribed   A term commonly used in legal situations to describe a prohibited action.

prospectus   The disclosure document required in conjunction with primary securities offerings and commodity limited partnerships (pools) that must register with the Securities Exchange Commission (SEC). *See* preliminary prospectus; statutory prospectus; summary prospectus; final prospectus.

proxy   A limited power of attorney from a stockholder authorizing another person to vote on stockholder issues according to the stockholder's instructions. To vote on corporate matters, a stockholder must either attend the annual meeting or vote by proxy.

prudent investor rule   Legally known as the Uniform Prudent Investors Act of 1994 (UPIA). A modern adaptation of the prudent man rule, which, as a result of the development of modern portfolio theory, applies the standard of prudence to the entire portfolio rather than to individual investments. It requires the fiduciary to measure risk with respect to return.

public appearance   Participation in a seminar, Webinar, forum (including an interactive electronic forum such as a chat room), radio or television interview, or other public appearance or public speaking activity.

public arbitrator   A person who does not meet certain standards regarding ties to the securities industry in a Code of Arbitration Procedure. *See also* nonpublic arbitrator.

public offering price (POP)   (1) The price of new shares that is established in the issuing corporation's prospectus. (2) The price to investors for mutual fund shares, equal to the net asset value plus the sales charge. *See also* ask; bid; mutual fund; net asset value.

public purpose bond   A municipal bond that is exempt from federal income tax, as long as no more than 10% of the proceeds benefit private entities.

publicly traded fund   *See* closed-end investment company.

pump and dump   A form of fraud, typically in connection with microcap stocks. By artificially inflating the price of a stock by making misleading statements (pump), the defrauder then sells inflated shares (dumps). Following the sale, the overvalued shares fall in value, and the investors lose their money.

purchasing power risk   The potential that, because of inflation, a certain amount of money will not purchase as much in the future as it does today. *Syn.* inflation risk.

put   (1) An option contract giving the owner the right to sell a specified amount of an underlying security at a specified price within a specified time. (2) The act of exercising a put option. *See also* call.

put bond   A debt security requiring the issuer to purchase the security at the holder's discretion or within a prescribed time. *Syn.* tender bond.

put buyer   An investor who pays a premium for an option contract and receives, for a specified time, the right to sell the underlying security at a specified price.

put writer   An investor who receives a premium and takes on, for a specified time, the obligation to buy the underlying security at a specified price at the put buyer's discretion.

QTP   *See* qualified tuition program.

qualified dividends   These dividends, if certain requirements are met, are taxed at a lower rate than an investor's marginal tax rate.

qualified higher education expenses   These include expenses for tuition, fees, books, supplies, and equipment, as well as room and board costs.

qualified institutional investor or buyer (QIB)   An institutional investor permitted under SEC rules to trade privately placed securities with other QIBs without registering the securities with the SEC. A qualified institutional investor must have at least $100 million under management.

qualified retirement plan   A corporate retirement plan that meets the standards set by the Employee Retirement Income Security Act of 1974. Contributions to a qualified plan are tax deductible.

qualified tuition program   The technical name for Section 529 Plans. *Syn.* QTP.

quick assets   A measure of a corporation's liquidity that takes into account the size of the unsold inventory. It is calculated by subtracting inventory from current assets, and it is used in the acid-test ratio. *See also* acid-test ratio.

quick ratio   *See* acid-test ratio.

quotation   The price being offered or bid by a market maker or broker-dealer for a particular security. *Syn.* quote. *See also* ask; bid; bond quote; stock quote.

quote   *See* quotation.

RAN   *See* revenue anticipation note.

rating   An evaluation of a corporate or municipal bond's relative safety, according to the issuer's ability to repay principal and make interest payments. Bonds are rated by various organizations such as Standard & Poor's and Moody's. Ratings range from AAA or Aaa (the highest) to C or D (company in default).

rating service   A company, such as Moody's or Standard & Poor's, that rates various debt and preferred stock issues for safety of payment of principal, interest, or dividends. The issuing company or municipality pays a fee for the rating. See also rating.

real estate investment trust (REIT)   A corporation or trust that uses the pooled capital of many investors to invest in direct ownership of either income property or mortgage loans. REITs that are traded on exchanges or OTC are considered very liquid. Real estate is not.

real estate limited partnership   A direct participation program formed to build new structures, generate income from existing property, or profit from the capital appreciation of undeveloped land.

realized gain   The amount earned by a taxpayer when an asset is sold for a profit. *See also* unrealized gain.

recapture   The taxation as ordinary income of previously earned deductions or credits. Circumstances that may cause the IRS to require this tax to be paid include excess depreciation, premature sale of an asset, or disallowing of a previous tax benefit.

recession   A general economic decline lasting from 6 to 18 months (at least two consecutive quarters of declining or negative GDP growth).

record date   The date a corporation's board of directors establishes that determines which of its stockholders are entitled to receive dividends or rights distributions.

red flags   Term used to describe potential warnings about an investment. Examples of red flags are promises of high returns with low risk and "don't miss this opportunity; get in now." The term is also used in conjunction with protecting against identity theft.

red herring   *See* preliminary prospectus.

redeemable security   A security that the issuer redeems upon the holder's request. Examples include shares in an open-end investment company and Treasury notes.

redemption   The last payment made by the issuer of a debt security. It would represent the principal amount plus the last interest payment (six months of interest).

Reg T   *See* Regulation T.

Reg T call   *See* margin call.

registered   The term that describes a security that prints the name of the owner on the certificate. The owner's name is stored in records kept by the issuer or a transfer agent.

registered as to principal only   The term used to describe a bond that prints the name of the owner on the certificate but that has unregistered coupons payable to the bearer. *Syn.* partially registered. *See* coupon bond; fully registered bond.

registered investment company   An investment company, such as an open-end management company (mutual fund) or closed-end management company, that is registered with the SEC.

registered options principal (ROP)   A principal at a member firm that supervises options accounts, transactions, and options-related communications.

registered principal   An associated person of a member firm who manages or supervises the firm's investment banking or securities business. This includes persons who train associated persons. Unless the member firm is a sole proprietorship, it must employ at least two registered principals.

registered representative (RR)   An associated person engaged in the investment banking or securities business. This includes any individual who supervises, solicits, or conducts business in securities or who trains people to supervise, solicit, or conduct business in securities.

registrar   The independent organization or part of a corporation responsible for accounting for all of the issuer's outstanding stock and certifying that its bonds constitute legal debt.

registration statement   Before nonexempt securities can be offered to the public, they require registration under the Securities Act of 1933 and/or the Uniform Securities Act. The registration statement must disclose all pertinent information concerning the issuer and the offering. This statement is submitted to the SEC and/or administrator in accordance with the requirements of their respective laws. If the securities are to be sold in only one state, by qualification, only that state's registration requirements apply.

regressive tax   A tax that takes a larger percentage of the income of low-income earners than that of high-income earners. Examples include gasoline and cigarette tax.

regular way settlement   The time when standard securities transactions are settled. The Uniform Practice Code sets the standard payment period. The type of security being traded determines the amount of time allowed for regular way settlement. *See also* cash transaction; settlement date.

regulated investment company   An investment company to which Subchapter M of the Internal Revenue Code grants special status that allows the flow-through of tax consequences on a distribution to shareholders.

Regulation A+   Provides two offering tiers for small- and medium-sized companies that will allow them to raise capital in amounts substantially more than the $5 million previously allowed under Regulation A. There are two tiers: tier 1 for offerings of up to $20 million and tier 2 for offerings of up to $50 million.

Regulation D   The provision of the Securities Act of 1933 that exempts from registration offerings sold in private placements. *See* private placement.

Regulation NMS   An SEC regulation that fosters competition between markets/exchanges and competition among orders.

Regulation S-AM   An SEC regulation that allows a consumer, in certain limited situations, to block affiliates of brokers/dealers, investment companies, investment advisers, and transfer agents registered with the Commission from soliciting the consumer based on eligibility information.

Regulation SHO   Mandates a locate requirement with regard to short sales. Before entering a short sale order, members are required to locate the security to be assured that delivery can be made on the settlement date. The locate requirement applies to short sales in all equity securities.

Regulation S-P   An SEC regulation covering privacy rules promulgated under the Gramm-Leach-Bliley Act. A broker-dealer must provide customers with a notice of its privacy policies and practices and must not disclose nonpublic personal information about a consumer to nonaffiliated third parties unless it provides certain information to the consumer and the consumer has not opted out of the disclosure. Rigorous standards to protect privacy are also required under the regulation.

Regulation T   The Federal Reserve Board regulation that governs customer cash accounts and the amount of credit that brokerage firms and dealers may extend to customers for the purchase of securities. Regulation T currently sets the loan value of marginable securities at 50% and the payment deadline at two days beyond regular way settlement. *Syn.* Reg T. *See also* Regulation G; Regulation U.

Regulation T excess   *See* excess equity.

Regulation U   The Federal Reserve Board regulation that governs loans by banks for the purchase of securities. Call loans are exempt from Regulation U. *See also* broker's loan; call loan; Regulation T.

regulatory element   The portion of the industry continuing education program that is a computer exercise taken by all registered persons. There are versions for Series 6 limited representatives, all registered representatives, and registered principals. One sits for the session within 120 days of the second anniversary of registration and every three years thereafter.

regulatory risk   The risk that changes in regulations may negatively affect the operations of a company.

rehypothecation   The pledging of a client's securities as collateral for a bank loan. Brokerage firms may rehypothecate up to 140% of customer debit balances to finance margin loans to customers. *See also* hypothecation.

reinvestment risk   The potential that a bond investor may not be able to reinvest interest income or principal in new bonds at the same rate of return.

REIT   *See* real estate investment trust.

remuneration   Money paid for work performed or a service provided.

repo   *See* repurchase agreement.

repurchase agreement   A sale of securities with an attendant agreement to repurchase them at a higher price on an agreed-upon future date. The difference between the sale price and the repurchase price represents the interest earned by the investor. Repos are considered money market instruments and are used to raise short-term capital and as instruments of monetary policy. *Syn.* repo. *See also* reverse repurchase agreement.

required minimum distribution (RMD)   The amount that traditional and SEP IRA owners and qualified plan participants must begin withdrawing from their retirement accounts by April 1 following the year they reach age 70½. Exceptions apply to those covered under a qualified plan who are still employed. RMD amounts must then be distributed by December 31 that year and each subsequent year.

reserve requirement   The percentage of depositors' money that the Federal Reserve Board requires a commercial bank to keep on deposit in the form of cash or in its vault. *Syn.* reserves.

reserves   *See* reserve requirement.

residual claim   The right of a common stockholder to claim corporate assets in the event that the corporation ceases to exist. A common stockholder may claim assets only after the claims of all creditors and other security holders have been satisfied.

restricted account   A margin account in which the equity is less than the Regulation T initial requirement. *See also* equity; initial margin requirement; margin account; retention requirement.

restricted person   As defined by FINRA, member firms, employees of member firms and their immediate families, finders and fiduciaries, portfolio managers, and 10% or more owners of member firms.

restricted security   An unregistered, nonexempt security acquired either directly or indirectly from the issuer—or an affiliate of the issuer—in a transaction that does not involve a public offering.

retail communication   Any written (including electronic) communication that is distributed or made available to more than 25 retail investors within any 30-calendar-day period. A retail investor is any person other than an institutional investor, regardless of whether the person has an account with the member.

retail investor   Any person other than an institutional investor, regardless of whether the person who has an account with the firm is considered a retail investor.

retail transaction   A trade in which an individual investor buys a security from or through a broker-dealer, or sells a security to or through a broker-dealer. *See* wholesale transaction.

retirement account   A customer account established to provide retirement funds.

return on investment (ROI)   The profit or loss resulting from a security transaction, often expressed as an annual percentage rate.

revenue anticipation note (RAN)   A short-term municipal debt security issued in anticipation of revenue to be received.

revenue bond   A municipal debt issue whose interest and principal are payable only from the specific earnings of an income-producing public project. *See also* double-barreled bond; general obligation bond; municipal bond; special revenue bond.

reverse churning   The unsuitable practice of placing a client who trades infrequently in a fee-based account rather than a commission-based account that would be more appropriate. *Related item* churning.

reverse split   A reduction in the number of a corporation's shares outstanding that increases the par value of its stock or its earnings per share. The market value of the total number of shares remains the same. *See also* stock split.

revocable trust   A trust that can be altered or canceled by the grantor. During the life of the trust, income earned is distributed to the grantor, and only after death does property transfer to the beneficiaries.

right   (1) A legal guarantee. (2) A security representing a stockholder's entitlement to the first opportunity to purchase new shares issued by the corporation at a predetermined price (normally less than the current market price) in proportion to the number of shares already owned. Rights are issued for a short time only, after which they expire. *Syn.* subscription right; subscription right certificate.

right of accumulation   A benefit offered by a mutual fund that allows the investor to qualify for reduced sales loads on additional purchases according to the fund account's total dollar value.

rights offering   An issue of additional shares of stock accompanied by the opportunity for each current stockholder to maintain a proportionate ownership by purchasing additional shares before the stock is offered to the nonshareholders.

risk   The possibility that an actual return on an investment will be lower than the expected return.

Risk Disclosure Statement   The document a customer must acknowledge in writing to confirm understanding of the significant risk of trading futures contracts or options on futures.

risk tolerance   An investor's ability and willingness to lose some or all of the original investment in exchange for greater potential returns. An aggressive investor, or one with a high risk tolerance, is more likely to risk losing money in order to get better results. A conservative investor, or one with a low-risk tolerance, tends to favor investments that will preserve the original investment.

RMD   *See* required minimum distribution.

ROI   *See* return on investment.

rollover   The transfer of funds from one qualified retirement plan to another. If this is not done within a specified time period, the funds are taxed as ordinary income.

ROP   *See* registered options principal.

Roth 401(k) Plan   A retirement plan that combines the characteristics of a Roth IRA with a corporate 401(k) plan.

Roth IRA   Allows taxpayers—subject to certain income limits—to save money for use in retirement while allowing the savings to grow tax deferred, with qualifying distributions being tax free.

round lot   A security's normal unit of trading, which is generally 100 shares of stock or five bonds. *See also* odd lot.

RR   *See* registered representative.

Rule 144   An SEC rule that sets the requirements for selling or purchasing restricted, unregistered, or control securities.

Rule 144A   SEC rule allowing nonregistered foreign and domestic securities to be sold to certain qualified institutional investors in the U.S. without a holding period. *See* ORF; QIB.

Rule G-37   MSRB rule prohibiting municipal securities dealers from underwriting securities issued under the authority of a public official to whom an associated person of the dealer has contributed money.

S corporation   A small business corporation that meets certain requirements and is taxed as a partnership while retaining limited liability.

SIMPLE Plan   *See* Savings Incentive Match Plan for Employees.

S&P   *See* Standard & Poor's Corporation.

S&P 100   *See* Standard & Poor's 100 Stock Index.

S&P 500   *See* Standard & Poor's Composite Index of 500 Stocks.

SAI   *See* statement of additional information.

sale   To convey ownership of a security or another asset for money or value.

sales charge   The term used to describe the cost involved in purchasing an open-end investment company. It is the difference between the public offering price (POP) and the net asset value (NAV). *Syn.* sales load; load.

sales charge   *See* commission.

sales literature   Any written material distributed to customers or the public by a firm in a controlled manner. Examples include circulars, research reports, form letters, market letters, performance reports, and text used for seminars. *See also* advertisement, form letter, market letter.

sales load   The amount added to a mutual fund share's net asset value to arrive at the offering price. *See also* mutual fund; net asset value; no-load fund.

SAR   *See* suspicious activity report.

Sarbanes-Oxley Act   An act that covers corporate accountability issues such as creating a Public Company Accounting Oversight Board to establish auditing standards and regulate accountants who audit public companies and enhance criminal penalties for violations of antifraud rules, federal securities laws, and other white-collar crimes.

satellite office   A member location not identified as an office of supervisory jurisdiction or a branch office, or held out to the public as a place of business for the member.

savings bond   A government debt security that is not negotiable or transferable and may not be used as collateral. *See also* Series EE bond; Series HH bond.

Savings Incentive Match Plan for Employees (SIMPLE)   A form of employer-sponsored IRA for businesses that have 100 or fewer employees who earned $5,000 or more during the preceding calendar year.

Schedule K-1   The form supplied by a partnership, LLC, or S corporation to owners indicating their proportionate share of income/loss to be reported on their Form 1040 tax returns.

seasoned issuers   An issuer with at least $75 million in public float value.

SEC   *See* Securities and Exchange Commission.

Rule 203   SEC rule requiring a broker-dealer to establish and further document a "locate" for a security to be delivered for a short sale prior to entering the sell short order into the marketplace. The documentation must include a tag number from the providing clearing firm.

secondary distribution (offering)   (1) A distribution, with a prospectus, that involves securities owned by major stockholders (typically founders or principal owners of a corporation). The sale proceeds go to the sellers of the stock, not to the issuer. *Syn.* registered secondary distribution. (2) A procedure for trading very large blocks of stock shares whereby the trade is executed off the floor of an exchange after the market closes.

secondary market   An aftermarket where investors buy and sell to each other apart from the issuer. Exchanges, such as Nasdaq, NYSE, and NYSE American, facilitate the secondary market.

Section 1035 exchange   A provision of the Internal Revenue Code that permits the cash values of insurance policies or annuities to be exchanged for a different policy or annuity issued by the same or different insurance company without current taxation.

Section 457 plan   A deferred compensation plan set up under Section 457 of the tax code that may be used by employees of a state, political subdivision of a state, or any agency or instrumentality of a state, and employees of certain tax-exempt organizations.

Section 529 plan   A state-sponsored plan to save for education. Contributions are made with after-tax dollars and grow tax deferred. If the money is used for qualified education expenses, withdrawals are tax free. Under securities laws, these plans are structured as municipal fund securities and, therefore, require supervision by a principal with either a Series 51 or Series 53 registration by an MSRB-registered broker-dealer.

sector fund   A mutual fund whose investment objective is to capitalize on the return potential provided by investing primarily in a particular industry or sector of the economy. *Syn.* industry fund; specialized fund.

secured bond   A debt security backed by identifiable assets set aside as collateral. In the event the issuer defaults on payment, the bondholders may lay claim to the collateral. *See also* debenture.

Securities and Exchange Commission (SEC)   Commission created by Congress to regulate the securities markets and protect investors. The SEC enforces, among other acts, the Securities Act of 1933, the Securities Exchange Act of 1934, the Trust Indenture Act of 1939, the Investment Company Act of 1940, and the Investment Advisers Act of 1940.

Securities Exchange Act of 1934   Federal legislation that established the Securities and Exchange Commission and aims to protect investors by regulating the exchanges, over-the-counter market, extension of credit by the Federal Reserve Board, broker-dealers, insider transactions, trading activities, client accounts, and net capital. *Syn.* Act of 1934; Exchange Act.

Securities Information Center (SIC)   The organization designated by the SEC to act as a central data bank for records of lost and stolen securities.

Securities Information Processor (SIP)   A market data vendor engaged in the business of collecting, processing, or distributing transactions in, or quotations for, any nonexempt security.

Securities Investor Protection Corporation (SIPC)   A nonprofit membership corporation created by an act of Congress to protect clients of brokerage firms that are forced into bankruptcy. Its membership includes all brokers and dealers registered under the Securities Exchange Act of 1934, all members of national securities exchanges, and most FINRA members.

securities record   *See* stock record.

securitization   Pooling assets that may be smaller or less liquid into financial instruments, allowing them to be sold more easily to investors.

security   Generally, an instrument evidencing debt of, or equity in, a common enterprise in which an investment is made with the expectation of financial return.

self-employed 401(k) plan (solo 401(k))   A 401(k) plan for self-employed persons who have no other business plan in place, and whose only full-time employees are the proprietor and spouse.

self-regulatory organization (SRO)   An organization accountable to the SEC for the enforcement of federal securities laws and the supervision of securities practices within an assigned field of jurisdiction.

sell out   The procedure that the seller of a security follows when the buyer fails to complete the contract by accepting delivery of the security. *See also* buy-in.

sell stop order   An order to sell a security that is entered at a price below the current market price and that is triggered when the market price touches or goes through the sell stop price.

selling away   An associated person engaging in private securities transactions without the knowledge and consent of the employing broker-dealer. This violates FINRA rules.

selling concession   *See* concession.

selling dividends   Prohibited practice of inducing customers to buy shares by implying that an upcoming distribution will benefit them.

selling group   Selected broker-dealers who contract to act as selling agents for underwriting syndicate members and who are compensated by a portion of the spread called the selling concession on newly issued securities. They assume no financial liability to the issuer, as opposed to a syndicate member.

selling short   A bearish investment strategy where an investor borrows then sells a security she does not own, with the anticipation that the security's price will decline, replacing the security at a lower price.

sellout   When a customer buying securities has not delivered the required funds by two business days after the settlement date, the broker-dealer must sell the securities (the sellout), charge the customer for any losses incurred, and freeze the customer's account for 90 days.

SEP-IRA   *See* simplified employee pension plan.

separate account   The account that holds funds paid by variable contracts issued by insurance companies. The funds are kept separate from the insurer's general account.

Separate Trading of Registered Interest and Principal of Securities

(STRIPS)   A zero-coupon bond issued and backed by the U.S Department of Treasury. *See also* zero-coupon bond; Treasury receipt.

serial bond   A debt security issued with a maturity schedule in which parts of the outstanding issue mature at intervals until the entire balance has been repaid. *See also* maturity date; series bond.

series   Options of the same class that have the same exercise price and the same expiration date. *See also* class; type.

Series 22   The Direct Participation Programs Limited Representative License entitles the holder to sell oil and gas, real estate, motion picture, and other types of limited partnerships and is used by many firms selling tax-advantaged limited partnership products. The Series 22 license can serve as the prerequisite for the Series 39 license.

Series 24   The General Securities Principal License, which entitles the holder to supervise the business of a broker-dealer. A Series 7 qualification is a prerequisite for this license.

Series 26   The Investment Company/Variable Contract Products Limited Principal License, which entitles the holder to supervise the sale of investment company and variable products. A Series 6 or Series 7 qualification is a prerequisite for this license.

Series 4   The Registered Options Principal License qualifies the holder to supervise the sale and trading of options. A Series 7 is a prerequisite. Every FINRA member firm engaged in trading options must employ at least one registered options principal.

Series 52   The Municipal Securities Representative License, which entitles the holder to sell municipal securities.

Series 57   A securities trader examination for those representatives executing transactions in equity, preferred, or convertible debt securities directly with other broker-dealers, not through a securities exchange. The SIE is a prerequisite.

Series 6   An Investment Company and Variable Contract Products Limited Representative License, which is required to sell mutual funds and variable contracts and is required by many firms that primarily sell insurance-related products.

Series 63   The Uniform Securities Agent State Law Exam, which entitles the successful candidate to sell securities in those states that require Series 63 registration. *See also* Uniform Securities Act.

Series 65   The Uniform Investment Adviser Law Exam, which entitles the successful candidate to give investment advice in those states that require Series 65 registration.

Series 7   The General Securities Registered Representative License, which entitles the holder to sell all types of securities products. The Series 7 is the most comprehensive of the FINRA representative licenses and serves as a prerequisite for most principal-level examinations.

Series 9 and 10 General Securities Sales Supervisor—This registration is appropriate for individuals required to register as principals to supervise sales activities in corporate, municipal, and options securities, investment company products, variable contracts, and direct participation programs. Series 7 is a prerequisite for this exam. Also known as the branch office managers exam.

Series 99 Operations Professional—The registration is for individuals who have senior management responsibilities over "back-office" functions such as collection and disbursement of funds, receipt and delivery of securities, and account transfers.

series bond Bonds issued in a series over a given period. All the bonds in the series have the same priority claim against assets. *See also* serial bond.

Series EE bond A nonmarketable, interest-bearing U.S. government savings bond issued at a discount from par. Interest on Series EE bonds is exempt from state and local taxes. *See also* savings bond; Series HH bond.

Series HH bond A nonmarketable, interest-bearing U.S. government savings bond issued at par and purchased only by trading in Series EE bonds at maturity. Interest on Series HH bonds is exempt from state and local taxes. See also savings bond; Series EE bond.

settlement The completion of a trade through the delivery of a security or commodity and the payment of cash or other consideration.

settlement date The business day on which delivery of a security and payment of money is to be made through the facilities of a registered clearing agency in connection with the sale of a security. Settlement provisions are standardized by the Uniform Practice Code.

settlement option (variable or fixed annuity) The annuitization selection made by a holder of an annuity.

settlor An individual or organization that gifts assets to a beneficiary by transferring fiduciary duty to a third-party trustee that will maintain the assets for the benefit of the beneficiaries. *Syn.* grantor, trustor.

share identification An accounting method that identifies the specific shares selected for liquidation in the event an investor wishes to liquidate shares.

shareholders' equity *See* net worth.

shelf registration (offering) Under Rule 415, an SEC provision allowing issuers to register a new issue security without selling the entire issue at once. The issuer can sell limited portions of the issue over a two-year period, and for WKSI companies, a three-year period without reregistering the security.

short (1) The term used to describe the state of not possessing a certain asset. For example, an operations person working in a "cage" cannot locate a security in the vault is said to be short. (2) An investor who borrows shares of stock from a broker-dealer and sells them is said to have a short position in the stock. (3) A producer of a commodity may short (short sell) a futures contract to hedge the commodity. *See also* long; short sale; short against the box.

short against the box The term used to describe the selling of a security, contract, or commodity that the seller owns but prefers not to deliver. Frequently, this is done to defer taxation.

short covering Buying securities to return those that were previously borrowed to make delivery on a short sale.

short hedge Selling options or futures as protection against a decrease in the value of a long securities or actuals position. *See also* buying a hedge; hedge; long hedge; selling a hedge.

short sale The sale of a security that the seller does not own, or any sale consummated by the delivery of a security borrowed by or for the account of the seller.

short-term capital gain The profit realized on the sale of an asset that has been owned for 12 months or less. *See also* capital gain; capital loss; short-term capital loss.

short-term capital loss The loss incurred on the sale of a capital asset that has been owned for 12 months or less. *See also* capital gain; capital loss; short-term capital gain.

SIC *See* Securities Information Center.

SIE A FINRA exam for prospective securities industry professionals. This introductory-level exam assesses a candidate's knowledge of basic securities industry information. The Securities Industry Essentials Exam is a corequisite for the many representative-level FINRA exams.

simple trust A trust that accumulates income and distributes it to its beneficiaries on an annual basis. *See also* complex trust.

simplified arbitration A FINRA program applying to arbitrations involving $50,000 or less, exclusive of interest and expenses.

simplified employee pension plan (SEP) A qualified retirement plan allowing employers to contribute to traditional IRAs (SEP-IRAs) set up for employees.

single payment deferred annuity Method of purchasing an annuity in which the annuitant deposits one lump sum of money into the account and elects to have the money remain in the account and accrue tax deferred until the annuitant elects to begin the payout phase at a later time (deferred).

single payment immediate annuity A method of purchasing an annuity in which the annuitant deposits one lump sum of money into the account and elects to begin the payout phase immediately.

SIP *See* Securities Information Processor.

SIPC *See* Securities Investor Protection Corporation.

SLP *See* supplemental liquidity provider.

small-cap A market capitalization range from $300 million to $2 billion.

social media The collective online communications channels dedicated to community-based input, interaction, content-sharing, and collaboration.

solicited order An order resulting from a broker-dealer recommendation. The resulting trade must be suitable for the investor.

solicited trade A trade that originates from, and is initiated by, a registered representative (recommending a securities transaction to a customer).

special memorandum account (SMA) A notation on a customer's general or margin account indicating that funds are credited to the account on a memo basis. The account is used much like a line of credit with a bank. *Syn.* special miscellaneous account.

special situation fund A mutual fund whose objective is to capitalize on the profit potential of corporations in nonrecurring circumstances, such as those undergoing reorganizations or being considered as takeover candidates.

specialist An NYSE American Exchange member who stands ready to provide automatically updated two-sided market quotations with size in all the appointed option series. The specialist's role is to maintain a fair, orderly, and competitive market. Formerly used on the NYSE. *Syn.* eSpecialist; specialist unit. *See* Designated Market Maker.

speculation Trading a commodity with a higher-than-average risk in return for a higher-than-average profit potential. The trade is effected solely for the purpose of profiting from it and not as a means of hedging or protecting other positions.

speculator One who trades a commodity or security with a higher-than-average risk in return for a higher-than-average profit potential. *See also* speculation.

spin-off A type of divestiture where a parent company sells all of the shares of a subsidiary or distributes new shares of a company or division it owns to create a new company.

split offering A public offering of securities that combines aspects of both a primary and a secondary offering. A portion of the issue is a primary offering, the proceeds of which go to the issuing corporation. The remainder of the issue is a secondary offering, the proceeds of which go to the selling stockholders. *Syn.* combined distribution. *See also* primary offering; secondary offering.

sponsor (1) A person who is instrumental in organizing, selling, or managing a limited partnership. (2) A term for the underwriter of a mutual fund. Another is *distributor*.

spousal account A separate individual retirement account (arrangement) established for a nonworking or low-income spouse. Contributions to the account made by the working spouse grow tax deferred until withdrawal.

spousal IRA A separate individual retirement account established for a spouse with little or no earned income. Contributions to the account made by the working spouse grow tax deferred until withdrawal.

spread (1) In a quotation, the difference between the bid and the ask prices. (2) An options position established by purchasing one option and selling another option of the same class but of a different series. (3) The price difference between two futures contracts. It involves holding a long and a short position in two or more related futures contracts, with the objective of profiting from a change in the price relationship.

SRO *See* self-regulatory organization.

stagflation A period of high unemployment in the economy accompanied by a general rise in prices. *See also* deflation; inflation.

Standard & Poor's 100 Stock Index (S&P 100) A market-value-weighted index composed of 100 leading U.S. stocks. The index is a subset of the S&P 500. *See also* index; Standard & Poor's Corporation; Standard & Poor's Composite Index of 500 Stocks.

Standard & Poor's Composite Index of 500 Stocks (S&P 500) (SPX) A market-value-weighted index that offers broad coverage of the securities market. It is composed of 400 industrial stocks, 40 financial stocks, 40 public utility stocks, and 20 transportation stocks. The index is owned and compiled by Standard & Poor's Corporation. *See also* index; Standard & Poor's Corporation; Standard & Poor's 100 Index.

standard securities settlement cycle *See* regular way.

stated value *See* par value.

stated yield *See* nominal yield.

statement of additional information (SAI) Part 2 of the registration statement for investment companies. This document is not required to be given when soliciting a sale but, if requested by the investor, it must be provided within three business days of the request.

static content   Social media format in which content can only be changed by the originator.

statutory disqualification   A person may be subject to a statutory disqualification (not permitted to work in the securities industry) if the person is enjoined temporarily or permanently from violating securities laws by a court of competent jurisdiction; is barred or suspended from association with a broker-dealer by the SEC, the Commodities Futures Trading Commission (CFTC), a self-regulatory organization (SRO), or foreign equivalent; or has been convicted of any felony or certain misdemeanors within the past 10 years. See Securities Exchange Act of 1934.

statutory prospectus   The official name for the full disclosure document for mutual funds.

statutory voting   A voting method that permits stockholders to cast one vote per share owned for each position. This method of voting benefits majority stockholders. *See also* cumulative voting.

stock broker (stockbroker)   *See* registered representative. *Syn.* financial advisor; account executive.

stock certificate   Printed evidence of ownership in a corporation.

stock dividend   *See* dividend.

stock exchange   Any organization, association, or group of persons that maintains or provides a marketplace in which securities can be bought and sold. Examples include the New York Stock Exchange (NYSE), the London Stock Exchange (LSE), and the Tokyo Stock Exchange (TSE).

stock loan agreement   The document that an institutional customer must sign when the broker-dealer borrows stock from the customer's margin account. The document specifies the terms of the loan and the rights of both parties.

stock options   Gives an employee the right to purchase a specified number of shares of the employer's common stock at a stated price over a stated time period.

stock power   A standard form that duplicates the back of a stock certificate and is used for transferring the stock to the new owner's name. *Syn.* irrevocable stock power; power of substitution.

stock quote   A list of representative prices bid and asked for a stock during a particular trading day. Stocks are quoted in points, where one point equals $1. *See also* bond quote.

stock record   A broker-dealer's accounting system that shows separately for each security all long and short positions, as well as the location of each security, the holdings of all customers, and all securities due from or owed to other broker-dealers. *Syn.* securities record. *See also* customer ledger; general ledger.

stock split   An increase in the number of a corporation's outstanding shares, which decreases its stock's par value. The market value of the total number of shares remains the same.

stockholders' equity   *See* net worth.

stop (stop loss) order   A customer order that becomes a market order when the market price of the security reaches or passes a specific price. *See also* limit order; market order; stop limit order.

stop limit order   A customer order that becomes a limit order when the market price of the security reaches or passes through a specific (stop) price. *See also* limit order; stop order.

stop order   (1) A directive from the SEC that suspends the sale of new issue securities to the public when fraud is suspected or filing materials are deficient. (2) A customer order that becomes a market order when the market price of the security reaches or passes a specific price. *See also* limit order; market order; stop limit order.

stop stock price   *See* stop order.

stop stock transaction   Any transaction in which a designated market maker (DMM) and another party agree that the order may be executed at a stop stock price or better. The agreement is for a short period.

street name   The security registered in the name of the broker-dealer on the issuer's books where the firm holds the security for clients in *book-entry* form. A book-entry is a record in the broker-dealer's books showing who owns the security. A stock or bond certificate is not delivered.

street name account   An account in which the customer's securities are held in the name of the brokerage firm to facilitate payment and delivery. The customer remains the beneficial owner.

strike price   *See* exercise price.

STRIPS   See Separate Trading of Registered Interest and Principal of Securities.

Subchapter M   The section of the Internal Revenue Code that provides special tax treatment for regulated investment companies.

subordinated debenture   A debt obligation backed by the good faith and credit of the issuing corporation that has claims to interest and principal subordinated to ordinary debentures and all other liabilities. *See also* debenture.

suitability   A determination made by a registered representative as to whether a particular security matches a customer's objectives and financial capability. The representative must have enough information about each customer to make a reasonable judgment.

suitable transaction   A transaction that meets or takes into account the investment needs of the customer. All solicited transactions must be suitable. *See* suitability.

summary prospectus   A disclosure document highlighting the summary of significant information provided to investors by mutual fund companies before or at the time of its sale. *Syn*. Rule 498 prospectus.

supervision   A system implemented by a broker-dealer to ensure its employees and associated persons comply with the applicable securities laws, rules, and regulations.

supplemental liquidity provider (SLP)   An off-the-trading-floor (upstairs) market maker who is incented by the NYSE to add liquidity. The SLP trades only for its proprietary account and may compete with the on-floor Designated Market Maker in a stock listed on the NYSE. The SLP must maintain a bid or an offer in an assigned stock at least 10% of the trading day.

supply   The total amount of a good or service available for purchase by consumers. *See also* demand.

supply-side theory   An economic theory contending that a sharp reduction in tax rates will stimulate productive investment by companies that benefit the entire society.

suspicious activity report (SAR)   Financial institutions, such as broker-dealers, banks, thrifts, casinos, must file a suspicious activity report (SARs) with the Treasury Department's Financial Crimes Enforcement Network (FinCEN) whenever customer activity appears out of the ordinary or illegal.

syndicate   A group of investment bankers (broker-dealers and banks) formed to distribute a security on behalf of the issuer. Each syndicate member is responsible for the sale and distribution of a portion of the issue. *Syn*. underwriting syndicate. *See* selling group; underwriting.

syndicate manager   *See* underwriting manager. *Syn*. Bookrunner; main underwriter.

systematic risk   The potential for a security to decrease in value, owing to its inherent tendency to move together with all securities of the same type. Neither diversification nor any other investment strategy can eliminate this risk. *See also* market risk.

systemic risk   The risk associated with the failure of entire financial markets. A single financial institution collapse, leading to another and another, cascading throughout a region or the world, is an example of systemic risk, not to be confused with systematic risk.

T-bill   *See* Treasury bill.

T-bond   *See* Treasury bond.

T-call   *See* Regulation T; margin call.

T-note   *See* Treasury note.

TAN   *See* tax anticipation note.

tax and revenue anticipation note (TRAN)   A short-term municipal debt security to be paid off from future tax receipts and revenues.

tax anticipation note (TAN)   A short-term municipal or government debt security to be paid off from future tax receipts.

tax basis   *See* cost basis.

tax bracket   A point on the income-tax rate schedule. *Syn*. marginal tax bracket.

tax credit   An amount that can be subtracted from a tax liability, often in connection with real estate development, energy conservation, and research and development programs. Every dollar of tax credit reduces the amount of tax due, dollar for dollar. *See also* deduction.

tax liability   The amount of tax payable on earnings, usually calculated by subtracting standard and itemized deductions and personal exemptions from adjusted gross income, then multiplying by the tax rate. *See* adjusted gross income.

tax-deferred annuity   *See* tax-sheltered annuity.

tax-equivalent yield   The rate of return a taxable bond must earn before taxes in order to equal the tax-exempt earnings on a municipal bond. This number varies with the investor's tax bracket.

tax-free bond fund   *See* tax-exempt bond fund.

tax-exempt bond fund   A mutual fund whose investment objective is to provide maximum tax-free income. It invests primarily in tax-free municipal debt. *Syn*. tax-free bond fund.

taxability   The risk of the erosion of investment income through taxation.

taxable gain   The portion of a sale or distribution of, for example, mutual fund shares that is subject to taxation.

tenants in common (TIC)   A form of joint ownership of an account whereby a deceased tenant's fractional interest in the account is retained by his estate. *See* joint tenants with right of survivorship.

tender offer   A limited-period SEC-registered offer to acquire a substantial portion of a company's securities (equity or debt). When a company seeks to acquire its own securities, it is referred to as an issuer tender offer. A filing is required to disclose the terms of the offering and information about the bidders, known as the Offer to Purchase, along with SEC Form TO.

term bond   *See* term maturity.

term maturity   A repayment schedule for a bond issue in which the entire issue comes due on a single date. *Syn*. term bond. *See* maturity date.

testamentary trust   A trust created as a result of instructions from a deceased's last will and testament.

thinly traded   A security with a low trading volume, generally with a wide spread between the quoted bid and ask prices.

Third Market   A trading market in which exchange-listed securities are traded over-the-counter.

third-party account   A customer account for which the owner has given power of attorney to a third party.

TIC   *See* tenants in common; true interest cost.

tick   A minimum upward or downward movement in the price of a security.

TIF   *See* Transfer Initiation Form.

time deposit   A sum of money left with a bank (or borrowed from a bank and left on deposit) that the depositing customer has agreed not to withdraw for a specified time period or without a specified amount of notice. *See* demand deposit.

time horizon   The expected number of months, years, or decades over which the investments will be made to achieve a particular financial goal.

time value   The amount an investor pays for an option above its intrinsic value. It reflects the amount of time left until expiration. The amount is calculated by subtracting the intrinsic value from the premium paid. *See also* intrinsic value.

timing risk   The potential for an investor to incur a loss as a result of buying or selling a particular security at an unfavorable time.

tippee   Term used in the Insider Trading and Securities Fraud Enforcement Act of 1988 (ITSFEA) to describe the person receiving material nonpublic information from an insider or other tipper.

tipper   Term used in the Insider Trading and Securities Fraud Enforcement Act of 1988 (ITSFEA) to describe the individual responsible for disseminating material nonpublic information.

TOD account   *See* transfer on death.

tombstone   A printed advertisement that solicits indications of interest in a securities offering. The text is limited to basic information about the offering such as the name of the issuer, type of security, names of the underwriters, and where a prospectus is available. *See* omitting prospectus.

total capitalization   The sum of a corporation's long-term debt, stock accounts, and capital in excess of par.

trade blotter   *See* blotter.

trade confirmation   A printed document that contains details of a transaction, including the settlement date and amount of money due from or owed to a customer.

trade date   The date on which a securities transaction is executed.

traditional IRA   A retirement plan available to any individual with earned income.

TRAN   *See* tax and revenue anticipation note.

tranche   One of the classes of securities that forms an issue of collateralized mortgage obligations. Each tranche is characterized by its interest rate, average maturity, risk level, and sensitivity to mortgage prepayments. Neither the rate of return nor the maturity date of a CMO tranche is guaranteed. *See also* collateralized mortgage obligation.

transfer agent   A trust or bank engaged by a company to maintain records of investors.

Transfer Initiation Form (TIF)   A form that facilitates the transfer of securities from one trading account to another at a different brokerage firm or bank. *See* ACAT.

transfer instruction form (TIF)   A form submitted to a new brokerage firm by customers who desire to transfer assets from one firm to another.

transfer on death   A type of individual (or JTWROS) account registration where the account holder designates a specific beneficiary or beneficiaries to receive the assets in the account upon the holder's death. No special legal documentation is necessary, and the assets pass without going through probate. *Syn.* TOD.

Transportation Average   *See* Dow Jones Transportation Average.

Treasury bill   A marketable U.S. government debt security with a maturity of 52 weeks or less. *Syn.* T bill.

Treasury bond   A marketable, fixed-interest U.S. government debt security with a maturity of more than 10 years.

Treasury Investors Growth Receipt (TIGR)   One of several types of zero-coupon bonds and notes "stripped" of their coupons and issued by brokerage firms and collateralized by Treasury securities. *See also* Treasury receipt.

Treasury note   A marketable, fixed-interest U.S. government debt security with a maturity of between 2 and 10 years. *Syn.* T-note.

Treasury receipt   The generic term for a zero-coupon bond issued by a brokerage firm and collateralized by the Treasury securities a custodian holds in escrow for the investor.

Treasury stock   Equity securities that the issuing corporation has issued and repurchased from the public at the current market price. *See also* issued stock; outstanding stock.

trough   The end of a period of declining business activity throughout the economy, and one of the four stages of the business cycle. *See* business cycle.

Trust Indenture Act of 1939   The legislation requiring that all publicly offered, nonexempt debt securities be registered under the Securities Act of 1933 and be issued under a trust indenture that protects the bondholders.

trustee (1) A person legally appointed to act as a fiduciary and make decisions in the best interests of the beneficiary. (2) A bank designated by an issuer of municipal debt as the custodian of funds and representative of bondholders appointed to ensure compliance with the bond contract.

trustor An individual or organization that gifts assets to a beneficiary by transferring fiduciary duty to a third-party trustee that will maintain the assets for the benefit of the beneficiaries. *Syn.* settlor, grantor.

TSA *See* tax-sheltered annuity.

two-dollar broker An exchange member (broker) that executes orders for other member (broker-dealer) firms when their floor brokers are especially busy. Two-dollar brokers charge a negotiated commission for their services.

type A term that classifies an option as a call or a put. *See also* class, series.

U.S. government and agency bond fund A mutual fund whose investment objective is to provide current income while preserving safety of capital through investing in securities backed by the U.S. Treasury or issued by a government agency.

UGMA *See* Uniform Gifts to Minors Act.

UIT *See* unit investment trust.

uncovered The position of an option investor who writes a call on a security they do not own (or put options without a short position in the underlying asset).

uncovered call writer An investor who writes a call option without owning the underlying stock or other related assets that would enable the investor to deliver the stock, should the option be exercised. *Syn.* naked call writer.

underlying securities The futures or securities that are bought or sold when an option, right, warrant, or convertible bond is exercised.

underwriter An investment banker who works with an issuer to help bring a security to the market and sell it to the public.

underwriting The procedure by which investment bankers channel investment capital from investors to corporations and municipalities that are issuing securities.

underwriting compensation The amount paid to a broker-dealer firm for its involvement in offering and selling securities.

underwriting discount *See* underwriting spread.

underwriting manager *See* managing underwriter.

underwriting split *See* underwriting spread.

underwriting spread The difference in price between the public offering price and the price an underwriter pays to the issuing corporation. The difference represents the profit available to the syndicate or selling group. *Syn.* underwriting discount; underwriting split.

underwriting syndicate *See* syndicate.

unearned income Income derived from investments and other sources not related to employment services. Examples of unearned income include interest from a savings account, bond interest, and dividends from stock. *See also* earned income; passive income; portfolio income.

unethical trading practices The use of any manipulative, fraudulent, or deceptive activity in selling securities. *See* front running, capping, painting the tape.

Uniform Gifts to Minors Act (UGMA) Legislation that permits a gift of money or securities to be given to a minor and held in a custodial account that an adult manages for the minor's benefit. Income and capital gains transferred to a minor's name are usually taxed at the minor's rate. However, if the child is under a specified age and has unearned income above a certain level, those earnings are taxed at the parent's rate. *See* Uniform Transfers to Minors Act.

Uniform Practice Code (UPC) FINRA policy that establishes guidelines for a brokerage firm's dealings with other brokerage firms.

Uniform Prudent Investors Act (UPIA) A modern adaptation of the prudent man rule, which, as a result of the development of modern portfolio theory, applies the standard of prudence to the entire portfolio rather than to individual investments. It requires the fiduciary to measure risk with respect to return.

Uniform Securities Act (USA) Template legislation written by the NCCUSL to serve as the basis for a state's securities legislation if the state wished to adopt it. It regulates securities, persons (broker-dealers and their agents and investment advisers and their representatives), and transactions in the securities markets within the state.

Uniform Transfers to Minors Act (UTMA) Legislation adopted in most states that permits a gift of money or securities to be given to a minor and held in a custodial account that an adult manages for the minor's benefit until the minor reaches a certain age (not necessarily the age of majority). *See* Uniform Gift to Minors Act.

unissued stock That portion of authorized stock not distributed (sold) to investors by a newly chartered corporation.

unit investment trust (UIT) An investment company that sells redeemable shares in a professionally selected portfolio of securities. *See* fixed unit investment trust; nonfixed unit investment trust; unit of beneficial interest.

Units   Compensation issued by an enterprise to an employee in the form of company stock. Restricted stock units are subject to a vesting schedule.

unlisted securities   Securities that are not listed on any registered exchange.

unrealized capital appreciation   An increase in the value of an asset that the owner does not receive because the asset has not been sold.

unrealized gain   The amount by which a security appreciates in value before it is sold. Until it is sold, the investor does not actually possess the proceeds of the sale. *See also* realized gain.

unseasoned issuers   Public companies that are required to file reports with the SEC but are not seasoned issuers.

unsecured bond   *See* debenture.

unsolicited trade   A trade that originates from and is initiated by the customer.

unsuitable transaction   A transaction that does not meet the investment needs of the customer. An example is the purchase of a municipal bond for a low-income customer seeking growth.

unsystematic risk   The potential for an unforeseen event to affect the value of a specific investment. Examples of such events include strikes, natural disasters, poor management decisions, introductions of new product lines, and attempted takeovers. *Syn.* nonsystematic risk. *See* systematic risk.

UPC   *See* Uniform Practice Code.

U.S. government and agency bond fund   A mutual fund whose investment objective is to provide current income while preserving safety of capital through investing in securities backed by the U.S. Treasury or issued by a government agency.

USA   *See* Uniform Securities Act.

USA PATRIOT Act of 2001   Stands for Uniting and Strengthening America by Providing Appropriate Tools Required to Intercept and Obstruct Terrorism Act. Congress enacted the USA PATRIOT Act to arm law enforcement with new tools to detect and prevent terrorism.

Utilities Average   *See* Dow Jones Utilities Average.

UTMA   *See* Uniform Transfers to Minors Act.

value fund   A fund and management style that focuses on undervalued companies.

value style investing   A management style that looks for stocks that have solid underlying fundamentals and are currently selling at distressed prices.

variable annuity   An insurance contract used to fund retirement. Cash values vary with the performance of a portfolio of investments. An insurance and securities license is required to present variable contracts.

variable annuity trust account   In some jurisdictions, the term used to represent the investors' accumulation units.

variable death benefit   The amount paid to a decedent's beneficiary that depends on the investment performance of an insurance company's separate account. The amount is added to any guaranteed minimum death benefit.

variable life insurance   Provides death benefits and cash values that vary with the performance of a portfolio of investments. An insurance and securities license is required to present variable contracts.

variable-rate demand obligation   Municipal bonds issued with variable, or floating, rates of interest. These securities offer interest payments tied to the movements of another specified interest rate.

variable-rate municipal note   A short-term municipal debt security issued when either general interest rates are expected to change or the length of time before permanent funding is received is uncertain. *Syn.* variable-rate demand note.

vesting   (1) An ERISA guideline stipulating that an employee must be entitled to all his retirement benefits within a certain period of time, even if he no longer works for the employer. (2) The amount of time that an employee must work before retirement or before benefit plan contributions made by the employer become the employee's property without penalty.

VIX   The volatility market index, known as the *fear index*, that measures investor expectation of implied volatility in the S&P 500.

VL   *See* variable life insurance.

volatility   The magnitude and frequency of changes in the price of a security or commodity within a given time period.

volume   The amount of trading activity, expressed in shares or dollars, experienced by a single security or the entire market within a specified period, usually daily, monthly, or annually.

voting right   A stockholder's right to vote for members of the board of directors and on matters of corporate policy—particularly the issuance of senior securities, stock splits, and substantial changes in the corporation's business.

warrant   (1) A security that gives the holder the right to purchase securities from the warrant issuer at a stipulated subscription price. Warrants are usually long-term instruments with expiration dates years in the future. (2) A debt security, usually a small amount, issued in certain municipal jurisdictions to pay project costs as they are incurred.

wash sale   Selling a security at a loss for tax purposes and, within 30 days before or after, purchasing the same or a substantially identical security. The IRS will disallow the claimed loss. *See* bond swap.

wash trade   Occurs when a customer enters a purchase order and a sale order for the same security at the same time. It is done to create a false appearance of activity in a security. This is a prohibited practice.

Web CRD   *See* Central Registration Depository.

Well-Known Seasoned Issuer (WSKI)   A company that is current in its 10K, 10Q, and 8K filings and has a more than $700 million market capitalization or has issued $1 billion in nonconvertible securities over the past three years.

wildcatting   *See* exploratory drilling program.

Wilshire 5000 Composite Index   A market cap–weighted market indicator composed of about 3,500 exchange-listed and over-the-counter common stocks. It is the broadest measure of the market. *See also* index.

Wilshire 5000 Total Market Index   Represents the broadest index for the U.S. equity market, measuring the performance of all U.S. equity securities with readily available price data.

wire house   *See* futures commission merchant.

wire transfer   A method to electronically transfer funds from one person or institution to another.

withdrawal plan   Benefit offered by a mutual fund whereby a customer receives the proceeds of a periodic systematic liquidation of shares in the account.

WKSI   *See* Well-Known Seasoned Issuer.

working capital   A measure of a corporation's liquidity—that is, its ability to transfer assets into cash to meet current short-term obligations. It is calculated by subtracting total current liabilities from total current assets.

working capital ratio   *See* current ratio.

wrap account   An account at a broker-dealer where a number of the firm's services, including advisory service, custody, and trading, are wrapped together for an annual charge based upon the assets in the account.

wrap fee program   Any advisory program under which a specified fee or fees not based directly upon transactions in a client's account is charged for investment advisory services (which may include portfolio management or advice concerning the selection of other investment advisers) and the execution of client transactions.

writer   The seller of an option contract.

written supervisory procedures   *See* supervision.

yield   The rate of return on an investment, usually expressed as an annual percentage rate. *See* current yield; dividend yield; nominal yield.

yield curve   A graphic representation of the actual or projected yields of fixed-income securities in relation to their maturities. *See* flat yield curve; inverted yield curve.

yield to call (YTC)   The rate of return on a bond that accounts for the difference between the bond's acquisition cost and its proceeds, including interest income, calculated to the earliest date that the bond may be called by the issuing corporation. *See also* bond yield.

yield to maturity (YTM)   The rate of return on a bond that accounts for the difference between the bond's acquisition cost and its maturity proceeds, including interest income. *See also* bond yield.

yield to the worst   The lowest of the yields calculated to the pricing to maturity, par, or call. A discount bond, for example, would be priced to maturity.

yield-based option   A security representing the right to receive, in cash, the difference between the current yield of an underlying U.S. government security and the strike price of the option.

YTC   *See* yield to call.

YTM   *See* yield to maturity.

zero-coupon bond   A corporate or municipal debt security traded at a deep discount from face value. The bond pays no interest; rather, it may be redeemed at maturity for its full face value.

INDEX

Notes

Notes

Notes

Notes

Notes

Notes

Notes

Notes

Notes

Notes

Notes

Notes